also by George Millar in Cassell Military Paperbacks

HORNED PIGEON (prequel to *Maquis*)

THE BRUNEVAL RAID

maquis

the french resistance at war

GEORGE MILLAR

CASSELL

To the inhabitants of the Franche-Comté, and especially
to those of them who live and who lived in the
unconsidered beauty of the valley of the Ognon.

Cassell Military Paperbacks

Cassell
Wellington House, 125 Strand
London WC2R 0BB

Copyright © George Millar 1945

First published in Great Britain by William Heinemann 1945
This Cassell Military Paperbacks edition 2003

3 5 7 9 10 8 6 4

This book was published in the United States under the title
Waiting in the Night

British Library Cataloguing-in-Publication data:
A catalogue record for this book is available from the
British Library

ISBN-13 978-0-3043-6543-2
ISBN-10 0-3043-6543-2

Printed and bound in Great Britain by
Cox & Wyman Ltd., Reading, Berks.

The Orion Publishing group's policy is to use papers that are natural,
renewable and recyclable products and made from wood grown in
sustainable forests. The logging and manufacturing processes are expected
to conform to the environmental regulations of the country of origin.

www.orionbooks.co.uk

MAQUIS

CHAPTER I

H IS face was a polished mask that might have been made originally at the Royal Military College. From behind the almost motionless mask his voice trickled. The words seemed to drop, then slowly rise like oily bubbles through the waters of an aquarium.

Indeed the room was an aquarium of a room, a dusty, empty, high and unhandsome room, in a house taken over from its human personalities for such impersonal interviews and the anonymous work that pulsed behind such interviews. The double casement windows were shut and bolted against the discreet humming of London's streets, the smoky smell of London's air.

He leaned back on two legs of his chair, and his little eyes wandered coldly over the fretted plaster circling the ceiling where now the spiders, undisturbed by the housemaid's feather brush, fought and copulated and spun their beautiful webs.

Above the deal table I saw the upper-half of his uniform. He had an industrious air. He was unlike the glittering young officers of my own and other regiments who, at that hour, would be congregating to meet their girls in the L-shaped corridor of the Berkeley Hotel. His unregimental uniform, shiny and crushed, carried on the lapels the General List insignia that the butterfly soldiers call "Crosse and Blackwells". His belt was not of shining leather, but of trouble-free cloth, its brass buckle sullenly dull and unclean. A contrast to his R.M.C. face.

His hands, suave, white like the under-belly of a coarse fish, with long, sharp fingers, rhythmically stroked the heavy briefcase that lay between us on the table. His hands accompanied the smoothly-bubbling voice and the eyes that wandered coldly among the spider colonies while his brain spun a web around me.

I sensed the web and offered myself to its folds. Like a girl dancer I wanted to put myself in one end of the web, and spin until it was sheathed around me.

"Yes, Major. I would be most anxious to do that. If you think I might be suitable . . ." I punctuated his words, I tried to accelerate his spinning. Now he spoke English, now French, and I answered:

"Mais oui, mon commandant. D'accord, mon commandant."

"Your accent is good for an Englishman," he said. (So was his.) "I think, yes, I really think, that you might work for us in France. That is, if you would like to?"

"I would like nothing better." I took the first strand of his web and gave it an extra half-hitch to fix myself in it the more securely.

I believed that he was offering death. And I wanted a useful death and then peace. How ridiculous it seems now. Then it was April, 1944. I was thirty-three and so unhappy that life was almost sense-free, almost sensation-free. I lived in a glucose unhappiness so thick that I barely perceived outside things. Things that had been very important to me, like the powerful kindness of my parent, were the things that still hurt me, for they stabbed me back towards life and the realisation of what I thought I had lost for ever.

"George Reid Millar," I signed at the bottom of the paper the major handed me.

"Please do not take this as absolutely final," he said, slipping the paper smoothly into the brief-case. "If you are not happy about the work you have a perfect right to draw back. If we become unhappy about you we have the right to get rid of you, or to give you a different kind of job. You have a lot of work ahead of you, my friend. Remember that although we are always sympathetic we may not always have the time to show it. We have no time for failure. Sometimes we fail when our men have already gone into the field. More often we learn that we have made a mistake before we send them there. . . ."

I knew that I was unfitted for his work, and afraid of his work. And I knew that I would hide my unfittedness and my fear so that I could get to France to do his work, and to get away from the cotton-wool smothering of unhappy security.

Outside in the bending, carpet-less corridor I secretly wrote his name down on a small piece of paper because at that time I was particularly bad at remembering names, and the impersonal major seemed to personify hope. Much more than the woman with a harp, sexlessly bestriding a globe, on the wall of the cook's bedroom.

At the Berkeley, among the glitterers that were so unlike the major, I wondered if I should ever see him normally in the street, walking quickly, swinging his black brief-case with the Royal Arms of Britain on it, carrying the signed pledges of people like me. The talk of the people with whom I ate, their

2

faces, the air I breathed there, all resembled a colourless fluid, liquid paraffin perhaps. I could not wait to get back to the empty, dirty waiting-room of the tall house where they ordered me on to the work they wanted me to do. How lucky I was. To be unhappy like that in war-time. If such unhappiness had closed down on me in peace-time I should have seen no flicker of light at the end of the tunnel, no livening glint of danger and excitement and usefulness. The unhappiness was worse than a disease, more numbing than paralysis, more abstract than the agony of cancer.

An American officer, a British officer, a French officer, two Intelligent Gentlewomen. They saw me and questioned me and told me that because I had already been a soldier and knew what it was like in German-occupied France my training would be rushed.

What fools intelligent people can be. The more intelligent they are the more capable they are of building an impression for themselves. With the usual bogus modesties I helped their picture-making, helped them to believe that I was brave by hiding my cowardice and fear. I allowed them to believe that I would succeed because I was determined and direct. But I knew that my only assets were my twistedness and cunning.

They were fooled, even the intelligent women, by my baby face and my open, frank expression. Sometimes I secretly laughed at them as they painted their phony pictures, and my laughter helped me, injected air bubbles into the glucose that stifled me.

There was the usual drawback to being considered frank, open, a shade simple. They thought that they could push me around. And (although I did not know this at the time) they were in a hurry to get me ready before D-Day. They ordered me about. They listened to my simple demands and said, as often as not: "No."

They kept me waiting for hours in the dirty waiting-room filled with age-old *Daily Expresses* and *France Libres*, and quite often with Frenchmen in battle-dress, who eyed my fair hair, British baby face (or sheep face, as an angry mother once neatly described it), and my unusual uniform with unveiled, pebble-eyed curiosity.

"Can this over-dressed, pale-haired creature imagine that he will do our secret, tortuous work?" the pebble-eyes demanded. And to satisfy their curiosity they would put a question.

3

"Would you have the kindness to direct me to the Waters?" Then the questioner would stamp off in his heavy, British boots, while the others savoured my French, turning it over and over.

Yes, they kept me waiting because they were over-worked. But if I arrived late there was trouble. Handsome Mrs. Pollock would glower at me from behind her flower and chocolate-laden desk and her pneumatic Jane, the American secretary in uniform, would pretend to be engrossed in her typing, so that she could spare no sympathy.

"You are late, Millar," Mrs. Pollock often snapped. And one of the majors took me aside to warn:

"Please be careful, my friend. You must not give a false impression of slackness, you know. You are being trained for a position of very great responsibility. Punctuality is considered most vital in this organisation. We demand the most absolute discipline and obedience."

When they had seen enough of me beneath the spiders they sent me off to a country house which was called a school. It was better than any other school that I had known. There were Frenchmen there, and a few of us Britons and Americans. We were lectured to in French or in English or, more often, in a mixture of the two languages. We were called students. In the main rooms, the outhouses, the fields and coppices we were taught to use firearms and clean them, to destroy things with explosives, and to carry out raids on interesting objectives like Gestapo jails.

Sometimes men who had worked in the field (in France) came to the school for so-called refresher courses. I noted that they wore no conquering hero airs. They were quiet, tired, and irritable. They seldom wanted to go back to the work abroad, but they waited with a doomed passiveness to be sent back. One of them was an American, a soldier of World War I who had settled in France, preferring that country to the strong artificialities of the big town where he had been born. Now he spoke English with a strong French accent, and French with no accent at all. He knew he would have to go back, and most of him did not want to go.

He had a beaten-bronze, countryman's face, and nippy, light eyes. Eisenhower had personally decorated him, they said. But he did not seem to remember that as he slumped in his chair and refused to go out on exercises.

"God damn you no," he said to the bossy young instructor from Edinburgh. "Make me do those things when there's no

4

Boches here, like as if it was a game. . . . God damn you, no."

From him I learned a lot that the intelligent instructors could not teach. The little French-American saw that I was sly. He knew me better than the instructors, who were efficient know-alls. So he talked to me.

He had arrived panting from his escape, sweating through the tongue from his fear and his escape, like an animal that had been run nearly off its legs and then, by some miracle, had found itself safe and lying beside a brook. They told him that he was wonderful. The Generalissimo pinned a medal on him and told him that he had helped to win the war for the great peoples. Then they gave him the icy douche of discipline, they sent him back to school. They tore him away from the brook while he was still thirsty.

They always gave this heat-then-cold treatment. A man who was puffed up by the things that Eisenhower had said to this little French-American was not going to be able to continue the work that had made Eisenhower say such things. The organisation needed more work from this man. So they helped first to inflate the bubble of his conceit, then they pricked it, and to finally destroy it they sent him back to school. Clever organisation.

My little French-American took it hard. I watched him sympathetically, trying to learn from him and his sufferings. They seemed petty beside my own unhappiness. When he was in the pistol-range the French-American became almost cheerful.

We were taught to use the forward-crouching stance and the quick, snap-shooting method. Some of us got so accurate with the pistols that we were like King George V knocking down driven grouse. The French-American danced. His legs were tense and springy, but above the waist, except for his straight right arm, his body was loosely balanced. As the targets popped up, or darted from one screened side of the range to the other, his stiff arm leaped to the horizontal and the automatic, a blue, shining continuation of his arm, spoke "crack-crack", and again "crack-crack".

Such training in these schools had saved his radio operator, he told me. When his circuit got "blown" the Gestapo had captured his operator, a young Frenchman. They searched him, but failed to find the small automatic hidden in a special holster. The pistol, following the rule of his master, my French-American, was ready cocked and at "safe". When they had

5

handcuffed him they took him away in a car. There were three Germans in the car. One beside him on the back seat. The radio operator had never fired a pistol except in England at the school where he had been taught like us to snap-shoot at cardboard targets. He was afraid that he would miss. But he was more afraid of what would happen when he arrived where they were taking him.

Despite his manacles he opened his buttons, pushed down the "safe" lever on his .38, and brought it to the point where it would draw freely. A glance around. The plain-clothes German beside him was watching the country flash past his own window. The car was rolling smoothly along a well-metalled Route Nationale.

He held his breath, drew, and fired as he had been taught. "Bang-bang". Two holes sprang red in the back of the driver's neck. The car overturned. He shot the other two. He escaped. He even returned to England, where he was sent back to school for a refresher course. They told me he was "an ordinary little Frenchman". I never met him.

"A man's second-best friend over there is his gun," the French-American decided.

"And his best?"

"His luck, touch wood."

The schools varied with their different commandants and instructors, although most of them were coloured by the aloof kindliness that gave a strange warmth to the organisation. They rushed me through the schools so that the picture of each one of them became blurred into a moving film and I learned for certain what I had always suspected, that Britain is strong because of her cranks. The most apparent factor of her strength is the steadiness of the stodgy, dull, ugly, ordinary people and their readiness to face all problems cheerfully, packed together in a cohesive mass. But in time of war, and especially in odd organisations like the one in which I found myself, the British crank makes himself felt, you see the importance of the great body of Britishers who occupy themselves seriously with crazy things.

There were many crazies in the organisation. It said much for the officers at the top that the crazies were permitted, if they were not encouraged. And for us students they gave a flashing background to a hardworking existence. It was exciting to hear strange noises in the night; to see senior officers who had

6

burned themselves playing with fire between tea and dinner; to watch strange weapons (which occasionally worked) being tried out with live ammunition beside the wallflower-beds on the lawn; to glimpse the colonel in something between a duck-punt and a one-man submarine among the water lilies on the ornamental pond.

One man stood out for me among all the teachers and experts. He was a huge man, an engineer. He had great dignity, and a face which might have belonged to a cardinal, or a thinking man with enough self-discipline to own coal-mines. He was a driving machine. He drove all with him and below him.

He taught me to destroy, and he gave me the first real hope that I had known since my unhappiness began. For the schools, like the spider colony in London, remained an aquarium to me. I was still only half alive. I was moving in something thicker than air. But this rock of a man, this pinnacle, this icicle of a man taught me that in plunging myself almost casually into the aquarium I had pledged myself to something that might *save* lives.

To explain this I must go back to the monastery of Padula in Southern Italy, during the summer of 1942. The monastery was then a Fascist prison camp for British officers. It was in those rather beautiful and peculiar surroundings that I began to hate Britain's bombing of enemy towns. In prison such a hatred can become an obsession.

Now, at this strange school in England, the tall engineer showed me that by destroying his way, by sabotage, I might prevent bombing. He gave me another incentive to go into the field. To be honest, when planted, his incentive was much weaker than my desire to burn out my own unhappiness by doing something violent. But the tall man's incentive remained when the other faded and died.

The tall man did not, like me, hate bombing for ideological or humanitarian reasons. He simply hated it because he considered it appallingly inefficient. It pained him to read of hundreds of tons of explosive being dropped on Germany from the air when a correspondingly minute quantity of similar explosive placed by saboteurs on the key machines would knock Germany right out of the war. He was a clear thinker with no orange filters on the lenses of his thoughts. He considered my thoughts on bombing "tosh", and he told me so.

We filed out of the big, cold house into the cars that were to dump us at the station, and because he was scrupulously correct

7

he was standing by the front door to shake hands and say good-bye individually.

Towering over me, with his big head hanging rather between his shoulders he urged me: "Destroy as we have taught you. Use your head and pick your objectives neatly. Pay not the slightest attention to so-called experts on the spot. Always try to reconnoitre the target yourself. Good-bye and make good use of what you have been taught."

A strange man. Most students were glad to leave his cold, spartan school. I was to be very thankful that I had been there. And I suppose many others also remembered his voice and his great stiff head as they waited in enemy country for a train or a convoy or as they worked and fretted around an objective. He is a difficult man to forget. As a schoolboy I had one or two harmless but odd habits. One of these was a liking for the sermons at evening services in the Presbyterian churches of Edinburgh, and I well remember this sentence from one sermon:

"The most remarkable thing about Christ, perhaps the only really remarkable thing about Christ is—we are comparing him to the other great and noble figures in history—was his singleness of purpose."

Christ would probably have disapproved of my small activities as a saboteur. But the tall man who taught me all that I know about sabotage certainly had singleness of purpose. Well, well. When we are short we want to be tall and when we are fair we want to be dark. Singleness of purpose may work for some people, but not for me.

Now the tempo of my training was increasing. I began to feel that I was sitting on a mat on top of a helter-skelter. That somebody would give me a push and I would be away with no trousers on and nobody at the bottom to pick me up.

I fell in now with a different type of student, a type that had been waiting a long time to go away, a type that had been through all the different schools (not just some of them like me) and had done full time in each. These people frightened me. They seemed so capable. They talked learnedly about queer things. They talked French among themselves. Even eating Welsh rarebits and drinking bitter beer they talked French. And called the Gestapo "la Geste".

One day when I was hauled out of a school with six or seven other students, mainly Frenchmen, I listened to a long talk by a major, a somewhat halting, very dry discourse on the work we would shortly have to do in the field.

8

It was the same room with the spider colony, but a month farther on, a month nearer my launching to the lions. I felt chilly fingers playing on my spine as this new major read from his well-considered, unstepped-up notes. He had a charming, sharp face with a small moustache, and when he looked around our seated circle his eye was carefully impersonal. I liked the man, yet I had a sudden craving to see him walking down Manor Street, Chelsea, eating ice-cream, or to hear him sing:

> "Git away, you bumble-bee,
> Git off my nose.
> I ain't no pray-ree flower,
> Ain't no something rose."

The whole, smoky room waited in heavy-breathing concentration while he talked of D-Day. His slightly-worried expression, the odd, halting considered speech, gave me a feeling of urgency, more of that feeling than the crisp vitalising sentences of an energy-giver. Then his talk was larded with words that worried me, puzzled me. Technical words for the things I had done and would do. Every sentence seemed to be heavy with portent.

There was also a weight of responsibility behind his words. It looked as though the work of those organisers in France was important to the troops thronging the whole of Britain, waiting to hurl themselves on the Atlantic Wall. Perhaps I had been a little hasty in wrapping myself in the first major's web. But with the genius for comfort of the truly lazy I told myself: "Don't worry. Nothing ever happens to me. . . ."

Mrs. Pollock, dark, aquiline, and good-looking as a gannet, pounced out on me from behind the roses on her chocolate-laden desk. She showed her teeth in rather a fascinating way when she talked English.

"Millar," she said (for she did not bother with little things like rank—if only there were more like her). "Where are you going?"

"Out to lunch."

"Why are you in uniform?"

"Because I am supposed to be in the army."

"Don't be flippant. Do you NEVER read our rules? Don't you know that when you are in London you should wear your foreign civilian clothes? . . . Don't? . . ."

"Doing what to what civilian clothes?" And then I realised what she was getting at. I was to parachute into France with

9

two suit-cases of civilian clothes, and more on my back. She wanted me to wear the clothes so that they would not look too new when I arrived in France.

"I have no civilian clothes," I told her triumphantly. (Now they could not send me to France).

She retired behind her desk, put a chocolate in her mouth, and considered this. Then I saw a smile of triumph between the roses, between two Frau Karl Druschkis and a clump of Madame Butterflies.

"Poor Millar," she said, and the soft shudder of her breathing caused three petals to float down into the chocolate box. "He has no foreign civilian clothes, so he will have no lunch. Jane dear, phone the tailor and the clothing store. . . ."

From then on I was a shuttlecock in London and elsewhere, hurled about by the charming Mrs. Pollock or one of the other powers that now threw me from office to office, preparing me to be handed, suitably seasoned with a dash of red pepper, to the Gestapo. I floated through the air in a daze, obeying the impulse that sent me out of one office, and homing correctly in the next office. And in a daze I went through the training.

Who was that German soldier who wore white tabs on his collar? Everyone knew but me. How did you get your tobacco ration in France? Everyone knew, and cared, but me. How did you kill a man without weapons, silently, with the edge of your hand? Everyone could do that, even the women it seemed, but not me.

Now I did not go to schools (I gathered that there was scarcely time for that) I went to courses. People were doing a lot of talking about "the moon". I knew vaguely that it was normally during the "moon period" that parachutists like me were dropped. But I was too lazy to find out when the moon periods began and ended. There is truth in my belief that if you want to know anything you need not inquire about it. Just wait. Sooner or later somebody will volunteer the information.

Sure enough. One day I went to see an Intelligent Gentlewoman in one of the offices. When she had paid my taxi bills for the week she said:

"By the way, I hope you are all ready to leave."

"Why?"

"Because you are going on the next moon."

"When is that?"

"It begins on June 1st. Have you got everything ready?"

"I seem to have nothing ready."

"Yes," patiently. "But you have got your clothes, have you not?"

"I collect them today."

"That's something," she made a note in shorthand. "Your next course will last seven days. After that you will do your jumps, and then you should leave immediately. Have you got your false papers and your cover story?"

"What is a cover story?" I asked.

"My God." She looked so queer that I thought for a moment she might allow herself to be human. But army bureaucratic training came to her aid, and she picked up a telephone to pass the baby. She handed me on to the Frenchman who had my cover story.

The moment I saw him I knew that I had seen him before. But somehow, in my semi-alive condition, I had never associated him with cover stories.

"I have a story for *you*," he began.

"How kind of you."

"It's a grand story. But you will tell me yourself that it is grand. . . .

"You, MAILLARD, Georges Henri, are born on the 19th of September, 1910, in the 8th arrondisement of Paris (I shall give you the exact address later). The son of Thomas Maillard, architect, and Marie Mortier, spinster without profession, you go at an early age to Australia, to the town of Sydney, where your father joins a building enterprise. You come back to France only on holidays and for your military training, which you go through at the Centre Mobilisateur d'Infanterie at Reuilly. Your regiment is the 46e. R.I. After the military service you return to Australia, where you go into the insurance trade. In 1938 your father dies, leaving you a nice bit of money. You return to Paris to blow some of it. You are trapped there, in Paris, when the general mobilisation arrived in August, '39. Unable to leave the country you respond to the mobilisation. Your military career as a private soldier I shall give you in detail later. Briefly, you fight your way back in rearguard actions to the Moselle, where you are made prisoner. After a short stay in the Frontstalag at Strasbourg you are taken to Stalag XIID at Limbourg. On January 2nd, '42, you are repatriated to the Centre de Repatriement at Sathonay. The reason for your repatriation is heart trouble. (Two advantages here: heart trouble will explain your abnormally high colouring, and I can give you complete repatriation papers, both French and German. These papers go down particularly well with the Boche.) Once repatriated you return to Paris, where you are employed by the Union, the big insurance company, as a publicity agent. Your work since then consists of touring the different regions of France, although your headquarters is in Paris, where you live in an apartment at 12 Rue de la Victoire, 9e. (Thus, if you ever approach a strange town you search previously in the directory for the name and address of the Union representative in that town. The Boche stops you. "Where are you going?" he demands. "To see Mr. So-and-so, number 6, Such-and-such street," you instantly reply.)

"Now go away and think it over," he urged me, all in the same breath. "In a few days I shall have the whole thing worked out perfectly with very complete papers. Then you must learn the story by heart and begin to live your new part. It is most essential to live the story. That is why I have made you a publicity man, not just a plain insurance agent. And the accent accounted for, and the heart trouble. Yes, I think it is good."

I thought so too, but it did not fill me with confidence.

At the phony-continental-clothes-and-accessories department I collected my new belongings. They gave me the lot in two suit-cases. All the cloak and dagger clothes were handed over by a typical British quartermaster's clerk. I don't suppose men ever looked less cloak and daggerish than he, with his wholesome, long face and his neat battle-dress with the trousers sewn into permanent creases, or than me, dolled up like a dutiful little officer with my correctly shining belt, hat and gloves.

The things he handed me were ugly, but of good quality. They had invited me to order two suits. I had only taken one—of a type their tailor called a "blue uncrushable"—and instead of the other I had chosen a dark grey leather jacket and brown corduroy trousers. I fondly hoped that with my accent and appearance I should be able to spend most of my time hidden in the woods. Then the organisation provided everything else, from winter and summer underwear to a "housewife". I had not been so completely equipped with necessaries and unnecessaries since the Nazis, marching across Europe, had begun casually to collect all my property on the way. It seemed a crime that all this stuff had to be parachuted with me. At that time I half thought that I should be obliged to jump with a suit-case in each hand and a brown-paper parcel under my arm.

Nothing in the suit-case was "Made in Britain". Most of it

was "Fabrication Française". Everything I had, from the long, over-waisted, blue overcoat to the last razor-blade was precisely listed with a blunt pencil in the normal illegible hand by the normal quartermaster's clerk and I signed for it in the normal Army manner. Then I drove away with my suit-cases and dumped them in the dirty house. I was thankful to be rid of them. The very sight of them put me on edge.

Before I left for the last course, to learn about the science of parachuting supplies, one of the majors said to me comfortingly: "Well, Millar, old chap, you must be relieved that all this tiresome period of training is practically over. Soon you will be at the real thing."

"Wonderful," I agreed, trying not to allow my tone to be too sepulchral. "If you like that sort of thing, of course."

"But you do like it. Why, your whole life shows that you like that sort of thing. The spirit of adventure is not dead yet in our young men, don't you think?"

Sometimes a careless remark like that makes you feel that you have influenza and frost-bite at the same time.

"I know one young man it's dead in," I told him. "Dead and rotting. Oh, by the way. Something wonderful happened today."

"What's that?"

"They gave me a cover story."

"Naturally," he drawled coldly.

Something else happened to me when I got back from that last course. It had been one of the best. Particularly interesting, and not far from a smooth-flowing river in which I could see my face reflected brown, swirling, not cherubic but devilish in the thick water's curving volutes. Between the waters of the river and the wonder of strange wireless apparatus I was in a human mood, for that time, when I returned at tea-time to my London hotel. There was a parachuting doctor there who told me that the previous evening at a big cocktail-party he had met B., a woman for whom, once in vain on the telephone and the rest of the time subconsciously, I had been searching since my hurt began.

The parachuting doctor, who walked cattily with his hips like Battling Siki did, took me to B.'s flat, where people like any other civilised people gave us war-time drinks. And my hurt began to change a little, and my mind, and the chemical composition of my body.

Walking home very late and alone that night from battered

Belgrave Square, I told myself how strange it was. It was as though my hurt had been a seething chemical mass enlarged a billion times and thrown upon a screen to show extraordinary patterns. Then an antidote or changing substance had introduced itself to one corner of the seething mass, and the forms and patterns began to alter, to mean something else. For strangers, watching, they altered so subtly that the pattern still looked the same. But the pattern was part of me, and I felt the change.

Dark, chalk-faced Frenchwomen watched me as I walked eastwards down Piccadilly, wondering. It was nearly dawn. An American was singing cowboy love songs in an upper room of the Splendide. My old night porter said as he swung back the creaking door: "Thought you was never coming home, sir."

"I haven't come home," I answered. I opened the black-out curtains so that I could watch the dawn on the bomb-scarred roofs and terraces outside my bedroom window. Before I fell asleep I realised that for ten hours I had not thought of my work or of the aquarium.

"Hey," shouted Mrs. Pollock. It was a carnation day. White ones and deep, dusky crimson ones gleamed on her desk. Their crispness dominated the smells of spearmint and American cigarettes.

"Do carnations always make you think of heifers before they have become cows?" I asked her. "Black ones without horns and with curly hair combed and brushed for the show. Virgins who have yet to smoke their first Mexican hemp, drink their first absinthe."

"I adore carnations. And I detest having to deal with mad boys who miss their appointments. Where were you yesterday evening?"

"With a girl."

"Nonsense. You were probably drinking. You were released from the course early to get back for an interview with someone-or-other, I can't remember who. I've been racking my brains all night." She changed her tack. "Why are you in uniform? Do you want to commit suicide? I order you to wear your nice civilian clothes."

"They are not nice. They are impossible. I refuse to go about London dressed like that. Everybody will ask: 'Why are you dressed like a publicity agent for a big Paris insurance company?'"

"I am not asking you, I am telling you to wear your blue suit."

I never wore the blue suit in London. Instead I evolved a technique for avoiding the woman by waiting in the hall until she was busy with somebody else and then insinuating myself on tiptoe into the inner parts of the building. She only caught me once in the few days that remained to me in England.

"Are you *still* in uniform?" she said. "Don't blame me if the Gestapo tear you limb from limb. Have a nice time at the parachute school. Think of me as you exit from the aircraft on your first jump."

The parachute school was the usual ugly country house. I had arrived late in the evening, but they put me straight out on the lawn with an officer in parachute overalls who (although he was British) looked capable of fighting Dempsey before breakfast and the Wild Bull of the Pampas before Dempsey. Mixed with the noble elms and beeches on the lawn were some nasty things they called "mock-ups".

By the end of the evening, with the help of mock-ups of varying heights I had been taught how to land in a parachute without driving my legs through my torso, and to exit feet first from a hole in the bottom of an aircraft, to exit as stiff and pointed as a sea bird diving (upside down).

Next day I did two jumps. The first was all right. The second began as a dive, but ended up safely. After a long train journey I reached London in time to see B. just after dinner. The change in my chemical composition was now so marked as to be almost visible. It made my going away easier, not more difficult. I began to regard what was coming to me in France as a severe test, not as the lethal chamber.

It appeared to be coming to me all right. There were six or seven appointments arranged for me on the day following my jumps. At the first of them a captain told me that they wanted me to leave for France in two days' time, on the evening of Thursday, June 1st. I was to be dropped near a village called Chaignay, about ten miles north of Dijon.

"Know that part?" he asked.

"No, not at all. But I know that it's a good part of France."

"Yes, and we're sending you to a friend."

"Indeed?"

"Yes, Albert. He went out two months ago. He's developed a big sector centring around Dole, dropping down as far as St. Amour to the south, including Dijon and Besançon to the north.

We dropped an American radio operator, Paul, to him last moon. Now Albert has asked us for a lieutenant. No use disguising the fact that the sector is tough. It's very far east, you see, and the area is full of Huns. Another organiser, Henri, worked there for some time, then he was wounded by the Gestapo, and was lucky to escape. He was followed by Pedro. Pedro was on his way to the Swiss frontier one day when he was shot and killed by the Germans at Montbeliard. Then, from Pedro's death to Albert's arrival, the Resistance carried on under two of Pedro's lieutenants, men called Gut and Petit Henri. Well, what d'you think?"

"The area would suit me all right. There's just one thing. I am no friend of Albert. I don't like him."

"Good heavens. You mean you'd prefer *not* to work with him?"

He hurried off to a conference. They probably decided that I only had cold feet, and would be all right if pushed along a little. The captain returned and asked me: "Do you refuse to work with Albert?"

"No, of course not. But I would rather not work with him."

"Are you unwilling to work with him because he is very young, and you feel that he is unworthy to command you?"

"Most certainly not. I formed a high opinion of his capabilities. I certainly consider him fitted to command me. But it might be unwise to begin an association with a chief whom I, probably quite unreasonably, dislike."

"You have some definite reason for disliking him?"

"Yes."

"What is that?"

"It is a personal reason."

"Ah." I could see a gleam of triumph in his eye. "But surely, Millar, you would not allow personal things to interfere with your job, with this job? If we ordered you to join Albert (of course we don't do things like that under these circumstances), but say we ordered you to join him, you would then work with him to the best of your ability?"

"Yes, I suppose so. But it seems stupid to put two people together who already have a personal antagonism, however small, between them. And how does Albert feel about it? Have you asked him whether he is willing to have me?"

"No, but we shall do that at once. In the meantime, unless you definitely want to back out, stand by to leave on Thursday."

I did not care for his "unless you want to back out". They

thought I had cold feet. Well, I had. And I did not want to go to Albert. But I saw that they intended to send me.

If I had been normal and keen I should have spent the next forty-eight hours in frantic preparation. I should have studied maps of the sector, getting road and rail networks into my head. I should have memorised intelligence data about enemy troop concentrations. With the aid of a large-scale map of Dijon I could have pictured the place where I was to be parachuted and determined what to do if I missed the reception committee. I should have wondered what sort of place Chaignay, the nearest village, was, and I should have worked out the route from there to Salins (a very long way), since the only address I had for contacting Albert was near Salins. Lastly I should have shut myself up and memorised my cover story which had been handed to me that morning together with an astonishing number of forged "personal papers" for Georges Henri Maillard.

Instead of all that, however, I telephoned B., left the office, and did not go back there until Thursday morning, the morning of my departure. I swept the whole thing clean out of my head. It is true that I went about London, as I thought for the last time, with a certain prodigality of emotion, and occasionally of gesture. Now that I really was on the helter-skelter looking down it was not worth bothering about being there.

On Thursday morning I got up very early and packed all my personal belongings which were to be stored by the organisation. The same captain who had argued about Albert told me that I was to leave that night.

"We have decided finally to send you, since Albert has raised no objections," he said, with a nice smile. "And since the nights are short now and getting shorter, and it is a long flight over enemy territory to your sector, we have made you priority for tonight. We are afraid that if you don't go tonight you may not go for a couple of months. Is there anything else you want to know?"

Anything else? In a glistening, shining, swirling rush all the things a bright young agent-about-to-leave ought to know filled my head. I mentioned five or six of them and he gravely made notes. That day, like any important murderer, I could get anything within reason that I wanted.

Before seeing anyone else I went to the reading-room and wrote to my mother. I was worried about her, for she had just heard that my younger brother had been killed in Burma. I wrote a carefully rushed-looking letter saying that I was being

17

sent away on "an intelligence job" for a few months, that I would be able neither to send nor to receive letters, that the War Office (actually one of the Intelligent Gentlewomen) would let her know that I was all right once a month, and that she must not worry since the country that I was going to was not a theatre of war (this was strictly true at the time of writing). I felt badly about this letter. So badly that I hurried out into the street to post it and to get it as much as possible off my conscience. Orders were orders, and I could do nothing else.

A terrible shock lay in store for me. I entered the dirty house almost gaily, and gaiety must usually be paid for in suffering. At my first interview the blow fell.

"Kindly sign your field name twenty times on this sheet of paper," said the interviewer, an English captain who spoke with a strong French accent.

"What is my field name?" I asked, for I had never bothered to find out. I could have known quite simply. It was written on one of the papers which they had given me several days previously. He searched on the paper in front of him. Then hit me on the nose with this sledge-hammer.

"Désiré," he said.

"Would you mind repeating that?"

"Désiré," he repeated, a little sharply.

Visions connected with this ghastly name flashed through my head. I saw stalwart foresters laying back their heads until the neck cords showed like bared intestines, but their voices came in a shallow unison pipe: "Oh, Désiré." I saw the German questioners in Gestapo headquarters. Their leader said: "We give you one last chance, Captain Er, Captain Um, Captain Désiré."

I saw a woman with gold teeth and dirty hair who came towards me asking: "Qu'est ce que tu désire, Désiré? . . ."

"I refuse," I shouted. "I will not go with that name. Find me another name and I will go."

He looked at me glassily, then down at his papers. He carefully drew a pig alongside a red "Secret" stamped on them. "Nerves," every hesitating stroke of his pencil seemed to say. He began to draw another pig as he spoke again.

"It is too late to change now. If you did not like the name you should have complained earlier. Sign twenty times. I am very sorry that you did not complain earlier."

He was right. It was my own fault. With a pen dipped in vitriol and an elbow that groaned I signed Désiré twenty times. It looked even worse than it sounded.

"What kind of people are called Désiré?" I asked him. He looked at me with an irrepressible flicker of sympathy.

"Certain senators and a few hairdressers," he replied gravely.

"And publicity agents?" I suggested.

"Rarely," he replied. "Very rarely."

One of the Intelligent Gentlewomen whom I next saw gave me a glimmer of hope.

"It *is* rather a dreadful name," she agreed. "Perhaps I might manage to get it changed."

She drew up my will for me, a new one. My whole life had altered since I made my other will. She had handsome, heavy eyebrows that were as poised as Georgian candelabra. She had an answer for everything, and I suspected that she knew all about my past and present. Something watchful and soothing about her eyebrows warned me that she was steering me through, that she realised what a fraud I was, and pretty tired of the war anyway, and frightened of everything, including making an idiot of myself.

When the ordinary business was finished she produced maps and talked to me about the region where I was going. It was Intelligence eye-wash, and I had been in France recently enough to know that most of what she said was nonsense. She was trying to comfort me, and she knew that I would want to hide with as many Stens between me and the Gestapo as possible. She brought it all out so calmly, and in such a smooth, fruity voice that I continued to be grateful to her and even raised her in my own seniority list for that organisation to the rank of *the* Intelligent Gentlewoman (which was something).

Down in someone else's office five minutes later she showed how sternly she merited her recent promotion. We were looking over some maps, deciding which ones I should take with me that night. There were two other people there, both of them, naturally, employees of the organisation. In front of them I mentioned the name of Lons le Saunier, a town in Albert's sector. The I.G. took me into a far corner of the room and spoke into my ear: "I know that you are quite unused to such work. But for goodness' sake *never* mention names of places or people."

You were perfectly right, Intelligent Gentlewoman, with your voice that reeked of the rightness of life, of tea in the nursery and snowmen with pipes in their mouths and Struwelpeter and Jemima Puddleduck to read. So right that afterwards, when discretion really mattered, I would go hot and cold and keep my mouth shut remembering your "for goodness' sake".

They told me to be back at five o'clock that evening. There was a general rushing round of agents. A tall officer darted at me and asked if I wanted to take an American carbine with me. At other times the little Winchester has seemed one of the best things on earth. Now I recoiled with a shudder.

"No weapons," I said. "Please don't thrust weapons or equipment upon me. If go I must then I will attempt to conquer more by charm and example." A small crowd of Frenchmen had gathered round. "Gandhi is the greatest general today," I continued. "He may carry off a permanent victory. He fights without arms, he fights with the will and the suffering smile. Christ taught the genius of counter-attacking by turning the other cheek. Christianity persists today. We shall win this war against Germany. But how long will our victory of arms persist? Perhaps twenty years. That is why it is important, even though we are committed to a war of arms, to fight according to the rules of civilised battle, to show the Boche that there exists among his enemies, even while they fight, a flowering of these softer and more charming qualities which he secretly so greatly admires."

Gentle pity (for me) shone in the eyes of a large English-woman who stood near-by trying to attract my attention, but the Frenchmen seethed like the inside of a heated boil.

"If I thought that you were going to talk like that in France, Captain Millar, I would kill you now before you could leave," hissed the first one to speak. "Let the Germans charm back my finger-nails." Three of the fingers on his left hand were without nails and were puckered at the ends like the mouths of aged crones before the invention of false teeth.

"Now, now. You know that Captain Millar is quite mad, and did not mean a word of it," said the Englishwoman in a thick finishing school French accent. "I must take him away now to look at his clothes."

My two suit-cases were laid out in the baggage-room. One was small and yellow and the other was big and brown and frankly not leather.

"What will you wear tonight, Captain Millar, the gent's suiting or the 'men of the Maquis'?"

"The latter. Comfort must come first, although it will be a little embarrassing going through London in that."

She began to repack my suit-cases, taking out the clothing I would wear and filling spaces with bags of tea and coffee and slabs of chocolate and razor-blades and packets of French cigarettes, Gauloises Bleues, manufactured in clever England.

"I don't wear woollen underwear except when I am a prisoner of war," I told her, for I was keeping an eye on the clothing she unpacked.

"You must wear it tonight, though, duckie," she answered firmly. "They all say it's perishing cold in the aircraft—all the ones that come back."

I was thankful to get out of the aquarium. I would have liked to have had the time to sit down and howl with laughter at myself. There were no taxis to be found that day, and I had forgotten to book a table for lunch, so we wandered round several restaurants before settling down in one of them to have a drink and wait. Leave had been stopped for the Americans, but London still bulged with them. When we got a table we were on a banquette alongside a young man who had worked with me in peace-time, and who had found himself a nice job (at least some would call it that) in a Ministry. However, he was not with his wife, but with somebody else's, and he appeared to pay little attention to us.

B. wore a frivolous white hat and was very serious. She said she was sure that I would be killed. I argued about this, but I secretly agreed with her.

We were lunching late. It was 2.30. While we talked the mechanics would be working on the four engines that were to take me and twelve containers and eight packages to Dijon and then drag the big empty aeroplane back through the sky to England. The waiter seemed to be French. I asked him where he came from. Bordeaux, he said, and gave us two lumps of sugar each with our coffee. I wondered if I was unhappy now because I had to leave B. I hoped so, for it is better to have something positive and fixed and worthwhile to be unhappy about. Something was dragging me towards the aircraft and the parachute, though. Perhaps it was only the departure urgency that affects everybody when there is a train or an aeroplane to catch.

Before I left I was taken to the most terrifying place in London, the dark, low place in Piccadilly, the cavern where women meet each other and have tea. I said good-bye to B.'s mother there. I remember that my anxiety about the night's work, the apprehension which had been building up for some

21

days and which I have made no attempt to conceal, did not prevent me from being terrified at entering that place and threading through the tables.

B. came with me in the taxi, and she cried when I got out at some distance from the dirty house so that she would not know where I had been employed.

They told me to hurry up and get changed.

"You leave almost immediately," said a young captain. "The R.A.F. have refused to take you, but the Americans say they will. Liberators. They are doing a magnificent job now. . . ."

"My God."

The big woman had put my clothes in the cupboard lined with mirrors which she called the "changing-room". I hid the thick woollen underwear behind one of the mirrors. Although hurried, I made a good job of this. They will probably find the underwear when that house is pulled down. My grey leather jacket and corduroy trousers looked so horribly new that I had twinges of conscience for the days in London that I had not given to the organisation. I really should have worn my civilian clothing.

Besides, they told me that I should see the colonel before I left. This was a particularly sympathetic and admirable colonel. His talents and industry and kindliness had coloured the whole organisation, and had done much towards keeping me alive during the past two months. I was scared of the colonel, one always is.

So I took off my leather coat and trousers, rubbed them on the filthy floor and walked and stamped on them. They looked better. When I had mixed some water and dust in the wash-basin and rubbed the mixture in wet they looked so much better that I did the same for my beret.

A vast American station wagon stood outside the front door. And three people, the colonel, the Intelligent Gentlewoman, and the young captain, were waiting on the pavement to say good-bye. The usual French words were exchanged that are supposed to bring good luck. The colonel said something very kind to me in his soft voice. I suddenly felt that I wanted to make a go of it, for him. While I was savouring this feeling he handed me an astonishing present, gold cuff-links, made from four great chunks of gold and two gold anchor cables.

"A small present from all of us," he said. "We like to give all of you men some little personal thing before you leave. Something you can use and think that we are behind you, with you in a sense. We are not all strong enough or young enough to go

22

into the field ourselves. You don't smoke, I know, so I bought these for you. They are gold and they have no English markings on them. So they might come in useful; you should be able to hock them if you run out of money."

I climbed into the car. It smelled shiny and well cared for. The three on the pavement were all tall. They were obliged to crouch slightly to shine their friendly smiles into the car. Suddenly the Intelligent Gentlewoman leaned closer and tapped on the window.

"Why, I nearly forgot," she said to me. "We have changed your field name to Émile."

"Hosanna in the highest. How can I ever thank you?"

One moment to be called Désiré, and the next to be called Émile. Life can be very wonderful. Émile. Liberating name. I will always love it in deepest gratitude.

We moved away. They all waved. A light rain was falling. It was five o'clock. The after-work rush for ordinary people was beginning. I suddenly liked all the ordinary people of London, a quite exceptional feeling for me.

I still clutched the massive gold cuff-links in my hot right hand. (I wonder what German has them now.) I stuffed them into my pocket alongside the long-suffering copy of the cover story I still did not know.

We were leaving the street where I should have worked, where I had failed to prepare myself for what lay ahead. The dirty house was small now in the tapering perspective. Three figures were moving slowly back, off the wet pavement.

It was good-bye to the aquarium.

CHAPTER II

THERE were three other passengers in the big, comfortable car. One was my old acquaintance, the French-English captain. He did not seem to like me any better now that my name was no longer Désiré. The other two were an American agent called Dick, and his radio operator, a young and lusty Frenchman, who had a curious way of flinging back his long, greased hair with a twist of the neck.

This pair sat in the back seat, immediately behind me, and as they gradually woke up—they began the trip in gummy-eyed silence, for they had been sleeping all day—they exchanged the wise-cracks for the sake of talking that men utter when they are tired and their nerves are stretched.

All the windows gradually fogged up as the gentle, wetting, spring rain poured down them. Like the windows of a fascinating fishmonger's shop that I had often admired as a child in Great Western Road, Glasgow. The captain lay in a dozing silence, punctuated with the smoking of Gold Flake cigarettes, a habit for which he had come ill-prepared, for he was obliged to ask me for a match every time he lit one.

But Dick, and his operator talked for the lot of us. They were due to leave from the same airfield as myself, and it was their second attempt. They had made this same trip the previous night, had left English soil at 10 p.m. in a Liberator, reaching out through thick weather to the place they wanted to go to, somewhere in the north-east of France.

But they had failed to find the lights of the people waiting for them. So they turned back, touching down in England at 6 a.m. They were in London for a late breakfast and here they were, tired and a little shaken, but bolstering their spirits with loud talk and forced laughter, and fully ready to try again.

They were a good pair. The American was, as Americans sometimes are, a shade loud-mouthed for our European taste. But I had known him for some time, and I knew that he was a good worker. I liked him better, too, in his funny civilian clothes than in his uniform. For in the American army he had been one of those parachutists who wear khaki pasha's pants tucked into high boots, and Dick had been an ultra, ultra-parachutist, hung with gadgets and talking the language. Why is it that one usually likes other men better in civilian clothes, and oneself better in uniform? Perhaps there is some of the jealousy of the fighting cock in this antipathy for the parachutist (the parachutist on leave, that is).

He was depressed about what lay ahead, Dick was. Perhaps more than me. He had had a good time in England. He was young, and had no unhappiness to get rid of. He spoke good French, and looked dark and un-Anglo-Saxon, but he thought he was going to a bad area. The radio man seemed calmer. This part of the work was easier for the Frenchmen. After all, they were going to their home-land, that gave them fifty per cent extra confidence.

Maddeningly, a Scottish tune that I had learned as a child came tripping through my head. Insistingly the words, stupidly heroic, beat into my head:

"Chains and slavery . . . Wha would be a traitor knave . . . Wha would fill a coward's grave . . . Let us do or dee . . ."

And again, perhaps by association, another, still more gooey:

"Bonnie Charlie's noo awa', safely o'er the friendly main. Mony a heart will break in twa, should he ne'er come back again . . ."

I wondered if B. was still crying, but comforted myself with the logical conclusion that nobody could cry steadily for one hour and twenty minutes, and now she must be faced with other people who did not know about us or me. The two maudlin old tunes came through my head, maddening me finally into a hearty disgust at myself. I realised that I was wonderfully, greedily hungry, hungry as I had not been for weeks and months. In fact, I had not been hungry from January 20th, when I arrived in Britain from Germany, until this spring evening, June 1st.

From my hunger I took heart. And something inside me stirred slightly at the thought of action and exercise and sunshine and darkness and rain. Simple physical things, so different from the things that life had offered me this time in Britain.

Grey and storm-tortured, the sky hung heavily over the fields, and the wet, black road that we followed seemed to wind up-country as though its destination was the sky. The captain ordered a halt to demand on the telephone if the aeroplanes really would take off. The car pulled up at a small, impoverished-looking inn.

"Don't worry about the looks of the pub, you can get whisky there," the captain assured us, with practical good sense. I realised then that he knew this route well. To him this was only one trip like many others. How many other men had he seen off on the strange one-way passage? Did it do anything to him to send them off like that?

He came back and drank his small whisky in quick sips. Between sips he told us, as though it were scarcely important, that our trip had not so far been cancelled. I think I was glad, for my hunger was growing, and Dick told me about boards groaning with American food at the airfield.

The sentry on the gates was huddled under a thorn tree for shelter against the wind and the rain. He knew the escorting captain. It was such a bleak place that all the kindly Americans in their leather jackets and squashed hats seemed like explorers to me, and the place as much an outpost of their Empire as a stockade with an arrow hanging from the flag and natives war-dancing outside. The mess, a long hut with bare board tables

and benches and dirty windows, thrumming with the rain.
heightened this impression. We ate enormously, a last meal in
England that had nothing English in it. In fact the only English
thing within miles seemed to be my accent. After the meal they
ordered the three of us off to the lavatory to empty ourselves
before being trussed up in our parachute clothes and harness.

What ghastly lavatories! Not even locks on the doors, or
room to move one's elbows; and the cheapest of cheap fittings!
It would have been well at such a moment to sit in a white-
enamelled palace with a glowing electric fire, and perhaps a
wonderful view like the one in Huxley's "Chrome Yellow".

After this ordeal we went to be dressed in separate little cells.
We were not only dressed, we were searched. I had a lot of
experience as a prisoner at the hands of Italian and German
searchers. The searcher this time was a quiet Britisher. He wore
civilian clothes and talked with some kind of soft West Country
accent. He adopted a motherly attitude and sprinkled his talk
with old-maidish expressions.

"Oh deary me, aren't we nicely fitted out now," he said, running his big hands swiftly, cunningly through my clothes. "Best
of the good old British wool, I'll bet, comes from Bonnie Scotland, I dare say. Did you say you were Scotch, Sonnie . . ."

"Say, Chan," shouted an American, shoving his head round
the door. "That the one who's going alone? Ain't you through
with him yet?"

"Nearly, nearly," said the searcher, tearing a price ticket out
of the lining of my beret, and starting on my maps with a
magnifying-glass he had taken from the pocket of his sedate,
dark waistcoat. "The horse Hurry always finished last. Now
what have we here? Money. Well, my, my, young man. You
could have a time with all them francs around Paree. . . ."

The money was arranged in a white money-belt. There were
great wads of it, for I was carrying a lot out to Albert as well as
what in peace-time would have seemed a fantastic sum in cash,
for myself. I put the money-belt on next to my skin, arranging
the bulging bits over my kidneys and adjusting the neat brace-
straps. When I had the rest of my clothes on a young American
officer came in and pushed me into my parachutist overalls with
a strange coat that buttoned between the legs and zipped everywhere else. The overalls were filled with special pockets, mostly
around the legs, holding hardware like a shovel, a parachutist's
knife, a small flask, my own .38 automatic and a tin of
emergency rations. Inside my trousers at the back they fitted

an enormous Sorbo rubber mat called, properly but inaccurately, a "spine-pad". Then they strapped me into my parachute harness, a harness so designed that once firmly in it you could not stand up straight owing to a strap coming from the neighbourhood of your shoulders which gripped you round the legs just below the rump.

At the last moment the French-English captain drifted in. He scooped my English belongings, money, note-case, clothing coupons, into a large envelope.

He handed me two celluloid containers. One had minute white tablets in it and the other had blue ones. He told me either that the white ones were for energy and the blue ones were a strong opiate (one tablet giving twenty-four hours' immediate sleep) or the other way about—that the white gave sleep and the blue energy.

(The trouble was that I could never remember which. As there was no point in putting yourself to sleep for twenty-four hours while running away from the Germans, and still less in giving a German sentry an "energy" tablet, I never tried them out. Except that in an effort one night to find out which was which I chose two bouncing young girls in the Landel's house at Loulans, and gave each of them a tablet, saying that it was an energy tablet. To one I gave a blue, to the other a white. They ate them after dinner, at nine o'clock in the evening, swallowing them with a sip of Burgundy. I expected to see only one of them at breakfast the next morning, but both turned up, neither looking excessively drowsy, and both complaining that they did not feel in the least energetic. After that I gave up.)

"You boys finished messing around?" the American shouted. "This guy is wanted outside."

"Who wants me?"

"The pilot, general."

They pushed me with great difficulty into the back of a car. Alone I could just fit into the space normally occupied by two people. It was still raining and, since it was now ten o'clock, the space of the airfield was shadowed and grey with pale curtains of thin rain sweeping it.

On one corner of the airfield were two Liberators, flying trucks, fat and solid-looking. Standing, most surprisingly somehow, near the Liberators was a girl in American girl's uniform. She had one of those wholesome, round faces with a short nose and wide eyes and mouth. The rain was running down her forehead and cheek-bones. She stood looking at me, frankly interested, staring. I looked into her eyes almost unconsciously as I passed her—for by this time I felt as though I were half drunk, and my parachute harness and enormous bulk obliged me to walk like King Kong—and her eyes gave me a nice, friendly smile.

"I might ask for your autograph if it weren't raining and you hadn't so much to do," she said. "What does doing what you are doing feel like to you?"

"I honestly don't know," I answered truthfully. The eight engines of the two Liberators were turning. The noise was terrible. Two pilots and other airmen came around me to shake hands in the rain. The captain from the Aquarium pressed forward and said good-bye. At least I thought it was that because his pale shout was submerged in the engine noises. Only two words came over from him to me. He put his head to mine and shouted in my ear:

"Don't forget." Then he went swiftly away to his big car. I don't suppose it would have made any difference if I had heard him entirely.

The Americans pushed and bustled me under the belly of the leading Liberator. With great difficulty I heaved my enormous bulk up through the aircraft's navel, and into the shed-like interior where the noise was mercifully lessened. There were two men fussing around in there, like grocers fussing in a grocer's shop. Another climbed in behind me and said:

"Guess that's about all now." He closed up the hole through which we had climbed, and went off through another hole, to his guns. One of the two men in the body of the aeroplane took me by the arm and led me to a package, a square packing-case, wrapped in a sprung container and with a small parachute fixed on the top. I sat on the parachute. They were piling all the packages forward of where I sat, to get them as near the centre of gravity as possible, for the take-off.

The small, rectangular windows were covered with blinds. When we taxied out on to the big wet airfield I lifted the corner of one of the blinds. The aeroplane's clumsy ground manœuvring showed me by chance the other Liberator lumbering out after us. We were going to the same place, but they were to leave ten minutes after us. I saw the shining tarmac running past, then the wing-tip gently lowering as the pilot turned in a wide sweep, circling the field until he struck off straight and climbing on his course to the southward.

Would I ever, from this secure little part of America, so typical a part of America with its carefully manufactured excellence and its neat little rivets, would I ever jump into the air and land in France? They had turned on a couple of tiny lights in our barn, and it was beginning to look quite attractive to me. A brown and beige attractiveness. The two Americans had finished tidying the place up, and I was able to take stock of them.

"I am the despatcher," said the taller of them, and he further told me his rank and his name; then added:

"And I come from Pasadena."

"Where the grass grows greena?" I asked, for I had always wondered.

"You French?"

"No."

"American?"

"No."

"Why then, guess you must be British. That's swell. Nice people the British. I only been over here three weeks."

"Nice people the Americans."

"You actually like them? Ever been over our side?" He sounded pleased, so I laid it on even thicker (although I was quite sincere).

"I've been twice in California. Sure I like them."

"Why?"

"I just like them."

"Good boy. Frightened? Guess you got a right to be."

"No," I lied. Now I reckoned that I could logically consider myself to be on friendly terms with the despatcher. The despatcher is a terrifying figure to the man-about-to-parachute. The despatcher is the person responsible for seeing that your parachute is correctly attached by its static line to the aeroplane, and for seeing that you go out of the aeroplane smartly whenever the bomb-aimer decides to drop you.

This despatcher was a pleasant-looking, red-haired youth with a good many freckles and a loose, tumbling body. He plied me with chewing-gum, chocolate and Chesterfield cigarettes.

"Later on, to wake you up a bit for your jump, we'll give you a nice cup of Java, strong and hot," he told me, with the accent on the last word. "Nobody makes Java like the boy friend." He waved an arm at the other man who sat silently there, saying never a word.

"He's the assistant despatcher. We don't normally carry an assistant despatcher. But this is his first combat trip and he's here for the experience. He likes the British too. Only arrived this side day before yesterday. . . ."

The assistant despatcher nodded gravely, without talking, at each fresh assertion regarding himself. He bored into my face with a pair of deep-set, small, very dark eyes. When he took them—like a navvy lifting his pneumatic-drill—from my face he fixed them on one of the little lamps and kept them there for a long time. He was a Red Indian. At any rate, he had the face of a Red Indian. A fine-bred, bony face. The kind of face I should like to have.

The aeroplane was running into bumpy weather.

"If it's like this over France we won't find no goddam reception, nor nothing else neither," said the despatcher. The inter-communication telephone spoke every now and then. By watching their faces (there were no head-phones for me) I knew when there was interesting talk going on. Strangely enough the listening look was more obvious on the Indian's face than on the ever-moving features of the red-haired youth.

"We're over the Channel now," said the despatcher after listening for a bit. "And don't leave your seat if you hear guns. This is where we test them."

After they had tested the guns the two men began to settle themselves down for the flight. The gunfire seemed to be the signal that the action was turned on. They put on their para-chutes, airmen's parachutes, smaller, weaker-looking than the massive thing I had on my back. They pulled out packages and settled themselves comfortably. They fixed their head-phones and filled their mouths with chewing-gum. The Indian showed massive jaw muscles as he chewed. They did not talk any more for a long time, except that the despatcher touched me on the leg once and said:

"Over France now."

Soon after this the flak began. Our strange, slightly vibrating barn began to pitch and roll and jump and fall in the flak. I watched the two others. The freckle-faced one seemed to be going to sleep. At any rate, his eyes were shut. The Indian still stared at nothing significant. His body swayed like a sack to the ungainly movements of the aeroplane. His jaw worked constantly, terrifyingly.

I saw the mouth of the hole that I would have to go out of. It was covered over with two traps, bolted together. On the side of the aircraft near the hole there were several little metal rail-ways for holding the fixed end of the static lines. If we found our objective I would jump down through the hole and, when I had fallen a little through the air, my static line would pull the case off my parachute, opening the parachute at the same time. When you thought it all out like that it seemed just as simple as stepping out of a train on to a platform.

Above the hole, on the port side, I saw two small signal lights. One of them should be red, the other green. When the aeroplane saw the correct light lay-out and signal letter flashing from the ground the pilot would make a long, careful circle, then, guided by the bomb-aimer, a straight approach up-wind at the lights. When he began this approach the despatcher would shout: "Running in" at me and I would sit on the end of the hole. The bomb-aimer would switch on the red light above the hole and the despatcher would shout: "Action Stations." I must then put both legs, feet close together, in the hole, my hands at my sides on the edge of the hole, and I must neither look down at the ground, nor at the light on the side of the aircraft. I must watch the despatcher's raised right hand. When the bomb-aimer changed the red light for the green one the despatcher would crash down his right hand and scream at me: "Go!" They were trained to do this scream in a most savage manner, like the scream of a maniac being hacked in half with a blunt axe. They had a theory that the more terrible the despatcher made his scream the easier it was for the man in the hole to do that extremely unnatural thing—launch himself into three hundred feet of space.

Then all I would have to do would be try to remember the things they had told me about "exits" in twenty-four hours at the school. Like that it would be easy. I had stopped being frightened about the thing. It was midnight and I was sleepy. I had eaten all the chocolate and had a huge wad of chewing-gum in my mouth. We were still crossing odd bits of flak, though it seemed less violent. Sometimes a package would slide a bit across the floor. Farther forward I could see the twelve big metal containers, stowed upright in the Liberator. They were shaking slightly in the bomb-racks, like very frightened old containers, although they were all brand new. They would have the privilege of dropping before me.

Still farther forward there was a glimmer of a light from the brains cell of the big aeroplane. I would have liked to go and see the men there and the things they were doing, and look out at the dark countryside below us (France, it really thrilled me to be flying over her, it really thrilled me that I loved her enough to be glad that I was there in the chilly, rocking barn in the sky). But I was too shy to push myself on the people who were working forward.

So I tried to think of B. and a few other people. But life seemed a little bit rushed for that. I was conscious of the enormous meal digesting quite reasonably well inside me. My legs felt good and strong when I stretched them out. The square-toed, imitation-French shoes looked a bit silly under the parachuting trousers, though. I had refused to allow them to bind my ankles. I drowsed off into good sleep.

He had been shaking me for some time. I thought it was the rocking of a boat, for I dreamed that I was somewhere on the sea.

"Hey," shouted the despatcher. "Wake up, buddy. Time to get ready. One o'clock. We should be there in a half-hour."

I could go from the forward edge of the hole or the after edge; at the forward edge there was only a narrow shelf to sit on, but I had firmly made up my mind to go from there. I knew from my two previous jumps and from parachuting talk that when you go from the forward edge the slipstream hits your back and it is easy to make a good exit.

They sat me down in position, hooking my static line, and then held it up to show it to me. Then they busied themselves with the eight packages, dragging them aft and attaching all their static lines. I soon went to sleep again.

The despatcher wakened me with a yellow, bakelite cup of indifferent coffee. I thought the Red Indian had fallen down on the job. This was not good Java. They lit a cigarette for me and stuck it in my mouth. They were mothering me.

"I'll probably have to open up the hole in a minute," said the despatcher. "Want more coffee, son? No? Feeling okay? Swell. I have to kind of admire you guys. You're my second. Makes me feel bad to have to send you out there in the cold. . . . Guess you won't need no shove. . . ."

The Red Indian thrust a little book into my hands, and a big fat fountain-pen. It was an autograph-book. I signed an assumed name, and glanced back through the pages. The only name I recognised was Aimée Semple MacPherson. I had a feeling that the rest were baseball names. Stars. I wanted to cry.

"Give us your hand, son. Happy landings," said the despatcher. "Here goes." And he began to open the hole, folding back one flap, then the other. I forced myself to look down after a moment of slight nausea caused by the inrush of cold, savage air.

It was a clear, a lovely moonlit night, and through the hole which was, I suppose, about four feet wide, I saw the fields and woods and farms of France. They were passing swiftly, for we were travelling low over some high ground. After a little I felt something urging me to look up. The Red Indian wanted to speak to me. He leaned across the hole and grasped my hand. I braced myself back, for I was afraid that his powerful hand-clasp would pull me in. His face looked like the Satanic face of a male ballet-dancer.

"Give 'em hell, pal," he said. I nearly fell in from astonishment. His voice was as brazen as the voice of Groucho Marx. The despatcher was gesturing wildly at me.

Down through the hole I saw lights. Four of them in the required shape, with one flashing an erratic "K", the correct code letter. We were really there. I simply could not believe it. I realised suddenly that quite an important part of me had been telling the rest of me that we should never find the dropping-ground.

Parachutes floating past beneath my feet roused me from an introspective daze. The twelve containers; good God, I was next. Without being told I took up the "Running in" and then the "Action Stations" position as I had been taught. Sure enough. The despatcher's right arm was raised. I stole a clandestine look at the light to my right. It was still at red. What were they playing at? I wanted urgently to go. I was going to be late. What were they playing at? We were leaving the lights well behind, surely. I thrust my head stiffly back and glared at the despatcher's hand. His hand was dropping, dropping very, very slowly, it seemed to me, and gently, like the whispered endearment of a loving aunt, the word "Go" came floating across the hole to me. Without waiting for any more nonsense I angrily shot myself through the hole. Next moment I was lying on my back in the air watching the fat round camouflaged belly of the aircraft passing above me. My parachute opened.

I felt cold and absurdly big in the moonlight. I knew that I had forty-five seconds to descend in. Forty-five seconds between free America and France in chains.

33

CHAPTER III

GOING down. I waited a moment to make sure it was really true. Yes, the big umbrella was open all right, and I was gently swinging from the lovely Nylon ropes that gleamed like silk wigs in the moonlight. So I waggled my bottom out of the strap that held it, swung up both arms in the rather affected arc they had taught me, grabbed the lines in each hand and took up the crouched, looking-down landing position. Now I could see the ground below.

All I saw was wheat, wheat blowing in a wind, sometimes showing partings like a woman's long hair in a wind. I had no time to be obsessed with the beauty of the wheat. Before I could be obsessed with anything I had made a reasonable landing, quite a fast one with a bump and a roll. Then I found myself being towed through the wheat. That wind really was strong. I sluiced round on one side, spilling the air from the big bag. The heads of the wheat lashed me about the face and eyes.

The parachute lay, a mighty, untidy dark splash of deadness on the living wheat. I got it into a straight line and rolled it, then twisted the lines into that in-and-out pattern they liked at the training school, climbed out of my parachuting clothes and rolled them into the parachute.

Now I had earned a drink. So I drank from the little flask they had given me. Rum it was, and good. British Army rum from the West India Docks. Not a soul was to be seen. That did not worry me because I knew they had dropped me late, and I had certainly over-shot the reception ground.

Here came my aeroplane on its final circuit. Beautiful in its queer heavy way, and powerful with its roaring, it crossed right over me, but a long time before it reached me eight white puffs magically appeared under its belly, as though it were spawning. The eight packages floated down, landing out of sight, lower down than my wheat-field.

"Hey," I told myself. "My two suit-cases are among all those." The Liberator was flying off, waggling its wings in farewell. I left in the opposite direction.

But three figures, in line, appeared ahead of me, like figures in a wheat-field in a Russian film. I sank slowly to my knees, then lower until I was completely hidden from the men who approached. They came on without caution, shouting to each other. This worried me a little. They were too far away for me to distinguish their shouting. I had been taught to believe that only Germans shouted, and that the Resistance worked slyly, silently.

So I took my pistol from my pocket and crouched there. Until I heard them say:

"I'd swear a container fell near here. It dropped after the others."

"Better go on a little farther. How in the name of God will we get it back? Can't bring a cart through this field because of leaving traces."

On hearing such reassuring talk in definitely non-German French, I rose from the wheat feeling like a rather washed-out Aphrodite, and gave them a hearty "Good evening" which, on second thoughts, I changed to a "Good morning."

Instead of replying the three Frenchmen vanished. They had flung themselves face down in the wheat. The following sound was unpleasant; it was the click of a Sten gun being changed from "safe" to the "fire" position. There seemed to be no alternative. I crouched down myself. The wind tore across the wheat-field, swaying the grain like silver-blonde hair.

"Who are you?" asked one of the Frenchmen.

"Who are you?" I answered, without raising my head.

"Come out of there and give yourself up!"

"Is Albert there?" I asked.

"Never heard of him. Who are you?"

Another Frenchman who lay slightly farther away now fortunately intervened.

"Perhaps he's a parachutist," he said. "I thought the last tube was a man. Not a tube," he added, to ram his point home.

"Yes, I am a parachutist." A long pause followed, then the first Frenchman said triumphantly:

"If he were a parachutist he would have a parachute."

"Yes, let him produce his parachute," chorused the other two.

I came forward holding my absurd bundle in front of me, and when they had inspected it they led me away, one holding me by the arm, the other two behind me with Stens at the ready. They were rough-looking men in caps and ordinary clothing.

We arrived at a wide space, lightly strewn with boulders. In the middle of it I saw a bunch of figures.

They were all making so much noise that they paid no immediate attention to our party. I just stood there while my guides or captors tried to shout louder than the others. At length one figure, stocky and powerful-looking, detached itself from the crowd and came towards me, followed by two or three others. This man was the chief. In that light I could only see that he had one arm in a sling, and wore a soft hat pulled forward over his eyes.

"They say you are a Boche spy, pretending to be an Englishman," he began. "You must prove to me quickly that you are English. We have much work to do here."

"Is Albert not here? I thought he knew I was coming."

"You know Albert?"

"Yes."

"Then what is the password for this parachutage?"

"I don't know. London gave me no password."

"He is a spy," said the first man who had spoken in the wheatfield. "We were all told that the password was 'Cambronne'."

This appeared to influence the chief in my favour.

"Shut it, loafer," he boomed at the last speaker. "This man is an Englishman, he speaks like Henri, and Henri was English, wasn't he. Excuse my left hand, Englishman, my right was wounded by a Schleuh in Dijon yesterday. My name is Jacques, do they know of me in London?"

"Yes," I lied, for I had never heard of him. "I call myself Emile."

"And you are a British officer?"

"Yes. But don't shout it around."

"Good. Very good. There is much work to be done." A chorus of approval went up from the uncouth men who crowded round us. I saw in the moonlight that some wore ordinary civilian clothes, while others were dressed in the odd scraps of rags, old uniforms, and leather coats that I had learned to expect in the Maquis. When everyone had shaken hands with me they returned to their work, arranging the twelve containers in one pile. They worked much faster than we had done in practice operations at the schools. They were strong. But they made a terrible noise.

A little goblin-like man came dancing up to me. He wore few clothes, and was so thin that I expected to see him carried away by the wind like the skeleton of a dried leaf.

"Petit-Henri," he said.

"Enchanted. Emile," I replied. "Are you the Petit-Henri who worked with Gut? Then I have heard much of you in London."

"Really heard of me in London? How wonderful. How wonderful. All that distance away. And you come in the big aeroplane and tell me." He was nearly weeping with pleasure. I saw that this Petit-Henri, *the* Petit-Henri, was only a boy.

"Tell me, Émile," he asked. "I was flashing the letter, the 'K'. Was it well done?"

"Yes. Well done. I saw it from the air."

"You saw it from the air, and now you are here with us. Fantastic. They told me 'Dah-de-dah' was 'K' so I flashed it, but I was relieved when the aeroplane came over and dropped the things. Well, I must go to my post now for the second aeroplane, and tomorrow, when you are rested we will have a long talk."

"Yes, indeed. Try to make your 'K' very regular if the other aeroplane comes. Count to yourself like this 'one, two, three, *cut;* one, *cut;* one, two three, *cut.*' But I do not think the aeroplane will come now."

"Why not, Émile?"

"Perhaps it failed to find us. They do not use wireless to plot their courses, because the Boche has many radio-locating stations. So the navigation is difficult. Also now there are many Boche night fighters, and the flak is bad for the aeroplanes."

"Poor things, what dreadful risks they run. Still we must wait on in our positions for them, must we not?"

"Yes, you must wait on for two hours. If they do not come then, something has happened."

The squat leader, Jacques, came up to me with a young boy, who led me away to the side of the field. The men were loading the containers now on two of the long French farm carts which they call "platforms". One cart had two horses in it, the other had a horse and a mule, sign of the occupation.

I walked easily and springily in the dark woods. My body felt good again, relieved of the bulky parachute clothes. Only my neck was a little stiff. I must have failed to relax it properly when I rolled out the landing shock.

Occasionally the boy asked me odd questions about England: were there still cinemas? were there still farms? was it true that most of the cows were milked by machines, and that the fields were fertilised not with dung, but with scented products manufactured in the cities? And of course the eternal question then: was there going to be a second front?

"Yes," I answered to this.

"Why do you say yes?"

"Because I have seen the armies massing in England, and

37

where you find armies massing you will always find war. France is the nearest country to England."

"But my father says that the only way to have peace after this war is for us to have a great and powerful army and air force. Surely that will not mean war?"

"Surely not," I said in a tone that ended conversation, for I suddenly felt tired and depressed and lonely in the bleak moonlight. The farm lay ahead. In the kitchen he lit an acetylene lamp, gave me a glass of Marc and a slice of the bread they make with honey, then led me up to the best bedroom. The double feather-bed looked good. I told myself it was risky to sleep in bed so near the parachutage, but I told myself too late. Before I had time to consider the problem and agree that it *was* dangerous I was in bed and asleep.

That is how people get killed.

A warmer sun than I was accustomed to was pouring into the room. I got quickly out of the feather-bed, and looked out of the window. There were fields and some big woods. I eyed the woods carefully, but saw no smoke, or other sign of the Maquis. There were three men in greyish shirts and faded blue trousers working in different parts of the field. I tried to attribute sinister, under-world motives to these industrious figures. But it was difficult to explain away their hoes, and bent, toiling backs.

My first reaction was to see either the dark hand of the Resistance or the dark hand of the enemy in everything I saw in France. This reaction lasted for about two weeks as far as the Resistance was concerned, and for about a month as far as the Germans were concerned, decreasing after that, but coming back strongly every time that they gave me a fright. These feelings were normal. Other people who did the same work always told me that they felt exactly the same way about things. Our organisation believed that it took a normal man about ten days to get settled in and begin working seriously. It took me longer, but I am of a naturally timorous disposition.

Down in the farm kitchen I washed myself. There was an old woman there, who seemed pleased to see me. She gave me a bowl of imitation coffee and milk and a huge round loaf of dark bread and about six months' British butter ration on a dirty plate. Lastly she put down a cardboard box of French sugar in long lumps. Not a bad breakfast.

Jacques came in to watch me eat. He had brought my two suit-cases, and was very impressed with them, even the imitation leather one. He set them down as though they contained diamonds or eggs, and asked the crone to get a duster and wipe them over.

"The second aeroplane didn't arrive," he told me, when he had accepted a packet of my cigarettes from England. "But we have a lot of wonderful things, Émile. Some things that we don't understand. We are uneducated men here, Émile. We have the spirit, but we need a man like you, someone educated."

"I am uneducated."

"Oh, then you don't know how to use the 'Arbalette'?"

"What's that?"

"The American anti-tank rocket thrower."

"Oh, the 'Bazooka'. Yes, I know how to use that, and I will show you and your men."

"And the English anti-tank mine, and to take the Bren gun into all its pieces, also the big 'Chassepot', the big American Colt."

"Yes, I know how to do those things."

"And you say that you are uneducated." His wolfish face broke into a charming smile. "Émile, you *must* stay with us. Your arrival puts heart into the whole band. The winter has been long. My hand hurts me, and now I think I will always have to fire with my left. But if you can stay here we will not only kill the Boche, we will *murder* him. Can you stay with us?"

"I don't know. Albert will say. I take orders from him."

"Albert will want you to go with him," he said moodily. He was a big, exaggerated child, now sulky, now friendly. His voice was like the deep booming voice of a huge Spanish priest I had met in an inn at Burgos. He was dark-haired and he had a white skin despite the gipsy life, a skin that shone with health where it was not covered with black hairs. There was a spot of blood forming at the bottom of his sling. I asked him how he had hurt his hand.

"Fired on, stupidly, in the street. After such a success," he answered sadly. "Such a success in the night. It was the nephew of the chief of the Gestapo in Dijon. He and his mistress. They thought they had laid a trap for us in their pretty bungalow. But Bobby (you will meet Bobby, he's good fun), Bobby and I decided to bait the trap ourselves. So we watched the bungalow and we arrived there, entering by a back window, two hours before our appointment. There was nobody there, but we already knew that. We settled down to wait, happily. For we had another pal with us, a 'silencieux' (silent pistol).

They arrived, the pair of them. They did not turn on the light. But our silent pal does not mind that, he has luminous sights. Bobby took the first shot. The man fell. He handed me the 'silencieux'. I shot the woman. She fell across her Boche. We left by the window. The bungalow was quiet. A real love-nest. Then I had to go and get myself shot in a street brawl.''

Our relations were strained when I had seen the containers that had dropped to Jacques' group with me. They had taken them into a thicket, only about two hundred yards from the farm where I slept. No attempt had been made to hide the tracks made by the carts. Nor to conceal the trail of broken branches and bruised grasses that led to the spoils of the parachutage.

"No danger in that. Ça ne risque rien,'' said Jacques, when I politely pointed out the lack of precaution. As the months passed with the Resistance I was to come to know this phrase: "Ça ne risque rien.'' "Ça ne risque rien,'' always the excuse of a lazy or a bad soldier, killed many a man in the end. Jacques did me a favour. He introduced me to the phrase when I had just begun work, when I was fresh from the principles and energy of London.

I went through the bushes, along the too-well-marked path to the containers. They had been strewn about in a small clearing. A lot of the contents were lying about on the trampled mud.

"What happens if it rains?'' I asked.

Jacques looked for a second at the clouds crossing the sky:

"I don't *think* it will rain,'' he said. "But as you say, we had better take our precautions.'' Within five minutes he had ten men stowing the material properly in container cells and tidying these up. He got his men moving by strong-arm methods when he bothered to put them to work.

In one corner I saw a great pile of parachutes. On the top lay my own (a parachutist's parachute, different from the others) still with the jumping-suit wrapped up in it. I gathered these things in my arms and went off to burn them.

"Hey,'' said Jacques as I stuffed all this then priceless Nylon into the farm incinerator among the burned-out refuse of cabbage husks and the only parts of sheep that peasants find inedible. "Hey, Émile. You gone crazy? That stuff is beautiful. You can't buy it here, you know.''

"Supposing the Gestapo pay a visit here, what will they find?'' I asked him.

"Everything,'' he answered immediately. "Mais ça ne risque rien.''

"But in ten minutes, when all this stuff has turned into tar, there will be nothing to tell them if they come that, along with the containers, there arrived last night a British officer."

"Huh," answered Jacques, and I could see that he thought I was over-scared. When the parachute had burned, in the sunny farm-yard I began to wonder how I would get back to Britain, if ever. I thought the answer then was "never". But there was plenty to do.

And I wondered how to do it.

Despite the protests of Jacques and his men, who could not understand why I wished to discard comfort for discomfort, I had Petit-Henri help me move my things to the shack in the woods where they lived. The shack's lineaments resembled those of a wigwam built in rectangular, instead of circular, form. It was long and narrow and pointed in section, being made of birch branches leaned together at the top to form a ridge. The interstices were blocked with lovely bright moss from the forest, and in places with none too clean-looking sacking. The floor, which fulfilled also the function of communal bed, was covered with fresh-cut hay.

Installing my things in this home, and unrolling a sleeping-bag alongside the space reserved for the chief, I committed what I think was my worst mistake in all my life in the maquis. I locked my suit-case. True, it had a million francs in it. But I locked it.

That evening, when the carbide light was turned low, and sixteen of us began, with difficulty in the narrow hut, to compose ourselves for sleep, I suddenly realised my crime. Being of Scottish parentage and origin, I believe in second sight, and I believe in speech that is unspoken. But I was not thinking of that as, bending beside my sleeping-bag I unlocked my suit-case. Nobody said anything, of course. They were terribly polite to me. Nobody even looked at me. I was thankful that the suit-case was of the one lock and two straps variety. The one lock, being strong and stiff, of best British brass, made a horrible hard click as it yielded to my gentle key. The click seemed to me to echo and linger in the strange hut like the quartz chuckles of Shylock.

I never locked anything again, in all my stay in France. No, never. If I had anything secret or terribly valuable I buried it under a bush or hid it in a hollow tree. Like that I only insulted myself. What a fraud I am.

Soon the hut was heaving with sleep, and reeking certainly

41

of garlic. I should care. I had eaten heavily at both lunch and dinner of this noble weed for which, unlike most of your gastronomically timorous Britishers, I have a profound and faithful liking. Over the irregular base of our bodies there was a little space, a kind of stratosphere of bluish light, then the narrowing top of our house was filled with a white, gently-moving cloud of pale grey tobacco smoke, bitter with the spittle of slobbery smokers.

It was too hot in my sleeping-bag. I rolled the top of it back. It was a feather-bag that had been made for a woman going into the field, then she had not wanted it, so I had profited. The inside was blue, azure blue, Mediterranean blue, and clean. Nothing could be nicer than my sleeping-bag then. I owe it everything. When the small of my back gets cold I can no longer relax. And when a man cannot relax he is wiser if he does not attempt to sleep. But inside this place it was too hot. The carbide was nearly finished in the lamp now. I fixed on two principles then and there. When in the Maquis I would try to sleep a little apart from the men. And if I had anything to do with the construction of huts like this I would have them made more on the shelter principle, with one side open to the elements.

Perhaps the men would feel the cold. But I would ask London for blankets. Clothing, they needed too, especially boots. London must send us that, and cigarettes and oil for the weapons. Fresh in the field, I did not yet think in perspective, and I imagined the whole of the supply system as waiting to parachute supplies to me.

Jacques groaned beside me as I lay and dreamed my tiny dreams of expansion. His hand wound seemed to be clean, but it was hurting him more than it should. The bullet-hole was too near the thumb-joint to look good. He was a leader all right, Jacques, I thought now. Just a little tired perhaps. . . . Just a shade lazy. . . .

The hunting-lodge in the woods reminded me of something. We took out our pistols and cautiously approached it, leaving traces on the grass still wet with morning dew. The door and shutters were closed, locked and bolted. The kennel at the back was empty, save for a few gnawed bones. There were big paw marks in the soft, sweet earth and tender grass between the kennel and the back door of the lodge. One of the shutters was warped. Thrusting the blade of my dagger in the slit I was able to swing the shutter back.

Inside were chalk-white walls, a black iron fireplace with a brass fender, a curving, old-fashioned arm-chair. Over the back of the chair was a brown velvet smoking-jacket, and on the small table beside the chair lay one of those heavy, complicated Bavarian pipes. Now it came back to me. This reminded me irresistibly of the hunting-lodge in one of the Ruritanian novels, I think the one in *The Prisoner of Zenda*.

This one belonged to a senior German officer.

"It is the one drawback to our Maquis," Jacques told me. "He comes up from Dijon every Saturday morning, and he leaves on Sunday night or Monday morning. Usually he hunts both Saturday and Sunday, but on the other side of the forest from us. Once he had other officers and perhaps some women with him, for it was here, behind the cottage, that we found the frilly woman's garter that the Squinting One showed you in the camp.

"They would be easy to kill, the pair of them. I have been waiting to ask Albert, but now you can tell me. Should we kill them, Émile?"

"No, leave them alone for the present. If you kill them you will have punitive expeditions here, and you are not strong yet, nor is your material well enough hidden."

"But we are hiding it now, Émile. Tomorrow it will be hidden. You will see. And supposing he finds us in the woods when he is hunting?"

"Then you must kill him, hide the body carefully, and strike camp at once. Move at least ten kilometres in the forest, and leave no traces. Before you move you must find the batman and kill him too, for the officer must tell him approximately which area of the forest he intends to hunt in."

Jacques sighed. He was a sentimental creature. "If only we could kill him now, Émile. Each time we heard his beastly gun go off I have trouble with certain of the men, with those who are too afraid and with those who are not afraid enough. 'Leave here now,' say some. 'Kill him now,' say others. I tell you it is getting me down."

He rolled himself a cigarette, sitting against the bole of a beech-tree at the edge of the glade, and I prowled about the lodge. There were faint traces of last week-end's tyre marks on the narrow white roadway. There was a good stock of wood, and a few potatoes lay in a wooden box that had once held German mortar bombs. I wondered how long the German overlordship of this difficult part of Europe would last. As though he sensed my thoughts Jacques said:

43

"If the invasion really comes and the Allies manage to land we will kill this Boche and his servant. You and I will kill them, Emile. Then you will take this house for your Command Post, and we shall form a mighty band in this Maquis. I can get all the railway workers from Is-sur-Thil and most of them from Dijon. The cultivators here are sturdy types. We shall be strong with you, who understand strategy and things. But first we will kill this Boche, eh, Emile?"

"Yes," I answered, but I did not mean it. The Boche who left the sordid streets of war-time Dijon to hide himself in his hunting-lodge with his pipe and his smoking-jacket was sympathetic to me. I hoped I should not have to kill him.

At the edge of the forest, five hundred yards from the hunting-lodge was a mighty rolling field that Jacques wanted to show me.

"It has been signalled as suitable for dropping a strong force of parachutists," he told me proudly. "It is big enough, is it not? And flat enough, without wires, or pickets, or other obstacles."

"Yes. It might do."

The field was high up. There was corn and wheat and hay on it. The land was good and the grain was high and thick. If a battalion of parachutists landed what could they do? I imagined myself just landed as their colonel, looking around the dark woods that surrounded the field like the thick brush of hair springing back from the forehead of a Neapolitan. Looking south, towards Dijon, whence I would swiftly expect the German armed answer to our hypothetical arrival, I saw bare sides of small hills among the forest, the whole sloping southwards. I saw no village, but to the north-east the gracious, slightly-Oriental steeple of a village church. Were I the colonel I should be glad of my compass, I decided. And I suddenly violently wanted to be the colonel, wanted to be a soldier again with fixed responsibilities and a definite task to accomplish, and men whom I had the right and the power to order and command. Only for a moment however.

"Let's go back to the farm," I said to Jacques, who stood politely watching my ruminations. "I am thirsty, Jacques, for some of the good coffee I brought from England."

"For breakfast! Real coffee. I told the 'cuistot' that we would keep it for a special occasion."

"Every occasion is a special occasion when the sun shines

44

and the wind is gentle in the spring morning and there is real coffee to be drunk.''

"If you put it like that, real coffee would be most acceptable.''

We walked across the broad field to the farm that sat on the crest of the hill. It was a fine building for a farm in those regions, solid and almost fortress-like.

The Maquis cooked in one of the outhouses in the yard, on an old kitchen range the farmer had fixed for them. That way no smoke was seen from the woods.

While they heated the coffee I washed myself outside in the yard. There was a fatigue already up from the Maquis, peeling potatoes for the midday meal. The two men doing the peeling watched me, their nimble fingers and blades working automatically.

"Where did you get your back so brown, Englishman?'' asked one who looked gipsy, small and nearly black-skinned, with a close-cropped prison hair-cut.

"Don't call him that,'' said the other, an older man with greying dirty hair and a 1940 wound scar on his chin. "He is Monsieur Émile to us.''

"Plain Émile, please,'' I said.

"Why?''

"Because I am one of you now, and because it is stupid to differentiate. There are no officers and men here.''

"What are there then?''

"There are leaders and men.''

"That's all right so long as the leaders eat the same food and share the wine with the rest of us.''

"They do, don't they?''

"Yes, but we thought that with your arrival all that might change. Jacques has arranged meals for you at the farm, and soon all the leaders will eat there too. Then the difference will begin and soon we will be split in two and weak, like the army of '39 and '40.''

"I have told Jacques that I will eat with you, and sleep with you, and work with you, and fight with you, that is, for as long as I am allowed to stay here.''

"So you don't want to stay?'' His eyes were hostile, but not intensely so. He was the old-soldier type, still smarting from the '40 defeat, still trying to parcel out the blame on every one else, on his officers, on Pierre Cot, on the English, on the politicians. It was just a frame of mind. He was a solid-looking desperado, and I knew we should get along. But his kind were always difficult to know, and when the work went badly they were apt to go bad on you. They had too many stock grievances. I preferred the young ones.

"Yes, I want to stay. I like it here." That was the truth. The first speaker now intervened again.

"Where did you get your brown back, Émile?"

"In Italy, lying on a rock inside a fortress," I told him.

"Which fortress?"

"At Gavi."

"Between Genova and Alessandria?"

"That's right," I said, and I eyed him more closely, for I knew from the way he pronounced the names that he was Italian. He knew that I knew. He looked at me in a troubled way and then dropped his eyes like a dog.

"I am French," he said softly. "And I will show that I can fight the Germans. I left Italy when I was young because I was so ugly none of the girls would have me. In Italy you must have girls. Here in France you can be a man. When the boys took off their shirts in spring-time in the fields in Lombardy, the girls laughed at me. 'Why do you keep your shirt on, Pietro?' they asked me. They knew I had been in an accident with the threshing-machine. Cruel, Italian girls are. The bitches. That's why I noticed your back."

The cook, a tall boy who had been at the Sorbonne, came out with my coffee.

"Pierre is obsessed with the ugliness of his back," he said. "That's why he makes himself so beautiful on the first Friday of the month to go into Dijon. A collar and tie. He never takes them off."

"Liar, dung-heap, 'putain'," shouted the Italian. "Here in France the women like extraordinary things on their men. At Marthe's they call me the Lord's Anointed. I hope that does not offend you, Émile, but you will understand when I show you." He tore off his shirt and showed his back. The scars, a puffy white on his dark skin made roughly the shape of a crucifix, the perpendicular curling up and half-encircling his neck like a tame snake.

"And I tell everyone that they are wound scars," he said.

"Cheat," said the older man. "You in the army. My God."

The woods still had that creepy feeling. I expected to see a German or Germans every hundred yards or so, and very often indeed I let my right hand slide down to touch the butt of the

46

.38 in my trouser pocket. Jacques had made his camp in a scrubby part of the forest, where there were stunted trees—few of them more than ten feet high—and thick undergrowth with a lot of thorn in it.

To get to it from the camp I followed a track for half a mile, then took small paths which first crossed a wide clearing covered with heather and then wound into the undergrowth. I noticed that the paths were well worn, and there were tracks of nailed boots all over the place. Here and there in the bushes I saw papers and once even a piece of "regulation flannelette", British material parachuted for weapon cleaning. When I got near the camp, although they had taken every possible trouble to camouflage the two huts (there was a second one ready for possible expansion of the Maquis), camouflage them both from the ground and the air, they posted no sentries, and as I approached I heard loud, rough voices, smelled cigarettes, and saw thin blue spirals of cigarette smoke rising into the sky. I was to get accustomed to this "ça ne risque rien" about the security of the Maquis. But this day I was profoundly shocked.

The Maquis of Jacques was no better than most in one respect. Coming through the fresh-smelling woods I was savouring with my over-sensitive nose the various delightful smells that one expects to smell. As I approached the camp I savoured others, less delightful, which, I confess, I also expected. By this time I had some idea of sanitary arrangements at the camp. They did not exist.

Mistake number two. Lesson number two perhaps. After this, if I were meddling with a Maquis, I tried to insist on the subject of sanitation before attacking the more ordinary aspects of a soldier's (or a guerrilla's) training. All that long, hot day I worked with Jacques and his men under the scrubby trees. We sat round in a friendly circle, taking the thick packing-grease off Stens, revolvers, automatics, grenades, mines, ammunition, torches, bazookas, rifles, Brens.

Dear old Bren. As I stripped it and explained its theory and its working, I saw how ideal the little gun was for the maquis. Strong and portable. Lovingly they looked at its shining innards. I did too. And I remembered the red-haired Aberdonian, Corporal Gordon, who first taught me how to strip the gun and then to use it. I remembered how Corporal Gordon watched Martin, the Englishman and the worst recruit in the squad, go through the "more gas" drill and said to him quietly at the end: "Ye might as well throw the bloody gun away."

Corporal Gordon would have found more apt recruits in the fifteen Frenchmen and the Italian with the scarred back who called himself French. They were quick with their hands, and they wanted to learn. I found difficulty in teaching them, since I had to pick up the technical language as I went along. I had not bothered to learn the French military terms for things like "safety-catch" and "firing-pin" and "used cartridge-case". I knew them better for the explosives because I had been trained on them along with Frenchmen, and frequently in French. As for the weapons, I had airily said in England that I knew them all, and indeed this was pretty well true,. so they had let me off that part of the training. Like most British soldiers I will do anything to go and fire a weapon and anything to avoid having to train with it. At any rate I began to pick up the correct names for the different parts. This period of training and talk was only spoiled for me by the smells that permeated the camp.

Thinking things over from the diplomatic point of view, I thought it unwise to broach such a delicate and important subject that day, in view of other upheavals which I had tactfully instigated. Most regretfully, but I think wisely, I put off the question of sanitation until the following day. Fortunately, too, the kitchen was not actually at the camp. Otherwise, we should certainly have had kitchen offal all over the place. At one o'clock sharp the cook arrived with an excellent meal in containers. This Maquis, being sponsored and financed by Albert, ate well.

We ate on a home-made table and benches behind the sleeping-hut. The table and benches were screened from air observation by a lattice-work of branches closely interwoven. Jacques and the man with the scarred chin were both air-conscious, like most soldiers who had been through the 1940 Battle of France. Twice during that day a Heinkel reconnaissance plane flew over us at the nasty height that might mean photographs. I knew that the Resistance was fairly strong on the other side of Dijon, and it was possible that the Germans might search for some sign of it in the neighbourhood of Chaignay. But from the Boche officer's unprotected hunting trips it looked as though they suspected nothing. And Jacques had so far been wily enough to resist the temptation to sabotage too near his own camp.

One thing stands out in my memory of this and other meals in Jacques' Maquis. We drank cold milk. We did it firstly because there was no wine, secondly because water was scarce, and thirdly because the farm had so much milk that it did not know what to do with it.

During lunch Jacques fitted up the British "midget" radio receiver, a type that was parachuted in fairly large numbers.

Jacques was listening to London all right for his parachuting message for the ground where I had dropped ("mon portefeuille est plein"). But although he was supposed also to be listening for the D-Day "action" message he did not know for certain whether or not these had been passed.

"Old So-and-So said the one about the railways was passed yesterday," he said vaguely. I was horrified. There was no definite listening watch.

Petit-Henri came back from Dijon with bad news. Gut, French Air Force officer, whose name had been given to me in London, had been taken by the Gestapo at Clairvaux, near Mouchard, the day before. He had been taken stupidly in a barber's shop. They had beaten him up before taking him away in a car. All the men sobered down at this news. They always did. There was not only the horrible agony which the comrade was probably suffering at the hands of those beasts. There was the danger that from that agony the Gestapo would extract information that would give them more victims. Max Gut was known as a calm and brave man. But many of the strongest had talked to the Gestapo, and who could blame them. And Gut had worked for a long time in the Resistance and knew everyone in that area.

Gloom settled on the encampment in the scrub. And during this gloom Albert arrived.

I heard his voice talking French when I was behind the hut, and amazement held me there for a moment to listen. I heard his voice all right. But he was speaking with an English accent nearly as strong as that of Winston Churchill.

I had met Albert before, once, in peculiar circumstances. I knew that he was the son of a French industrialist, that he was in the early twenties, and that he spoke very little English. I walked round the hut. There he was. Much thinner and wilder looking than I remembered him.

"Hellow owld boy," he greeted me, putting both hands on my shoulders. This was followed by a flood of the most extraordinary language (which I later learned he had picked up from the lips and sprightly conversation of his American radio operator, Paul). At any rate, Jacques and his gang were almost overcome with delight at such a touching "Mr. Livingstone, I

49

presume" scene in their own Maquis. All in a language they did not understand too.

"And they say that the English are undemonstrative," said Petit-Henri.

Albert manœuvred me behind the hut, and away from the others, when he immediately became intelligent and intelligible.

"Forgive me for all that," he said with great charm. "I must first of all explain that here in France I pass as an Englishman. When I was parachuted in I adopted this role for two reasons. Firstly, because I am very young, and I felt that as an Englishman I would have more weight with my work. Secondly, because if the Gestapo catch me they will take me as an Englishman. I can then say: 'What, me a British agent. You must be mad. I am one hundred per cent French and I can prove it.' I should then give correct details of my parents and education. Like that I might get away with it.

"And believe me," he changed from French into English as Jacques came round the corner. "This area is plenty hot. Pll-enny."

He ate a rather extraordinary meal of four eggs fried without pepper or salt and some potatoes. I saw that Albert was a good actor, and carried his role to completion in everything.

"Émile is a queer Englishman," Jacques told him. "Sometimes we wonder whether he is an Englishman. He even eats garlic, and drinks wine."

"Garlic, how repulsive," exclaimed Albert.

"Don't you drink wine?" I asked him (restraining myself from adding "now").

"Can't touch the beastly stuff," he answered. "Gin and whisky are my two drinks."

This seemed to me to be the height of devotion to duty. But Albert was such a strange person. Perhaps he really meant it.

There was a little man who had come with him. A little man who smiled all the time and said: "Yes," whenever anybody else said anything. Thus when Albert said:

"I am astonished that they have sent you, Émile. They told me that they were sending a helper and a first-class instructor who did not speak French well."

"Yes," said the little man (although he knew nothing about it).

"I had intended to leave him here," Albert went on. "Because this sector is too far away from my centre round Dole, and I cannot get to it often enough. But this is too small a job

for someone of your experience, and you really speak exceedingly well." (We were still being polite to one another.)

"Yes," interjected the little man, helping himself to a steak.
For although he was odd in other respects he ate voraciously
and more normally than Albert.

"So I am going to take you away with me now," said Albert.
"To a place near Dole. We can be together for a time at any
rate. I know how puzzling all this is at first."

"I should be quite happy here," I said, a shade regretfully,
for the thought of the big outside world terrified me.

"Yes," said the little man. But Albert was determined that
I should go with him, so I said the usual "Good-bye, see you
all again soon," to Jacques, Petit-Henri and the rest of the
Maquis. Jacques, strangely enough, was nearly in tears. He
was a pleasant brigand.

At the farm I began the process common to all who did this
sort of work, the process of shedding belongings. I left there
my big suit-case, with the waisted overcoat, the waterproof, and
most of the clothes London had provided me with. I dressed
myself in the blue suit which, although I had refused to be seen
in it in London, looked too incredibly smart in the part of the
country where I now found myself. In the small yellow suit-
case which, with a brief-case for my money and toilet things,
was all that I took with me, I packed the battle-dress that
London had ordered me to take, and the leather jacket and cord
trousers, also a couple of shirts, some socks, and of course, my
sleeping-bag.

We left on three bicycles, wobbling dangerously along the
rutted track and then descending swiftly to Chaignay. I felt
new and vulnerable. Like a lobster without a shell, and I confess
to a twinge of more than conscience at the thought that I had
not really learned my cover story backwards (or even forwards).
I ran it over in my mind, and it seemed all right. But the experts
said that to withstand that Gestapo questioning it had to be a
part of you, you know, *ingrained.* Nobody could call my cover
story a part of me. The trouble was that, for security reasons,
I had been obliged to leave the typewritten copy behind me in
England. So I knew that I could never really learn it.

Outside Chaignay, Albert and I waited beside a duck-pond
which was screened from the road by some thick bushes, while
the little man went to find the truck that was to take us on our
way.

We sat down on the muddy side of the duck-pond. There

had been a dry spell and the waters had receded, leaving enough space for us to place our feet. Here we had time and privacy to examine each other, and here there came over me the feeling that things might go well between us.

His slightly wild and suffering look influenced me more to this than anything else. He spoke of our former meeting and of the danger of our present association.

"What on earth made you come back here?" he asked. "Are you mad? Don't they know in London what is going on here? Gut has gone now. Any day it may be one of us. Do you think D-Day is coming?"

"Yes, very soon."

"If it does not come soon we are all sunk. If it does come soon we are sunk if they will not, or rather cannot, send us more arms and stores. With the exception of a group at St. Amour, in the south of my sector, the Maquis you have just seen is by far the best armed in the whole area. And the roads are getting so dangerous. The Boche puts restriction after restriction on the traffic. We are going to a village called L'Eglise, not far from Dôle. We shall travel in a van which has very good papers, papers of the French secret police at Dôle. Also there is a good hiding-place for our stuff in the floor of the van. But it is a long way, and we shall be lucky if we are not stopped. If we are stopped they may search us from head to foot, and even if they find nothing suspicious they may take us away to Dijon or Besançon for further questioning by the experts. All right. If it is so difficult for us to travel by road, how do I transport arms? How am I supposed to move those arms that arrived with you? The answer is that it is so risky as to be nearly impossible. We must have our parachutages, then, where the men are. We must have lots of parachutages. But this happens to be June, and next month is July, months when we have been told we cannot have deliveries because of the short nights. Boy, it stinks."

Our van, a blue-grey Renault, burning charcoal and wood chips, chugged up to our pond. We put the bicycles in the back and opened up the secret trap in the floor. The driver was a great bull of a man in faded blue overalls.

"Don't you worry, boys," he growled as we hid our money and weapons along with my suit-case. "It's a long way, but we'll get there. This tin bath [slapping the Renault] is not a tin bath, it's a tank."

"Good-bye, Jean," Albert said to the little man, who was going off in the other direction on his bicycle. "Shall I see you on Wednesday?"

"Yes."

"Do you really mean yes?"

"Yes."

"Well," Albert said. "Now there is nothing to keep us. Let's go."

We all three piled into the closed driver's cabin, with me in the middle, ridiculously smart in the blue suit. After one minute we cleared the woods and moved on steadily towards the village and the open country beyond it, France.

CHAPTER IV

DESPITE its strange fuel the engine was powerful, and the driver was full of bravura in the villages and on the curves. He lit, and even rolled cigarettes with the accelerator pedal firmly pressed down on the floor-boards, and me holding the wheel with one hand.

Chaignay village, to my relief, looked like no village that I could possibly have imagined. It was a village with a lot of curves in the street, and the children all seemed to have running noses. After Chaignay the country, rich in vineyards and in grain, poured past the windows.

Albert, on my right, closed his eyes and dozed. He was hatless, with a lot of dark auburn hair springing back from his forehead. His face was a proud young face. Proud, striving to be hard, but betraying nevertheless much strain and suffering. I remembered him as a haughty young man. I found him greatly changed, and the change was good. I remembered him as a spruce young man, with thick, cable-stitched white stockings and the bottoms of his grey flannel trousers rolled up to show them off, and perhaps to show a manly turn of leg into the bargain. Now he was dressed in clothes made by the same tailor as my own blue suit. I even recognised the greyish-blue tweed of his suit, and the cut of his trousers. His clothes were carelessly worn and shabby. His trousers were crushed. They even looked a little frayed over the heels of his shoes, and there was a cigarette burn on one leg. I had seen cleaner shirts. And there was at least one hole in his socks. Those things drew me to him. Prepared me to believe what London had told me, that he

53

had worked like three men for the past two months.

He slept. Except through the villages. Then the shaking of
the abominable roads (unrepaired since the war, but much worse
in the villages than elsewhere owing to the heavy agricultural
traffic) often woke him and he would watch the road ahead like
me, eyes searching from side to side of the road like a dog hunting, with this difference, that our eyes were searching for what
they did not want to see. We took the smallest roads possible,
avoiding main roads, since those were the ones which the Germans used and controlled.

A certain exhilaration mingled with my fear. It seemed that
tension in the air added to my appreciation of the country's
charms, as though every mile I was driving to fight a duel, and
appreciating the sky and the grass and the smell of the earth for
perhaps the last time. And tension added to my feeling for
the animals. In the eyes of a brown-and-white cow or a fat-
bodied, small-headed, stupid sheep there glowed no cruel
hatred. After my time in prison camps there seemed to be
something ridiculous in man's hatred for man. In the lust for
blood that still obsessed my fellow-creatures.

Sometimes I would get an idea like this: "Supposing the Germans did take me, they might not torture *me* because I have
fair hair and blue eyes, and look so innocent." But common-
sense would answer: "Yes, they will torture you, because it is
their way of doing their job, and the men who torture are the
men without pity."

Sometimes then, on my first drive, we passed odd German
soldiers on bicycles or on foot. Once an infantry platoon on a
route march. They were marching at ease and two or three
even smiled at us. These men were not the torturers, the men
without pity; but had they known that I was a British officer
they would have killed me. They would have feared me, and
they would have killed me. The thought came strongly to me
that the German reign of hidden torture in France was the expression of Germany's fear of France. And it was our (my)
strongest ally.

And I was to think about torture with Albert during the next
few difficult days. I thought then, in the van, that we were
going away to discuss things and settle where I was to work,
and generally have a restful time. I had learned even in the
Maquis that the Germans knew that there was a British officer
(Albert) working in and around Dôle; Albert had been warned
by the French secret police that he must lie low for some time,

54

and trust nobody. So we were to have a few quiet days, and get things settled. This was the evening of June 3rd, 1944.

Going through the last village before l'Eglise both the driver and Albert startled me by a sudden outburst of swearing. This was caused by a handsome and apparently care-free youth who passed up the street in the opposite direction on his bicycle.

"What's the matter with him?" I asked.

"He's a militian home on leave," said Albert. "He knows who this van belongs to. And he saw me in it yesterday. Saw me exactly here, and going in the same direction. Damn and blast his eyes. . . ."

The militian had looked just like anyone else to me. Those were the people I was frightened of. They were the people who led you to the Gestapo. For I knew that I could pass as a Frenchman before almost any German, even a German who spoke perfect French himself, but I knew that a real Frenchman would smell me out at once. If you could call the militians real Frenchmen. Scum of the jails, brutalised of the most brutal, cream of the offal, they worked for money and food for their carnal appetites; they worked for German money. And he had looked fresh and normal on his nice clean bicycle. I suddenly felt that I would like to kill him (an unusual feeling for me unless I have someone actually in the sight of a weapon). He had made the trees, the bushes, the cottages, that railway bridge across the road seem sinister.

"Stop," said Albert just before the bridge. We pulled into the side of the road. "We get out here," he went on. "The house is only 300 metres further on, but of course we cannot drive up to it in the daytime. We must hide your things here in the bushes and come back for them after dark."

While I was in the back of the van Albert whispered to me to come out quickly with the jack and anything else that might look necessary for changing a wheel. An old man was hobbling along the road. Agonisingly slowly he passed us, so slowly that I had to lie in the road in my new suit to put the jack under the axle. He might have been playing the part of "suspicious yokel" in a bad film. Why he even stopped to tie his bootlace, and while he did it he looked back at us under his arm. I could have murdered him. I seemed to be getting bloodthirsty.

Albert and I strolled along the road. The van had turned round and departed. We went under the railway. There was a small village ahead, perhaps six or seven houses in all. On our left a wood, on our right a swampy field. A youth passed us with a stare. We talked about Insurance, me keeping my voice low and indistinct.

"That's it, God how I hate it," Albert said, pointing at the first house on the left. It looked good enough to me. A biggish house set well back from the road with an orchard and hens and rabbits and ducks playing around the front door.

There was a man standing in the hall. Albert brushed past him with a "Good evening" and put on with me an elaborate pretence about only going up to see if mademoiselle had any eggs to sell. At the top of the stairs stood a slatternly, blonde, young woman who greeted us with her widest smile. Albert put his fingers to his lips and led the way into a small bedroom which held (but only just) a double bed, a large wardrobe, a small table and a chair.

"This is home, at any rate for the moment," he said. "Make yourself comfortable, but for the Lord's sake don't make any noise. That buzzard you saw in the hall is the landlord. He's an artist. He lives in the house. And he wants to get rid of these people with whom we stay, who lease from him the garden and four rooms. If he knew what we were he might denounce them. You never know. We shall have to stay here for a few days. I have given this address to several contacts, and I must wait for their news. We shall even have to sleep in the same bed. What a life."

We ate dinner with the family, father, mother, and daughter. The daughter was the slattern we had seen on the stairs.

"She's in love with Paul," Albert told me. "Can you beat it. She makes me sick. I can scarcely eat. And the food is such filth."

As a matter of fact, the food was reasonable, there were even extra luxuries like butter and wine, rare at that moment, and bought with the money Albert was paying for our board and lodging. And the young woman was kind. But Albert was bitter and by nature and upbringing too fastidious for such a life.

The father, a tiny red-faced creature, was Albert's favourite. The mother, grey-haired, handsome and with a good job teaching in the town of Dôle, we saw only in the evenings. She was completely ruled by her cock-sparrow of a husband.

"He is a great man," Albert said of the little man. And he told me this story about our host:

One night he was coming home in alcoholic semi-stupor from

the big café in Dole. A German stopped him, asked why he was out in the streets at midnight, an hour after curfew, and then demanded his papers. While the German examined his papers the little man looked around. The enemy was standing with his back to the canal and there was nobody about. So he grabbed hold of his papers, gave the Boche a tremendous kick in the stomach, climbed on his bicycle and rode home. For weeks the whole town was in an uproar over the "Canal Murder". The Gestapo claimed that the German had been set upon by an armed gang of terrorists. The little red-faced man was a fire-brand.

"If every Frenchman were like me there would be no Germans in France," he said.

"And no British either?" I suggested.

"Oh, the British are all right, within reason. It's those German buggers boozing all our wine. That's what gets a man down. And what they don't booze they send off to their factories in tanker wagons to make explosives with. The vandals. As for the cognac! They pour it down their great gullets without even swallowing. A whole burgundy glass at a time. Only a Boche has the right to wake up with a sore head in the morning. Why, for ten months now I have not kicked the wife out of bed."

"No, you little devil," said his wife.

"Thank God, I may be sixty but I still have my strength."

"Strong as three big ones," said the daughter complacently.

Before the end of the meal the little man was beginning to slip off to sleep at the table. His red-veined face nodded to a less and less obtuse angle with his body. Twice or thrice he straightened his neck with a jerk as whippy as the flick of a trout that is dying. Then he let his brutal round-muscled chin lie on his chest and frankly slept.

"Pa's away again," said the daughter.

"If he would only stay like that all night," her mother said. "Many and many a time I wish the drink would come back into the cafés. He's a demon when he's drunk, but kind of happy and good-hearted with it all. The little beast."

After dinner we got our belongings that we had hidden in the bushes that evening. We hid all the incriminating things in a hiding-place below the stairs. We kept out one pistol each, however, with three magazines. Albert liked the big .45 automatic whereas I preferred the less cumbersome .38.

"You can always hide a pistol in some odd corner if they search the house," Albert said. "And I am determined not to

57

be taken alive. If something slipped up outside they would come here directly for me, and hiding everything incriminating would not save us, we should just have to shoot it out, and hope we got killed in the fight.''

"Will you kill yourself if they take you?"

"Most certainly I will," he said. "I have made up my mind to do it at once if they catch me."

"Why? You ought to have a good chance if they think you are English.''

"I just kid myself with that to keep up the morale. They are too smart to be taken in by that. I'll cut my wrist damned quickly, and to hell with it, to hell with everything. Otherwise I know I would talk. I can't face the torture. Nobody can.''

"Have you no other responsibilities? Do you not have to try to live as long as you can for other people, for your parents?''

"Don't let's talk about that. All we can hope for is that we shall see the end. But we won't.''

"Why do you say that?"

"Because hopefulness brings bad luck, and in our case it would be ridiculous. There is too much to go wrong. But pay no attention to me. I am perhaps over-tired. Let's go upstairs. Tomorrow people will be coming here, and I am going to go over the detail of my sector with you.''

We closed up the hole under the staircase. It was a solid oak staircase running up between two walls and the hole was formed by lifting out one of the treads. Through the space thus formed a man. could wriggle. When the tread was replaced it was wedged into position with two little sticks of oak.

"They discovered the hole quite by accident while Paul was here," Albert told me as we undressed. Three days after they found it Paul was obliged to spend most of one day in there.

"This was the first house that I put him in. He had arrived, like you, I expect, all puffed up with the pep talks London had given him. First thing he did was to get out on the roof and fix up an outdoor aerial. Quite unnecessary of course, but he had been taught that it was a good thing to do, and he had great difficulty like most operators in making his first contact with London. Now he works on an indoor aerial and he never misses.

"Well, one day he was working, and the daughter came running in. She told him that there were hundreds of Germans surrounding the houses. He did not believe her until he looked out of the window. They were everywhere, even in the orchard in front of the house. He took it for granted that he was finished. But the girl showed plenty of energy. She was in love with him, don't forget. They always are.

"Within five minutes she had Paul and all his belongings under the staircase, and the hole solidly closed. The aerial on the roof of course they had to leave. Paul thought that was as good as a fifty-foot-high arrow in Neon lights. It was the only outside aerial in the village.

"He lay in the darkness, stretched out on a blanket, his head on a pillow, his gun in his hand, waiting for the sound of German boots on the stairs, ready to shoot the moment the hole was opened.

"Meanwhile a messenger had come rushing to me in the house where I was staying at the other side of Dôle. 'Move Paul at once, this moment,' he told me. 'We've just got a red-hot tip that the seven hundred Boche infantry who are parading in the barracks are to do an operation against l'Eglise.'

"I jumped on my bicycle, and I borrowed another one for Paul. I thought I would move him to Salins, where I already had another set hidden, waiting for him.

"Outside l'Eglise I was stopped by a German officer who had ten men with him. 'Where are you going?' he asked. I gave the name of the next village. 'Why are you leading another bicycle?' I said that was why I was going to the village. I had borrowed the bicycle from a friend there to get back before the curfew the night before. He let me pass.

"So I had to cycle slowly past this house. I saw Boches everywhere. The pickets on the roads even had fires going, and were preparing to eat there. It was evidently something serious. I was certain that they had located Paul with their direction-finding apparatus. I was certain that he was as good as dead, or worse, alive in their hands.

"I rushed round the circuit all day, warning everybody who had had contact with Paul, or who might go to this house. Then that evening an extraordinary thing happened. Two men who had been hiding in an attic of one of the houses tried to escape through the Boche cordon. The pair got through the first ring all right, but the Boches are thorough in these things. They make a wonderful job of surrounding a house or a village. And this place is so small. They were four rings deep. The second ring fired on the two men and brought them down. I did not even know them. They had been denounced for something. Perhaps they were important even. I suppose the Resistance has a good many facets. Paul just could not believe it when we fetched him out. He was like a man who had been doped."

After that Albert had moved Paul to a big house near Salins, a house that the fastidious Albert liked because there was running water in the bedrooms and they ate with clean silver and clean napkins, but which Paul, with his grosser appetites, hated because there was very little to eat. Paul did a lot of work there. So much that he was picked up within a few days, apparently, by the German direction-finding stations which, we were told, could place an operator within an area of twenty square miles. Into this area they sent special closed vans which were able to narrow the suspected area down from twenty to three and a half square miles. The vans were reported all right by Albert's scouts. They were disguised as ambulances. But ambulances do not make strange, radio howling and squeaking noises. And ambulances go directly from one point to another instead of stopping at intervals to work at the roadside.

Although warned of the false ambulances, Paul had a lot of work to do. Albert was sending it to him by messenger. He thought he would risk it for another day or two, when he expected Albert to return, anyway, and take him somewhere else.

So one morning he was working at the top of the large house. There was a fine view from his window. As he tapped out his message to London he glanced out of the window and his hand stiffened on the key. There was a man in a dark square-looking overcoat walking down the edge of a copse towards the house. Strolling down the main road there was another stranger in an overcoat. Both of these men had the collars of their coats turned up, and occasionally they glanced down into their chests, where small direction-finding sets were hidden. Their soft hats were pulled right down to hide the head-phones screwed into their ears.

Paul packed up his set and hid it, went down to the back door with nothing incriminating but his gun in his pocket. And there he met Albert. For Albert, who was something of a genius, and already an old enough hand to know that it was best to obey his instincts, had felt uncomfortable somewhere far to the south of Salins, and had taken the first train north.

He whisked Paul away to another hiding-place. Another house. Another place that might be located, might be encircled. I remembered an American captain who had spoken to me in London, just before I left.

"When you see little Paul tell him we know he is doing a swell job, and we are gunning for him. We hope to make him an officer," this officer had said. And he was a comfortable-looking American soldier. I wondered now, sharing a small double bed with Albert (a large man) in the very house where Paul had been under the stairs all day, I wondered whether they did realise just how nauseating Paul's swell job could be. If there is one thing I dislike it is sharing a bed with a man. Albert obviously felt the same way about it.

Next morning I was awakened by an arrival. A man with dark hair, a round face, and a quizzical look for me, was in the room. He did not take off either his hat or his waterproof.

"You will be Émile," he said. "What are your politics?"

"I have no politics."

"Oh, like Albert. What is the matter with you people. You are not politically conscious."

"Not when there is a war. Then we are nationally conscious. Albert and I are both soldiers. We have nothing to do with politics."

"Albert is a pretty remarkable fellow. I am sure that he hates Communism since he obviously comes from the looking-down-their-noses classes. But he works with us as well as with anyone else. Better in fact, since we are the best workers. I am a Communist," he added.

Albert, always a heavy sleeper in the mornings, now woke up.

"Hullo, Georges," he said, yawning. "Still trying to talk politics before breakfast. What is the news?"

"Both good and bad. Gut's out. Escaped . . .

"Don't ask me for details," Georges went on. "All we know now is that the Boche is consumed with rage, he's trying to trace Gut and he's trying to hush it up at the same time.

"Now for the bad news. Three thousand Cossacks are coming today or tomorrow to the forest of Chaux here. As you know, this village is actually in one corner of the forest. We think it highly probable that they will clear out the whole village to use it as a headquarters or at any rate that they will search the place."

Albert considered this in silence for a moment. Then he gave Georges some instructions and some money and sent him away.

"That's one of the best men I have," he told me. "I wish there were more like him. He and his men are steady workers, although they do waste a bit of time with politics. In some

61

ways he was right when he said the Communists were the best people in Dole. . . ."

"Oh, I thought you were asleep."

"No, I was listening. I wanted to see how you would get on with him. Especially if or how you would blank off the political angle. That is most important here since the Communists call themselves F.T.P. and refuse to join the F.F.I. So I have a schism in my sector. When I arrived the two were at logger-heads, and although both wanted to work with me, neither wanted to if the other did. Well, I have just worked on regard-less of politics. Those were the orders from London, were they not? I take on whatever bodies of resistance exist and accord-ing to their military merits as I judge them I demand arms from London for them. The arms are not arriving, of course. Not yet, at any rate."

"Are we staying on here?" I asked, for I had expected him to begin packing whenever Georges had left.

"We must. I have other messengers coming here. We cannot move before the 7th of June, that's the day after tomorrow. I place considerable faith in this place, though," he went on, screwing up his long nose as though he were actually smelling the dangers in the air. "I have some faith in the 'cachette', the hiding-place. Not many houses have one of those. I have still more faith in the fact that the Boches were here a short time ago, and when they have stirred up a village they usually leave it quiet for some weeks."

If Albert had faith in the "cachette" it was more than I had. In the fortress at Gavi they had routed out Wally Binns of the East Yorks Regiment and myself when they had to break down five-foot thick walls to do it. I had no faith in half-inch oak planks, and a hiding-place under a staircase always proclaims itself. I remembered also at Gavi how Tom Murdoch of the Warwickshire Yeomanry and Richard Carr of the Long Range Desert Group had been cemented in under a stone staircase. That was an elaborate hiding-place. They had liquid food pumped in through a rubber tube. And they had a somewhat similar arrangement for pissing. But the Germans broke all that down in a few minutes. No, I hated the idea of the "cachette". But I did not like to say so. I had much more faith in Albert's sense of danger.

We had a lot of work with maps and papers to do together. As we did it I could see that one of his main ideas in asking for a lieutenant had been to ensure that there was someone to take over in case of accident or disaster to himself. He had done a formidable amount of work in the two months. And he was naturally proud of his work, did not want to see it wasted. He had a sector so big that you could not drive from one side to the other in one morning in a fast car. He had established numerous groups, and he found himself obliged now to spend most of the time travelling from one group to the other. Travelling was becoming increasingly risky. Dôle station, for example, was being watched for the "British officer". All cars or trucks on the roads were now suspect. Bicycling was too slow for his big sector and big responsibilities. What was he to do?

We argued it out. My point of view was that he would be better to consolidate, to make a strong point of Resistance in one part of his sector. To gradually move all his arms and even the men from the outlying parts into his "strong area". Albert, however, held that it was better for the future to go on building weak cells everywhere in the hope that some day Britain would be able to introduce blood to the cells, in the shape of arms and material, and that the whole would form a strong body. His plan was certainly the more ambitious. And naturally, after all the work that he had put in, he could not bear the idea of scrapping some of his groups. He was an ambitious young man. And as I talked to him and argued with him, I began to see that he was a good person, even in some ways a fine person. In a message back to London that night I said: "Don't worry about my relations with Albert. I am proud to work for him."

We were interrupted once more during the morning. A young man, hatless, with long wavy hair descending over the collar of a dirty waterproof came drifting in. He had a quiet, almost whispering way of talking. And the face of a Puck or perhaps the face Boucher might paint on a Cupid, intelligent, sensual and laughing.

This was Bobby, the man in the secret police who shot the nephew of the Dijon Gestapo chief in the dark bungalow, then handed the silent pistol to Jacques. He confirmed the arrival of the Cossacks and advised us to move. Then he told us the story of the escape of Max Gut, an escape destined to cost the Germans dear.

He was less than half-conscious, was Gut, as they carried him off in their "traction avant"—the front-wheel drive Citroën, the French car the Germans in France preferred to all others—and he did not know where they were taking him. His huge body was one mass of bruises and cuts, for when they had beaten

63

him to the roadway with blows about the head and shoulders they had kicked him savagely with their high nailed boots.

He did not know where he was, but it was an unfurnished room in, apparently, an empty building. A German guard shared it with him. He heard another guard in the passage outside. The door of the room was locked. They opened it to pass rations to his guard.

Consciousness had come back to him with waves of pain and sickness, but he managed to fight down the discomfort that made him ache to toss and turn and touch himself. For he saw that his guard was sleepy, and he realised from the blood that had dripped to the boards beside his head that he must seem to be finished at any rate for that night. At length the German walked over and kicked him. He managed to stifle the cry of agony that bubbled to his lips. His reward came promptly for the German retired to the other end of the room, lay down on the floor, and almost immediately was asleep.

Cautiously Gut reconnoitred the room. The barred window was impossible, but the door looked old and weak. For a long time he listened at the door, watching the German who slept within a few feet of him. He thought he also heard the deep breathing of sleep from the passage. And there was no noise of shuffling feet, no clatter of a rifle-butt.

In one corner of the room lay a heap of iron, the remains of an old bedstead. Gut took off his heavy boots now, so that he could move silently. He chose the longest and straightest piece of metal in the corner, put it under the door and heaved. A man of less than his mighty strength would perhaps have failed. Gut lifted the door half-way off its hinges, and the lock disengaged. This was done with a good deal of noise. The Germans still slept. He tiptoed along a stone corridor, down a staircase, opened a door which gave on to a street that he knew. There was no sentry outside. He had escaped!

Then he had a shock. He was standing, swaying from weakness and fatigue in a cold, empty street at four in the morning, and he had no boots on. Sorely wounded as he was, filled with the urgency of flight as he was, Gut returned past the still sleeping sentries, picked up his boots from the floor that was stained with his own blood, and then escaped all over again. In the street he put on his boots, cut down an alleyway, took to the fields, and thence to the Maquis where the Germans never saw him for dust, or rather for fire and smoke and the rattle of small arms. He was a great leader.

"Extraordinary," I said, when Bobby had finished a very full recital of this story. "Amazing."

"Yes, Max is a queer fellow," said Bobby.

"Queer isn't the word," Albert said. "To leave those two sentries sleeping without killing them."

"Incredible," said Bobby.

"But that is not what strikes me as peculiar," I told them. "I think it odd that he should have gone back for his boots. Were they new boots?"

They both stared at me as though I were very young and did not yet fully understand life. But Bobby kindly explained:

"No, they were exceedingly old boots. But you cannot live without boots. And where is a man to find new ones here?"

The wonder of Gut's escape remained with us for days, and probably longer. It seemed to hold out hope for anyone else who might be taken, and I expect many a man in that area as he bore the first brutal blows of the beating-up prior to being carted off by the Gestapo remembered the courage and the luck of Max Gut and took a little hope from them for himself.

That evening Albert had a further warning from a good source that he must lie low, and not show himself in the neighbourhood of Dôle. It was said that the Gestapo had a fairly accurate description of him. He did not seem to worry personally about these warnings. It was late at night that he talked about the torture. When the weather was bad, as it frequently then was with rain beating on the windows and the wind rustling the trees outside and shaking at the shutters, the temptation to think back to home and conversely of the horrors that might lie ahead was almost overwhelming.

On the night of June 5th we received our action messages.

That meant that we were supposed to attack instantly railways, the roads, and also open a guerrilla offensive.

How? We sat into the night discussing this. Excited, desperate to do something, conscious that this was a great night in history, that while we spoke the first Allied troops were probably across the Channel. Of course we had had no idea that the invasion was scheduled for the early morning of June 6th.

In pauses in the talk I occasionally wondered at the change I saw in myself. Before leaving London I had taken this job as a medicine for my own hurt. Then, just before leaving, I had found another doctor, and I had not wanted to leave. Now, having landed myself properly in the middle of it, I was think-ing, despite my fear, in terms of responsibility. But perhaps after all that gives too intense an impression of my feelings. I am a muddler-through if ever there was one. And if I have any confidence in myself it comes from two things alone. I am confident that I can withstand physical hardship when need be, since I have a type of physique and mentality suited to such small tests; and I am confident that I can, given the necessary time, find my way slyly round the more obvious obstacles of life. With this type of confidence (a poor type, I am sure) I faced June 6th, and the battles that would ensue.

Surrounded by the Cossacks as we were, for we had seen them move into the woods around us that evening, it would have been foolish for Albert or myself to go out that night. And once out, what could we do? The leaders of his different groups already had their orders to attack the moment they heard the action messages. And they had targets allotted to them on the railways and telephones. They would attack those that night.

In fact, as we talked we heard occasional explosions. Also tumultuous noises from the bedroom next door, where the little red-faced man, despite his sixty and more years, was evidently fulfilling his functions as a husband.

Finally, around the time when the Allied assault on the beach-head was beginning to develop, as we afterwards learned, we went to bed with the feeling that although still a little puzzled, still not completely changed over from before-D-Day to after-D-Day thinkers, we should be nearer that the following day, when everything that we had discussed would be crystallised. There is no disguising the fact that we were a puzzled organiser and his puzzled lieutenant.

We were indeed less puzzled as the news came pouring over the Allied radio of successes on the beach-head, and the mightiness of the occasion and the reality of it was rammed home to us poor mortals in that French kitchen.

In the first place we were less puzzled because our own situation was precarious. There were a great many Cossacks around the place. These dirty, hairy, fur-hatted little soldiers, traitors to their own great country and mercenaries in the armies of the Reich, had a peculiarly loathsome reputation at that time and in that corner of France. At St. Claude, to the west of us, they had carried out the reprisals that followed a successful Maquis attack on a German column in a mountainous valley. There the Cossacks, when they had overcome all resistance, not only raped women and burned houses and farms, but also killed men with extreme savagery, often putting their eyes out, or pegging

66

them down to roast over slow fires. Even Albert did not relish having these creatures around the house. He was anxious to depart. He was more anxious, however, to see that his sector started properly on its post-Invasion work.

In the second place we were less puzzled about the work because we had reasoned out what we could not do. London had given us orders to attack the railways and telephones. We would do that. But we could not allow the men to attack the railways every day or night because there was an insufficiency of explosives in the region. London had ordered that we attack the roads. We would not do that. We were not strong enough to do it, and the only weapons we had, being, with few exceptions, short-range weapons like Stens and pistols, were unsuitable for road blocks. In this region the enemy was particularly strong, and the Resistance, since the area had not long been organised, was comparatively weak. Resistance strength lay in a certain respect which the German had for us. He thought we were stronger than we were. We could not afford to let him measure our weakness by inviting direct contact with him, by attacking him on the roads. The same argument ruled out the possibility of guerrilla activity.

So we both decided that it was best to work on steadily with training and the development of organisation, to increase immediately to the maximum our attacks on the railways and the telephones, and to disregard for the moment "action" messages two and three. At the same time Albert was panting to get to Paul to send messages demanding, praying for arms and supplies of all kinds. He decided to leave l'Eglise the following day.

We had red-face with us all day, and his wife. There was no suggestion of their going to work on such a momentous day. We had champagne for lunch, and all the time a kind of white-hot speculation. These French people had hoped for the invasion for so long that they had finally and for ever given up hope. Now their feelings were an alternating current. One second they thought that the Allies were bound to be hurled back into the sea, the next that all France would be liberated and the French armies entering Berlin within a few hours. It was really most exhausting.

Reports of the first sabotage activities came in, grossly magnified as all such reports were. They nevertheless showed that a blow had been struck at the railways passing through the sector. German reprisals were expected. Would they materialise? We thought so. Would the Germans begin systematically to round up all Frenchmen (and supposed Frenchmen), particularly the young men? We thought so then. It looked as though the first month or two after D-Day would be spent by us in a struggle to exist. We bitterly envied our counterparts in Normandy and the north who not only had the hope of quick freedom but also the possibility of getting many supplies owing to their position close to England, and importantly near the fighting.

The little red-faced man brought home some bottles of wine for our last night there. He plied us, and himself too, with drink before, during, and after dinner. Albert coldly refused his hospitality, so I felt bound to accept it. Fortunately, like many exceedingly strong men, our host had a weak head. And after dinner he quickly went into the heaviest of heavy sleep. Once, while we talked to Georges, who had come in with messages for Albert, the little man jumped up and made this speech:

"It grieves me deeply to see two young strangers go out alone into danger. If, therefore, you find before parting tomorrow morning that you have need of a good man, take me with you. Please take me with you," he repeated, and burst into tears. "Please, please. I do so want to kill some Germans. . . ."

His wife and daughter applauded this righteousness.

"In vino veritas," said the wife, the school-mistress. "He has his good points, has my little man."

Later I often wished that we had acceded to his request, but I am afraid that he would have been too hot-headed for those early days. When he had spoken he laid his head down upon his dirty plate and resumed his slumbers. Shortly afterwards he piloted himself to bed without bothering to shake hands or to say good night. I never saw him again.

Late that night I slipped out silently to the earth privy in the garden. It was judged unsafe to go there during the day. A grave pity, for it had an enchanting view, including an acacia and a cherry tree, and a wire cage full of yellow ducklings.

A nightingale was singing in the trees. And a little farther away some Cossacks were singing too, an odd and pleasant moaning song. I could see the light of their fire reflected on the lower branches of a chestnut tree. The last nightingale I had heard was near Andover in Hampshire.

Before leaving the next morning I shed a few more belongings. Albert had given me a rucksack, a pale blue one, the type that a woman might carry on a small, comfortable walking tour. Into the rucksack and my dark grey brief-case (Continental model—and I prefer a lofty French name for this article of luggage—"valise diplomatique") I packed the minimum of belongings. My battle-dress, spare shirts and other odd things, I put away in the yellow suit-case, and this I hid under the stairs. Now I had no suit-case at all. How wonderful.

We left soon after breakfast. Georges had come for us, and he told us that the van in which we had come to l'Eglise was about one mile down the road. There did not seem to be any Cossacks about. They were away on manœuvres or punitive expeditions.

It was a heavenly morning, balmy and cloudless, and neither of us was sorry to leave this house. Albert and I set out in the highest spirits. At least I was in irrepressibly high spirits, and Albert seemed to allow himself to be warmed by them into a smile. But it is dangerous to feel too good. You may quickly touch the other end of the scale.

A few yards from the house Albert remembered that he had forgotten his bicycle. Accordingly he returned to fetch it, and I walked on alone, feeling conspicuous but enjoying nevertheless the freedom of walking by myself in enemy-occupied territory. The road passed under the small railway bridge which I have mentioned before. Although I knew that there had been sabotage cuts on this railway less than one mile from the bridge I carried on towards the line with never a thought of danger. Poor fool.

My pleasure in my own company was rudely shattered when two men in uniform crossed the railway, and began to slither down the embankment towards me. They were still about twenty yards from me, so I pretended to carry blithely on my way, I even managed to whistle.

A hoarse shout broke into my pretending.

"Where are you going, young man?"

"Down the road to get my bicycle," I shouted back. "I had a puncture back there, but I'd left my repair outfit at home, so I had to walk on and borrow one." This was the best I could think up on the spur of the moment, and I was rather proud of it, but not confident.

"Come here at once, and let us have a look at you and your papers."

Heavily aware I was of my odd luggage; the rucksack stuffed with new things; the "valise diplomatique" full of all sorts of queer illegal belongings such as an enormous sum of money, a dagger, about fifty pounds of pistol ammunition; most of all,

69

aware of the nice blue little Colt nestling in my right trouser pocket.

As I walked slowly, non-committally as I hoped, towards them I was able to take stock of the two men. So far as I could see they were just two gendarmes in the khaki uniform these men wear in summer. One was an N.C.O., a *brigadier*. He was old and cloaked in the sort of liverish anger that policemen assume quite automatically when they smell a malefactor. His companion was tall and surly-looking with the purplish face of a Frenchman who drinks too much too often. With all the talk about other things I had not had time to ask Albert about the feelings of the local gendarmes. But I had heard somebody, Georges I thought, say that they were a bad lot.

It was fairly obvious why they were there. They had been looking at the damage on the railway. They would think I was a saboteur. They would almost certainly search me.

I presented my papers with a forced smile. As I did this I made a mistake that might have cost me my life. I put my right hand in my trouser pocket. Somewhere above us I could hear talking on the railway. Albert flashed by on his bicycle. We were standing away from the road, and screened by the trees of a small wood. He did not see us. But for the voices above us I might have tried a stick-up. The old one did not bother much with my papers. He had made up his mind to search me. He nodded to the other, who took his gun out from the leather holster and stood back a pace. The old one searched me quickly.

"Ah," he shouted, and pulled out my pistol. "You were going to shoot us."

"Certainly not," I answered.

"Yes, you were going to shoot. You had your hand in that pocket. You were holding your gun."

"I had my hand in my pocket, but I always put my hand there. If I had wanted to shoot you I could have done it."

"All this has got to be cleared up," said the older man, scratching his grizzled head angrily as stupid men will. "We must take you along to the Gendarmerie with us."

"But who is he?" asked the younger one. He had edged up to me, for I could feel his spittle on the back of my neck. In the manner common to policemen all over the world, he also was working himself into a passion. Suddenly he put his hand on my shoulder and spun me round so that I faced him. The older one moved round me and took out his gun. The younger one stood slightly below me, but he was taller than me. I looked straight into his bloodshot eyes. Things were looking bad.

"Who are you?" he said fiercely.

"Georges Maillard, of Bourg," I answered him. And I looked round the blue empty sky. It was so beautiful. Was I destined to be caught stupidly like this?

"Who are you?" he shouted. He shook my shoulder with one hand, at the same time drawing the other back to strike me.

No answer. All I could do was stand and look at him. Incidents and people flashed through my mind. I was hot and angry like a beast that is cornered after a very short chase.

"Who are you?" he shouted again, and this time I knew he was going to hit me if I did not answer. "Tell me if you are German," he added in a softer voice. I waited for a fraction of a second and then whispered:

"I am no German. I am English."

The two gendarmes stood as though they were turned to stone. Sweat broke out on the vinous face close to mine. The bloodshot eyes stared anxiously at me.

CHAPTER V

FOR a long time we stood thus in silence. The two French-men stared intensely at me, and occasionally shot rapid glances at each other and around them. At length the old one whispered:

"Could they hear us from the railway? Has anybody passed while we were talking?"

"No," I answered him too quickly.

"Yes," the younger gendarme contradicted me. "One man passed on a bicycle. But I do not think he saw us. As for the railway workers, they may have heard us."

"What do you think?" asked the old one. "I think he is lying, he has no English accent."

"But he has an accent. He's foreign all right. What about taking him into the wood and searching him?"

"All right. Come on, look sharp, you. One dirty trick and we finish you off." With this kindly injunction to me the old one led the way into the wood. There they unpacked my ruck-sack, sleeping-bag, cord trousers, leather jacket and all. They saw nothing there that interested them. But the "valise diplo-matique" astonished them. First of all the enormous roll of thousand-franc notes.

"Where did you get this?" asked the stupid old man. "No honest man would have so much money."

"I brought it with me," I answered. "And I need it for my work."

"To finance the Maquis?" the younger one suggested. I saw that he was beginning to believe me. His voice had changed. He was impressed by my kit. Now he drew out my dagger.

"Why, you bloody murderer," cried the older one. "Razor sharp too. God in Heaven, what could you want with a thing like that."

"I use it to castrate Germans," I lied, for I thought that might be the sort of talk they liked.

"He's playing a part," the old one said. "Now look what you've done, Erneste, with your stupid idea of bringing him into the wood. Much better have taken him to the Gendarmerie."

"We couldn't hand an Englishman over to the Boche," the young one replied. I almost loved him.

"Perhaps not. But I don't believe he's an Englishman. He's a Boche. If we don't kill him he'll report us."

"Do you spik Ongleesh?" the young one now said to me.

"Yes," I answered in English. "Yes, yes, yes. Of course I speak English."

"He speaks English," said my new friend, but the other only replied sourly:

"All the Boches speak English. I don't like it, I tell you. We can't take such a risk as to believe him. Hey, you," he shouted at me. "How did you get here, anyway? Explain that if you can."

"I dropped by parachute, then I came here by car."

"What car? Whose car?" He had played into my hands.

"I cannot repeat the names of Frenchmen who risk their lives to help me," I said. A bit of that stuff always made an impression, and, true to form, they did look impressed. I now peeled two thousand-franc notes off my mammoth roll, and asked each of them to buy a present for his youngest son. After some polite refusals they pocketed the money, and the young one went off to the road to see that there was nobody about while I dressed myself and repacked my things. We shook hands warmly, and I walked away. Just through the bridge I saw Georges, pretending to blow up one of the tyres on Albert's bicycle. I passed him without a sign, but the gendarmes suspected that he knew me. They whistled to him, and beckoned, and obediently he cycled back to talk with them.

Georges overtook me as I reached the van. It was well hidden in a thicket and Albert, most nervous about my disappearance, was pacing up and down the narrow, dusty road. "We have two new recruits for the Resistance in Dôle," said Georges. "Two gendarmes. They both say they want to work, and must see the chief as soon as possible. They will be useful if they are honest. We always thought that brigadier was a bad lot."

The three of us crushed into the cab beside the driver. Each of us had a gun in his hand, and the driver had his ready above his head, hidden above the anti-glare shield. Warily we took the small tracks that cut through the forest of Chaux to the south. The forest frightened us twice. Rounding a bend we came on a gleaming black Citroën parked by the roadside, a car that screamed "Gestapo"; but it belonged to a mere wood exploiter. And again, roaring through a farmyard, we had to stop with full brakes. A German army lorry blocked the road. It was only a few soldiers out on a black market foray, probably searching for eggs and butter. They allowed us to pass without even a curious look. Stupid fools.

Georges dropped us with our luggage in a wood not far from Mouchard. It was rumoured that the Germans had put up a road-block in Mouchard that morning, and were stopping civilians and checking their papers. It was damp in the wood. Albert and I sat on my leather jacket, and he fitted up a midget wireless set so that we could listen to the news.

A stranger was with Georges when he returned. A peculiarly thin man. His hair was cropped so that you saw every bone on his skull. He wore a long-barrelled German Luger thrust openly through his belt, and he eyed us and our belongings coldly, taking in everything in detail, especially the small wireless set. His eyes were wary and showed none of the easy enthusiasm that I was accustomed to see burning in the eyes of Frenchmen at that time. This was a Communist, Mathieu, leader of the F.T.P. band of Mouchard.

Albert had a different way of dealing with people from me. He ordered, that is his nature. I humoured, that is mine.

Now I saw Mathieu stiffen under Albert's words, like a horse that finds his bit too heavy. Albert was brisk and energetic. He asked Mathieu for figures about his men and his attacks. The replies came coldly, factually. Mathieu was not trying to make an impression. There came a question which he did not answer. An awkward silence under the trees.

Georges intervened. Mathieu, he explained as tactfully as he was able, did not necessarily allow us any authority over his group. He was only too willing to co-operate, to accept any help we might be able to offer. But it must be clear that we were only acting as advisers and had no right to command Mathieu or his men.

Albert swallowed any annoyance he may have felt, and explained with a softer manner and semi-ironic politeness that he could not guarantee for his part to help Mathieu and his men, but that he was most willing to have a look at them, and possibly if he thought it worth while try to arrange supplies for them from England. He did not care for politics; the only aim was to beat the Boche, and so on. Albert, although his lifted left eyebrow and his imperiously curving lip appeared often to belie what he said, was a master with the honeyed word. A very clever young man.

We climbed into the back of the van. We were going to Clairvaux to pick up Paul, and since that area was judged dangerous, they asked us to lie down on the boards, and not let ourselves be seen on the roads or in the villages. The last cargo had been charcoal. Some of that newness they had so hated in London began to wear out of my blue suit.

"Now you understand a little what I meant when I said that the Communists were difficult," Albert said to me. "They are so suspicious of us that it is often difficult to do anything with them. You would think that they had been doing courses in Goebbels' anti-British propaganda, followed by a course in Vichy's 'Evils of the Democracies and the Great Trusts'. To Mathieu, I am afraid, we are two sinister figures representing horrid designs either on his country or on the freedom of the French worker. It really is too silly. Yet it's like Hitler—it's silly, but serious. We have to be diplomats as well as everything else."

Paul came down the high steps of a house in Clairvaux. Three women clustered on the top steps, their faces obsessed with the sadness of his departure. He was a small, but exceedingly well-built American with the pasty, slightly yellow skin of a youth who has lived much in cities. He wore a soft hat and a long blue overcoat like the garment I had left at the farm. Heaving in his luggage, two large suit-cases, one of them holding his set and equipment, he climbed nimbly in himself and lay down between us. His face was pointed and slightly spotted from his shut-in life and too rich feeding. It was not a

74

handsome face, and for some time I failed to understand why the women all went mad about him, unless it was his smallness and neatness that made them feel protective. Then I saw that he had a bubbling vitality. It was as though an electric vibrator were drumming inside him all the time.

And his eyes were the eyes of a siren. They were Egyptian, or Eastern, it seemed to me in the consciousness of their seduction. Shaded by immensely long and curving brown lashes, much darker than his brilliantined, curly, auburn hair, the eyes were wide and sharply pointed. Strangely, although they gave an Eastern impression, they were blue eyes, intensely blue. Yes, it was his eyes that knocked them down. That and his dangerous job. The romance of the mixture.

There was nothing romantic about his talk. It was the brisk, unnaturally bright talk of a precocious child of the American masses, mixed in with a good many French words which he had picked up from the different strata that he had lived in. His mother was French, or French-Canadian perhaps. Paul's French was a strange brand, spoken rapidly and brokenly, with a great many almost prehistoric expressions from Canada, where the language is still the ancient French, and a great many modern expressions which I had not often heard.

He showed signs of nerves, like Albert. The pair of them smoked incessantly, and were greatly out of sorts if they could not get cigarettes, which were then extremely difficult to find. They both slept badly through the night and heavily in the mornings. Sometimes they ate voraciously; at other times they could scarcely bear the sight of food. Neither liked drink, although I had seen Paul drunk in London, and he told great stories, which included, with the other delectations of life, rivers of whisky and gin. Neither of them could read a book or stay doing any one thing for more than a few minutes. They led, at that time, the lives of hunted gangsters with an unbelievable fate around the corner.

They took us in the van to a celebrated beauty spot and fishing centre, the village of Port Lesney. There, in the village street in broad daylight, we bundled out of the van and into a house. All our belongings were whisked upstairs after us, and into a small room on the first floor back. The landlord, a large man with the face of the fat boy at school, a rosy, tubby face, pointed out to us two escape routes beginning from the back window. The open country only a few yards from the window looked almost intolerably entrancing. I was already beginning to find a persistent weariness in this shut-in existence.

Paul was scheduled for an emission that afternoon. There was a couple of hours' work before the emission, writing the messages and coding them. Then he got a wooden table and screwed his morse key on to it, fixed up a single-wire aerial criss-crossing the room (an aerial that any B.B.C. listener in Surbiton would certainly have sniffed at), opened up the suitcase containing his set, and got to work. The set made some noise in the room.

Albert had arranged for patrols on bicycles supplied by Mathieu's group to watch all the roads around the village for German radio detection men either in trucks or on foot. The village, the sort of place to which the bourgeois used to motor in peace-time to eat well in the little restaurants beside the river, had a bad reputation as a centre of Gestapo work.

"No good will come of our arrival," Albert warned us. "To arrive in a new place like that in broad daylight was the height of stupidity. If it had not been for the emission I should have waited for darkness. I don't like this place at all." He wrinkled up his long nose in the sniffing movement I had noticed before.

That night we went out to try to work a little. The objective was Mouchard railway station, we were told. It was Mathieu's team who were attacking the station, but they had agreed to let Albert and myself go along as observers. Fat-face, wearing a raincoat and a slung Sten gun, called for us at II p.m. Albert and I, both in our leather jackets, looked like the film conception of a couple of Soviet agents going out to work. Each of us carried a big .45 automatic with three magazines. I wore soft shoes. At night I detest making a noise even if I am with a lot of other people who do. And I was coward enough always when I went out on night jobs to envisage the possibility of having to run away. I had already had experience against the German at night, and knew that the nicest thing about him was his refusal ever to discard his own heavy, noisy boots.

Taking field paths after one hour's walk in the moonlight we reached Mathieu's house, one of a row on the outskirts of Mouchard. It was already after midnight, and there was nobody about in the streets. But there was quite a crowd in Mathieu's cellar, where they were making up the charges.

If instructors from the training schools in England could have seen these Frenchmen making up charges the cellar would have looked to them like Dante's Inferno. Every conceivable school "don't" was being done. And we were unable to say a word.

The atmosphere was so strained that if either of us had merely uttered a "Don't you think that perhaps it might be better to . . ." we should have been forbidden the trip. I personally was consumed with a passionate curiosity. Curiosity to see whether these odd, sausage-shaped lumps of explosive would really blow things up.

In a choking voice Albert, who took those things much more seriously, asked Mathieu if we could have a meeting to discuss the operation the following day, and if he and I could then make suggestions about anything that we might find to criticise on the night's operation. Mathieu agreed to this brusquely, but, to my mind, with little intention of arranging any such thing.

When the young man who had been making up the charges, a long thin village Don Juan, had flung them roughly into a dirty sack, we left on the job without any orders whatsoever. I choked with laughter as we moved down the road in a clattering huddle. We were all armed with pistols, Stens, or rifles. But there was no scout ahead. And since it was a built-up area they made the most appalling noise with their nailed boots.

Every hundred yards I picked out a line of retreat or some cover on both flanks. I knew that if anything happened like meeting a German patrol (a not unlikely eventuality) the whole lot would break, and run, since nobody had been told to do anything else. It was better to be prepared.

However, we came without incident to the railway station, which is some distance away from Mouchard. We left the station on our left, crossed the rails a little farther on and came to the signal-box. It worried me that this should be the objective for all those vast, sausage-shaped blobs of explosive. However, I followed Mathieu, like the rest. We trooped into the signal-box where the man at the desk in the corner said the French equivalent of:

"What ho, Mat."

"We've come along to blow up your box."

"I say, hold on a minute. The 1.15 passenger isn't through yet."

"Imbecile. What d'you think we are, murderers? We'll send it up when the 1.15 has passed."

"Agreed. You going to tie me up?"

"Just as you like."

"Yes, best to tie me up good and proper and put me in the station-master's office. No immediate hurry, of course."

"Mind if we place the charges?"

"Make yourselves at home, boys."

At this the tall Don Juan shook his explosive out of the sack. With that amount I could have made a start on the Forth Bridge. There was certainly twenty times too much for the signal-box. Don Juan stood looking at the line of levers. Mathieu had gone out of the little building to place sentry posts on the railway to either side of our secret and dangerous work. So Don Juan, a perfectly normal and confused young man, with fewer "no-meddlers" principles than Mathieu said to me:

"Eh. Emile. How do we do this?"

Having already thought out this simple problem, I was able to place three of his charges in a minute or so, and link them up with detonating fuse in the best manner (except that we were taught in the British schools to double everything, and in the field there was a shortage of material so we always used it single). Impressed by the showy way that I did these things—they had to drag me to the schools, but I had not been there for nothing —the tall young man invited me to help him place the other charges. It was raining when we went out. We had some difficulty in keeping the detonators dry. Don Juan hitched some strange charges round the telephone-posts. They were like gargantuan pearl necklaces with blobs of explosive strung on fuse. I then placed the remainder of the charges in the hearts of the points. We put them there because these steel castings were extremely difficult to replace since hundreds of thousands of them had been destroyed by Allied bombardments of marshalling yards and stations.

While I had been doing all this, and getting wet, dirty, and bad-tempered in the process, Albert and Mathieu had been down looking at the station. There they had found fifteen German soldiers who were waiting for the 1.15. The 1.15 was late and everyone was angry. I went along to have a look at them. Five of them were labour corps youths in dirty uniforms, slouching about, anyway, with down at heel boots and rusty rifles. The other ten were S.S. men in thick greatcoats. They paid less attention to their compatriots than to two French women who were sitting at the back of the platform, waiting also for the 1.15. The S.S. men—enormous in the half black-out with their padded shoulders and high hats—strutted back and forth in front of the Frenchwomen, who looked stonily into the darkness.

They paid no attention to us. No more attention than British

78

troops would have paid in their place. Albert wanted to kill them. He had a blood lust.

"It is much more important to block the station," I said.

"But so much less amusing, Georges."

"Does it really amuse you to kill them?"

"Of course. Think what they are doing to my mother."

"Killing these ones won't get her out of prison."

"Be damned for a sloppy Englishman. Do you never want to kill them?"

"Yes, if I see them hurting someone, or destroying something. And when I have them in the sights of a weapon, or when I am frightened of them."

"Look at that now. Does that not make you angry?"

One of the Germans had approached the women. He leaned forward to speak to them, and the light shone for an instant on his handsome, loose young features. He wore his hair long, and his face was pointed. He drew back, offended, and his raised voice reached us across the platform.

"I am not German, I am Austrian, mademoiselle," he said, and he walked off after his friends, who greeted him with a salvo of coarse laughter.

"French soldiers would do the same thing to German women, or French women," I said to Albert. "I cannot see anything wrong in that."

"Sometimes I think you went out of your mind in prison. But thank God, here comes the 1.15, over two hours late."

When the train had slowly drawn out of the station I went around all the charges initiating them. I had often done this in England, placing dummy charges on machines or railway engines. And I had imagined that it would be different when the detonator was attached to one and a half pounds of violent explosive instead of a lump of plasticine. All I found was that it was more difficult to make a mistake, for a mistake might mean instant disintegration. I walked round with Don Juan in the dark. Being untrained, he was a little afraid of this part of the work. He watched closely everything that I did, although he was too proud to ask questions.

We walked back from the station in the same muddled way.

Our first charge went off. A flash in the sky, then a roaring explosion. The road trembled under our feet, for the charges had been fairly far apart and there was a good interval of time between initiating them and leaving the station.

They quickened their pace a little. The noise would draw

any German patrol that might be about. It was after four o'clock, a favourite hour for the Germans. Once a car's lights came shining on the top of the houses in the street we were in, gradually lowering as the car mounted the curve towards us. They broke and ran then almost in a panic, ran for any sort of hiding-place on a piece of waste ground. These men needed instruction and leadership. Guerrillas need leadership more than soldiers. Explosion after explosion shattered the silence of the dawn. With each one our spirits rose.

Mathieu thanked us at the door of his house. There was a car there, behind the house alongside the wood-pile. A French Ford, a reasonable car and in good repair.

"I have had my eye on it for a long time," Mathieu told us. "It is good now to have a car hidden so that if one has to run one can run on wheels. Tomorrow I will send two men out to get some petrol from another collaborator."

"Another?"

"Oh yes, the Ford belonged to an officer who worked in with the Germans and denounced one of my men three months ago. And the petrol belongs to a butcher who kills and sells only to the Boche."

"So you just—take these things."

"Yes. Now our day is coming," said Mathieu, with a wolfish grin. "They don't even complain when we take them, just stand and watch stupidly." And he drew the long Luger slowly from his belt, for he was going to bed.

The dawn was moist and clean-smelling. I walked on ahead to try out my legs. They were untired, but there was a hot tickling behind my eyes. I was relieved that my feet had not softened too much. They felt good in the rope-soled shoes that I had extracted from the big woman in London. But the shoes were already coming to bits. I sat down to wait for the others, thinking, as I sat there in the sweetness of the dawn, that if the life were all like this, genuine boy scout stuff, I could live it for a year. It would be good to have other little boy scouts with me, though. Boy scouts who knew how to move without being heard, and knew how to stalk the red deer. The wetness of the earth soaked through the seat of my trousers, and the soles of my shoes. I was nearly asleep when Fat-face came up panting in his coat followed by Albert, who was holding his heavy pistol in his hand.

"This damned thing hurts my stomach when I carry it in my belt."

"Shouldn't have such a big stomach."

Paul opened the thick curtains of his lashes when we walked in.

"Never leave me alone like that again," he said. "I tell you I can't stand it."

He had packed our things, for we were moving immediately to another house, a house that pretended to be empty, and belonged to a widow woman whose husband had been killed in the Air Force.

She was waiting up for us, a neat little woman with black hair pulled down on either side of her forehead in a smooth line. She had a charming squint too. She fussed around us. Fatface, with his Sten, was going to sleep in the hallway, on a mattress stretched on the floor. There was a bedroom for us, and a dining-room, and a kitchen. The lavatory was forbidden, because she shared one with another family where there were children. Too dangerous. We must use a bucket with a lid on it in the kitchen cupboard.

Our bedroom had one double and one single bed. I made them draw lots for the single. Had I won I should have taken it. Since I lost I elected to sleep on the floor in my sleeping-bag. I like sleeping on hard surfaces, and I cannot bear to share a bed with a man. They thought I was mad. But I was content alone in my sleeping-bag, shut off from the world, and tired.

A scene of enthralling interest lay before and below me the following morning when I pulled down the elaborate black-out (for since the house was "uninhabited" we must show no light). Through the net curtains I saw a small bit of a French village street. There was a grocer's shop on my right, and a little farther up the street a "bistro". Our little widow with the squint was standing talking outside the "bistro" to two other women. She had dark wine bottles in her hands, and I was sure that they were for us. But more interesting was the left side of the street. Most of this was taken up by a huge barn with a very pointed roof running parallel to the street. And against the wall of the barn two urchins were playing a game that I had played with my brother in Scotland, in a farmyard in Speyside, when I was eleven years old.

It was an interesting game. The urchins had made two light bats about the length of tennis-rackets and the width of cricket-bats. They had a rubber ball, which they bashed against the wall, taking it either volley or on the bounce, any bounce. The point was lost when the opponent managed to hit the back line, the opposite side of the street, with the rebounding ball. These two boys played with an intensity most rare in Latin children. One was tall and rangy and obviously considerably the elder. He would be about ten. He played carefully, getting about the road fast and using his long reach to advantage. His opponent, much smaller, was a fattish boy of about seven. Fattish, but springy with energy. And he played this rude game with the poise of athletic genius. Often played it with too reckless abandon, slashing crazily at difficult shots. It was a joy to watch him. Nobody did though. The villagers were so accustomed to the two boys with their game that they never looked at them.

And the village traffic, with occasional traffic from outside (or "abroad", as the villagers called it), passed through the game, making additional hazards and increasing the factor of luck. Hand-carts, hay-carts, oxen, horses, pigs, an old man in a bath-chair, a baby carried in a laundry basket, passed across the court and were skilfully played over, or under, or round.

Four Germans stiffly sitting squashed in a square black Peugeot whisked through. They had not sounded their horn, the Germans never did, and they arrived without warning. For once the smaller boy was put off his stroke. He stood looking into the German's dust for an instant, as though wakened temporarily from the drugged sleep of his game.

Both boys were burned nearly black with the sun. They wore faded blue shorts and had bare, dusty feet. I wondered if we should hear later of a tennis champion from the village of Port Lesney. Probably not. Life is hard in the villages. There is much work to be done in the fields. When they come home, the young men, there is not much energy left for more than skittles or bowls or the urgency of love-making. Then they feel like having children, and they are married. No time for fripperies like tennis.

Albert and Paul slept until lunch-time, so I sat all morning behind the net curtain, trying to project myself into the sunny street, wanting to bathe myself in the peaceful industry of the street, and in the unthinking energy of the two young boys. And at school I disliked games. Since the war, too, any game with a ball had seemed ridiculous, a waste of time. I told myself that I was interested in the game only because the boys played well, because the co-ordination of their movements was beautiful. They were called in by their mothers at midday.

82

"Claude, hurry thyself, unless thou hast no hunger," a woman in sandals called from beyond the barn. The smaller boy missed a shot, and he practised a few drives against the wall before he carried the ball and his bat into his home. The smells of cooking filled the street.

The little widow woman flitted round the table while we ate, apologising for every excellent thing that she had cooked. Her husband had been a fighter pilot, and he had been killed in Belgium in January, 1940. Immediately after the war she intended to make a pilgrimage to his grave. They had told her there was a cross on it. She wanted to send money for flowers. . . .

Was it my imagination, or did the widow woman reel slightly as Paul lifted his blue pointed-sided eyes to glance at her. He had to get his things ready for an emission. So he left the table, and she was safe.

That night I put on a pair of "espadrilles" that the widow woman had found for me on the black market. They were good ones, with solid, rope soles and good canvas uppers. We were to go out again with Mathieu and his men, and this time the programme was more exciting. A derailment. We walked a long way to an old chapel in a field. Paul had refused to stay at home, and now Albert had to order him every two minutes to keep silent. The American could not stop talking. He was excited.

Mathieu's small stock of parachuted explosives was kept hidden in the loft over the chapel's baroque, pale blue and gold altar. The building smelled strongly of incense. I kneeled down on the old, yellowish, brick floor and made up two small charges which we were going to use on the engine's cylinders if the derailment did not smash it completely. Don Juan gave me light, holding two long candles from the altar, candles that burned with a yellow light, and occasionally sputtered and spat wax on to my head.

"Even the candles lack fats these days," said Don Juan. "Why don't you want to blow up the bridge we spoke about, Émile?"

"It takes too much explosive, and it is easy to repair. The Boche has got material all ready for the bridges. Some things like the 'cœurs d'aiguilles', the points, have run right out of his control because everybody all over France is attacking them at the same time. The Boche engineers are skilful. A small bridge is child's play to them."

83

"Think of the bang that bridge would make," said Don Juan sadly. "And the fine effect upon the morale of the populace. My little 'gonzesse' asked me what we had blown up last night. A signal-box and some silly lines and telephone-posts make bad telling. It would take a man to blow up a bridge. A bridge is something, Emile. Although the signal-box was wonderful indeed. I went to see this morning. Yesterday there was a building, today there is a hole in the ground."

Mathieu had gone by himself to Mouchard station. He was going to stop a goods train passing through there at two o'clock in the morning, threaten the driver with his long Luger, drive the engine himself one mile out of Mouchard station, and then launch the train full-speed on the cut we were to make. We got to the appointed spot, a deep cutting between pine woods and with a high little road bridge crossing the line. Putting a sentry on the bridge, we soon had two sections of rail unscrewed, working hard in two teams of four and using the heavy tools parachuted from home. We completely undid only one end of each section, the end farthest from Mouchard, the train's starting-point; this end was wedged outwards towards the centre of the cutting, leaving a six-inch gap for the wheels to quit the track.

Waiting in the darkness for Mathieu's signal, two toots on the engine's whistle, we heard the crunch of two men walking on the line. They were railway guards, "gardes voies", Frenchmen in civilian clothes with white brassards on their left sleeves. These men had been put on the job by the Germans, and they were well paid. But they normally either did not care or did not dare to do the job properly. This pair walked under our bridge, arguing. One was pointing out volubly the merits of a Belgian cyclist who could, he claimed, do most obscene things to every French rider in any "Tour de France". His companion seemed to take this as a personal, not a national, affront.

They did not notice the rails which we had undone. But one hundred yards down the line they had a shock. For soon after they had passed we heard Mathieu's signal, and almost immediately the sound of a rushing engine. With ever-increasing speed, for it was a down gradient, a vast locomotive dragging an insignificant train came towards us. Flames and steam belched from it. Its rocking wheels struck sparks from the lines. Shuddering all over with its effort, almost jumping from the rails with its own excess of power, it dashed past us and quickly vanished into the distance.

Screams of rage greeted this terrible anti-climax. Great sobs broke from the beard of the grey-headed Maquisard, a local railway worker in peace-time, who had directed our unscrewing operations.

"Look," he cried dramatically. And he ran down the line to shine his torch on the wreckage of a locomotive that lay on its side twisted and deformed among the bushes. "That one was caught in our trap, and it was only doing half the speed. I had hoped that the two would be joined. Why did this not happen?" He sat down by the track and swore hysterically.

What had happened was that our attack on the points at Mouchard the night before had obliged the railway people to run single-line traffic. The normal up-line, where we had made our cut (trains in France travel on the left as in England) had been discarded, and the train had passed safely on the other line.

"The Resistance has taken to playing practical jokes," our widow woman said next day. "They took the driver and fireman off a train at Mouchard and put so much coal in the thing that it ran more than half-way to Dijon before it stopped. It ran through the stations so fast they thought it was a phantom.

"Just as well though," she ran on. "Although it was a goods train they had added another coach on behind at the last moment. Thirty passengers, there were. . . ."

We looked at each other in horror—and in relief. There was a law that trains with French passengers on board were never derailed.

I was watching the two boys at their game, and it was another sunny morning. One of Albert's liaison agents was in the diningroom. He was a pale man who looked as though five hundred leeches were working on him under his shirt. And he smelled unpleasant, like an old Belgian I once met. So I had gone to the bedroom to check over some batteries that I had left charging there. And once there I could not resist watching the game in the street.

But something else began to draw my attention. Behind the game two villagers were standing, deep in conversation. While they talked they looked down the road away from my window towards the river, and the edge of the village. There was nothing much in that. But something uneasy in their attitudes conveyed itself to me. And the uneasiness urged me to pack the few things I had lying around. (I always tried to make a point of living fully packed and ready to move with all my things.) Then I tidied up all the apparatus and aerials and earths lying around the room and put my own gun in my pocket, with its three spare magazines.

When I looked out of the window again there were five men, not two, standing in the street. The game still went on. A shining black car came tearing round the corner, scattering the five men and darting between the boys. It passed my window, braking heavily to take the corner. There were four big men inside with cropped hair, and the car was a "traction avant". Gestapo for a million.

A grey car, a Ford V8, nosed round the corner and edged down the street towards our house, coming so cautiously that it looked as though it were prepared to dive into any of the house doors at the slightest sign of danger. The boys stopped their game to look at it. There was only one man inside, a Frenchman in a cap. That was very unusual, a petrol-driven car with a poorly-dressed Frenchman driving alone.

It was Mathieu. He had hidden the car down the lane beside our house.

That could only mean one thing. I clicked a shell into the breech of my gun, stuck it in my belt, and began to get all our belongings into the corridor.

Albert came running down the corridor, followed by Mathieu and Paul.

"Everything down to the side door into the lane at once," Albert ordered. "The Boche surrounded the farm at the other side of the village where Mathieu was last night. They have begun to search the village.

"Paul, keep a look-out from the bedroom window.

"Emile, help me get the things in the car. We are going to try to get out by the field tracks this side of the village. They are only Gestapo so far, plain clothes and uniformed Gestapo. Mathieu doesn't think they have enough men to put a cordon round."

"Who are they looking for?" I asked.

"British officers," said Mathieu laconically. "They thought you were at the farm. I expect it's your buzz-box," he added, meaning the radio. Mathieu might have been going out for a drive in the park. "I'll go and keep watch while you load the car," he said.

"Get Paul," Albert said to me. All our things were in the back of the Ford. Paul came running through the house, a tommy-gun and two magazines in his hand.

"Just seen two Boches at the top of the road behind the ball-

86

game," he reported. We jumped downstairs. Mathieu came slinking fast, but not too obviously, round the corner, and sprang into the driver's seat.

"All in?" he asked. "Don't shut the doors. There are two Boches within sixty metres of us, but they can't see us yet. They could hear us though." As he spoke he let the Ford slide down the lane, slipping her into second gear. I glanced round once, back into the sunny street.

The game was still going on, and beyond the two bounding figures I thought I saw a grey uniform.

But the car started easily and silently as Mathieu let in his clutch.

"Get ready for action," he said. "I am going to try to take the tracks, but I have never been this side of the village before." I opened the windshield and stuck the barrel of a French light machine-gun out in front of me; the butt rested on my knees. In the back seat Paul and Albert, jammed in among the luggage, had lowered all the windows. Albert had taken the metal shoulder-piece off his Sten, so that he could use it more freely.

We were nosing along tracks through the fields, tracks that had certainly never seen a car before.

"An odd thing in the village street," I said. "That those two boys should have gone on playing like that. They were still playing when we left."

"Were they, that's good," Mathieu said. "I told them to. The small one's father was killed not long ago. Murdered by the Nazis." He was so politically minded that he used the word Nazi. All the others called the Germans either Boches, or Schleuhs (the name of the savage Moorish tribesmen who mutilate their enemies), or Stols or Schloks (names that sounded good, but I never understood their origins), or Fritz.

Mathieu had certainly risked his own skin in coming with the car to fetch us. He could have escaped easily on foot, or hidden himself among the other Frenchmen in the village. We owed him our lives.

"It was good of you to come for us," I said to him.

"You're not clear yet." He gave a shadow of his wolfish smile. "Leave you there in the widow's house with all your buzz-boxes and things. Three of you and the buzz-boxes. If they'd taken you there wouldn't have been two sticks of all Port Lesney standing this evening. Now we must get clear of the ring. There's a block on the main road up there to the right. I mean to try to take the small road up the hill there, and hide

87

you in the woods. But we'll have to follow the main road first for all of three kilometres."

It was lucky that Mathieu's men had taken the Ford, two nights before, and had found the petrol at the butcher's house. There was no ignition key on the dashboard. Contact had to be made by joining two wires together.

Mathieu drove very fast down the main road. But at each blind corner he slowed down to a crawl. He was afraid of German road blocks.

"Going slow round the corners we have time to get back out of it if they begin shooting," he said, then, flinging an almost humorous sideways glance at me: "By the way, Émile. We blew that bridge last night."

"Oh did you, Mathieu?"

"Yes. The whole bridge came tumbling down. We cut both sides. Now the railway is closed."

"For how long will it be closed? Did you cut it by any chance, Mathieu, because I said it should not be cut?"

"Yes, I did, at least I think I did. I appreciate your presence here and I am showing now that I will help you all, do anything for you. But I won't have any damned foreigners ordering my men around."

"*Any* damned foreigners?"

"What exactly do you mean by that?" he said sharply, and as he said it he swung the car off the main road, round a hair-pin bend and up a track that diagonalled the hill-side.

"I mean that if we came as Communists, still as foreigners, but as Communists first and foreigners afterwards. What then?"

"You would still be foreigners, I think. I am a Frenchman first."

"So you fight for national, not international ends?"

"Be damned to you with your sly educated words. Do you think I don't see your little trap. We fight, don't we? Is that not enough?"

"And we want to help you, don't we? Is that not enough?"

"Huh. This is the danger spot now. They can see us if they're sharp. Look down there. You can see the Boche road block."

The car was struggling up a steep incline, climbing a bare face of the hill. There were trees ahead, five hundred yards ahead.

"Yes, I can see them," I told him. "But they are small and distant. They do not inspire fear at such a distance."

"Telephones inspire fear, and radio, and aeroplanes," he answered. "If the Boche sees us from down there and suspects, then he can make things sticky for us, Émile. For we are driving into a bottle. The bottle is the narrow valley that runs up to Ronchaux. The Boche could make it as sticky as a bottle of beer is sticky for a wasp."

"I can smell freedom in the rain," I said, for it had begun to rain heavily, solid perpendicular rain.

"Freedom is what you British are always yapping about," he said angrily. I think he hated optimism in any form, identified it perhaps with stock markets and capitalism.

"We were right to 'yap' about it in 1940, were we not?"

"Yes, I don't deny you have done a good job, you British. You are stubborn, and I admire that. That stubborn thing and the Russian blood have won the war."

"And the Americans too," I said.

"Be damned to the Americans. They think of nothing but money. They are the enemies of the workers. Paul talks of nothing but the amount of money he makes. He is overpaid. He is making more money now, as a soldier, than he did before the war. So he does not want the war to end. Do you see what surfeit of money does? This American does not want the blood-bath to end."

"I dislike the surfeit of money too. But you must admit that Paul does his work well, and it is dangerous and difficult work. If he speaks too much about money that is a fault in education and upbringing. Those are faults that can be changed. The fact that he does his work well is much more important. America has something that all of us lack, a power, a vitality, a freshness in her industry that we lack."

"Which do you admire most, the Russian blood or the American vitality?"

"I admire the Russian blood the most. But then I could never help feeling sentimental about Russia. And vitality may be more important than blood even—I mean for winning the war."

"The war, the war. Have you a family, Émile? No. Well, I have three children, and a good wife of whom I am fond. But I like the war better. Yes, I like the war now that we can fight a little and risk ourselves a little. And then after some months of this fighting I shall want peace again to enjoy my children and the friendliness of my wife, and a glass now and then in the café. One of the troubles with war is that it is too permanent."

He slowed down and turned the car, then backed it down a narrow track which ran through a field, backed it until the first

trees and bushes of the wood closed over it. When the engine
shut off we heard the drumming of the rain on the metal roof
and on the trees. Mathieu sat considering at the wheel. At length
he said:

"I am going off to find out what is happening in the region.
Don't worry if I don't get back till evening. When I am gone
you had better camouflage the car as well as possible." He
walked off into the rain. It was so heavy that it created with
its splashes a kind of aureole around his narrow body.

We worked for an hour, hiding the car. We got twigs and
switched the grass track through the field until it showed no
suspicion of tyre tracks. With an old rag Paul wiped at the
road until there was no sign of the car's stopping. Then we went
back into the wood behind the car and cut branches and whole
shrubs. With these we entirely closed up the space by which
the car had entered. Despite all these precautions I personally
made certain that my ruck-sack and the "valise diplomatique"
were ready in case Germans appeared on the road. I had no
intention of losing all my belongings. And going for branches
I had already reconnoitred a suitable line of retreat. These things
had become more than second nature to me, for if you divide
men into categories, I belong to the hare rather than the lion
category.

We were hungry. All the food that we had was three boiled
sweets, which still remained in a paper bag in my pocket. These
despatched, I smoked my first cigarette in France to stifle my
hunger. The sequel to fear with me is usually a kind of cold
shuddering feeling in my weak spot, the small of the back, and
this is accompanied by an intense hunger. I was amused to find
now that I had been afraid during our get-away and during our
trip while I talked to Mathieu. It was a fear which would never
have occurred to me if I had only been facing the normal things
a soldier faces, death, wounds, or imprisonment. So I realised
that all this build-up of the torture business at nights with Albert
was doing me no good. That, and being hidden in houses. It
was not a life for anyone; but certainly not for me. I must
change it.

Paul, lying back beside Albert on the front seat, began to talk
of his past life in the States. His little story, a great story, came
to me in snatches over the rain's drumming. Sometimes the
bitter cigarette smoke was so thick in the car that I felt it stifling
me, sickening me. It was cold.

He described a tenement in an American town. His mother

beat him when he came home late from school. Then one day he found he was strong enough to beat her. After that he came home when he pleased. He ran away, joined a travelling circus; worked his way up in the circus until he had a stall, a stall that sold popcorn, peanuts and toffee-apples. The tricks of this trade mastered, he bought an automobile. Then a trailer caravan.

"Boy you should of seen that caravan. All chrome and mother-of-pearl. . . ."

Albert listened entranced; his family had two or three châteaux.

"The bed folded in, and I had those rubber sponge cushions on it, you know, all soft. . . ."

He had made good. He had had two, three stalls even in the same show, all taking big money. There was a success story too. One day the circus was playing his home town. Business was great. In the heart of the rush on popcorn he saw his sis' with the kid brother. He gave her the nickel change before she looked up. She hardly knew him. He hadn't intended to go home, at all. Too busy adding up the takings and fixing up for the next town on the list. But he did. The old girl was kind of glad to see him. All the same she chewed him off just like she used to. Only now he kind of liked it. Then the war came and one night when he was drunk he had to go and volunteer for the navy. Then they offered big money and plenty of glamour to radio operators who wanted to go to Europe as parachutists. He went along just to be with the boys. He was proud to be in the navy. But it had a drawback. Promotion was difficult. He was still a leading seaman. He thought he ought to be an officer.

We thought so too. I suddenly remembered, and told him they were "gunning for him" in the London office. Paul was unimpressed by this news.

"I would just like to be an officer, somehow," he said. "Why, dames doing my job in London are officers. Why should you be an officer for sitting on your fanny in London? When you do the same job out here you're a sergeant. Course, the money's good. But I'd take a little less money to be an officer."

"You mean you would pay to be an officer?" I asked.

"Sure I would."

"That is the system in the British Army."

Paul was being paid three times more than either Albert or myself. He was leading seaman, second class, and we were both captains. But I did not envy him. It took too much courage to do his job. It gave me the jumps to be in the same room when his wireless was buzzing and whistling and the German d.f. stations were listening. At least one always thought they were listening.

A car stopped on the road outside. Albert and I got out fast with our weapons. Three men were approaching our imitation "impenetrable bush" in front of the car. They were approaching carefully, one with a Sten held across his body and the other two with heavy revolvers in their right hands. They were dirty and dressed in tatters. Despite the rain, one wore no boots. Their car, standing in the road, was a handsome "traction avant", dark blue, with crimson wheels.

When they had come to the other side of our screen they still did not see us. They began to pull it down.

"Stop that," said Albert, and their Sten went "click". The man carrying it had half-raised it to the firing-from-the-hip-position. It had misfired. The magazine had not been pushed right home. Albert, talking faster than normally, explained that we were friends. We got back into the car, for it was still raining. They talked to us, sticking their shaggy heads through the windows. They reminded me of the outlaws in the film "Robin Hood" or revolutionary "ruffians" in the play "The Only Way". Compared to these Maquisards the men of Jacques were sleek and well-groomed. They had not tasted tobacco for ten days. They came from an F.T.P. Maquis on the hill. They had been down to the valley that day to steal the Citrœn in which they had arrived. They had been pursued by Germans on the road. They had approached our wood with the idea of hiding their car there. Two of them now went off to get another hiding-place.

The third had been in the navy, and had been in England, in Portsmouth, at the time of the Armistice. He had a round face, with a slobbering mouth and small, shifty eyes.

"We were betrayed by our officers," he said. "They said it was our duty to go back to France. . . ."

I slept, and I was cold and stiff when Albert shook me. The car had sunk into the leaf mould up to the back axle. We had to lift her out. Mathieu had arrived in a truck. It was night already, and he had brought food for us. A round loaf of bread with an omelette "fines herbes" stuck in the middle of the loaf. And a bottle of strong red wine.

When we had eaten we moved off again. Mathieu was again beside me, driving. We closed the windshield because of the cold night mist. It was hard to see with the headlights. We mounted for a bit, in second, then dived down into a deep narrow valley. Mathieu drove fast, accelerating hard on his corners. His driving seemed to have a kind of gallantry to it. It pumped oxygen into my lungs and blood into my heart. Often I could not see the road ahead, but Mathieu seemed to feel it through the wheel.

We stopped at last in front of an isolated house. Mathieu went in and some minutes later the light went on upstairs and a young man and woman came down to the hall-way. The man had bare feet, his hair was tousled, and his eyes were still full of sleep. The young woman, his wife, was dark, curving and coquettish, with long black eyes that seemed to leave a damp imprint when they landed on your face. She put dirty glasses in front of us. No two glasses had the same shape or texture of glass. This was in the kitchen, on the first floor. There was a small radio. The wife found love songs in a Southern accent from Radio Toulouse. The husband looked mistrustfully at us.

Mathieu emptied his glass of red wine.

"I'm off," he said. "Sleep well."

"Where are you going? Home?"

"Home! Did I forget to tell you? The Gestapo visited my house this afternoon. Until the end of the war the woods are my home. But I have the car to sleep in."

I wanted to leave with him. I did not want to stay in the house. Much better to go out into the woods. But I had to stay with Albert, I thought. The man showed us to our room. It was his mother-in-law's room, stale and pompous and fussy, with a great, ochre-coloured bed, and a small iron bed in another corner. This time Albert won the toss, and took the iron bed. I let Paul take the big yellow one alone and lay down in my sleeping-bag on the dirty floor.

There was a lithograph of "Balaclava" over my head, but there were Frenchmen in the picture, not our Light Brigade. I pointed this out to Albert, who said haughtily that he had never heard of any British cavalry in that particular battle. A long argument ensued on the evils of history as taught in the French schools. Paul did not listen to this sometimes acrimonious discussion. He lay stretched out on his bed, his big set beside him and the headphones stuck just over the fronts of his ears.

He talked to himself, rather than to us. He said things like: "That's real music." Sometimes he laughed at something somebody had said in London or New York. When I awoke in the morning Paul still had the headphones on, and noises were still coming from them. But he slept in his big-striped pyjamas like a little, yellow-skinned satyr. In the other corner of the room Albert slept more pompously. The chatter of children's voices came from directly below us. We were living over the village school. We had to be careful not to make a noise when we moved about. Albert and Paul went in their socks from breakfast to dinner, and I wore the "espadrilles" the widow woman had bought me.

Outside our window there was a beautiful green field with cattle in it. Then a line of fruit trees, then the valley began winding up and away with little woods and vineyards and good fields queuing up all the way along the bottom of the valley. The whole narrow twisting valley rang with the bells of the cows in it. The bells, reverberating from the sharp ridges on either side were sometimes so loud in the early mornings that they woke us from sleep.

In the school intervals the Ronchaux children played under our window. Played around the two old stone privies that the commune had put up in the yard, and played on the edge of the field bordered with fruit trees. Serious, slightly pasty-looking French children. Often they walked in pairs, usually two boys or two girls together, with linked hands. There seemed to be a great devotion or a magnetism flowing through the joining of their hands. Even doing something difficult like climbing down the steep bank from the field that ended in a wall, they would keep their hands linked.

The schoolmistress had a harsh face and reddish hair. But she was young, and the children loved the school. Often when the midday break came I would escape to roam along the common land that followed the ridge on our side of the valley. But I had to be careful, for the children, instead of taking the full two hours of their break for food, would often come back to the school after only half an hour's absence.

Three little girls had a house among the vines that grew from the side of the school into the garden. There were nasturtiums all round their house. If it had come to making a break from the Gestapo we should have had to jump from the staircase window right through their house. At nights I used to go down there with a torch and clear away the little bits of crockery and glass the girls brought there every day for their "house-keeping". The crockery would have made a noise crunching under our feet.

When Paul worked on his radio we had to shut the window

94

to keep our noise from the children and their noise from us. Usually when he worked I climbed the hill behind to keep a look-out for Germans. It was good on the hill. There were bracken and long grass and heather in some places. There were goats with small goatherds, but these I was obliged to avoid.

On the main road that paralleled the valley, about a thousand yards from the ridge, I often saw German military traffic. Once a convoy of tanks on transporters passed. There were Panzer men sitting on the tanks, aft of the turrets, lounging in nonchalant healthy postures. Still the monarchs. Not many people around us thought the invasion was going to be a success. The bridgehead seemed to be well contained.

I sunbathed on the ridge, hiding myself in small spaces surrounded by bushes and taking off my shirt. I lay in the June sun until I sweated and then went back to our room, filled with smoke, Albert lying on one bed and Paul on the other.

People came to see us from Albert's different sectors, but in none of them could we find any prospect of a job for me. The days drifted past at Ronchaux, drifted in an agonising sameness. The work was going on around us. Small sabotage groups were going out almost every night. But since the Port Lesney morning when, apparently, the Germans knew that they had nearly caught us, the enemy supervision had grown tighter on the region. It was agreed with the local chiefs that we should lie hidden for at least a week, and try to use the radio as little as possible. I could see no opening for myself, and I knew that I could not go on indefinitely with this existence. It was too unhealthy for me. In the mornings, before the school-children arrived and while the household slept, I got out of my sleeping-bag and did half an hour of exercises, just as I used to do in prison. I cut my eating down to a minimum.

"Preparing for what?" Albert asked me. "You know I want desperately to give you something to do. But what? None of my Maquis groups are big enough or important enough for me to risk you there. You could have helped me with the whole sector had the invasion come a little later. Now it is too difficult and too late for you to get to know all my people."

"Something will turn up," I told him.

It came from young Don Juan of Mouchard, a surprising messenger. He arrived late one evening when we were drinking French tea in coffee-cups. He told Albert that he could put him in touch with Colonel Morin. Albert arranged a rendez-

vous in a wood, down the road, a wood where we had already
met Georges and other liaison men.

Two days later we waited in this wood for the Colonel. Albert
had been told that the Colonel was a difficult man to deal with.
But he was certainly an important man. He was chief of the
French Forces of the Interior for an enormous area—the regions
of the Haute-Saône, the Doubs, and much of the Jura.

This great man arrived in an old car driven on wood gas, a
"gazogene", with a taxi sign hanging on behind. He was
followed by Mathieu, Don Juan, and two more of the F.T.P.
band in Mathieu's Ford. One reason for bad reports of the
Colonel was obvious to us both from the start. The two car-
loads of men did not mix. They stood apart in two tight little
groups glaring at each other. The woodland glade was warm
and dappled with sunshine, but the colonel invited Albert and
myself to sit with him in his dusty old taxi. Once inside he
closed the windows so that nobody should overhear.

Colonel Morin, a regular soldier and a 1940 colonel of
colonial infantry, looked like a little peasant in a dirty suit. A
suit striped and spotted with food, bicycle oil, and all kinds of
dirt. A suit faded by the sun, the wind, and the rain, and
crushed by the many nights the colonel had slept in it. Above
this monumental suit there balanced an incredibly weathered
face. The features of a soldier who had faced all kinds of
weather, and all kinds of enemies, in almost every country in
which a French officer could serve. In two nests of wrinkles
were set a pair of mercurial and inquisitive grey eyes. Close-
cropped, grizzled hair showed above his slightly pointed ears,
but was otherwise hidden by an extraordinary filthy beret. He
opened on Albert at once.

"Fine people you associate with," he said in a loud, hard
voice. "Those F.T.P., I mean. I am late for this appointment
for this reason, that when I called as arranged on the dark lad
there [indicating Don Juan through the window] I found him
stripped to the waist and in bed with a 'gonzesse'. Furthermore, he did not even get out of bed when I arrived." He
paused to lower a window, spat, closed the window and lit a
short, squat, and revolting pipe.

"You are in grave danger," he continued. "Why? Because
you are working with the wrong people. Look at them there.
They are in a car that runs on petrol, and they are dressed like
a cross between burglars and big-game hunters. No idea of
craft, of concealment. Now look at me. Dressed like an old

peasant; with the ugly mug of an old peasant, and the ugly
clothes of one. Haven't had my boots off for sixteen days.

"I travel in an old taxi that just gets me around. But if the
Boches stop me I get past them, for my story is prepared and
all is in character. And to the French people I am just an old
wood merchant. There is nothing suspicious about me at all.

"Now who is right, young man? Me or them?"

Albert, doubtless piqued by the Colonel's "young man",
answered stiffly that monsieur the Colonel was perfectly right.

"You have been in with the wrong people from the very
start," the Colonel told him bluntly.

"Meaning, my Colonel, that they are wrong because they do
not work for you?"

"I mean that any good Frenchman should fight now as a
Frenchman, and if he is a communist he should drown that for
the present and fight with the F.F.I. Politics were the downfall of France in '40, and unless we are firm about them they'll
be our downfall in '44, and afterwards. We want men who'll
fight now, and discipline, and proper officers. That's how the
F.F.I. has to be in my area. Like the army."

"Anybody who will fight, and who is worthy to carry arms,
will get arms if I have my way," said Albert. "For your
politics I don't give a damn. All I am interested in are results
and how to achieve them. Here, in this part of my sector, I
have armed the communists, because here the communists are
the only people I know. I have tried to get in touch with your
people. If you can now help me towards that I shall gladly
have a look at them, and if they merit it I shall try to get arms
and material for them."

"You shall see them tomorrow," said the Colonel, and he
opened the door to introduce us to a lieutenant who worked
there in the locality, an aviator with smooth, shining black hair.
"From now on we shall help you," the Colonel went on. "Anything that you want you will only have to ask for. If you need
a car, a sensible car like this that can travel without risk, you
will only have to tell us. Tobacco, food, books, clothes, anything we have we shall give to you. But for God's sake be
sensible how you carry on with these cut-throats."

Albert asked the Colonel if he had any job for me, as an
instructor or organiser.

"Jobs everywhere," answered Morin. "But I would
particularly like to put him in the Haute-Saône."

"I fear that is impossible," Albert countered. "Emile must

work somewhere in my sector, and the Haute-Saône is too far north. I don't want him to go north of Besançon.''

"Well, you must ask Barthelet," the Colonel said. "He'll come and see you. Barthelet has been in command of this Salins area, and now he's moving up to Besançon to be military governor of that town. That makes you snigger, eh? I know there are three thousand Boches in Besançon still, but one day we'll burn them out and put our military governor in." How far away that day seemed.

Albert and the Colonel did not like each other. They were both too downright, and too easily offended.

"See all the promises he held out," said Albert as we walked back along the ridge towards the school. "They will do anything to get us to give arms to them, as opposed to the other bunch. That's why they are polite to us. Because we get them arms. Or may get them arms.''

"Yes. But will they use them better than the other bunch?''

"We shall see. These F.F.I. people depend entirely on their leaders. Sometimes they are reasonable. Sometimes they are appalling.''

Next morning the shiny-haired lieutenant picked us up in another "gazogene". This one was even more picturesque. For the back windows were covered with ply-wood and the back part was curtained off and fitted with hangers for women's dresses. It was a commercial traveller's car.

The news was bad.

"There are a lot of Cossacks moving into the area," the lieutenant told us. "It is said that they are going to search the village down the valley from Ronchaux. That's only the wildest rumour, but it's extraordinary how frequently these rumours come true.''

None of us risked much should we meet the Cossacks on the way. Albert and I had left our pistols at Ronchaux, and were travelling as strictly bona fide civilians. We dropped down the little road past the hiding-place where we had spent the day in the Ford. When we came to the main road our driver pointed out black tyre-marks where fast-driven cars had bitten into the surface as they made the turn.

"You see what that gangster driving does," he said. "If the Boches were really intelligent they would follow those marks, those arrows you might say. They would lead them to you.''

We cut through a small village where all the men seemed to be sawing wood and turned up another and much wilder valley, at right angles to the one we were living in. Driving up this road we came from behind upon three men, Mathieu, Don Juan, and another. They carried heavy sacks of provisions. Mathieu also carried, slung openly upon his back, an American carbine. I suddenly wanted violently to be with them.

"Are you not going to give them a lift?" I asked Shining Hair.

"Oh, not worth it with all that stuff they're carrying," he answered. "They have begun to form a Maquis on the hill, up there, not far from ours. Since we met you they seem to be working in better with us. We have helped them a bit with provisions."

So we passed, and I was only able to give them an impersonal wave. Mathieu's bony face was bare of expression as the rock he stood beside, but I expected to see the half-smile come on it that would mean: "That's right, let us drop now, spawn of a capitalist. You'll get more out of the new ones you've found."

I knew that Albert would never let Mathieu drop. The thin man had been working like a madman the last few days. Getting material for his Maquis. He was an outlaw with a German price on his head. His wife and children were still at Mouchard. But they expected arrest and imprisonment any day. Mathieu had had every hair shaved off his head, and looked leaner and wilder every day. He had some sixteen men and several cars under his orders now. But he was taking too many outside chances. Albert did not give him long to live.

Standing beside the rock on the roadway there was the last I was to see of him.

A Maquis in a village was what Shining Hair first showed us. About a dozen men occupying a deserted farm-house. They were all clean and tidy and polite and disciplined. Their deserted farm-house was well swept and neat. When we arrived they were washing themselves under the village pump.

"They have all done their military service," said Shining Hair proudly. "We insist on that, you know." Their chief was myopic, with a bony and non-muscular bare torso. He wore glasses and shorts with a clasp-knife hanging from them.

Something about this Maquis displeased me. At the time I did not know what it was. Now, from greater experience, I know when I look back. These "Maquisards" were all of the clerk or "petit bourgeois" or "member of mountaineering clubs" type. Not the best type for the Maquis. Something rougher was needed. This was too nice. But we had to praise of course. One must always praise cleanliness and order, two admirable qualities, especially when they are founded on strength. They asked me to show them how the phosphorous grenade worked and was thrown. It occurred to me that if there was one thing more droll than myself—law-abiding and baby-faced—teaching them this efficient but ghastly weapon in that place it was my audience. They looked like a benevolent society or a ramblers' club at a rest-house in Sussex.

We ate with Shining Hair and the myopic chief in a hut buried in a basin in the woods. In the stable annexe to the hut there were another dozen men, lying on the straw. They had a recuperated French heavy machine-gun there.

Half-way through the meal a youth came in, a communist, sent by Mathieu to say that about eight hundred Cossacks had begun to beat the wood at his side, and might be expected to reach us in about two hours' time. The tactical weakness of the siting of this Maquis was now shown. We found ourselves at the bottom of a big and well-wooded punch-bowl. We had no idea what was happening around us. The place had been chosen because the road in and out was easy to cut. It had been chosen by two officers in the French Army. But one had functioned in the artillery and the other in the engineers. The real defence problems were infantry ones.

We left, Albert, Shining Hair and myself, in the commercial traveller's car, going, since that was as good a shot in the dark as any, to the north. On the way we had bad news. Another detachment of Cossacks with some Gestapo had surrounded By, the next village to Ronchaux. We made a big, wheezing detour in that appalling car and came to Ronchaux from the north. There were neither Germans nor Cossacks in the village. We walked up to the school, leaving Shining Hair and the car in some trees.

Paul was at the back of the house, by the wood-pile. All our things were ready to move. The news that "la Geste" was in By had cleared every "terrorist" out of Ronchaux except poor Paul, who had been obliged to await our return. The school was in session, but there was no time to be lost. Despite the teacher's cries, all the children crowded to the windows to watch us load our gear into the "ladies' gowns" compartment of the car, which Shining Hair had backed up alongside the schoolroom wall. Paul and I sat in the back. The slow old car negotiated endless hills and finally, late in the evening, deposited the three of us in a wood beside the main road running north out of Salins. Our wood was on such a steep hill-side that you had to put a leg on either side of a tree to prevent yourself from sliding downhill. No sooner were we deposited there than it began to rain.

We lay there and laughed for half an hour. Laughed at ourselves for our misery and our rage at the stupidity of being chased all over the countryside by an enemy whom we never saw. When we had finished laughing Albert and Paul both coughed. And both of them had red spots on their cheek-bones. They were sickening for a chill. The memory of Mathieu and the other two men carrying their supplies up into the woods came clearly to me. That was the kind of life I wanted if I had to be in the war. I wanted to sleep out in the woods, and to work in the woods among the damp smells of the fungi and the dry smells of pine-needles. That type of running away and hiding might suit me. Hiding in houses did not.

After dark Shining Hair and the myopic chief took us to another farm-house. Another hole to hide in. And what a hole. Albert's face grew stormier and blacker as we passed out of the midden into the kitchen where the dried mud had been swept into the corners until it formed miniature ski-ing slopes for the ants and cockroaches, into the sitting-room with its dirty red plush sofa and a big feather-bed (unmade) in one corner, and finally into the bedroom, our bedroom, with two feather-beds side by side, two enormous Normandy wardrobes full of ancient peasants' Sunday clothes and hats, and one tiny hole of a window covered with a curtain of cobwebs.

"Here you will be safe," said the myopic chief.

"Safety is not all," replied Albert. "I am afraid this will not do. It is too depressing. We should go mad here."

"Too depressing?" they echoed, for they had not thought of that.

"I will bring you some books," said Shining Hair. "Books in English."

Albert shuddered. We looked around us at the hideousness of everything. This was a time when death seemed preferable to sordid discomfort. The smell of wet clothes began to fight the resident odours of the farm-house.

Shining Hair and the myopic chief went sadly away. They had promised to find another house. At first they had said it would be another farm-house.

"Not a farm-house," said Albert. "I loathe farm-houses."

They thought we were old-maidish and over-fussy. But they would find something better, a little better, anyway. The farmer's wife, an old woman with a body that slipped down on one side, brought us our evening meal. There were mountains of food. She had heard that Englishmen ate whole animals at a sitting. Almost everything that she put on the table was encased in fat; there was fat mutton, fat hot sausage swimming in its own yellow grease, and a fat salt ham. Albert left the table to be sick. Paul followed him. I was left sitting in front of all this food. The tragedy of it came bitterly home to me. If only that highly coloured fat could be transported to the children or the young factory-workers of Paris, or Athens, or even of Birmingham. I drank some of the red wine, which was excellent, and ate some salad, rather rancid with its colza oil dressing. The table looked like a ghastly Victorian still life. Albert had taken one segment of ham on his plate, and had begun to cut the lean from the fat before the full horror of the table had possessed him. Paul had dropped his greasy knife and fork on the floor as he left.

"What *will* they eat then?" asked the farmer's wife. I told her to give us eggs and butter in future and very little else, for that seemed to be all that Albert ate. "And I gave you all the *best* things," she said sadly. Paul and Albert had both gone to bed. They had doped themselves with aspirin or something similar and they slept thickly in the feather-beds. I put down my sleeping-bag as near the window as possible. That farm might be safe, but one had an impression of danger. It was only fifty yards from the main road, and much traffic passed; civilian traffic during the day, but military traffic that night. I hoped that no German vehicle would break down near our farm. For if they came through to look for a bed we had much incriminating material lying about, pistols and wireless parts, and torches. Even my sleeping-bag looked too military. What were the Germans doing, moving convoys at night? It was mainly north-bound traffic. I supposed they were bringing reinforcements up for the big battle in Normandy. Both Paul and Albert groaned and muttered in their sleep. The heavy Diesels shook the farm-house as they passed. No Germans visited the farm that night.

Next day a Frenchman visited the farm who was to change the immediate course of my life. His name was Barthelet, Joseph Barthelet, and he called himself Boulaya, which he told us signified "beard" or "bearded one" in French North Africa.

CHAPTER VI

HE looked amazingly healthy, this Boulaya. That was the first thing that struck me about him. Healthy and free, somehow. Not shut in by fears or inhibitions. And he walked with the devil of a swagger. It was almost a strut, for a middle-aged man.

He came in talking. A characteristic entrance. And I saw Albert stiffen and concentrate. For the newcomer spoke good English, much better English than Albert's. He spoke it with a London accent and a lot of slang of the kind that you find in grammar books, just a shade too vicar-at-a-tea-party. Apart from a few English expletives, therefore, Albert had to content himself with talking his native French.

Boulaya was on the tall side for a Frenchman. A thin man in the late thirties or early forties, who gave the impression that he had been fatter before the war. His face was constantly in movement. When he talked or laughed everything moved, nose, cheeks, ears, everything from his slightly receding chin to the top of his head where the fluffy fair hair, worn short and soldier-like, was going thin. He had blue eyes. One moment his bright look had settled on you, then in a flash it was curtained, then it was back on you, or it had darted away to another resting-place.

His clothes were appalling, yet he wore them with a rakish air, as though they were a flag—as indeed they were. They were the badge of his dangerous life. The uniform of a captain in the Resistance.

He wore a garment of blue wool, something between a coat and a cardigan, shaped in a tricky, double-breasted way, with the twin sets of large buttons opening out from the bottom pair in an exaggerated V to beneath the wide and lasciviously pointed lapels. Below the pinch waist of this article of clothing he showed a pair of blue, city-slicker trousers, nearly thread-bare and pinned tight over the ankles with big safety-pins (for he had arrived on a bicycle). His boots, encrusted with mud and worse, were of the solid German pattern. Unlike any of us, he wore a tie. And although the whole rather dashing ensemble and bearing of this man seemed to scream "Resistance!" or the German word for it, "Terrorist!" his clothes were neverthe-less well in keeping with his role of a commercial traveller operating on his bicycle around Besançon.

Shining Hair and the myopic chief arrived. He held the same rank in the Resistance as the myopic chief, yet there was a difference, a superiority, tacitly recognised by both of them, particularly by Boulaya.

"I failed to recognise you without the fungus," said the myopic chief.

"They hunted Boulaya without a beard, so Boulaya grew a beard," replied that worthy, who was evidently fond of his nom-de-guerre. "Now they hunt for the bearded Boulaya, so I have discarded the fungus, as you so familiarly name it."

"Not disrespectfully, I assure you. It was a good beard."

"It was more than a good beard. It was a beard that held something of charm and seduction. Had I worn it just a shade more as a 'boucle' I believe that it would also have held a distinction that is difficult to obtain. After the war, although Madame Barthelet is massing her forces in opposition to this, I intend to experiment with beards."

"You are confident that you will see the end of the war?" asked Albert. "I would like to meet a man with such confidence."

"If such a thing would not draw bad luck I would answer 'Yes'. I will content myself with the observation that it will take a shrewd blow to overturn Boulaya. I am an old hand, and experienced at this game. Why, today, for the first time in six months, I am going to see my wife. I tell myself that I am crazy fool to go and see her. So I am. But how many Frenchmen would stay away from their wives and children for all of six months just because the Gestapo is after them? You are right. Damned few. That's how we all get caught. But six months is a long, long time. And my wife is clever too. She does not know that I am coming, but she has thrown the Boches off her trail. And I will not stay with her. Only the one night. Tomorrow I return north to my new sector, the Besançon area."

"How is your new area?"

"It is going to be splendid," Boulaya answered.

"You mean that at the moment it is—backward?"

"I mean that it is the most important area in the whole of Colonel Morin's command. Besançon is the key to the area. The Resistance around Besançon must be built up until we are in a position to take the city. I shall form a company myself, a picked company of men who have served in the 'Corps Francs'. The Boulaya Company will march first as liberators into Besançon, and Boulaya will himself be at the head of the company. I am a native of Besançon, a real Bisontin, although I have lived and worked much in other towns and even countries. But the liberation of Besançon, that is the task that I adore."

"Have you got some Maquis up there?"

"Two. Best in the whole of France."

"Do you want a good instructor? What about Émile?"

"I should be honoured and delighted," said Boulaya, then he paused and considered. We all knew that he had exaggerated the strength of his forces for the sake of a few resounding phrases. Now he might slide out of it. Refuse to compromise himself, to give himself any extra trouble. But no, not the ardent Boulaya.

"I will take Émile up there with me tomorrow," he said, and he talked on, but I did not hear him, except as the low 'cello accompaniment to my thoughts, to the rhapsody of my thoughts on freedom and movement under the ægis of this debonair swashbuckler.

"You will only have to get a bicycle," he said to me. "And in two days you will be in the Maquis."

"Would he get through on the roads all right?" asked Albert. "Things are not easy between here and Besançon."

"I, Boulaya, guarantee that he will get through."

"What would my position be in the Maquis you speak of?" I asked him.

"You will be chief of the two Maquis. You will have under you an adjutant, a French officer who knows the country better than his bed and who has been personally responsible for enrolling the men. He will look after the administration of the Maquis, the commissariat and things like that. You, Émile, will be the chief of the 'Équipes Boulaya'. You will command them, and lead their operations. Why," he continued, working himself up, selling himself the idea, as it were. "Why it is the best thing that could happen. Your presence there will be an inspiration for the whole sector (though of course no outsiders must know that you are there). With your technical knowledge we shall build up great 'équipes'. You will become a kind of hero, a kind of God. . . .

"Upon my soul," he said, wiping his forehead with a red handkerchief. "I positively regret that I must spend tonight with Madame Barthelet, and I have promised to lunch with my dear father tomorrow. I would like to be off with you now, this very moment."

"Please excuse us for a second," Albert said, and he took me into the dark bedroom where Paul lay groaning in a feverish delirium.

"For my part, you can go, Georges," Albert said. He did not want me to go, and part of me was reluctant to leave him. He had nursed me through the beginning of my new life in France. He had been kind to me, and I was grateful to him. Now he was in danger, he was ill, he needed the safety-valve of my companionship. I felt that for his sake I should stay.

But behind these prosy, and I am afraid insincere, reasonings there was a wilder, stronger feeling pushing me, the urge to get out into a wider existence, the urge to get away from this district where I had been obliged to hide indoors, and defecate in slop-pails behind cupboard doors.

And then, tugging in the opposite direction, striving to keep me at Albert's shirt-tails, in the security of his judgment was my fear of the roads where one might meet a Gestapo man or a militian. My fear of capture and torture, my fear of the unknown and my fear of details. For example, Albert had told Boulaya that I was a good instructor. I knew that I did not come into such a category. In the first place I was not even an instructor. I had not been trained as an instructor. Was I capable of leading two Maquis? Was I capable of leading two men? Was I capable of following Boulaya up there, riding beside him on a bicycle, passing controls perhaps? Did he realise that I spoke French with an accent?

But the urge for freedom, stimulated by twenty months as prisoner of war, which were still a fresh memory, the urge was stronger than all my fears.

"I would come back if you ever needed me," I said oilily to Albert. "I shall be so sorry to leave you, but I feel that I am only a drag on you, an extra responsibility."

"So you want to go," he answered. "Well, I can't say I envy you. Living with these beastly people in the Maquis is not a life that I could endure for more than a day or two. . . ."

"But I *like* that part of it," I assured him.

"Well, if you can stand the dirt and the discomfort of it, that is not all. Those people cannot talk to you about anything interesting or civilised. They are the scum, the people who have no life worth living, so they sink into the Maquis, to live like jackals in the woods. They may steal from you. They might even murder you. . . ."

"You make it sound too thrilling."

"What do you think of Boulaya?" He changed tack.

"I like him. He amuses me."

"Yes, he seems all right. But he might be a bit harum scarum."

"Dashing perhaps. But the Resistance can do with a bit of dash. Besides, he would not have existed so long if he had been harum-scarum. So I can go, Albert?"

"Yes, go on. But come back when you get sick of it. We shall soon have a lot of work here." He led the way back into the sitting-room. Boulaya and the other two were sitting smoking. Boulaya had a beastly little pipe with a hexagonal bowl. There was a tiny silver star inlaid on each face of the hexagon. "I feel that I must get out and about now," Albert continued. "I must go back alone into Dole, and see all my people again. I've been too long away. When they don't see you for a few days they begin to think that you have lost heart, or they get nervous, and think you've been taken. Maybe I'll grow a beard or something. I look ghastly in a beard. Paul must soon be placed somewhere else. Perhaps you'll be able to find a place for him, a good, reasonably comfortable house at least thirty kilometres from here. He has worked far too much in this area, there is hardly a village here that hasn't been burned."

"Why don't you allow me to help you," Boulaya said, making a large sweeping gesture with his star-studded pipe, a gesture which seemed to encompass all France. "I could put him, put you both if you like, in a château, a château belonging to a general at La Chevillotte. That's more than thirty kilometres from here. A lovely place. Two charming daughters, a good library, everything."

"I would prefer it without the daughters," Albert answered. "Not for myself, of course, but for Paul. He has such an incredible effect on women, and any kind of love affair is dangerous in our job. But it sounds most suitable. We'll consider it tonight."

"Love is dangerous," agreed Boulaya. "It is a luxury which we of the Resistance cannot afford to offer ourselves. The pose of the stony heart is just one more gift that we must offer to the sacred cause of freedom. It is by no means the least costly gift. Life can be sombre without love."

"When do we leave?" I asked him.

"Two-thirty tomorrow afternoon. You must find a bicycle and you will need a bicycle-licence. Carry no arms, of course, and nothing incriminating if you can avoid it. Now that everything is so delightfully settled I must be off. Madame Barthelet must be impatient; she has been waiting a long time for her souse—you say souse, I think?"

"Spouse."

When he had gone the room seemed to darken, as though his departure had taken a few million candle-power out of the sun. In this half-gloom I had to persuade Shining Hair and the myopic chief to find, procure, or steal a bicycle for me, a task more difficult than it sounds since, at that period sans cars, sans buses, and with a railway system that was fast disintegrating, bicycles were gold.

They did find one, and sent it up that evening with the farmer's son. They did not even forget the licence. It was a bicycle belonging to the son of the mayor of Salins. He loaned it to me on the understanding that I would return it when I had reached my immediate destination, near Besançon.

A shining grey machine with a three-speed gear and those hand-screw things at the sides of the wheels, and rakish, low-flung handle-bars. I had never had a bicycle like that before. It was a machine that my schoolmasters or parents would have considered flash and ungentlemanly. Each little spoke was encased in a glittering sheath of chromium. And the red Michelin tyres, they told me, were "nearly new". They looked thin and fragile tyres to me. But tyres were even more difficult to find than bicycles. And then it had a little bag hanging behind the saddle with a REPAIR OUTFIT. When he saw this rarity the farmer's son was overcome by the generosity of the mayor's son. But no more overcome than I. No boy ever contemplated his first pony with more reverence and love than I accorded to the grey bicycle in the byre to the north of Salins. Its very name inspired confidence and affection. It was a "Corsair", and this fact the manufacturer had proclaimed in large, baroque letters.

A doctor who spoke with a German accent and reminded me of a newspaper man had come to see Albert and Paul, while I was waiting impatiently for Boulaya. It was three o'clock on the day I was to leave. The doctor was Alsatian, with hair worn "en brosse" in front and extremely short behind. He reminded me of a newspaper man whom I had known in Paris at the outbreak of war, a French reporter who worked for Havas. Waiting to go out into the wet world outside, for it had been raining since the early morning, I wondered if I should ever see Paris again, or work in my old civilian job. I did not think that I could survive to the end of the war. Perhaps, instead of standing there looking at the rain through the bedroom's miniature window, I might take my things into the byre and fix what I could on the back of the bicycle.

For this new development I jettisoned still more of the luxurious equipment given me by London. I had discarded my small short-wave radio receiver, my two pistols with all their ammunition and magazines, my dagger, and the maps which were photostatic copies of French Michelin maps. I had left to Paul also every bit of clothing which I believed I could spare, cutting myself down to the minimum of two shirts, four pairs of socks, and four handkerchiefs. For the road I wore my leather jacket, invaluable garment, and the trousers of my blue suit. These I pinned tightly around my ankles, following Boulaya's example. I wore a tie too, and my beret, which now had a weathered look. The remainder of my clothing was packed in the blue rucksack. My other belongings were stuffed into the black "valise diplomatique", which I intended to fix to the carrier of the bicycle with some rubber-covered wire stolen from Paul's aerial. The "valise diplomatique" hid the one thing that worried me—my bankroll. For although a publicity agent for the Union insurance might carry a considerable sum, he would scarcely have as much as that.

Secret information which I had not had time to memorise, the co-ordinates and radio messages of Albert's grounds, and other things and addresses, I had put into code and copied with a mapping-pen on to a piece of paper about the size of two postage-stamps. I put this paper under the collar of my shirt, fixing it with two stitches. In case of danger I would rip it off and swallow it.

One other thing might give me away. My knife. This was of the type issued to British parachutists, of the type the French call a "cran d'arrêt", that is to say, with a blade which fixes with a catch when it is opened. The blade was two-sided at the point, and it was altogether a beautiful and practical knife. I could not bear to part with it. What a miserable agent I made!

Boulaya was standing there in the stench and the steaming half-dark, standing just far enough inside to be clear of the fine rain which was driving in. He came forward at once to shake hands. He was dressed exactly as the day before, and he wore a woman's small claret-coloured rucksack on his back. His bicycle stood beside mine.

109

"Please do not think that I was late," he said in English. "I arrived here half an hour ago, but I saw that the doctor was here. He is a splendid fellow, and thoroughly trustworthy, but one cannot be too careful. A doctor sees too many people in the course of his day. It is better that he should not know that you are leaving with me, or even that I have been here."

Albert himself now appeared, jumping daintily in zigzags towards us.

"The doctor says that Paul must stay in bed for a few days," he said when he had shaken hands with Boulaya. "And then that he should be moved, if possible, to a better atmosphere. I should like therefore to accept your offer. Both of us will come to the château at La Chevillotte in a week's time. If it is not too inconvenient I should like to see both you and Émile again when we reach La Chevillotte. We shall drive up there in the van. If we run into any Boche we'll just have to shoot it out, as we'll have all Paul's equipment with us."

Boulaya agreed to this, and they said good-bye to each other.

"If anything happens to me you will know what to do," Albert said to me. "You must come back here and take over my area, no matter how interesting your own work up there may seem. I have told all my people that you will do that. Agreed?"

"Yes, agreed."

"You promise?"

"I promise. But I hope it won't be necessary."

"Don't worry. It will."

"Well, good-bye and many thanks."

"Thanks for what, you oaf? I've done nothing. Good luck and be careful."

Boulaya had already taken his bicycle outside. Feeling rather clumsy about it, for I had not handled a bicycle for years, I seized my machine and followed. The rain settled coldly on my face. As I mounted Albert called to me:

"What is the name and address of this B. woman you talked about? If I get back to London I think I'll look her up. Perhaps she might interest me. You won't get back. I'll tell her about your last days."

"I can't remember her surname," I answered.

"Bah. You're jealous. Let me know if you change your mind."

But it was true. I could not remember her surname. Yet I had thought about her many times each day, thought about her as a feeling, an impression. As I followed Boulaya down the dreadful quagmire of a lane which he had elected to follow rather than the main road, I pondered this mysterious thing. If I had forgotten her name I might never be able to find her again. Suddenly, it came back to me. But I decided not to send it to Albert. He was decidedly good-looking in an up-stage way. And French. And rich. My God, what a combination. No, I would not send him the name. Infinitely better that she should get a cold communication, a "we regret to inform you" from the War Office.

It was with such lofty thoughts that my mind was occupied as I set out on my crusade to liberate the French city of Besançon. Furthermore, my trousers were most definitely wet when I had been pedalling for five minutes, and the saddle was sharp under me.

"Sorry to take such a road," Boulaya called back to me, in French now, for he was too discreet to speak English out of doors. "But it would have been imprudent to be seen leaving the farm together. Ah, here is the good road."

We turned now on to a fairly large, well-metalled road. He stopped to take some small papers from his pocket and hide them inside the rubber hand-grip of his bicycle.

"Nothing incriminating on you?" he asked.

"No," I replied, then I felt bound to say: "I have a fair amount of money."

"Not too much of it in those five-thousand franc notes is there?"

"Oh no," I lied. I was frightened that he would send me back.

"That's good. The Boche is always most suspicious of those particular notes. Name of God. I have forgotten my raincoat. I must go back to the farm for it. Will you hide here in the wood and wait for me?"

He turned and pedalled painfully up the hill we had been swiftly descending. I dismounted in the wood. The rain poured steadily down on me. I began to wish that I had not left my own raincoat in the farm near Chaignay. And to wish that I could still carry a pistol. When you have got the habit it is uncomfortable not to feel that heavy metal thing dragging at your trouser pocket. Supposing anybody came into the wood and tried to get tough with me. I am a good enough shot. But when it comes to physical violence I am repelled. I wished that it were still an age when a man could carry a sword or a rapier without attracting attention. I am no true-blue Britisher. I believe that fists are the most uncouth, the most unsatisfactory, and the most unfair of weapons.

Paul, a Corsican whom I had known and admired in Lyons, had shown me a foreigner's viewpoint regarding the absurd British or Anglo-Saxon boast that we are the cleanest fighters because we use our fists.

"Two men are enemies," Paul said. "They decide unanimously to kill each other. One is big. The other is small. They fight with fists. What happens. The small man cannot get near the big man. The small man is the more nimble. But the big man chases him. Eventually, he should catch him, and kill him. Now give to each man a knife. The small man is still at a disadvantage. The big one has more reach. It is difficult to penetrate his wide guard. But the small man is the more nimble. His thrusts are the quicker. And knife fighting is a question of courage. Perhaps the big one feels faint when he thinks he may die. Or when he sees blood. The battle is more even. It is more dirty to fight with fists than with knives. To attack another man with fists is a dirty trick, requiring little courage, but only bestial strength."

This Paul was biased, being an expert with the knife he carried and ate and shaved with. It was a long curving blade, with a delicately curved, black bone handle, I recall. But I thoroughly agreed, and agree with his sentiments. To hell with adventure novelists who decry every man who draws a knife and who lionise honest John, the bulldog who fights with his fists.

I heard a few bars of *Carmen* whistled with great feeling. This was the agreed signal for my emergence from the wood, and when I emerged Boulaya was there, looking rather too comfortable for my taste in his long raincoat.

"A dreadful thing happened to me last night," he said, when we were once more travelling along. "I got to my father's house. My wife was upstairs making her toilet. I took the stairs four at a time. I could not wait to take her in my arms. I did so. She looked charming, charming.

" 'Jo,' she said, withdrawing herself from my embrace. 'You smell like a soldier.'

" 'I am a soldier, my love,' I answered. But all the same, I stripped down and made a thorough toilet with some perfectly marvellous scented toilet soap that this most magnificent of women had somehow managed to unearth from somewhere.

"Ah, Émile, my friend. It was difficult for me today to tear myself away from the soft atmosphere of my family, from my dear wife, from my children; from my elderly father and mother, disillusioned and unhappy so late in life.

"And I must say that I get no excess of sympathy. Madame Barthelet is too damned intelligent. Do you know what she said when I departed? She said: 'It's no use your pretending that you don't want to go, because I know better. This ghastly horrible war with the hiding in holes, and the simply idiotic way you generally pass your time, suits you better than any other kind of life you ever had. Confess now,' she said. I denied it, of course. I painted a picture of a soul in agony, separated from his loved ones. But she was quite right. Damn the woman, she was right.

"This life has made a new man of me. The uncertainty of the life, the glamour of it. Just think, if we introduced ourselves into any honest house in France and gave our correct titles to admission and friendship—British captain and French captain, chiefs of the Secret Army etcetera—why we would be most warmly received. Perhaps too warmly by the women, for that is dangerous."

"Very dangerous," I agreed with him. "I was taught that before I left England."

"I expect you are the traditional cold Englishman, impervious to the attractions and blandishments of women other than your wife," he fenced.

"I expect so," I parried.

We cycled on in silence. Boulaya did not believe in going fast, and this was all to the good for me then. My muscles and my seat were unaccustomed to this exercise; and London could scarcely have sent me to a worse area for bicycling. If there are no major mountains in the Franche-Comté, there yet seems to be always a hill or succession of hills between points A and B.

When we came to a village which had a bad reputation or to a road junction where there might be a control, or once when we were obliged to follow a main road for two hundred yards, Boulaya had always warned me about a mile before the spot and I followed him at a distance of anything from three to five hundred yards. Should he see anything dangerous he was to give me the signal to turn back and hide. The signal consisted in his taking his handkerchief from his trouser pocket and blowing his nose. All went well, except that the rain continued and my seat got sorer.

"What a welcome you will receive," he said to me, as we pushed our bicycles up a steep hill beside a small torrent which might have been any burn in Scotland, were it not for the heavily mansarded château on the opposite bank. An old man was fishing near the château. He was well-dressed and by the appearance and behaviour of the rod in his hands it might have been made at Alnwick. "Our hostess is a charming women," he continued. "She has one weakness. She is Anglophile to a degree. She is ever trying to master the English language. I have assisted her in this to the best of my ability, and in a limited time. Her husband, Hunblot, is a great fisherman and a tax-collector when he has to work."

Before reaching Ornans, where the Anglophile and her husband lived, we stopped for a moment beside the noble river, La Loue, whose clear waters pass that charming little town. A German officer was bathing in a great pool not far from the road. Three others in waterproof capes stood on the bank, watching him and laughing. It still rained. He stood stiffly self-conscious on the bank and dived in with an exaggerated posturing. It was a good dive, but over-stiff and he swam stiffly, like an automaton with a great agitation of the water. The water was swift and deep. He had to exert himself to reach the bank again. The others threw clods and small branches at him. He climbed out and ran around them, frisking like a very stiff and self-conscious puppy-dog.

"Absolutely revolting," said Boulaya.

The German was stark naked.

We came to Ornans. Hunblot, a strong figure with his shirt-sleeves rolled back to show massive forearms, was standing in the doorway of his house, and waved us in. It was a pleasant little house with a courtyard separating it from the road. Alongside the house was a garage big enough to take a medium-sized car. There were some flower-beds in the forecourt, well cared-for flower-beds too.

"Just like any tax-collector's house," thought I.

We hid our bicycles in the garage beside the small Renault, laid up for the duration. The family were sitting down for dinner. Madame Hunblot, the Anglophile, came darting out to meet us at the top of the narrow staircase.

"My God," she croaked when Boulaya whispered to her that I was British. "My God, how terrible that he should arrive to-day. You stupid man," she turned on Boulaya, stamping her foot. "Three hundred and sixty-five days in the year, and you have to bring him today, when I have this accursed ailment and Susanne is here for dinner. Damn you, damn you, damn you." ⌒

She was dressed in an ancient greyish-black overall and, fresh from her heavy evening's work in the small kitchen behind her, she carried the odours of garlic, parsley and heated cooking fat and butter. Her "ailment" was something to do with her throat, which was greatly swollen on one side, and she evidently had difficulty in speaking.

Not a whit put out by her vehemence, Boulaya patted her benignly on the shoulder.

"There, there, my lovely one," he said soothingly. "Run along now and change your clothes and generally doll yourself up for the Englishman. Do not be afraid of him. See, he is gentle and good. I dare say that Hunblot can give us an apéritif while you titivate yourself."

"But Susanne. She must not know that Monsieur is English. Of all the women in Ornans, she is the most indiscreet."

"She will never know," said Boulaya. "This Englishman speaks the most perfect French." With an admonitory look at me he swaggered into the hot kitchen. An old lady, Hunblot's mother, another elderly woman whose heavy make-up was streaking in the steamy air, Susanne, and a few children had actually begun to eat. Now the two women fussed around preparing yet more food.

We had begun to eat soup when Madame Hunblot, metamorphosed, made her entrance. She now appeared as a tall, willowy and handsome woman in a flowered silk dress. Somehow she had managed to do her hair and her face, and with the studied carefulness of gesture of an intelligent Frenchwoman she kept her hands swiftly moving or out of sight. The swelling still defaced her long and probably graceful neck, but as she talked and drank a little of the good wine, her voice gathered power and her head pulled over to one side by her malady came back nearly to the vertical. Most of my attention was occupied with Susanne, who insisted upon talking across the table at me. She called me "jeune homme" and I played for her benefit the part of a timid youth. She did not notice my accent. I was glad of her stupidity. It gave me confidence with my French.

After an enormous meal washed down copiously with wines and then liqueurs (there is some good kirsch in the neighbourhood of Ornans) Boulaya and I went out with Hunblot. We walked through delightful streets. To our right and left citizens bowed politely to our host. I realised that tax-collecting is a profession that carries a certain amount of jam with it. One man asked the collector obsequiously if it would please him to fish a certain water that week. Another told us that his cherries were going to be magnificent; would the collector like some kirsch? It would be better than that of 1941. But perhaps I am exaggerating the worldliness of these offers. Perhaps they were the spontaneous offers of friendship.

He took us to a dark room over a bicycle-shop, the home of his father and mother. The mother was still at the other house, clearing the wreckage of our meal. The father was a bony veteran of the Franco-Prussian war. He was preparing to listen to London, humouring the controls of his radio set with old corny fingers. He greedily accepted a cigarette from Boulaya, stuffed it, paper and all, into a cherry pipe, pressed in on top some green tobacco grown by himself, and when the mixture was burning turned to eye me shrewdly.

"Typical," he said.

"Typical what? Typical Englishman?" I asked.

"Not necessarily that, despite your hair. You are a shade full about the mouth for the Englishmen as I knew them. But man, you are typical of the English officers. Why, we demanded something fierce from an officer. We liked him with big, bold moustaches and a brazen voice that breathed brassy fumes all over the platoon. But your English 'poilus' want a baby boy of an officer. They want an officer they can look after and be fond of. What strange animals are the English soldiers. Coarse and brutal, too, and they don't know how to eat, nor how to drink. And women, they are devils for women. The one thing about the English soldier is that he is a little likable. There is something human about him. If it were not for that he would be nearly as unpleasant as the Boche. . . ."

"My father is dreadfully outspoken," said Hunblot. "He is an old and bitter man."

"Bitter, yes. And old I am. But I will live to see the Boches chased out of here and their blood staining the waters of La Loue. Please the troutsies, that will. Cannibals they are. They like a bit of blood now and then. Why, my brother Alphonse, who was the greatest fisherman on this valley, he used to counsel taking a bloody sheep's head and immersing it in the water above where he intended to spin for trout. Maybe I am like the fish myself. Guess I could swallow a drop or two of Boche blood. But failing that—don't know what you young men are

116

doing with yourselves letting them strut around like that, I'm sure—we'll just have a drop or two of Marc.

"It's the strongest Marc in Ornans," he said as he filled our glasses. His old gimlet eyes were friendly as they rested on me.

"I don't hold with the British too much, as you can see," he said when we were leaving. "But as long as they are working like you to get the Boche out of our country, or like those brave little bastards of yours who have landed in Normandy, why then, by God, I say that I am with you, and I would give my old carcase if need be to help you, or to keep you going in your work. If you ever need a hidey-hole you just come back to Ornans. You'll remember the bicycle-shop. There are only two of them in Ornans. And the other has no petrol-pump in front of the door."

As though I would forget. Already, after less than twenty-four hours with Boulaya, I had three possible hide-outs. I was learning from him all the time. Watching his reactions on the roads I learned where danger might lie, watching his behaviour in the friendly houses we visited I learned the kind of things people liked to hear. And he was good to me. As we rode along he pointed out the geography of the district, and passing through a village he would often say: "The priest is trustworthy here, you could hide with him or stop for a meal any time with half an hour's wait before eating," or: "Ask for the doctor here, we can depend on him," or: "That 'Hôtel de la Poste' is secure and they would give you anything, just mention my name; but beware of the 'Hôtel de la Gare', there are often Boches there." I knew that although I had changed the life in hiding for a life in movement, I must constantly have a hiding-place at hand. Instinct told me that.

Instead of going to bed when we returned to Hunblot's house I was obliged to work until three in the morning. Hunblot's garage, despite its bourgeois appearance, was not just the ordinary tax-collector's garage after all. For he fetched two bulging sacks of explosives from a greasing pit underneath the sump of the eleven-horse-power car. We sat down in the kitchen with a selection of five different liqueurs (most extraordinary profusion at that time) and I instructed our host in the explosives racket. He took voluminous notes on everything that I explained, and we even made up charges for two jobs he wanted to do, made them up on the kitchen table with the tall willowy wife watching us and occasionally helping to bind something neatly together with adhesive tape. Before I went to bed I had to submit to being kissed by the lady as "the first Englishman I have seen since 1940".

"When is this going to end?" I asked Boulaya as I undressed. "I am not sure that I like being a National representative for osculation."

"End?" he smiled, a shade vindictively. "Where you are going the excuse holds. It is just beginning. But women do not kiss you because of such patriotic or national feeling. They will kiss you in front of their husbands for two reasons. Firstly because they like doing it in front of their husbands, and that is a twisted, a perverted joy for a married woman. Secondly, they will kiss you because all women have got the 'gout de l'étranger'. This hankering to make love to foreigners, to make love to the unknown, as you might say, is stronger in woman than in man. Man is usually, in my opinion, a lustier creature sexually than woman. But woman is naturally more depraved, her appetites are more 'exotic', shall we say, to put it politely. Now look at man in the colonies, for example. See how disgustingly he behaves. See how developed is his 'goût de l'étranger'. And woman is—returning to my first reasoning—even worse than this bestial thing that we call man. Ye Gods."

He had talked himself out of the room undoing his tie. He was unbuttoning the big buttons of his blue garment as he came back.

"You are an amazing man, Boulaya."

"In what way?" he asked modestly.

"I asked when this was going to end, the international osculation, I mean, and you have delivered part of your notes for a lecture on perversion. Let me remind you now that it was you who reminded Madame of her vow to embrace the first Englishman. Please don't do it again."

"But my dear Émile. I enjoyed it so much more than you. I enjoyed watching you. The faint blush (how do you do it at your age?). The swift glance at the face of the husband. The hesitant offering of your face. It was perfect.

"Another thing that I forgot to mention. You don't think that they would bother to kiss you if you were physically repellent to them, do you? If you don't want them to, you must dye your hair and change your innocent expression and wear dark glasses to hide your Nordic eyes. Although some women are so funny, with some women it is only necessary to be a hunchback or have only one leg in order to have an instantaneous success. Why, with your thick lips *and* a hump you could have every woman in the Franche-Comté at your feet. Except Madame Barthelet of course, for I except her from all my generalisations on her evil and interesting sex."

He wandered out again, and this time I heard him settle into bed. I was to sleep on a divan in the drawing-room. I had clean sheets and a couch that was too soft for my taste. We had drunk more, much more than I was accustomed to. I knew that I should wake early, and with a hang-over which, with me, takes the form of an excess of nervous energy.

Boulaya was up almost before me, we reached the wash-place at the same time, about seven-thirty. He was less talkative than a few hours before.

"I feel rotten, rotten," he said. "I don't like drinking, I am really a most temperate creature in all things, except my hatred for the Boche. And it is raining too. Well, we might as well make an early start, we have the devil of a way to go before lunch. And the father and mother of all 'côtes' to surmount almost immediately on leaving here."

Boulaya bicycled because it was the most intelligent and most certain way of getting around the occupied country. Not because he liked it. His deepest enemies (after the Germans) were the diabolical hills that exist for the cyclist in Franche-Comté. Before setting out he always reckoned up—for he knew the country perfectly—how many of these "côtes" there were between him and his destination. According to the number of "côtes" to be surmounted he would at the start be either morose or gay. A few minutes later his mercurial spirits would begin dragging him off towards the other extreme of temperament.

"Don't go back to the Hunblot's if you ever have to hide here," he said to me as we rode off in the rain. "Go to the old father. Hunblot himself is apt to be blown since he is head of the local Resistance group. They have not much to do now, since there is no railway, but this delightful town holds some black hearts. Hunblot has enemies. He risks denunciation."

We passed four or five gendarmes at the outer edge of Ornans. They eyed us closely, but did not stop us. Boulaya looked back to see that they were not still watching us when we took our road fork that climbed up the hill to the left.

"After six months of being hunted in the Resistance I still cannot bring myself to trust the gendarmes," he said. "Perhaps it is wrong of me, but since I feel that way I act on my feeling as though it were a principle. I have noticed also many gendarmes who were the enemies of the Resistance who are gradually changing as the international situation becomes more and more unfavourable for the Boche.

"I fear, I fear that we must class all policemen in the same group, Émile. A policeman, no matter what his nationality may be, is big, bold, and stupid. Furthermore, he is often a sadist. Then, he is inclined to drink a lot. He often shows this in his rubicund complexion. And a man who drinks talks too much. The gendarme spends all his days seeing people. Instead of confining himself to one village he goes around several, and in each of them he talks to his friends and cronies and the people who are profitable to him. Therefore I say that I have a basic mistrust for the gendarme. And even if I feel like making a friend of one I should be loath to do so at this moment. And no matter how friendly I might be, I should never, never confide in him. All this is correct reasoning. But our position is more complicated than that. For we need the gendarmes. We need their help to obtain false papers, to keep a feeble kind of contact with the Boche. You will soon see how all this works out, and that there are good and bad gendarmes just like every other profession. Still, I don't want you to come in contact with any strange ones before we arrive in our own country."

We had now dismounted, and were pushing our bicycles up an interminable hill, and through dark, rain-sodden woods. Boulaya suddenly startled me by making this extraordinary statement:

"I am in the Resistance to fight one half of me for France, and the other half for England."

"How odd," I said, when I gathered my wits. "I am here to fight one half of me for Britain and the other half for France. But then I am quite frankly a Francophil, a not uncommon thing to find in Britain. Your statement, coming from a Frenchman, is most extraordinary, to put it mildly."

"I lived in England," he said, with deep feeling. "I lived there and I was happy there for years. I still have property there, my house in Ealing. And I hope to go back there often after the war.

"In fact I should probably be in England still if it were not that in January, 1938, my elder son came into the drawing-room in Ealing and said to his mother: 'Maman, the kitchen is absolutely full of flies.'

"That was enough for me. My son was speaking French with an English accent. Up to that time I could only think of the advantages of their speaking English without a French accent.

Why, I myself had spent hours, weeks, at elocution classes, and all that to improve my own accent in English. Madame Barthelet spoke with fluency and with a strong French accent which all found attractive. But I was seduced by your noble language. I worked to perfect myself in it, and I rejoiced that my sons would speak it with a perfection which I myself could never hope to attain. Then this brat walked in and shattered my dream with his:

" 'Maman, la cuisine est toute pleine de mouches.'

"This ordure was a child of mine, was my heir. He could not speak the language of his fathers. My mind was instantly made up. At great sacrifice I closed down or sold my businesses in England. I left the town and the country that I had learned to love and took my family to Metz, where I opened a college to give business training to young women.

"Metz is Germanic, as you know. And at first sight its architecture is heavy, pompous, and grim. It looks like one thing that I could never like in England—those red steamed puddings. When my wife and I arrived in our house in Metz we wept. After the gaiety and camaraderie of Ealing, this. But when my wife entered she flung her arms around my neck, she wept frankly, and this time in happiness. For I had had the place furnished with pieces bought from your Maple's in London, and to be inside it, with this splendid, lustrous and comfortable furniture was like being back home in London again.

"All went well in Metz, but this is where I kick myself, and I reserve a still harder booting for the whelp who forced me to leave England with his snivelling: 'Maman, la cuisine est toute pleine de mouches.' This is what maddens me. In '39 war broke out, and look where I found myself. Thanks to the flies in the kitchen I had placed my family on the doorstep to Germany. If we had still been in England I should have left my wife and family there in peace. My wife, who is an exceedingly capable person, would have been able to look after my interests, and I should have joined my regiment in France with a tranquil mind.

"Instead of this ideal situation, what happened? I joined my regiment, and I had a good war. I was a Captain in the 'Corps Francs'. We made successful patrol sorties all through the first agonising period when the war refused to move and sat staling on the West Front. Apart from a quarrel with my General and his staff (but remind me to tell you of that another time) everything went well for me. Then the débâcle came. The German avalanches swept over us all, and naturally first of all over my new home in Metz. They made me prisoner, but I escaped. When I went home after the Armistice to pick up the bits and pieces I found nothing, *nothing*.

"Those robbers, those murdering, blundering, ridiculous, hateful, rapacious Boches had simply walked away with everything that was mine. Where was my linen, my old family linen? Where was my new Maple's furniture? Where was the English bed with its patent springs? The carpets, the curtains, the cutlery? It was all in Germany. It had been carted off in lorries, carted off by individual Boches who had occupied my house. Individual thieves. Where was my office furniture, all those typewriters, those irreplacable typewriters. They were all in Germany or serving to type out muster rolls and account sheets for the 'Wehrmacht'.

"Sadly, bitterly indeed, I dragged myself back, as a man does when he feels old and beaten, to my home town, Besançon. There, with my dear wife and my children around me, wholly dependent upon me, I began again wearily to make a livelihood. It was hard going. But I managed to organise the same kind of thing at Besançon that I had begun at Metz. We took an enormous flat, the kind of flat a princeling or a profiteer would occupy. In the big empty rooms of this place I put the few typewriters that we managed to find in such difficult times. My wife was magnificent, magnificent. Together, to supplement our income, to buy food for our children, we began to give individual lessons in English to young people who wished to learn that language. Then I saw an opening. England alone at that time was carrying on the war. She and the General de Gaulle were the torch that all good young French men and women were looking to, even when they did not recognise it. I let my wife continue to teach the younger children. Myself I formed classes for more advanced pupils, mainly for young women who had just left school, and who wanted to continue with some studies like music and a foreign language. There are many rich people in and around Besançon. The Boche made efforts to seduce most of them, to encourage the teaching of German and the so-called German culture. I was able to fight this. I taught in class by my own conversational methods, unconventionally. Success began to come again to me. But seeing the hated enemy in the streets of my own town, seeing my home cafés filled with his extravagant uniforms, seeing some of my boyhood friends and schoolmates imprisoned and vilely tortured by the Gestapo, there grew a hatred in me that would not be stifled by my own family activities. My friends taken by the Gestapo were flung into cells in our own home-town jail, La Butte. I had played outside it as a boy, maybe I had even kissed a girl in the shadows of its walls. Brought up strictly as a lawful little citizen, I had been taught to regard 'La Butte' as a monument of justice, and its inmates, apart from the prison staff, as wretches who threatened the decency and security of France. Now they flung my respectable friends into it.

"The climax came one day when I saw one of those friends being taken from 'La Butte' to the 'Feldgendarmerie' for questioning. I recognised him only by his hat. Only by his hat, I tell you, and because I was waiting on the roadside to see him pass. I saw his face all right, but there was no skin on it, and he could not see me. Both his poor eyes had been closed into two purple and yellow bruises.

"I began to work for the Resistance. To work earnestly, for although I know that I give an impression of flippancy I am an earnest man. I had to hide this from my wife. I did not dare to confess to her that our new, hard-won, our glorious little family security was in the most dreadful danger. I refused to allow myself to realise that my conduct was endangering the lives of my wife and my children, yes, and of my old parents too, and all the other families whose husbands I had drawn in with me. Do you English people who have fought so gloriously, who alone in 1940 and '41 gave us the possibility and the hope of ultimate victory, do you realise what it means to risk not just your own life but the lives of all your womenfolk and children. Do you?"

"No, Boulaya, we do not."

"I shut that side of it out of my consciousness. I went on with my teaching and I gave all my spare time to my new work. Strangely enough my oldest son was the first to guess it. I had had a meeting of Resistance officers in my flat. He came to me afterwards and said: 'I know you say you were talking about local government with these men, but I also know the truth, papa. They are the Resistance, are they not? And you are too.' There was so much pride in his voice and his eyes that I nearly said 'Yes.'

"At that time, despite my energy and my reasonable army career, I was still small fry in the Resistance movement itself, or the 'Armée Secrète', as we then called it. But I put in so much hard work on the thing that I became unofficially a kind of organiser or secretary. Then, just over six months ago, a terrible blow fell. The Gestapo, through an informer or perhaps just as the result of an indiscretion on the part of one of us, had uncovered the whole net.

"I happened to get warning in time. The wife of a friend who had just been arrested came flying to my office. She had been present when they asked the first questions of her husband. They were after me, and also after another mutual friend. I left my office as I was, not even waiting to pick up my hat and coat. I ran to my friend's office. He was sitting at his desk. I began hurriedly to explain to him. There was a knock at the door. It was the Gestapo. They came in and they arrested him. While they did this I, the next name on their list, sat down at his secretary's desk and pretended to write a letter. To the Boches I was just an employee in the office. They left.

"I dared not go home. I fled the town and hid. I had said nothing to my wife and this was all to the good. The Gestapo, enraged at my absence, seized her and took her for questioning. They questioned her twice, the second time for nine hours on end. But this peerless woman knew nothing. You see, I had been right to tell her nothing. And she had been right to ask no questions. That was six months ago. The night before last I saw her again for the first time. She did not ask me a single question about my work. I told her nothing, nothing. A truly wonderful woman.

"But the purge that nearly caught me smashed the whole organisation in Besançon. They took a few and tortured them, then some more, then more torture, more arrests. In all we have lost forty-five officers, and who knows where it will stop. . . ."

"Forty-five officers! Are they still in 'La Butte'?"

"Most of them are, so far as we know. Plans have been studied for their rescue. But the jail is pretty well impregnable. And they even have a heavy machine-gun facing each line of cells. The slightest semblance of a rescue attempt and the Boches will shoot the lot."

We climbed in silence for a bit. The rain had stopped, and the morning was warm and muggy. Forty-five officers. It seemed a terrible total. What had I let myself in for?

"Have you been on the roads like this often in these six months?" I asked.

"Yes. I had the Salins sector for some time. But Colonel Morin is an energetic man, a fine commander. He stirs up his sector commanders. Now he has given me this new job. We have to pull the Besançon command out of the fire. I say 'we' because we will do it together, Émile. It is something worth doing. Besançon is a noble old city, solid and fine, a great city. And the people are fine too, stocky, almost stolid people for Frenchmen. I've been on the roads all right. It has been a struggle to keep things going. Just before the invasion there was a big Gestapo drive. We are badly armed. We have so little material. And the Besançon people are naturally law-abiding. They are told by the Boche that we are 'terrorists' and bandits. Sometimes that is true. Sometimes there are brigands and bandits in the Maquis, and their misdeeds are always magnified by the Boche and their press. Yes, Émile, our work is not going to be easy. But not so difficult that good luck, good will, energy, and then a bit more luck will not conquer."

We struggled on up the hill. It really was interminable. Suddenly Boulaya shot this question at me without preamble:

"Do you know Mr. Rose, Émile?"

"Mr. Rose? of where?"

"Mr. Rose of London."

"I used to know a Mr. Rose of London. I think his first name was Geoffrey, he was a barrister and he was Recorder of some town or other . . ."

"That's right," Boulaya cried, delighted. "That's *the* Mr. Rose. The Mr. Rose I know."

"This Rose used to be keen on skating. I met him and his wife at Wengen, in Switzerland. . . ."

"That's right, it's the same. How wonderful and how small is our great world. Mr. Rose was president of my club. The skating club in London. They had an examination, a test, before they would allow you to become a member. You had to be able to waltz and tango, etcetera. It was chic, the club. For weeks I had to practise, then, when I was not on the ice I would practise in the drawing-room and do leg exercises until Madame Barthelet would think I was crackers. Ah," said this incredible man. "Those were the great days."

It was a dream surely. Here was this leader of the Secret Army who thought that the great days had been the days in the ice club in London. And me, what did I think the great days had been? I could not really think of any particular batch of great days, anything great enough to match against his ice club. That was it; apart from people I had known I had nothing definite like an ice club to pull out of the bag. The difference was that Boulaya had managed to keep his illusions about his ice club. I was disillusioned about anything I might match against him. So he won. It is bad to be disillusioned, it is a loss. Walking up the hill beside him I admired him, an older man, for keeping something that I had lost.

"It was beautiful at nights, skating in evening dress. A tango on the ice with a beautiful woman, that is something. . . ."

And we had been joined together through space first by hazard, helped by the Aquarium in London, then by the strange impersonal tie`of the Roses, casual acquaintances of my youth.

I had seen them first on the rink at Wengen, a shortish figure, that was Rose; and his wife, slightly taller, if I remembered correctly. We used to watch them from above, two figures tirelessly making their endless convolutions on the ice that lay far below the Palace Hotel. They stayed in the hotel too. Later I went up from Cambridge to dine at their house near the western end of Kensington Gardens. And once to a dance there. I remembered that they had framed maps hanging on the walls of the room where we danced. . . .

"Ah, Émile, when we go together to London you will telephone Mr. Rose, and we shall go to see him together. Yes?"

"Yes, Boulaya." Rose probably would not remember my name. After all, I had not seen the Roses for over ten years. But wait; yes I had. Once when, for some reason, I had gone to the Westminster Ice Club. I had seen Mrs. Rose circling with graceful competence. That must have been about five years before. She had barely recognised me.

This vague connection seemed to wrap us round like a warm blanket with a Union Jack on it. We sat down at the top of the hill to rest. He smoked powdery grey tobacco in his star-studded pipe, and I lay back at his side. We steamed in the misty rain. I was feeling better already from the exercise, and with my improved health came more confidence in myself. And perhaps an increased fear of the dangers of the roads.

Boulaya never relaxed his precautions, and the roads were reassuringly empty. Few people could afford the wear on bicycle tyres for ordinary travel. They stayed at home. My "Corsair" was a good runner. On the hills it easily outstripped Boulaya's "Jupiter". The previous day I had fingered the brakes to keep tactfully at his side. But now that we knew each other better I felt that I could let the "Corsair" go without risk of offending him.

Rushing down a big hill soon after passing a village called l'Hôpital, "Corsair" was leading "Jupiter" by nearly one hundred yards when I suddenly found myself avoiding a Gestapo car which was swiftly mounting the hill. I had time to see that the four short-haired men inside eyed me closely. Then we were far apart. Their cars moved so silently and swiftly that they were suddenly on you without notice. At the bottom of the hill Boulaya overtook me, pedalling furiously.

"Hurry on, please," he said. "I don't like meeting those cars."

A little farther down the road he pulled off on to a track that led through the woods. Well out of sight of the road he dismounted, got out his torn Michelin map, number 70, and worked out a different route to Naisey, our immediate destination. From then on, throughout the morning, I noticed that he was a shade more jumpy. So was I.

"Naisey has been my Command Post for some time," he told me as we rode along. "So I think you had better drop behind now, for the next two or three kilometres. When you reach the outskirts of Naisey wait by the roadside and pretend to do something to your bicycle. I shall enter the village by a back way, and if all is clear I'll come out for you."

I did not feel inclined to do anything to the bicycle, which was thickly splashed with mud, since the lanes before Naisey had been more like morasses. Boulaya kept me waiting in the rain for nearly an hour and he looked worried when finally he rode out to me.

"There is nothing definite," he said. "But I have the feeling that this place has been blown. All there is to go on is that a Gestapo car came slowly through three days ago, and then again yesterday. And a stranger on a motor-cycle, a tall, dark man in riding-breeches, has passed through nearly every day for a week.

"Mistrust all motor-cycles, Émile. Well, I shall have to spend the afternoon here, clearing everything up. But I don't like it."

The Command Post of Boulaya was in the low, dark house of Monsieur Plançon, the wine merchant. An enormous man, with a heavily astute face and a square black moustache, Plançon gave us a glass of still champagne before lunch. I was shivering with the damp, and had to go off and put on dry trousers and socks and my "espadrilles". Plançon's large and blooming daughter, all bosoms, put my shoes under the range to dry while she cooked for us. While we ate, a motor-cycle of the small kind known as a "petrolette" arrived at the house. A pale young man came in. He looked wretchedly ill, and indeed he told us that he was to go into hospital to be operated on for duodenal ulcer. He was a liaison agent working for Colonel Morin, whom they spoke of always as "le patron". The young man carried a great sheaf of messages for Boulaya. This surprised me. He could never have destroyed them in time, had he been stopped. Boulaya proceeded to write out a lot more messages.

"You write all those things in 'clear'?" I asked.

"Yes," Boulaya answered. "We have no code. The 'patron' says code wastes too much time, and verbal messages are too unsure. He is a regular soldier. Like most of them he is a slave of 'paperasserie'. What do you call that in the British Army?"

"Bumph."

The frail young messenger drank some milk as medicine and rode away. Boulaya slid one of the messages he had received across the table to me. It said: "Warning. Frederic La Marche, a tall dark man, brown eyes, hair slightly greying on temples; poses as an ex-officer in the French Army wishing to join the Resistance; often wears riding-breeches and rides a motor-cycle. This man works for the Gestapo of Besançon and is *extremely dangerous*. His wife also works for the Gestapo. Both should be executed if taken, but not before they have confessed their crimes and given all possible information. . . ." The message contained a list of La Marche's aliases.

Boulaya took me away to a farm to see a man called Tom. It was a pity that he took me. Tom was hidden in a big, dirty farm-house a few miles out of Naisey. He was a big, rather flashy-looking young man with a thin line of dark moustache over his mouth. He was a ranter, was Tom. He told us repeatedly how greatly he resented being ordered by the "patron" to remain in hiding, how fundamentally he desired to go out and kill Germans.

"I hope that you *are* keeping quiet now," Boulaya said severely. "I don't like the atmosphere around Naisey. It is blowing up for a storm. But if you keep well hidden here you should risk nothing."

"Don't worry about me," replied Tom airily. "I've still got my gun. If they come for me they'll have to fight for it. As for keeping quiet, I haven't stirred outside the place since

I last saw you. My one amusement has been playing football
with the farm boys."

"Football!" said Boulaya sharply. "What do you think you
are doing? Fool. Who ever heard of ordinary farm people
playing football. Remember, too, that there is a big arms dump
not far from here. That is your responsibility, as well as your
own miserable hide. The 'patron' gives me this message for
you: You are to clear out of this country immediately, and
take yourself off, as far away as possible. I take upon myself
the responsibility of amending that order. If you stay here
quietly that will do. But no tricks remember, and none of your
loud-mouthed boasting."

Before we left Tom gave us bowls of grain coffee, and bread
and butter in the farm parlour. He pulled out a swagger note-
case in crocodile leather, edged with silver, and showed me
proudly a note which he took therefrom. It was the address
in Scotland of a girl called Jenny Something. Jenny had written
her note while she was packing containers to be parachuted into
France. She had written below the address: "I'd so like to
meet a boy in the Maquis, brunettes preferred."

"Think I'll do?" Tom asked, preening himself. He was the
type who enjoys successes with easy women. "Anyway, I'm
going to see Jenny as soon as the war's over. What d'you
say? We might go together. You're blonde, so I'd be all right,
eh?"

We left this big, bouncing young man standing waving
heartily at the farm gate.

"What do you think of him?" Boulaya asked.

"I don't like him."

"Quite right. If we were coldly methodical like the Germans
we would shoot him. He is terribly dangerous."

"How is he dangerous? Does he know anything?"

"Anything! He knows everything. And you can see for
yourself that he is conceited and a coward at the same time. His
conceit will give him away and his cowardice will make him
spill everything to the Gestapo, mark my words."

"Well, why don't you kill him? Or have him killed."

"I cannot, I cannot. I am too soft, Émile. And the 'patron',
although he is hard as steel in other ways, cannot give such
orders. He simply passes the responsibility on to me. Besides,
Tom worked well enough for us at the outset. He was able to
drive all over the country in a van. He aroused no suspicion.
He was here, there, anywhere on business. We used him a lot.

We made him a lieutenant and put men under him. That did not last long. Almost his first action was to make tracings of a map showing his Command Post, arms dump, and other important things. He gave one of these tracings to each of his 'sous-officiers'. The fool. Within a week the Boche had captured one. The man was killed. The area was blown. So was Tom. This is the second farm I have had him hidden in. The first one became hot because the idiot took it into his head to go to Mass on Sundays. Imagine that! Mass. The one place where a stranger is instantly picked out by everyone, friend and foe alike. Now he is playing football. Yes, this evening I feel like shooting him myself."

We went to another house in Naisey to sleep. Plançon's might be unsafe at night. We slept together in a double feather-bed. There was an old man sleeping in a single bed beside us.

"I could kick myself right out of bed," Boulaya whispered to me. "God knows why I told Tom that Albert and Paul were coming to La Chevillotte."

"But you also told him to stay where he was."

"You don't imagine that an oaf like that will stay hidden if the weather is fine and he has half an excuse for a joy-ride."

The next morning was fine, and the June sunshine was warm on my face and my hands. I was able to travel in shirt-sleeves, and when we had climbed out of the mud and slime of Naisey, we found ourselves on a wide and noble prairie rolling north to the dark hills separating us from the river Doubs.

"This is all my territory now, our territory," said Boulaya.

"It's beautiful. Like Siberia, this bit, with all the waving grain and the wild flowers."

"That ruined castle on the top of the long hills over there is my Combat Post. It's roughly in the centre of the area."

"But surely the more important part is north of the Doubs, on the other side."

"Yes," pleaded Boulaya. "I know, I know. But it's such a lovely Combat Post. So romantic. And so easy for the liaisons to find."

"And so easy for the German mortars to find."

"Damn you, Émile, for a practical Englishman."

But I could not have felt less practical as we bicycled along and the sunshine dried the dampness out of me and caressed my skin. Why, passing through the villages the women and children all smiled at us. They knew, or appeared to know, that we were fighting for them. Our wheels seemed to rotate more easily, more sweetly than ever before. The flowers and trees were fresh after their drenching. Our progress should have been made to a whirling musical accompaniment.

"When shall we get to the Maquis?" I asked.

"This afternoon," he answered. I was eager to get to work. Occasionally, when the sun shines and I feel that I am alive and living, I get such crazes.

"That is we shall get there this afternoon if the tunnel of Champlive, up there, is not guarded," said Boulaya. "Sometimes the Boche put a post on it, or on the big bridge below it."

He showed me the mouth of the tunnel, a black, forbidding hole in the green hill-side ahead. Then he left me and mounted alone, pushing his bicycle. A brave figure he made, crawling up the hill-side, smaller and smaller, until he was a blue smudge and then the blackness of the tunnel swallowed him. I waited another quarter of an hour, lying in the sun beside the road. Then I followed him.

It was nearly black darkness inside the tunnel. But it was straight and you could see a bead of light at the end. And it was slightly down-hill. I ran through at high speed. There was no control, but it was obvious that it was a danger spot, as Boulaya had said. Perfect for an ambush. Cold drops from the barrel-vaulted roof fell on my face and my bare arms as I passed through. I free-wheeled quickly down beyond it, now on the other side of Boulaya's ruined keep of a "Combat Post", down to the broad river Doubs. The bridge was unguarded too. Beyond it, dismounted, and toiling up the 'cote' I came upon Boulaya. He chose the small roads. But by lunch-time we were on the outskirts of Marchaux.

We left our bicycles in the cabbage patch behind the Gendarmerie and went into that long yellowish building. A burly gendarme blocked the passage that ran past doors marked with family name-tags. But he knew Boulaya and he let me past with a handshake and a "Bonjour, jeune homme". Boulaya led the way into a kitchen, where Madame Chapuy, a fine, strong woman and the wife of the *Brigadier* Chapuy, was giving lunch to her two daughters and another little girl, a refugee from Paris.

"The 'Chef' is in Besançon," she said, meaning her husband. We ate lunch with the family. It was embarrassing. Madame Chapuy had little indeed to offer us to eat. It was a difficult time of year. The potatoes were not yet ready and vegetables were scarce. And a gendarme's pay is not enormous. I was amused to hear that in the case of Chapuy, Boulaya apparently had gone against all his expressed rulings regarding policemen.

"I have good news for your husband," he told her. "He is now an officer in the Resistance. His promotion has just been confirmed by the 'patron'." Before we left the kitchen Boulaya advised me to leave nearly all my money with Madame Chapuy. She put it away in the drawer of an old bureau.

"Better not to take too much money into the Maquis," he said to me when we had left and were climbing up behind Marchaux towards another long, wooded crest. "You never know. The men come from all sorts of 'milieus'."

"But I thought you said that one should never make confidants of gendarmes."

He laughed. "My dear fellow. Chapuy is quite exceptional. He has been doing the work of a lieutenant here for some time. And it will be an important step up for him. Then, when we have conquered, I hope that he will keep his promotion I have confidence in him." A slight pause, and he added slowly: "Although he is apt to be too talkative."

Between the village of Marchaux and the much smaller village of Champoux there is a kind of sloping prairie. Marchaux lies in a valley and clings on either side of the big secondary road that runs north-east out of Besançon to Rougemont, and on towards the sinister name of Belfort. And Champoux is stuck up on the hill-side, far away from anything as mundane as the Besançon-Rougemont road. Much of the prairie between them is well cultivated by the villagers. But higher up there is a delightful piece of common land, fringed by the white old military road that cuts in zigzags up through the woods, and then down the other side of the "côte" to the village of Vieilley.

Leaving his bicycle on the edge of this common land Boulaya broke into his song from *Carmen*, and wandered towards the thick pine-woods. Sometimes he sang, sometimes he whistled. But there was no response.

"What are you looking for?" I asked him. "The nightingale?"

"No, the Maquis. Often on a fine afternoon like this they come down into the shade and perfume of the pines to sleep. But either they are not there, or they are very soundly asleep."

We left our bicycles in Champoux. Champoux is the real "bled", a dirty little village hidden away from everyone and everything in the lands that its villagers work. If it had not been for the war I should never have seen Champoux. I might have passed in a car along the road from Besançon to Rouge-mont, but what could have drawn me to Champoux? Not the scenery, for that is beautiful in a shy and secret way. Not sports or pastimes, for at Champoux man is living off the land and the trees, not off tourists. Not even the people, for they have rough exteriors, and they are shy with strangers. Later, I was to think that the war had broken the thread of my life, but that I was grateful to the war for showing me Champoux and other villages like it.

On this first visit I noticed only that there were many fine-looking cherry-trees around the village, that the brown and white cattle looked extra fat and ruddy, and that the village looked extra squalid. A long path climbed through woods to the Maquis of Champoux. And when we came to it I saw a dirty hole in the ground. It was a grave disappointment to me.

It was a natural hole in the ground. Before the coming of man it had been a leafy bowl under the great trees. But the Maquis had changed all that. There were about twelve of them in that place, and to my mind they could scarcely have in-stalled themselves worse. The bowl was about thirty feet in diameter. In this space the men cooked, disposed of the offal from the kitchen, lived, washed and slept.

Amid the once-fresh trees and bushes immediately surrounding the bowl it was only too plain that they did all the other things necessary in human life.

Since the weather had recently been wet, the floor of the bowl was deep in mud, and a slight film of mud, now dry, now damp, coated every bed, every article of clothing, every cooking-pot and every weapon. Boulaya, also apparently struck by the squalor of the scene, administered sharp rebukes to the Maquis at large, and particularly to the chief, Jean Buthot.

Buthot, an impressive-looking figure, whose head and build reminded me of pictures of the old bare-fisted pugilists, answered back in a slightly cowed, slightly bitter manner. From his gloomy answers I drew a sad picture of the life this "best Maquis in France" had been living before our arrival. They had been given no explosives, and they would not have known how to use them anyway. They had done some sabotage nevertheless. The chief, Buthot, was a railway worker and knew the lines well. About a month earlier they had derailed a train in a tunnel near Besançon, on the Belfort line. Since then they had been resting on their laurels, and existing in spite of the rains. There had been quarrels. Several of them had packed their things and gone home. Others had taken themselves off to the Maquis of Vieilley, on the other side of the "côte". They had no tobacco. They had no wine. Their clothing was wretched. Most of them had no boots, and were obliged to paddle through the mud in slippers or rope-soled "espadrilles" or summer sandals.

They were a bedraggled and bitter lot. Just one thing about them pleased me. They did not look like a Benevolent Society. In fact, in their misery and their bitterness they looked more like murderers. And we were going to need some murderers.

Their attitude towards myself was exceedingly friendly. Boulaya, generous as ever, gave me a glowing introduction. As far as I could make out, I was a cross between The God Mars, Lady Luck, and the British Red Cross. Still, everyone seemed delighted.

How could their squalor be ameliorated? Short of moving them from their hole it looked an impossible problem. They had built a long bed made of wattle-work covered with hay, and above this was stretched on heavy cross-pieces supported by trees a big black railway tarpaulin (which leaked, they said). This bed held twelve of them sleeping cheek to cheek. The remaining four were disposed on two other low "double beds", built up a little from the mud and in the lee of the tarpaulin. Within three feet of the two smaller beds the cook worked on a big open fire covered with a sheet of corrugated iron. The peelings from vegetables and the bones and remains of meat and fish were flung to the other side of the bowl, or were trodden into the ground where they fell. Little attempt had been made to accommodate the weapons. These were hung about anywhere by the individual owners, and once, when my boot struck something solid in the mud, I unearthed a British hand-grenade covered with rust and filth. Their total armament consisted of five Sten guns, five revolvers, three French or Belgian automatic-pistols of small calibre, two long "Lebel" rifles of the French Army, and a few hand-grenades, which were unlikely to work if needed.

Boulaya saw me looking angrily at the weapons (it annoyed me to think that Allied airmen had risked their life to drop

134

material which was being mistreated), and he spoke seriously to the men, telling them that the place and the arms must show improvement the next time we came. We would return in a few days.

While he was haranguing them I noticed that the chief had gone a bright crimson. Appearing from the bushes behind the bowl came a blonde woman, she was followed by an extrava- gantly muscular red-haired little man. Despite the mosquitoes, which were naturally so thick in the bowl that we literally breathed them, this newcomer wore no shirt and his white-skinned torso was covered with coarse tattooings. His bull-neck and flattened nose proclaimed the boxer. He was "Chocolat" Missana, an Italian.

The appearance of the woman was the last straw for Boulaya. The "best Maquis in France" was not living up to its reputa-tion. The woman, he was told, was Madame Missana, and she had come to the Maquis for the first time that afternoon to fix up a false divorce with her husband. It was known in Besançon that he was in the Maquis, and to avoid unpleasant repercussions the pair had decided to pretend to terminate the marriage. They had to decide whether it was necessary to specify an infidelity or seek separation on the grounds of deser-tion or mental cruelty. Before we arrived she had called on the Maquis to vote on this, and the voting had been even in favour of infidelity and desertion. She now asked Boulaya to make the casting vote. He refused to do this, asking the lady politely to take herself off, and never to come back to the Maquis. He now addressed the Maquis at some length and with great heat.

"Remember you are soldiers," he began.

Leaving the place after shaking hands with everybody, I saw another tarpaulin which they had spread out to dry in the sun at the edge of the wood. There were two fresh and enormous cowpats in the centre of the tarpaulin. That seemed to express everything.

Then, when we got down to Champoux, we found that both tyres on my "Corsair" were flat. Boulaya had to get back to Marchaux for a meeting with the "patron" in the Hotel de la Poste. He had to fly, for he was already late. So he left me to mend my punctures, surrounded by a number of aged peasants and young children, who regarded me in what I then mistook for a quizzical and hostile manner. I had everything that was necessary to perform this task, the repair outfit, and a trough of water handy. I remembered that water was necessary to find out by the bubbles where the puncture was. But beyond that I could not remember how to begin, and what to do. Had I been alone I should have settled down and worked it out quite happily. Because there was a gallery I began to wonder whether it was necessary to take the wheels off the bicycle or not. Hopelessly, I searched the dusty files of my childhood memories. It was certainly about fifteen years since I had mended a puncture, and probably more like twenty. I was saved by "Chocolat" Missana, who, unknown to me had been watching my quandary from the window of the mayor's house. He now darted out, and quickly mended both tyres. I was so grateful that I gave one thousand francs to his wife to buy tobacco for the Maquis.

As I left two men arrived on bicycles and Missana introduced me as "the new chief". One of them, tall for a Frenchman, powerful and hairy, with a blue jowl, was René Berger, known in the Maquis as "le gros Berger". I paid little attention to him at the time. I was annoyed and frightened by Missana's airy way of introducing me in front of a lot of strangers. At this rate every peasant in the Doubs would soon know that a British officer who looked like a sheep had arrived. And finding a sheep-faced officer in the Doubs would be child's play for the Gestapo.

Boulaya was waiting for me in Marchaux under three lime-trees just beyond the hotel, which was shut since it had run out of every beverage, including lemonade made with saccharin. He had a tall young man with him whom he introduced as Gros-Claude, the schoolmaster from Rougemontot, a village to the north, and another lieutenant in the Resistance. I rode away with this new acquaintance down the Besançon road.

Boulaya was going to finish his business with the patron and then they would join us. Gros-Claude, in the most tactless manner possible, began our friendly conversation by telling me with a smirk that he was an officer in the French Air Force, and that he had bombed Gibraltar, obeying the orders of Vichy. Fortunately, I am unbiased about such things, and we soon got the talk going on more normal lines, discussing the methods of blowing things up. Gros-Claude had an arms dump near his village and had the idea of forming a small Maquis group. I promised to visit him and give instruction. Then he left. He looked the kind of man who would wear a net on his hair when he bathed.

So I waited, hidden in the bushes at the side of the Marchaux-Besançon road. It was an important and busy road, and I regarded it with great awe, being careful to duck whenever any vehicle or any human being passed.

⊘ Colonel Morin, or le patron as he preferred to be called, came riding up the road with Boulaya. He told me that he would get me a new bicycle from the big Peugeot factory at Montbeliard, a factory well disposed towards the Resistance.

"A brand new machine, exactly the same as mine," he said. I looked at his bicycle, and liked it less than the "Corsair". His was definitely a war-production machine, without chromium plating even on the handle-bars, with wooden, instead of rubber hand-grips, and without those wonderful hand-screw things at either side of the wheels. He ordered Boulaya to see that I was "most comfortable" and that I did not sleep outdoors in the Maquis. Then he departed, cycling alone down the road to Besançon.

"Where is he going?" I asked.

"Besançon," said Boulaya.

"Indeed." The little colonel in his spotted and faded old suit seemed a very big man to me as he cycled away. It began to rain.

CHAPTER VII

WE put our bicycles in the white-painted rack that paralleled the front of the hotel. Behind the rack stood two bright-green lemon-trees in pink wooden tubs. Baby lemons were already formed on the trees. And behind the trees the hotel appeared to bristle with its sense of being an extremely clean and complete hotel, with its door and three windows looking straight at the road.

It was self-assertive, like a toy house built of bright red bricks and white mortar in the London toy-shops at Christmas-time. Or like the façade of a house that a child draws happily before he has forced himself to learn the photographic laws of perspective, a functional house with bricks, stones, four steps and a door, three windows, a roof with slates in it, and a slightly top-heavy chimney (with smoke coming out).

When the "patron" had cycled off into the rain, Boulaya said to me:

"How do you feel after seeing the first of your Maquis, Emile?"

"Frankly, depressed."

"So do I. There is but one reply We must prescribe for ourselves a good dinner, a good bottle to follow it, and then a clean bed. We must go to old Letallec, but I warn you it is twelve kilometres from here, and he might be full up, or have Germans there."

Letallec, proprietor of the "Hotel de la Gare", opposite the wayside station of Rigney, was an old soldier with a grey, fiercely-waxed moustache, and that hawk-like type of French face that seems to be dying out. He had two professions. He was photographer as well as hotel-keeper.

They are two professions that go admirably together. His dark room was the hotel cellar. And when I entered the shining kitchen I saw a rack of his plates washing under the tap, while another rack stood between the pastry that his wife was making and a four-pound pike, fresh-caught from the River Ognon.

You walked straight into the café by the front door and I had to wait there and drink an apéritif brought by Mademoiselle Letallec, while Boulaya went into the kitchen to spy out the land. Then I was whisked into the kitchen, and into the parlour beyond. It was a parlour filled with strange weapons collected by Letallec in his foreign service, and with stuffed birds from the woods and fields of the Doubs department.

There was a distinctly communist, or equality flavour to the atmosphere of the "Hôtel de la Gare". The owner was fierce and imposing, but his small round dark wife and his small round fair daughter were at least equally fierce and active. There was no background in the family, their life was like a horse-race, with all three running always neck and neck.

I know enough about kitchens to know when a cook is "making do". Madame Letallec found our arrival a heavy strain on the commissariat. There was little food in the place. But neither of us dared to remonstrate with her generosity.

After dinner we drank a bottle of Côtes du Rhône with the three of them. We sat at one of the shinily varnished tables in the café, the café with its "zinc", its white-scrubbed floor, its walls covered with Dubonnet and St. Raphaël advertisements, and warning notices in German and French. The warnings about closing-time came from the German military authority, and the warnings against alcoholism and selling drink to young people came from the Vichy Government. There was a big picture of Marshal Pétain behind the bar.

The Letallec family grew quickly excited when Boulaya revealed my identity. I had spoken little, and they had failed to remark my accent.

"Now you are here, are we going to start setting about the Boche?" asked old Letallec.

"Don't stay too long in this neighbourhood, you'll be sure to get yourself shopped," said Madame Letallec.

"Don't eat too much of the bread here, it will simply ruin your inside," said Mademoiselle.

"Why are we backward around here?" demanded Letallec, angrily waving both hands across the table. "It's true that we've had one or two parachutages. That was enlivening. But what are we doing about winning the war? I am in the Resistance, and I demand to be put into action."

"Father, Father! Calm yourself. You are sixty-two," said Mademoiselle. "If people would spend more time in doing the things that had to be done, and went more regularly perhaps to Mass, instead of telling the others what ought to be done."

"The trouble is the towns-people," said Madame. "Coming rushing out into the country with their money, sometimes even with money that's tainted by the Boches. The towns-people think they can come into the country and buy everything. The Bisontins are bad. So are the Parisians. Yesterday there was a woman came in a taxi all the way from Besançon. 'I would like to stay here with my little girl,' she says as sweet as honey. 'Indeed, madame, and what will you provide for the hotel?' I reply. 'Provide?' she says. 'Oh, I will pay you anything you ask.' 'So you will pay, then pay me in bread and pork and ham and butter and eggs and chickens and potatoes,' I tell her. 'And, furthermore, for your ration-cards, you might as well use them as curl-papers, my dear; yes, and your bank-notes too.' And believe me or believe me not that woman was wearing sables that must have been worth hundreds of thousands—except that nothing is worth anything. Oh, what a puzzle life is. One considers oneself rich if one has a pig."

"Enough, woman," screamed old Letallec. "Your gross talk makes me vomit. France suffers and you can talk of sables and of pig. These gentlemen are here to settle the big questions."

"The big questions, the big questions," interrupted Madame.

"Yes, a man talks all the time about the high-faluting business, but he forgets all about it quickly enough if the kitchen lacks fats."

"Every Frenchman has the right to fight to wipe out the shame of conquest and betrayal," continued the old man. "I regard myself as a soldier, bound by the same duties and loyalties as forty good years ago. My pack is ready, my rifle is greased. When I get the order I march. Am I or am I not a member of the Rigney group? a group that is officially recognised by the likes of Monsieur Boulaya here. Why don't we *do* something?"

"What?" asked Boulaya.

"Kill every Boche that passes through Rigney or orders a drink here in my café, or travels on the railway."

"But if you kill one Boche they will burn the whole of Rigney, station, hotel and all. We are not strong enough to begin to fight them openly. Remember that this is a main garrison area of France, and every barracks within one hundred kilometres of us now is absolutely stuffed with the swine. He is numerous, powerful and ruthless. What does he care that your village is the product of centuries of steady family labour, that your grave-yards mean more to you than a million years of his brazen victories could mean to him. If he has to punish you he will punish not only you, but all generations that are destined to follow you, who have the right to know the village of Rigney as you have known it, to see the old walls and to drink at the iron fountain, which is good, because it has slaked the thirst of their ancestors.

"We will fight him with guile. That is why we have come. Émile and Boulaya will flay the Fritz from the rich valleys of the Doubs and the Ognon, and you, father Letallec, faithful soldier of France, will march with us in the victory parade through Besançon. Now have faith in your leaders, and wait."

"I have faith, much faith," said Letallec. And I thought that he would need it. His wait would certainly be long.

They showed me to "the Blue Room" because it was the best room, and because its windows opened on to a roof which sloped down to the back garden. This was the room that Boulaya normally occupied, but he was the most generous of men. It was a sacrifice to give up the best room to a comrade in those days, but to give up a room with a way out over a roof was more than a sacrifice.

I opened the window wide. We had arrived at Rigney on June 15th, and the moonlit nights were ended. But in the light from the kitchen window below me I saw a stoat slide from the haricot beans into the wheat-field, and he was carrying something heavy in his mouth. There was no black-out in my sector.

Boulaya had left me in a hay-field while he went on ahead to investigate conditions in the village of Moncey, three miles from Rigney. I was hidden from the road by a few trees and, since the sun was warm, I had taken off my shirt and lay happily upon it, using my rucksack as a pillow. My bicycle stood behind me under trees, its precious tyres shielded from the sun.

We had breakfasted late in the "Hotel de la Gare", and now we were to see the second and last of Boulaya's Maquis. I was not looking forward to this, and I had every intention, if it were no more promising than the one I had seen at Champoux, of returning south to Albert. Boulaya was so kind to me and so delightful a companion that I could not feel angry with him for exaggerating the merits of his Maquis. But he had drawn me north under false pretences. However, lazy as usual, I decided to see what the day would bring forth, and relaxed to enjoy the sun.

"Hey, Émile. Really, you should not do that," Boulaya said when he came round the corner of the wood.

"Do what?"

"Why, take a sun bath, of course. What an extraordinary thing to do. Only the Germans do that sort of thing around here. One might conceivably do it on the river-bank. But to take a sun bath in the corner of a field. No, really. Otherwise you are such a sensible fellow. But you already look a little odd, you know. I mean with all that fair hair cut in the English way. You look a shade Germanic (pray forgive the insult). You must therefore be scrupulously careful not to behave like a Boche. . . ."

After this homily (I think it was the only one he ever gave me, but he had strong ideas on nudism out-of-doors) he told me that he was going on himself to Vieilley to see the other Maquis, but that Vieilley was a dangerous village at that time, frequently visited by the Gestapo and the Militia, and that he did not care to accept the responsibility of taking me there immediately. Accordingly, I was to lunch in Moncey with a young woman who had attended his English classes. . . .

"A charming young person, and madly anglophile. Her mother also is a most delightful person. Her father is head of the aluminium factory in Moncey. I have not met him, but I know that he is sympathetic to the Allied cause. I will meet you at three o'clock under the lime-tree five hundred metres before Vieilley. Take the normal road from Moncey to Vieilley. The only village you must pass through is Venise. Now. Walk warily. Eat well. Seek to charm."

Turning these orders over in my mind (I could not help thinking that some newspapers might have called mine a "phony war") I cycled to the outskirts of Moncey, where a dark, scared-looking stranger standing alone by a road junction gave me the agreed pass-word "Grenouille 36". When I had replied with the counter: "Thirty-six frogs have sixty-*three* legs," he told me to follow him at a distance.

He had a pleasant house under the beetling old château in the centre of Moncey. You entered his garden by an iron gate in one corner of a court-yard where there were always women gossiping or mending clothes; it was a court-yard with a lot of doorsteps and windows around it, and two or three barking mongrel dogs in the centre.

A large weeping-willow stood before the front door of his house, its branches trained and imprisoned to reach the ground. In the arbour thus formed he hid my bicycle, then led me through French windows into a salon furnished with the expensive kind of tables and chairs that you used to see at "Arts Decoratifs" exhibitions in Paris. Seating me reverently upon a sofa he held out a plump hand and said:

"Dardel. Enchanted to make your acquaintance."

"Émile," I replied. "Highly honoured by your kind invitation."

He was a man in the late forties, a heavy man with a thick moustache and black hair that grew low down upon his forehead. He was a solid, slightly self-important man who yet gave the impression of being a naughty boy. Thus he made my arrival the excuse for drinking a Pernod, and to the act of opening a bottle of this, then unprocurable alcohol, he contrived to give an irresistible air of debauchery.

When he had wiped two glasses with a silk cloth, set them and the drink upon a heavily engraved glass tray at my side, he ran to the French windows and called loudly to his women-folk. Instead of calling as most men would have done: "Come up at once, I have a surprise for you," or words to that effect, he merely shouted rudely:

"Am I supposed to starve while you women work down there. I am hungry, I tell you."

Returning to me, he said: "Won't they just be mad with me. Because I shouted like that they will delay over returning. Actually they detest the work they are doing, and they are dying to come up for luncheon. And that will give us the time to tranquilly drink at least two Pernods each. Then they will have to go and change of course when they hear who it is. . . . Silly pigeons.

"As for my daughter, Janine, I really cannot think what she will say or do. Cry, I shouldn't be surprised, or just go straight off her head. And my wife. But there they are."

Two women came to the door. Rather small, very dark women with enormous deep brown eyes. One carried a rake and the other a hoe, and these they concealed behind them as though they were the badges of shame whilst they peered from the sun-drenched garden into the cool darkness of the salon. They wore faded linen dresses, floppy straw hats and they had "espadrilles" on their feet.

"Come in, my dears, come in," said Monsieur Dardel, with his naughtiest smile. "Permit me to present to you the Captain Émile, officer in the Royal British Army."

Two small screams rang in the warm garden air and the doorway was empty.

"Fools of women," said Monsieur Dardel. "Always thinking of clothes. Now I suppose they will be hours late with luncheon."

Already, while drawers banged in the bedrooms overhead, I heard madame issuing her "action" orders to the kitchen. They were given in a shrill shout with scarcely a pause for contemplation, a string of admirably concise, unmistakably clear orders. And in a short space of time we were all four seated around a civilised table with white linen and gleaming silver and eating ultra-civilised, though perhaps a shade too copious, food. My hostess and her daughter now wore the fresh and coquettish dresses that a French townswoman likes to wear in the country. Both had admirable figures for their separate ages (the mother was forty, the girl, twenty) with slender waists and nervously slim legs terminating in graceful wooden-soled shoes.

This was a rich bourgeois family. They were more impressed by me, and more polite with me than the other French people I had met. The girl, too shy to speak the English she had acquired

143

in years of study, sat and drank me in with her great brown eyes. Being drunk like this, while it was not actively disagreeable to me after the many days which had been spent among rougher females, yet reminded me that I was a fraud. And when these women told me that I was courageous or admirable my inside wanted to guffaw, and it was all I could do to go on eating their food. They spoke cultured, intelligent French; that only made it sillier.

Madame Dardel was at pains to eradicate the "bad impression" she felt I must have got from seeing that she and her daughter had been working.

"What a terrible life," she wailed. "Obliged to work in the fields; who could ever have imagined such a thing. But if you want potatoes and vegetables you are obliged to grow them yourself. And where, may I ask, is one to get labour? I assure you, to me it is absolute agony, this appalling manual labour. To think that as a little girl I was brought up to admire, yes, admire, Millet's picture of the Angelus, with its perspiring peasants. I tell you the peasants are only too delighted now to see us obliged to work in order to eat. I can sense them sniggering when they see me going down to the field."

"Hush, hush," said Monsieur Dardel, and I had the impression that he was smiling, although his face was solemn. "My dear, you will give Monsieur Émile the impression that you detest the peasants. They are the backbone of France, you know—or at least we are always told so."

"But I do, I do," she cried. "The war has been a good thing for the peasant, the cultivator. The war has only meant that he gets enormous prices for everything that he grows or every animal that he fattens. And it has killed his jealousy. Before the war he was jealous of the city worker or people richer than himself because those people had cars and beautiful clothes and fine houses and holidays while he had only hard work in his fields. Now the others have less than nothing, and they have to come to him and beg him for food. And he revels in it.

"And don't you talk to me about work, my friend," she continued acidly to her husband. "I don't see you in the fields that you bought in order that *we* should cultivate vegetables and potatoes for *your* meals. It's not as though you were doing your ordinary work, with the factory shut down most of the time, and you up at Martin's Hotel playing 'belotte' with your cronies."

With them I was away from the Resistance. Listening to their talk was like listening to the talk of ambitious people in almost any small town in Europe. Behind the talk was the French genius for "making do" or "System D.", as they called it In the intervals of her lively talk Madame Dardel went out and cooked the lunch herself. And despite her avowed hatred of labour, her garden was well kept and in the outhouses she had cages and cages of tame rabbits for eating. The main difference between this and the working-class houses or small farms which I normally visited was that in those other places the daughter would have done the cooking and would have been expected to do more running about than her mother. With the Dardels the daughter was expected to play the piano and be well educated and well dressed. The mother was at the same time strict and friendly with her daughter, trotting her out almost as though she were showing the tricks of a favourite poodle, and calling her by a number of silly pet names such as "Poulette" and "Cocotte". I imagined that occasionally I noticed a rebellious smoulder in the dark gaze of the girl's meek eyes.

My trip, on leaving the Dardels' hospitable table, was the first bicycle ride that I had undertaken alone. Mentally stiffened by the profusion of refined alcohol which Monsieur Dardel had insisted on my drinking, I yet felt a strong nervousness. I now know the road so well that it is almost shocking for me to think back to that afternoon and realise that then it was strange to me, that I was surprised to find a sharp turn in the village of Venise, and wondered if I were on the correct road as I pedalled with difficulty up-hill with rolling fields and then a railway on my right beyond the line of apple-trees that bordered the road, and on the left the ground rising at first in gentle cultivation and then in steep wild woods to a high ridge. But it was only a short ride after all. And surmounting the crest between the two villages, I saw the spire of Vieilley church, and between me and it the lime-tree, with Boulaya resting peacefully in its shade.

"All is well," he said when he had politely asked me if I had enjoyed myself. "Give me five minutes' start then follow me into the village. Go to the first house on the right after the fountain."

So I entered Vieilley for the first time, riding on a bicycle, alone, and unknown to any of the villagers. There were people who eyed me suspiciously as I rode in; an old man putting two horses away in a farm on the right, an old woman attending to her bee-hives, children clustered around the fountain and a peasant who came out of the "bistro" wiping his unshaven lips with his shirt-sleeve. It looked even more of a quagmire than the other villages. The house where I was to stop was a superior kind of place. The front was freshly painted, and the wooden railings enclosing the little space of ornamental pebbles between the house and the roadway had been painted with an imitation wood grain and then varnished.

Boulaya took me into the back room of the house. It was a kitchen, and there was an eighth of an inch of dust over everything, including the pots and pans. It had the smell of a room that is not lived in.

A quiet man stood by the table. He was Georges Molle, the owner of the house. He poured out three glasses of the white alcohol that they called "la gnole" or "la goutte". I did not feel like drinking, and putting out my hand clumsily, I knocked the glass off the kitchen table to the stone floor.

"That brings good luck," said Georges politely as he picked up the fragments. He had a slow voice with the accent of the countryside. He began to tell us about his house. It had been ransacked by the Gestapo five weeks previously. Nothing had since been altered in these back rooms. The front rooms were occupied by Poirier, the "garde-pêche" and his family. The Gestapo had left the Poiriers alone. They had not even disturbed the back rooms much. He took us into the dining-room which you entered through a doorway from the kitchen.

Lying in the thick dust on the round walnut table was a note written in clumsy French. The note said:

"Will Monsieur Molle, Georges, please kindly to call as soon as possible at . . ." here followed the address of the Gestapo in Besançon. On the sideboard the Gestapo had searched a big box of snapshots taken of or by Georges during his life in the French Air Force. Most of them showed him posed stupidly in front of dated aeroplanes or more sensibly crouching with a shotgun in rushes or camel scrub.

"La Marche." The name that I knew startled me. It figured in the story Georges was telling. He told it quietly, calmly. I could see that he was a steady character and unexcitable. He had been working for a long time for the Resistance one way and another since his squadron had been broken up. There was not much to do, but when he could see something to do he did it. Anything. Perhaps it was only hiding some war material from the Boches. Perhaps it was only assisting at a parachutage and carting the material up through the woods on his back to hide it. Perhaps it was only talking to the young men, telling them that it was treason to go and work in Germany.

One day a tall, dark stranger came into the village and asked for Georges Molle. He introduced himself as an ex-officer named La Marche, and he invited Georges to drink a glass with him in the "bistro". La Marche said that he had fought in the infantry but that in the previous war he had been in the Air Force. What aeroplanes had he flown? Georges asked. La Marche "could not remember". Georges knew that an airman always remembers his aeroplanes. His own, from the little Potez 63 back, were engraved on his heart, and were often on his lips. So La Marche was lying. Next time the ex-officer came to Vieilley the wily Georges was aware that he was there, and watched his movements. All that La Marche did was to enquire if his old friend Georges Molle was at home. He was answered in the affirmative. Instead of going to the house by the fountain La Marche jumped on his motor-cycle and roared out of the village. Three minutes later two Gestapo cars, with their engines cut, glided swiftly to the front of Molle's house. Seeing a peasant leaning on the railings, one of the Gestapo men asked:

"Is Monsieur Georges Molle in his house?"

"This is his house," replied the peasant, with a strong accent. "And you won't find Molle there, for he is behind the house in his garden digging. I've just been speaking to him."

The Gestapo men drew their guns and raced through to the garden. But they found nobody in the garden, and nobody except the tenants in the house. The peasant who had directed them was Georges Molle.

After this story I felt uneasy in his house, and I was glad when Boulaya suggested that we might go to see the Maquis. I paid little attention to Georges. He was such a quiet person compared to the more florid personality of Boulaya. He seemed to melt into the background. His clothes helped this impression. He wore a very old browny-green tweed coat and trousers and down-at-heel brown boots. He was smaller than Boulaya and myself with a square, agile, build. His movements were peculiar. They were lithe and performed with perfect muscular control, and yet there was a hint of awkwardness in them. Later, when I knew him well, I thought that the awkwardness came from his habit of watching the ground as he moved along with a motionless head, but with his eyes darting from side to side looking for places where hares had lain or passed or where a wild boar had dug. He had spent so long in the woods—he was known as the leading amateur poacher in all the valley of the Ognon—that he seemed to take the woods with him wherever he went.

He was a fine-looking man, unobtrusively handsome, to a man's way of thinking (though apparently obviously so to women). His face was wide and pleasant, slightly spoiled by teeth that had been mended with much gold.

We walked out of Vieilley by a lane that twisted from the back of the village and then ran parallel to the ridge behind it. After a quarter of an hour's brisk walking we turned up a small path which mounted rapidly through the trees. Georges here took the lead, and his smooth strides left me breathless behind him. It was an ordinary woodcutter's path that we followed. Soon we stopped climbing and turned to the right along another still smaller path which slid down a miniature precipice and came to an end. Here Georges parted some bushes to disclose another path turning away sharply to the left, and following what had once been the bed of a small stream. We walked up this, brushing through the bushes and lashed about the faces and bodies by whippy branches.

At last Georges pushed his way into a clump of pine-trees and gave a two-note whistle. At the same time my over-sensitive nose picked up a hint of Maquis smell, and the tang of wood-smoke.

There were only four men there. Jammed into a narrow space between the pine-trees. I was introduced to the four. Buhl, the Pointu, the Frisé, and Philippe. Buhl, who appeared to be the leader, was older than the others, probably about my own age. He had a thin, weak face with a small moustache and large dark eyes. Boulaya told me that he was a noted "killer". The "killer" himself seemed pleased at this description. Then, remembering his grievances, he told Boulaya that he was going off to spend a day or two with his wife near Besançon. When were they going to get more food? and perhaps some wine? The tobacco was nearly finished.

I was sorely disappointed. Was this all that there was to the second Maquis? Four uncomfortable men, three of them very young. It was hot under the pine-trees, and the ground was none too clean. They had fixed a big mirror with a mahogany frame on one of the trees. They slept on beds made up of branches. They slept apparently in pairs, except for Buhl, who slept alone, and over each rude bed they had tried to make a rainproof roof with great thicknesses of cut pine branches. There was no room to move around. If I stood up straight the branches pricked my cheeks and eyes.

An old sack of explosives lay under a tree, beside it were three large round loaves of coarse bread and about six pounds of fresh farm butter partially wrapped in dirty greaseproof paper. The surface of the butter was deeply scored by the knife-blades of the Maquisards, who, when they felt hungry, cut off a hunk of bread and spread coatings of butter on it.

"Nothing but bread and butter to eat," Buhl ended his catalogue of woes. "I tell you we can't go on like this."

Boulaya took me away quickly, saying that we would return to eat at noon the next day. On the way back to the village he asked Georges to see if he could get them some more food, particularly for the following day. "I'll buy a rabbit, anyway," said Georges. "And they can often get eggs from the farms."

That night we ate and drank with Monsieur Marquis, one of the leading men and leading patriots of the village. He was a grey-haired man with a small saturnine face and the square stooped body and gnarled neck and arms of a man who had done heavy outdoor work all his life. We ate in the inner room with him, while the remainder of the household, deaf Madame Marquis, the two daughters, the farm labourer and the orphan boy, ate at the long oilcloth-covered table in the main room, the kitchen. Marquis had many fields in the village land, and some of the best vineyards running up the hill-side behind the church. Then he was rich for a cultivator, since in the winter-time he exploited the timber on the "côte" above the vineyards. After dinner we went to sleep in a bedroom over Marquis's stables, on the opposite side of the road from his house. To get to our room we traversed a squalid hallway where the labourer and the thin orphan slept the sleep of complete physical exhaustion. Boulaya gave me the larger of the two beds, his manners exquisite as always. I could not find it in myself to be angry with him, but I had been a poor companion all evening. Was this really all that there was to his Maquis? The first one at Marchaux was the dirtier, but at least there was something there. This one at Vieilley seemed only to consist of a man and three boys. Then there was Georges, of course. He was the "adjutant" of whom Boulaya had spoken to Albert and me. There was only one thing that I liked about it. And that was the effrontery of Boulaya; the cool way he carried the whole thing off, and his easy optimism. Such a man might be capable of anything.

A morose and unwilling guest, I accompanied Boulaya and Georges to the Maquis. It was a fine fresh morning, and pleasantly warm in the sun. Even my state of mind could not entirely sour me against the beauty of the valley and the hill behind the village. But I hated turning into the damp trees away from the sunshine and the spaces outside. I never got over this hatred. I have lived too many years in London, and I shall never appease the constant hunger for the sun that those mist-soaked years gave me.

When we reached the Maquis I asked to be shown the dump of parachuted material which I knew existed near-by. Georges led us up a path so nearly perpendicular that I had great difficulty, and Boulaya even greater, in getting up at all. I made up my mind there and then that I must have nails put in the soles of the square-toed shoes London had given me. I remembered as I struggled up the path that when I got my clothes in London the French-English captain had tried to insist on my taking one pair of heavy boots. I had refused because I hate wearing heavy boots, even for hard walking in rough country. I wondered if the captain had not been right. Certainly the Maquisards were surprised at my light shoes, and my feet would often have been drier in boots.

At the top of the small hill he had climbed Georges dived into seemingly impenetrable brush, and he soon disclosed the arms and explosives depot, a part of the material from one small parachutage. The material was in a bad state. It had been exposed to the weather for some months, stored merely in sacks shoved under a ledge of rock and covered over with moss. Bit by bit, crouched double to avoid the branches, with muscles already creaking from my climb and now cramped maddeningly, I pulled out the material. Rage consumed me as I handled rusted grenades and explosives soggy with moisture. Everything was in such a wet condition that in England it would have been unconditionally scrapped.

I was careful to conceal the main seething of my anger, but my questions and exclamations grew colder and more bitter. Georges' face grew long, and Boulaya injected the strained talk less frequently with his maddeningly optimistic remarks.

"There is not enough explosive to do much work," I said

at last. "And from the look of it, I doubt if it will work. We shall have to take the lot down to the Maquis and dry it. Then I shall test it. It's quite hopeless to store this material out in the woods without protection. Why was it not stored in the container cells? They were designed for that purpose."

Georges was unable to keep quiet any longer.

"That is all that remains of that parachutage," he said coldly. "Except for the Sten guns and pistols, all of which were given out, it was split into three parts. The other two parts were stored as you advocate in the woods on the other side of the 'côte' in the container cells. And this part is the only part that remains. The Boche captured the other two dumps. All this was carted in rucksacks over the hill, a distance of sixteen kilometres through the snow by myself and Barbier of Thise. Weinmann helped us to begin with, but he was ill and he had to stop after one trip because he was spitting blood. If you think it was easy . . ."

I interrupted him:

"It looks as though you might as well have spared yourself the trouble. Or taken a little more trouble and endeavoured to make this dump waterproof. Now if we can get all this down into the sun we shall see whether some of it will still work."

They agreed with frigid politeness.

While the atmosphere was strained I decided to strain it further.

"In the British Army," I began maddeningly. "In the British Army we have a rule for any formation, no matter how small, that goes out by itself. Say it is a section. The section arrives to take up a position. The first thing to be done is to post sentries. What is the next?"

"Next they make some tea perhaps," suggested the intellilent Boulaya.

"No. They dig two holes. One is for rubbish and the other is a latrine."

"Exactly," said Boulaya. "We have the same procedure in the army. But of course it is impossible in the Maquis to have quite the same standards." He had understood. We left it at that.

Down in the Maquis they organised carrying-parties with three men, the whole strength apart from Philippe, who was "attempting", they said, to cook the meal. Buhl had departed to see his wife, but another man had returned, Maurice. When the material had all been spread out in the sun to dry, a sorry sight, we ate squatting on our hunkers like savages beside the beds of pine branches. The food was revolting, for Philippe was no cook and all the cooking utensils and the French Army dixies from which we ate were greasy and horrible. There were two fried eggs for each of us, followed by segments of tough rabbit burned nearly black.

It was getting hot and airless in the woods and we were thirsty after the work. We drank water from the old water-bottles, water with a queer dead taste. After the meal, while I worked with the explosives we had spread out to dry, I began to instruct the four young Frenchmen in the use of these strange things.

And suddenly, from their eager questions and their enthusiastic attention, I picked a flicker of hope. All through the long afternoon I talked to them in my halting technical French. Talked to them until I was hoarse, asked them questions to see that they understood, made each of them handle the explosives, and finally listened to their talk, struggling with their strange language spiced with the "argot" of the Maquis.

Who were these four young men? They were four youths of the working classes. Their faces and hands and habits were rough, none rougher. When they talked a girl was called a "gonzesse", a hand-grenade was an "orange" or a "lemon", a Sten gun might be a "petrolette" or a "clarinette", and the big Colt automatic was a "chassepot". They were dressed in a mixture of clothes with khaki from the French and German armies, the predominant motif. All four wore khaki trousers of cheap stiff German cloth, trousers stolen from the Wehrmacht. Their boots were in a terrible state, although Georges had recently had them patched in the village. Toes and heels showed through holes in the leather. They had no socks.

They were dirty, all four. They sprawled over the ground, and when they came close to me I smelled their bodies. Especially that of the Pointu, who wore no shirt.

The Pointu was thus called because he was a tall, lanky youth, of the type that has outgrown his strength. He was an unnaturally serious twenty-year-old. His weapons were well-cared-for, and I noticed that he was careful, though clumsy in his work.

Philippe was still younger. He was a handsome boy, his blond good looks were just beginning to coarsen with his environment. He had a strangely deep and resonant voice for his age.

The Frisé (I suppose in our Army he would have been called "Curly") had been a sailor in 1940. He was an old twenty-two-year-old, tough and cheeky but intelligent. I saw that he was the only one who had closely studied the instruction booklets which were parachuted in every container. The Frisé really knew something. Boulaya and Georges, who had also read the pamphlets, still knew nothing. The Frisé learned easily. And his personal weapons, a Sten and a Colt, were in perfect condition. He was a strange-looking young man. Powerfully built but with short legs and a huge head that looked even bigger because of the enormous thickness of dust-coloured curls surmounting his high forehead. He spoke some English too, and maddened me frequently by flinging mispronounced English words into our conversation.

While the Frisé, in his odd tough way, gave me a perfectly correct first impression of brilliance, it was Maurice who interested me most of the four. He was older than the others, in the middle or late twenties, and he had a family in Besançon, a wife who was enceinte. He had been a house-painter, and a Communist. But he never spoke about these things. He had been in the Army, a noncommissioned officer in the "Corps Francs", the volunteers who did patrols against the German lines and outposts in the opening "dead" period of the war. He often spoke about his life in the army. He was single-minded and solid. He had already paid the price of his front teeth in the battle. The stumps of them and some ragged, strangely white edges showed when he smiled, which was frequently. The Germans had broken his front teeth with hammers to teach him a lesson when they had caught him trying to sabotage in Besançon station. Maurice was a wide man. He was not short, but the great width of his shoulders made him look almost squat, and his face was round and wide, so that when I remember him it is as though I remember him in one of those convex mirrors that broaden every object they reflect.

Those were the four young men who formed that day the Maquis of Vieilley. Georges was not really a part of the Maquis. He made its existence possible by holding the goodwill of the village and by getting food and supplies for the Maquis. But he was no more a part of it than I, a foreigner, was part of it. Georges was a poacher, a man who walked alone.

Something about them inspired me. They were ordinary young men. They were the youth of France. And they were good material because they were excited and eager and fresh.

That was it. They were fresh. The whole situation suddenly turned round like a revolving stage in my mind, a stage that showed one instant a gloomy set, dark and hopeless, and the next instant a fine light set with a wide road leading into the distance. I saw that Boulaya had done me a favour in bringing me here to work with him. Here was the best way to begin his celebrated "Equipes Boulaya", to begin them with only ourselves and the four youths who lay around me in the pine-trees.

Everything fell into the picture. Perhaps in the gloom of the previous night's sleep my mind had already been working things out.

We would build Vieilley into the centre of our area. Then we would strive to dominate, first by sabotage, later by force of arms, the two valleys, the big valley of the Doubs running north-east from Besançon to Belfort and the valley of the Ognon, which runs approximately parallel to the other. The two valleys were the key to the town of Besançon. We would make Besançon our objective. Boulaya would march through it at the head of his men—perhaps.

Vieilley would do for the headquarters, the pine-trees would do to begin with. Already I had three useful houses in and near Vieilley, houses to hide in or to seek help from. Marquis at Vieilley, Dardel at Moncey, and Letallec at Rigney. I would keep the Dardel house separate from all my other activities, and secret from all save Boulaya. For Dardel, being cautious and "safety first" by disposition, was not connected in any way with the Resistance. I could go to earth in his house in case of danger. And his timid daughter with the unblemished reputation might be used to carry messages.

The first thing was to get the confidence of the Maquis. We must sleep there that night, Boulaya and I. And we would do a sabotage attack with them the following day. If the attack succeeded my new plan was on.

I questioned and requestioned the Frisé about the big station and railway depot at Besançon. He had worked there as a "garde voies" for the Germans before he had run away to the Maquis. He was able to draw me plans of the depot.

The others began to pay thrilled attention to my questions. Excitement grew under the pine-trees.

CHAPTER VIII

AFTER talking over with the Frisé all possible targets in the depot, I decided that the best would be two big turn-tables (called by the French "plaques tournantes") used to empty the locomotives from the round-houses.

I chose the turn-tables for several reasons. Both the Frisé and Maurice knew that part of the depot well and thought that the job could be done. The Frisé had a friend who owned a small café just across the wall from the turn-tables, and whose son was a "cheminot" employed in the depot. The son would be able to give them last-minute information on the positions of the German guards. And the turn-tables were an important target. If they were put out of action up to seventy big locomotives vital to the Germans would be imprisoned in the round-houses. I should have preferred to make a bigger attack to begin with, but I was pressed for time and short of men. I could only stay one more day at Vieilley. Then I must leave with Boulaya to meet Albert and Paul as promised at the château of La Chevillotte.

So that evening I sent the Frisé away to study the situation. He left in a rush and flurry on a brand-new woman's bicycle that he had "found" in Besançon. To go to the city he altered his toilet only by perching an extremely dirty beret on top of his curls. Maurice was to join him in the morning to make the final reconnaissance, then they were to return in the afternoon to report to me. They swore that they would be able to examine the turn-tables from close to. I wanted an actual description and drawings and the diameter in centimetres of each of the big central pivots. A turn-table works on balance. There is a central pivot underneath and there are two outside wheels, one at each end of the platform. When the locomotive is driven on to the turn-table it balances on the pivot and the two wheels do not touch the steel runway beneath them. One charge on the pivot therefore can knock out the whole turn-table, and repairs are extremely long and difficult.

I wondered if the Frisé and Maurice would come back and say that the job was impossible. It was not unlikely that this would happen. But I had a feeling that they were determined young men.

At two o'clock the following afternoon they returned. Maurice was a shade nervous about things. But the Frisé swept all objec-

155

tions aside. There were fifty-six big locomotives in the round-houses and more expected in the evening. What if there were German guards in the round-houses? They never stirred outside, did they? He had not seen them come out once the night before. And there were only three, or five at the most, if the other two from lower down came up that way to chat to their friends. As for the "gardes voies", they would not dare to interfere. And they would take the Pointu with a "clarinette" to guard the gate into the lane, and Philippe with another to stand well down the lane and give warning if a patrol came. He described the vital pivots in some detail. I had the impression that he was lying when he stated categorically that he had seen them from close to (why, he had "even touched the thrice-defiled things"). But he gave me a careful description of them with dimensions which I have now forgotten. The Frisé was irresistible.

By this time I had checked over and tested most of the material rescued from their dump, and I was staggered and proud to find that all of it worked, a mute tribute to the British armament industry, which I had hated so much in peace-time. I reckoned that this would give us in all about fifty "standard" $1\frac{1}{2}$ lbs. charges—enough to hit the railways a good thump while I was trying to get some more explosives.

Squatting in the middle of the pines, with the excited Frisé breathing anxiously down my neck, I made up the two big charges. I made them as neatly as we had been obliged to make them in the training schools, each charge a long and perfect cube of explosive, with two nice white primers nestling inside and a two-foot tail of detonating cord coming out of its end. Now there was a small problem. In England we always wrapped our charges in waterproof material and fixed this up solidly with rubber solution and adhesive tape. Here, in the field, there was hardly any adhesive tape and there was no material and no solution. So I cut up an old French Army linen flea-bag, had the Pointu dye it with ink, and sewed the charges into two solid little bags.

They dressed themselves up for the long walk over the hill, over past the Vauban fortress of "La Dame Blanche" at the top, and then down through the other side of the forest of Chailluz until they struck the suburbs of Besançon. They would reach Besançon before curfew and would carry their weapons and charges through the back streets in two haversacks. By curfew-time they would be hidden with the Frisé's friend, the café owner. From the upper windows of the café they could watch movements in the depot. They were to attack at 2 a.m. Pointu and Philippe gave their Stens a last rub and polish, broke them down into three pieces, and packed them with their magazines, one in each haversack. The Frisé and Maurice carefully adjusted their massive charges in the haversacks on top of the Stens. They ate a light meal of bread and cheese, standing up, looking at each other and at us excitedly.

Boulaya and I walked with them as far as the fields.

"Remember now," I said. "Place the charges properly inside the steel lattice-work and against the pivot proper. Wedge the charge against the surface of the pivot, then light your fuse, and don't pull on the fuse as you light it. The moment it is lit move away individually for the gate. Don't run away. Walk. Once at the gate, run down the lane. And take cover when you see the flash of the explosion in the sky, those charges are big, there will be much metal flying."

"Yes, Émile. Thank you, Émile. Au revoir."

I watched the four of them cross the field, striking up diagonally towards the forest that came pouring down the side of the ridge towards us. Boulaya put his hand on my arm.

"Well, Émile," he said. "Tonight a start is being made."

He was dreaming again that Besançon would one day be free. The four Maquisards had disappeared from view. The evenings were still chilly, and dew was beginning to fall. I closed the fastener on the front of my leather jacket. Boulaya had the great hooded blue cape that he had worn as an officer in Morocco. He used this to cover him when he lay down on the pine branches beside me. I was in my sleeping-bag. We used the "bed" of Maurice and Phillipe since it looked like rain and their bed appeared to have the most scientific "roof" over it.

"Shall we hear the noise of the explosions, Émile?" Boulaya asked.

"Yes, we should hear them, although the hill is between us and them."

"That will be wonderful."

He slept. I was glad of his heavy breathing beside me, and of the wind moving the tops of the pines. On my face I could feel the dampness of the dew-soaked air, but my body was warm and comfortable in the sleeping-bag. The pines smelled good. Perhaps that was the deciding factor, perhaps it was the smell of the pines, the antiseptic, Lysol, pine-tar-soap smell that had decided me to try to work with the Maquis of Vieilley.

I told myself that I would work with it only if the attack succeeded. I was fifty times more nervous than if I had been on the job myself. I pictured again and again the dark depot, a lurid light showing here and there from the cab of an engine, the air full of the hiss of escaping steam, the smell of heated oil and coal smoke. Would the Frisé and Maurice have the courage to go through with it?

It was easier to think of home now, and of the people I loved and had loved. There is something soothing about sleeping outside, provided you are warm enough. Lying under the pine-trees, alone but for the sleeping friend at my side, I could take the broad view of people I loved and had loved, people who had been kind to me and people who had hurt me. I wondered, as wanderers do, whether anybody at home was thinking of me now. If they were it would be sure to be somebody unexpected. Not B., but Violet the char, who used to come for an hour each morning in 1938 and clean the flat in Chelsea. Not my friend Geoffrey, but Saunders, who had cut my hair until 1939 and then disappeared into the Middle East in the Tank Regiment.

Before going to sleep I set the alarm clock in my head. For 12.30 a.m. I set it, just in case it worked unsatisfactorily, or in case the Frisé and Maurice got impatient and decided to do the job before two o'clock.

I awoke at midnight. Boulaya still slept, but uncomfortably. A light drizzle was falling. Not enough to penetrate our roof of pine branches, but the kind of drizzle that is normally prelude to something worse.

At 12.30 to the second I heard the first thump. It was like someone beating a giant metal tray in the distance, and it was followed immediately by its own echo. I timed it on the luminous face of the watch London had given me. Thirty seconds passed. One minute; the second one should go now. Ninety seconds. Two minutes. Something had gone wrong. I tore myself from the sleeping-bag, and sat up naked in the cold. But I still gazed despairingly at the dial of my watch. Two and a half minutes. I strained to hear small arms fire, although I knew that the depot was much too distant for that to be possible. I pictured the four youths there, surrounded perhaps. Perhaps even at that moment being clouted to the ground by brutal "Feldgendarmes". Two minutes forty-five seconds. Even as I decided to wait till three minutes had elapsed I heard the second explosion. It was much louder than the first, but there was no echo. A wave of gratitude to the young Frenchmen swept over me, a warm feeling that possessed me and gave me peace and a longing for sleep. Should I waken Boulaya? No, I would keep this to myself. If I woke him he would want to talk, and he would certainly roll himself a cigarette and drown the smell of the pines.

Why had the second explosion been louder than the first? The charges were exactly similar. Possibly one or both had been badly placed. But I realised that, bad soldier as I am, I did not care so desperately whether or not the two turn-tables were destroyed, what mattered was that the Frenchmen had not failed. They had the courage to do big things.

I went to sleep again, but not before I had made up my mind that I would go to see Albert at La Chevillotte only to ask him if I might return to Vieilley. And whenever I got back to this little Maquis I would do a big attack.

They came in at 6.30. In the rain. The hair hung damp on their foreheads. Their feet were blistered and their leg muscles were reacting in the almost drunk way you see when unfit men are exhausted. None of that worried me. But there were only three of them.

"Where is the Frisé?" I asked.

"Oh, we left him coming through the forest, in the wood-cutter's hut beside the well. His feet and legs were so bad he couldn't keep going."

"How many people are there in the hut?" Boulaya asked.

"Oh, not many. The father and mother and the son and his wife and three or four children."

"Children! But the Frisé might shoot his mouth off."

"He will, indubitably."

"Name of God, why did you leave him there?"

"How were we to stop him?" Maurice asked. "As for talking. I was greeted when I arrived at my home in Besançon yesterday morning by my wife, greatly excited. 'Maurice, my cabbage,' she cried. 'It is too dangerous. I forbid it. Think of the unborn child.' 'Forbid what?' I asked. And she answered: 'Don't go trying to deny it now, idiot. Why, all Besançon knows that you and Frisé are going to blow up the turn-tables tonight, and that you have an English officer with you who is planning your coups. Why, half the young men in Besançon were queueing up in the bistro by the depot last night to buy drinks for the Frisé.'

"And it was quite true," Maurice added, with a smile (for he did not appear to dislike the notoriety). "Frisé has only the one vice. He is a gabber. No use trying to shut his mouth. As for women or drink, he is just not interested, but talk will be his downfall."

"That must be changed. But the turn-tables. Why did the second charge go so much later than the first?"

"Well," said Maurice, a little timidly. "We realise now that your plan was the best. I mean for me to go into one pit and the Frisé into the other and light the charges almost at the same time. But, as you may realise, it's one thing to agree before or after which plan is best, and it's another to do the actual job.

"We were waiting in the café. Midnight had struck. Jo-Jo, that's the son of the café proprietor, had just come in to say that all seemed to be well. The depot looked sort of spooky, you know, full of long shadows. Suddenly we decided two things. That it would be too long to wait until two o'clock, and that the Frisé and I would lay the charges together. Lighting the first and then going on and doing the second. So we did that. Another thing. Philippe wanted to actually come into the depot instead of waiting outside in the lane. So we let him. The poor kid was going to feel kind of out of things.

"It was no easy job wedging the charge in behind the steel lattice-work. Frisé held the charge while I lit the fuse. Then we went on to the next. Philippe stopped a little by the first turn-table to see that nobody interfered with it."

"My God."

"Yes, but there were quite a lot of workers about. Some Schloks too, but they paid no attention to us. They were playing cards in the hut. We had tied white handkerchiefs around our sleeves, so they would think we were 'gardes voies'. Well, we could not run from the first turn-table to the second. There were too many people around. We walked across together and we had not got the second charge in place when the first one went off. Name of God, what a bang. There was metal clattering down for nearly five minutes, it seemed. We lay under the shelter of our turn-table, and when the metal stopped falling around us we placed the charge and I lit the fuse.

"Frisé now made his big mistake. That boy really is indiscreet. 'Philippe,' he shouted across the station. 'Are you all right?' As though half the cheminots in the depot did not know young Philippe. Then he shouted to the station at large: 'Keep in cover, there's worse coming.' Just then the air-raid sirens went, for they thought the first explosion was a bomb. There was not a soul, not even a Schlok to be seen around. They had put out the lights. We beat it for the gate, picked up the Pointu, and threw ourselves down in the lane when the second explosion came."

"It was louder than the first?"

"Yes, much louder."

"Were the two charges placed the same?"

"Yes, exactly the same."

"Do you think the attack succeeded?"

"Yes."

On this we shook hands all round, and realised that there was nothing, absolutely nothing, to eat for breakfast. Boulaya, beside himself with joy that the first attack had succeeded, was sorely vexed that he could not feed his men.

"One of the great events of the war for Besançon," he exclaimed. "And the men who did it return to find that there is not a crust of bread, not even a drop of warm coffee for them."

But the men who did it were going to their rude beds, too tired and too happy to talk much or to mind the rain. Before they slept Boulaya produced a small bottle of extra-strength Marc, made by his old father from the fine grapes of Salins. In this wonderful beverage we all toasted the successful beginning of Boulaya's campaign to liberate Besançon.

And later Georges arrived with eggs and bread and ground and roasted wheat for making "coffee". While the others ate "breakfast à l'Anglaise", Boulaya and I discussed with Georges plans to put the Vieilley Maquis on a more permanent basis. The three maquisards ate like wolves, especially the Pointu, who needed a lot of nourishment. Before they had finished the Frisé came hobbling in. He had news of the result of the attack.

There were sixty-three locomotives in the trap. One turntable had been lifted right up in the air, its pivot was smashed to bits. The other, the second to be attacked, had suffered more damage to the structure as a whole, but it was judged that the pivot could be repaired. The German engineers thought they could have that one moving with hand-gear in a few days. The other would be immovable until a new pivot could be cast and transported, that would certainly take weeks, perhaps months.

All eyes were turned on me while the Frisé recited this.

"The charges were not big enough," said the Frisé.

I turned this statement over in my mind. It was fairly clear to me that one charge, the first one, had been properly placed, and the other had been less carefully placed, because the pair were interrupted by the first explosion and the turmoil that it caused. But if I made public this opinion I would only arouse a storm of argument, and I would lose some of their faith and liking. Much better to turn the Frisé's accusation (for that was what it amounted to) to my own profit. Accordingly, I replied with every appearance of sincerity:

"I am very sorry indeed. I would like to congratulate you all and thank you all for a fine achievement and a brave deed."

A stunned silence greeted this. They tried to work it out for themselves. Was the foreigner actually accepting the responsibility? They had been certain of a good argument.

"They seemed on the small side, those charges," Pointu said, just to make sure.

"Yes, perhaps they did," I answered at once. "One is always liable to make a mistake. Explosives are queer things."

"And pray do not let us quibble," Boulaya said. "For the coup of the 'plaques-tournantes' will long be remembered. Émile and I must leave you now, but soon we will both return, and then deeds, military actions, will prove to the Boches that there is a serious menace for them hidden in the forest of Chailluz. We shall make the Maquis of Vieilley famous for all time.

"But not famous now, Frisé. I am appalled at your lack of discretion in Besançon. Do you realise that your loud mouth has endangered the whole Maquis and especially our friend Émile? You go around telling every low person of your acquaintance what you and your comrades have been ordered to do, and worse still, you declare that those orders were given by *an officer in the Intelligence Service*. Don't you understand that if the Boche has wind that there is a British officer in the forest he will encircle the forest, if it takes three thousand men to do it, and he will tear it apart, branch by branch, until he has got every one of us, Émile included."

The Frisé was too tough a bird to be put out by words.

"Who says that I said anything in Besançon," he said through the mixture of egg, bread, butter, and coffee that filled his mouth. He allowed his hard grey eyes to play around our circle.

Nobody said anything.

"Besides," the Frisé added, when he saw that nobody answered his challenge. "Surely the thing is to get strong enough to make it impossible for the Schleuhs to get at us."

"Enough," cried Boulaya. "Shut it, Frisé. You have done a good job, but you know nothing and you will accept orders. All I say is that from now on the actions of my Maquis must be purely military. You men will have to accept military discipline. For you, Frisé, I have two orders of the day. One, you are hereby promoted to sergeant in view of the successful operation on the 'plaques-tournantes'. Two, you will refer to the Germans as Boches, Schloks, Fritz, Stols, Têtes Carrées, or any other name you like, except by the name you have just used, Schleuhs."

"I would like to add something," I said. "I am not in the Intelligence Service." An incredulous silence greeted this. Then sly smiles spread on their faces, for the Intelligence Service, often shortened to the I.S., was a myth widely spread in France. "I am just an ordinary soldier," I insisted. But their smiles replied: "Ah, foxy, foxy, you don't deceive us." Too maddening.

Maurice also was promoted. Then we departed. Since my new bicycle had not arrived, and another was unobtainable, I had to cling to the "Corsair", which by this time was looking much the worse for its stay in the wet woods. I felt a little guilty about "Corsair", and so did Boulaya (his father and his family were both living at Salins, and the son of the mayor might be a dangerous enemy). "Corsair" was beginning to made odd groaning noises as we rode along. These noises worried me, unused as I was to bicycle travel. And the noises worried Boulaya, who sometimes muttered darkly that one day it would be necessary to clean our bicycles.

I was thinking of this threat as we cycled out of Vieilley and dismounted to begin the two-mile climb on the small road that crosses the "côte" to join Vieilley and Marchaux. This is a beautiful road if you like trees. It runs through woods for the whole distance, until it descends to the plateau behind Marchaux, the plateau separating that village from Champoux. It is a terrible road if you dislike pushing a bicycle up-hill. I was thinking that perhaps after all bicycle cleaning need play no part in the brave-new-world existence I was planning to build on the bravery of four young men in the Maquis.

"Boulaya," I said as we climbed. "We are coming back to the Vieilley Maquis, are we not?"

"Yes, indeed we are. At any rate you are, I hope. That is, if you feel that it is good enough for you, Émile."

"I think that it could be perfect. I think that we could make something big, centring on that Maquis, making that forest our headquarters, installing ourselves cunningly there. But we would have to fix the Frisé first. The men must not blab all over the Doubs that we are there, and they must not know our plans. We must be a little apart from the men, yet with them; and we must give them orders, not plans and intentions."

"You are right, Émile. I too have been thinking. Behind the château at La Chevillotte, the patron and I had a small hideout. There were two tents there (he used the colonial soldier's word 'gitounes'). We shall bring the tents back and establish a command post a little apart from the Maquis itself. I know how to make myself comfortable in a tent, for I have soldiered enough in Morocco to know all that sort of thing. The best thing is to dig a deep trough so that you go down steps into the tent. You then have enough headroom, and you are protected from winds and therefore perfectly warm. . . ."

He continued on this subject for some time, but since I had, like most men, my own definite ideas on tents (which did not correspond with his) I paid little attention.

"We could do with a man to look after us, couldn't we," I said, remembering the dirty bicycle.

"Yes. Someone honest, and intelligent and discreet."

"The last quality is difficult to find."

"Agreed."

We left our bicycles as before behind the mayor's house at Champoux. I wanted to carry my rucksack and "valise diplomatique" with me, but Boulaya would not let me.

"What do you fear?" he asked. "Nobody would steal a pin from us in the village, or indeed in any of the villages. There is a great honesty in this part of France." So we left all our possessions lying in the lane beside the bicycles. And the priceless bicycles themselves were left unlocked. Later on I was to become blasé enough about such things. But at this time wartime London, with its hurly-burly of sharks, foreign and domestic, was still fresh in my mind.

The path up to the Champoux Maquis worried me. It was an extremely muddy path through the woods, and no attempt had been made to disguise the tracks of the Maquisards. Yet it was not the type of path that would be used by anyone but Maquisards, since the woodcutters were not working at that time. It presented a contrast to the Vieilley Maquis, which had at least some security in that its approaches would be difficult for the enemy to find. This was due of course to Georges, the poacher. The Maquisards at Champoux were mainly townspeople, drawn there by the leader Jean, a "cheminot" and a Communist.

Jean's men had progressed since our recent visit to his Maquis. The horrid bowl in the woods had been much tidied and generally spruced up. There were proper racks for the weapons now, and the beds and shelters had all been improved. A stand had been made for the cooking utensils, and the ground had been levelled and cleaned.

"The big Berger did all that," Jean said generously, when we complimented him on the changed aspect of the place. "A demon he is for straightening up a place."

Berger, the tall swarthy man whom I had met as I left Champoux the last time, shuffled and hung his head modestly at such praise. He was a man of great strength, a law-abiding citizen, and a house-painter in civilian life at Montbozon, some distance, to the north, in the department of the Haute-Saône. I had heard about him from Maurice, at Vieilley. Maurice knew him well, because they both followed the same trade.

He had told me tales of Berger's strength and of his gentleness. Berger had come into the Resistance mainly because of matrimonial difficulties. He and his wife sought a divorce, but were finding it unobtainable under the rigid rules for the sanctity of marriage laid down by the Pétain government. Driven from his home by his wife's shrewish tongue, Berger had travelled south to take to the Maquis because the Resistance in the Haute-Saône followed more gangsterish lines than that of our contiguous department, the Doubs; and Berger was a very respectable man.

It so happened that I was interested that day in a pump at the station at Loulans, in the Haute-Saône. This pump provided water for the trains travelling north from Besançon to Vesoul, and if the pump were destroyed big locomotives pulling the important freight trains would find the up-hill journey nearly impossible. Since Berger knew that district particularly well, I asked him to go up and find out exactly how the pump was guarded and what type of pump it was.

We had carried over some explosives from the other Maquis. I gave Jean and his men a couple of hours of instruction before we ate. But here I did not get the same return spark from the men that I had noticed or imagined at Vieilley. Probably it was my own fault. I may have been affected by my repulsion for the mud bowl as compared to the slightly-antiseptic pine-trees of the other Maquis. At any rate the men were duller here. There was no Frisé eagerly hanging over me to pull the facts out of my mouth. I admired Jean Buthot as a man—he was one of the leaders of the Popular Front in Besançon, and he had done much to build up the first Resistance and encourage the young men—but I sensed in him a certain mistrust of me. Boulaya, like me felt, I could see, that Jean was a chief who required pushing. Like me, but secretly, Boulaya preferred the élan of the youngsters. He would always deny this, saying that the older and steadier men were the more valuable, especially the ones with military experience. That was only his French brand of Conservatism.

We ate extremely well with Jean and his men. They obtained everything that they wanted from the patriotic village of Champoux, and they spared no pains to make themselves comfortable. We were told, for example, that the Italian pugilist, Missana, and two others were away on a two-day trip. They had not gone to attack some railway or telephone line but to hunt for sugar and to spy out the tobacco situation. I contrasted this too with what I had seen of Vieilley, and I preferred the harder life at the smaller Maquis.

Since I was not smoking myself at that time, the tobacco situation horrified me. Under the occupation, with the absurdly small tobacco ration allowed by the Germans, almost every Frenchman had turned into a tobacco fiend. British men would have been the same had there been the same shortage, I knew. Tobacco became one of the main problems in the Maquis. Some cigarettes were sent by London in every parachutage, but not enough to make any difference to the general situation.

Later we managed to work out our own solution to the problem. But at the time of which I write, when the meagre tobacco supplies for the civilian population came into the tobacconists, these supplies, or parts of them, were taken over (or stolen, which ever way you like to look at it) by the Maquis.

Boulaya's solution to the problem was a logical one under the circumstances. He only allowed them to take tobacco from places at least ten miles from the Maquis itself (for both diplomatic and security reasons), and he insisted that they pay the regular price for all tobacco taken.

Even this solution appalled me, and every time I arrived in a Maquis and heard the fatal words "bureau de tabac" I had to fight through a coldness that shut me off from the utterer and his companions.

"More Maquis are lost through hold-ups of 'bureaux de tabac' than through contact with the enemy." I don't know how often I heard Boulaya repeat this. For although Boulaya was a swashbuckler by nature, he had a great respect for the law, and he often reminded his men: "We are the French Army in France, and we have a right to the necessities of life. Tobacco is regarded as a necessity in the life of a soldier, so we have a right to that too. But never forget that we shall be answerable after the war for our actions during the war. We must try to confine ourselves to military objectives. Every 'bureau de tabac' is a debit entry on our balance sheet." When he dealt with such questions I realised how lucky I was to have fallen in with such a man.

Somewhat bloated after our meal, we descended slowly to Champoux to pick up our bicycles. We were not looking forward to the long hot road to La Chevillotte. As we came into the village a boy ran up to us.

"Better hurry, and get out of here, messieurs," he said. "They've just arrested the *Brigadier* Chapuy."

"Who have?" asked Boulaya.

"The Gestapo, of course. They came in a big car to the Gendarmerie at Marchaux to find him, and one of the other gendarmes, stupid fool, told them truthfully that he had gone into Besançon. So the Boches just drove slowly down the Besançon road and picked him up when they met him. They've taken him to 'La Butte' for questioning."

"When did this happen?" snapped Boulaya.

"An hour ago. The mayor here was warned only five minutes ago by one of the other gendarmes. Capitaine Chantecleer telephoned Marchaux from the Gendarmerie at Besançon to warn them about it. Better look out. They might be coming up after the Maquis now."

"He's right," Boulaya said. "If they knew of Chapuy's work they would know of the Maquis. Damn him, I always said he talked far too much, that Chapuy. Did they make a perquisition at his home?" he asked the boy.

"No. Nothing like that."

"Good." He sent the lad off with a message to the Maquis to be on their guard and post sentries day and night, and a note to Jean asking him to warn Georges Molle immediately of what had happened, and to inform Gros-Claude, the schoolmaster of Rougemontot, that he must now take over Chapuy's command. "If they have not perquisitioned at Chapuy's place your money is bound to be all right," he said to me. "Madame Chapuy will have it well hidden by now. For us the best thing is to clear out while there is still time, in case they put the screw on Chapuy immediately and come for this Maquis, or the other."

"Will the Maquis be all right."

"All right? It would be exaggerating to say that. But they should always be prepared for these eventualities. They should be able to look after themselves. Each Maquis has men who know these woods better than their home villages. Besides, I doubt if Chapuy will talk. He is a hard case. And I believe that the Boche still has some respect for any uniform. They might not dare to offend all the gendarmes and Chapuy is a popular figure. They may not 'friction' him."

On this note of negative optimism we departed.

"What was Chapuy's exact position?" I asked Boulaya.

"He was in charge of this sector, the sector including the two Maquis and the depot of Gros-Claude, also another arms depot near Marchaux."

"But I thought you were in charge of all that."

"So I am; but Chapuy was in command under me. My position is really military governor of Besançon, and these Maquis come into my province. But as you know, I am a new arrival, I worked until recently in another sector, and Chapuy had the main command here. His capture endangers both Maquis."

"I wonder why they picked him up."

"Maybe because he talked and boasted so much. Oh," wailed Boulaya. "I could kick myself. What an ass I am! To think that only the other day I said that Chapuy was the exception to my ruling about gendarmes. But what am I saying. He *was* an exception. He was a fine fighter, and he has done a man's job for the Resistance."

"You don't think he was denounced?"

"Yes, very probably denounced. But they may easily have been watching him. He was proud of being a leader of the

Resistance. He was not wily enough. The trouble with these arrests is that you only hear of one at a time. Chapuy may be only one in a long string. For all we know they are after the whole bunch of us. I only hope the bridge at Laissey and the tunnel at Champlive are not ambushed.''

Boulaya scented trouble in the air, and I grew nervous from the extreme vigilance he kept up along the route. He insisted most of the time that I follow him at a distance, and he gave me some nasty turns when he inadvertently pulled out his hand-kerchief (thereby giving our danger signal), but only to mop his brow. He travelled faster than usual. Both of us were wet with sweat when we had traversed the dark tunnel at Champlitte, but both of us were much relieved to be safely through that sinister place.

From there Boulaya took small roads, tracks, and footpaths cutting south directly towards La Chevillotte. Some half-hour's journey from the château he drew off the road into a dark wood beside a pond.

"I think we should rest here for a bit and take a nap," he said. And he took from his rucksack a pint bottle of his father's splendid Marc. This was unusual, for he was a most abstemious man. "Something tells me, Émile, that we are in for a bad spell. I don't know what it is, but I feel reluctant to go on to the château. How absurd I am. Just think. In an hour or two we shall be sitting down to a beautiful dinner with highly-civilised people. But I don't mind telling you that I shall take peculiar care how I approach the château. I feel uncomfortable about things. Maybe I am getting stale.''

So many mosquitos persecuted us in the wood that we were obliged to give up all ideas of sleep, and we continued almost immediately on our way. The last few miles to the château were made in a series of "bounds", like infantry scouts working up to an enemy position. Boulaya's caution astonished me, for I was conscious only of being tired and hot. I intended to ask for a bath when we reached the château, and I was glad that I had a clean shirt in my rucksack. I thought that Boulaya was only nervous by association of ideas with Chapuy's arrest.

But when we approached the château we knew at once that something was wrong. The big building—it looked like an enlarged Swiss châlet, and had a disused hard tennis court in front of it—appeared to be uninhabited. All the shutters were closed, no smoke came from the chimneys. We stood in the wood and stared.

"I wish I had remembered to bring my binoculars," Boulaya said. "But perhaps your eyes would do. Have you extra good eyesight?"

"Fairly good."

"Then look carefully at the right-hand gate-post, and tell me if you see anything."

"I see nothing. But wait. It's only a small thing. There is a fairly long bit of white cord, or perhaps thin ribbon tied around the top of the post."

"Thank God we didn't ride up on our 'velos'. That is the danger signal I arranged with the young Marquis. We must get out of here cautiously.

"But where to?" he asked himself. "The trouble with this hunt is that you never see the hounds until it is too late. I must find out what has happened. We'll hide the bicycles here and I'll go off and see if I can get hold of the factor. His house is not far away. You must hide yourself carefully, and remain hidden no matter what happens. If I don't return try to get back to Vieilley."

"What about Albert and Paul? They should have arrived here in the truck yesterday."

"It looks bad. Au revoir." He shook hands. (I don't know why, I suppose he was thinking of other things) and went off on foot, skirting the edge of the wood. It was already seven o'clock. I was hungry. From where I lay I could see the château, but there was no movement there. It was a still evening. Even the leaves were motionless. And when I moved a colossal rustling seemed to fill the wood and move out in waves towards the sombre château and two farms further away, and then the big woods beyond.

A little boy came along the edge of the wood. He stopped a short distance from where I lay hidden and said in a soft voice:

"Monsieur Émile. Is Monsieur Émile there?" He was a well-dressed boy, with long curly hair and a petted mouth.

"Yes, little one."

"Boulaya says you must lie hidden. He will come for you after dark. Tom has been taken."

Evidently it was something serious. I took a good drink out of the small silver flask that had parachuted with me. About ten o'clock Boulaya came blundering along the edge of the wood.

"We will ride on without lights," he said. "We must keep

close together, otherwise you'll lose me. The news is very bad, but I think Albert and Paul are safe. The first thing is to get away from here while we can. Ordinarily, I hate travelling on the roads at night, one simply puts oneself at the mercy of any Boche who happens to be around. They wait beside a road and they shoot first and ask questions later. But it's most important that we should not be seen here."

Shortly before Naisey the road ran through a large wood. Boulaya turned left up a small path into the wood. We followed this path for nearly five hundred yards. It was pitch-black here, and we had to use a torch masked with a handkerchief to avoid bumping into the trees. We cut branches off some pine-trees and made a bed to lie on. Then Boulaya lay down and talked and held the light for me while I built up a rough screen and cover against the cold north wind. Tom, who had been caught, he told me, was the boaster whom I had seen in the farm near Naisey.

"You see what we get for being soft?" Boulaya said. "Yesterday was a fine sunny day and milord Tom thinks to himself: 'I'll just pop over to La Chevillotte on my "velo" and see how preparations are going for the English guests they're expecting.' So off he goes, accompanied by Jacques, one of the boys at the farm. Riding down the road that passes the front gate of the château, they are stopped by three men in civilian clothes. These men carry arms and they order Tom and Jacques to descend from their bicycles. They comply, but Tom seeing that the men are Germans, drops his bicycle and makes a run for it. The Germans have sized up their prey and they shoot into the air. After the third report Tom stops and puts up his hands. How typical of this creature. He had excellent false papers on him, and he had altered his appearance by growing a moustache and putting on weight. If he had stopped calmly with Jacques and shown his papers, all might have passed off well. But no. He has to do the spectacular thing and run for it. And then he has not the guts to carry it through. He walks back to the roadway, his hands in the air. The first German hits him in the face. The second hits him in the face. The third hits him in the face. Tom drops to the ground, moaning. The first kicks him, the second kicks him, the third, then the first again, and so on. A young girl rides down the lane. Her name is Marie. When she sees him lying there she cannot control herself, she releases a choking cry: 'Tom.' The Gestapo men take her from her bicycle. One of them puts a hand on either shoulder of her dress. 'You are working with this terrorist,' he says, and he rips her dress from the neck-opening right down to the hem of the skirt. The dress falls on the road. The Germans strike the girl, who weeps and screams. She falls beside the dress. Her father watches this from his house near-by. Most of the people of the village see it all. The shame of the thing. They arrest the young Marquis in the château. The servants are out, also the lady mother of the Marquis and one of his sisters. The other sister is there. They arrest her, though without mistreatment. They pile all the victims they have gathered into a big truck. Then they go to the house of the father of the girl they have stripped and beaten. Two of them hold the father stiffly in an upright chair and the third puts the barrel of his pistol on the old man's forehead. 'Your daughter worked for the terrorist, Tom. Tell us all you know, or this gun will accidentally go off,' says the man with the gun. 'I know nothing, and if I did I would not tell you, you swine,' the father answers. 'He is speaking the truth,' says the Gestapo man, and they leave the house laughing, without even hitting him. They are peculiar brutes, these Germans. Sometimes they appreciate courage, and sometimes it maddens them. Just as they are preparing to leave the château another truck is seen approaching. It is a blue-grey truck, and there are four men in civilian clothes in the cab. Some of the villagers think it is a Gestapo truck, but others think it is the Resistance. The truck stops to ask the road for the château. One villager comes forward and tells them the road: The Gestapo are at the château,' he adds. 'Then let's get to hell out of here,' shouts a man in the blue-grey truck. He speaks with an English accent. It is Albert. The blue-grey truck turns and hustles back towards Naisey. Just as it disappears the Gestapo truck comes and takes the other fork for Besançon. The villagers think the Boches left two men in the château.

"That is a reconstruction of the story," Boulaya ended. "And what a mess we are in. Do you see the whole tie-up? This is why Chapuy was arrested."

"Do you think so?"

"Think so! Why nothing could be more obvious. Tom would talk and talk and talk. He will have told them everything, and he knows nearly everything."

"And the girl they took? Was she really working with him?"

"Yes, that's the asinine part of it all. This fool, this triple idiot was actually carrying on a clandestine correspondence with his own wife. With his wife; could anything be more dangerous? And the girl was the go-between. It was she who carried the letters. First he goes to Mass on Sundays, next he writes letters to his wife, and of course he has to put an address on top of his letters. He does not put the address where he is staying. Oh no, he is too cunning for that. He simply puts 'Château de la Chevillotte'. Then, culminating idiocy, he has to go there himself on a bicycle. Here is our whole organisation gravely threatened by this lunatic, this weakling, this 'fumier'."

"Thank God Albert was not taken."

"Yes, but what will he think of us, Albert? He will think we invited him to a trap. I guaranteed the château. It seemed as safe as anywhere. It's always like that. But Albert will be mad. We must get a message to him. We must get messages to everybody. The poor 'patron'. Tom knows all his addresses, knows even the house of Père Janet on the outskirts of Besançon, where the patron is staying now. What are we going to do?"

That was the question. We talked it over from all angles. I had never seen this Boulaya before. But then I had not had the experience of seeing forty-five of my comrades arrested by the Gestapo. He took a most gloomy view of everything. He had intended to return with me to Vieilley after seeing Albert, then to leave me in charge of the Maquis operations and move himself to Besançon or to the west or south of Besançon. Now he was certain that the enemy would obtain from Tom full details of all his haunts, of the houses where he spent a night here and there, of the places where he stopped to eat.

"Did Tom know the exact locations of the two Maquis?" I asked.

"No, but he knew that they were near Vieilley and Champoux."

"Did he know of Georges Molle? And the Marquis house in Vieilley?"

"No, I don't think so. He knew Chapuy. And the Gestapo know of Molle already."

"Did he know of the Père Letallec's hotel at Rigney, and of your association with the Dardels?"

"He knew of the hotel at Rigney. Not of the Dardels."

"Then it seems to me there is only one answer. You must

come back with me to Vieilley and we will go ahead with our plans there. You will probably have to live all the time in the Maquis now until the end of the war in France, since we have the bad luck to find ourselves in what will probably be the last bit of France to be liberated."

"Maybe you are right. But it seems to me, Émile, that we shall need all our luck to get back to Vieilley. The Boche is sure to be jubilant at getting Tom. He will be on the watch. Anyway, we must sleep on it and see what we can think up in the morning. I'm hungry."

"So am I."

"That farm we passed—you saw the light just before we entered this wood—there are friends there. Only it was the first farm that Tom stayed in. Perhaps it is watched. We'll see in the morning."

It was a noisy night, with a strong wind and much barking of dogs and ringing of cow-bells. We slept with the tension of men who imagine themselves in danger. And at six o'clock in the morning, chilled and hungry, we stole across the fields to the farm. The fields were full of beautiful mushrooms. I ate a handful of them as we walked. My trousers were soaked to above the knees by the copious dew. There was a massive and ferocious "loup" dog in the farm-yard. He was attached on ten feet of chain to an overhead wire, which gave him the run of the yard. Boulaya's swashbuckling walk carried him safely past this monster, but it went so far as taking the heel of my shoe between its teeth, and I was thankful to reach the safety of the house. There was a tall, fair girl inside. She knew Boulaya and she gave us a lot of food, not only bread and butter and cheese and wheat coffee, but ham and sausage and bread to carry away with us. She showed me the walls of the kitchen, which, she told me, Tom had painted when he was hiding there. She spoke well of him, and I thought she must have been slightly in love with him. There was a rumour that Tom had escaped.

"Huh. Tom. Not likely," was Boulaya's comment.

We chose a place on the map, a corner of a forest, for a rendezvous and I cycled on alone there, passing through Naisey on the way. Boulaya was going to make some calls, and get warning messages out to the F.F.I. He calculated that Tom's arrest put some fifty people in grave danger. It was early to be on the roads, and I arrived in the forest having seen nobody, except a few people waiting for a funeral in Naisey itself.

Among them was Plançon, the wine merchant, a great bunch of wild flowers in his coarse hands. We affected not to see each other.

Carefully hiding my bicycle so that even I could not see it from a few feet away, I made myself a kind of miniature clearing, surrounded by low dense bushes. On the ground of the clearing I spread moss and on top of the moss a layer of clothes. Then, stark naked, I lay down to sunbathe. It was only nine o'clock when I lay down, and I did not expect Boulaya to arrive before one or two in the afternoon. But sun has a bigger vitalising effect upon me than alcohol or foods. And I felt that it might be my last opportunity to take any sun. A few feet away from my head as I lay was the small road leading north from Naisey. It was the road that I expected Boulaya to arrive on. And it was now streaming with country people dressed up in their Sunday best and carrying flowers. They were people from Bouclans, the next village, going to the funeral at Naisey. They rode in farm-carts or buggies or on bicycles. Occasionally, a car passed too, but I let the sun dope me, and put the Gestapo right out of my thoughts. Finally, even the spiders and ants failed to keep me awake.

Boulaya, tunefully whistling some bars from *La Boheme* (he was so security-conscious that he had changed operas), awoke me. I put on some clothes before calling him over to my hiding-place.

"God, you are brown," he said. He had brought me a picnic lunch from Naisey, and he was in high spirits for no reason whatsoever except his mercurial temperament, for he disliked the hot sunshine, and the news was bad.

"Tom has given to the Gestapo descriptions of both of us and certainly many others as well," he said. "The Boche made enquiries about us two in Naisey yesterday. They visited chez Plançon, but they got nothing out of the old boy, except a bottle of his worst wine. I have sent off messages all round, and I now see only two courses open. First: we go to Bouclans, hide up with the Curé there, who is a really splendid fellow; and at night we go to the arms dump on the other side of Naisey and try to organise its removal. Second: we go straight back to Vieilley, and hide in the Maquis there. What do you think?"

"We should go to Vieilley."

"Right. But it means sacrificing the Naisey arms dump. Tom is sure to give it."

"We can get more arms, but we cannot get new skins and bones. It should be healthier on the other side of the Doubs."

"Right, Émile. And by the way, Tom has described us rather fully. Don't take your beret off on the roads. That beautiful blond hair is too conspicuous. And better hide your leather jacket in your rucksack."

Once more we safely traversed the cold tunnel at Champlive, but the bridge below it at Laissey was guarded. Boulaya's caution saved us from attempting to cross. Spying from the woods one hundred yards from the bridge, he saw a militian stroll out from the far side, spit into the swiftly-flowing Doubs, and retire again into the shadows. So we turned and rode up-river on small tracks. The next bridge was not guarded. A boat-load of young girls had passed underneath just before we crossed. They were squeaking with laughter at each other's rowing and letting their hands trail languidly in the brown water. They were well-dressed children. Boulaya had noticed them too.

"The summer holidays have begun," he said. It seemed almost incredible that such things still went on. They came from the château stuck among yew-trees by the river-side above the bridge. As we rode past the château garden a tall woman appeared with a long basket of picked flowers. She looked cool and clean and competent, just like any other woman doing the flowers. She was within easy hailing distance and I wanted to ask her for a glass of water. But I remembered that I was covered in dust, that my clothes were crumpled, that I had not shaved that morning, that I had an English accent, and that we did not know the lady's sympathies. We climbed up out of the Doubs valley with parched throats, and at the first village both Boulaya and myself flung ourselves on the trickling fountain which the Germans had condescendingly tested and marked "Trinkwasser".

We made a big circle to get back to Vieilley, for Boulaya wished to pass by Rougemontot to see Gros-Claude, the young schoolmaster-airman. We found his house shut, and the neighbours told us sourly that he did not live there any more. But the mayor, who knew Boulaya, came to the edge of the hamlet with us, and said that if we wanted we would certainly find Gros-Claude with the schoolmistress at Cendrey.

"Mademoiselle is Parisian, and *extremely* gay and attractive," he told us with a wink. "Many of the Schleuhs would like to get their hooks on her, but she is a true Frenchwoman, and they say affianced to Gros-Claude."

Boulaya made a fierce gesture at this, and I thought he was angry at Gros-Claude's way of passing an afternoon. But I was wrong.

"You cannot keep young men away from women all the time, Émile," he said. "Nor can you blame them for finding complete continence impossible. But it does complicate the Resistance. Talkativeness is the curse of our race. At least it is a curse while there is secret work to be done. And a young man will always talk too much to his woman in order to impress her."

"Then it was the word 'Schleuhs' that annoyed you?"

"Yes. That word maddens me when it is applied to the Boche. The true Schleuh fought fiercely and well against us French until we conquered him. But now he fights equally well for us. He is a fine person. I would not have him disgraced by this link with the Boches."

It was late when we rode into Vieilley, and we were weary. We had been sorely tempted to stop at the hospitable station hotel at Rigney, but Boulaya refused to take the risk. We ate some food with the Marquis, who said that all appeared to be quiet around, except that some Maquis had shot up the "bureau de tabac" at the village of La Bretenière the previous day.

"Not this Maquis, I'll be bound," said the thin daughter, Camille. "Here they're a decent bunch of lads. Only that Frisé is a bit wild, and he's got a good heart in him."

We refused the Marquis family's pressing offer of the beds we had occupied once before.

"No beds for me from now on," Boulaya vowed. "I shall be much happier sleeping in the woods. A village or a house is too easy to surround."

"Do you think it was the Champoux Maquis that did the 'bureau de tabac'?" I asked him as we walked up the hill behind Vieilley. "They were out of tobacco the last time we were there."

"I know it was," he answered. "As a matter of fact, I knew it already. The mayor of Rougemontot told me about it, but I was ashamed, and I thought I would keep it from you. It was Missana and two or three others. The tobacconist refused to let them in, so they fired a few rounds into the place. They got away with a good deal of tobacco and many packets of cigarettes, the devils."

Georges was still with the Maquis when we arrived. They were sitting round the dying embers of a big log fire in the reconstituted "dining-room", a hollow where the trees were big and wide-spaced before they ended in the fields at the side of this tongue of the forest. They were handing round a bottle of "la goutte" which Buhl had brought back from his home. Perhaps it was the alcohol that made Buhl particularly talkative, perhaps jealousy because the "plaques-tournantes" coup had been done without him.

"I could have told you that it was not worth while doing the 'plaques'," he said to me. "One of them is already working by hand. All Besançon is saying the charges were too small."

"That is a lie, and nobody will repeat it in front of me." It was the Frisé who had spoken. Now he glared round the small circle crouched by the fire. "The second charge was badly placed. We were flustered and we did not take the necessary time. Is that not so, Maurice?"

"That is the truth."

"And if any 'couillon' thinks he could do better than we did, let him step forward," said the Frisé. Nobody moved.

"But tomorrow I hope we shall do something more important than the 'plaques'," I said.

"More important than the 'plaques'!" They had expected the attack on the 'plaques' to be a nine-day talking wonder before anything more was attempted.

"Steady, Émile. We ought to sound out the situation with regard to Tom's disclosures," Boulaya said.

"Best to lie low for a bit after the 'plaques' and give the depot time to settle down," said the cautious Georges.

"Can you take me into Besançon tomorrow morning, Frisé?" I asked.

"Sure. I'll take you in your uniform, sword, medals and all if you like. I'll show you the whole town. I'll . . ."

"If you lose Émile with your madness, I'll skin you alive," Boulaya interrupted. "Now we must all go to bed. Is there any more of 'la goutte' in that bottle? It takes the tiredness from my bones. Remember, I am not so young as any of you. Well, not quite anyway.

"Oh, and Georges, before you go away to sleep by yourself, I must go over the hill to the other Maquis tomorrow morning, first thing. To give them hell. It was Missana who did the 'bureau de tabac' at La Bretenière.

"Oh, and I must take one man with me. There will be a lot of tobacco and cigarettes to bring back. Since the job is done, it is done. And the tobacco will come in damned handy. It's share and share alike in my Maquis. On a purely military basis. . . ."

CHAPTER IX

WE were lying under a shower of huge rain-drops. The shelter of small criss-crossing pine branches, which we had erected over our couch, served to keep heavy rain off for about ten minutes. Then it was wetter underneath than it was outside. Lying in my feather-lined sleeping-bag, I managed to keep in a steamily warm condition. But poor Boulaya was cold as well as wet. He lay beside me drawing at a crooked and yellow-looking home-rolled cigarette. Then an extra large drop fell on the end of his cigarette. It fizzled and went out. He put it away in a tin. (Later, when the sun came out again, he could dry it.)

"Merde!"

He was thinking, I knew, that there might be months of this existence ahead of us. Out-of-doors life is all right when you can organise reasonable cleanliness and comfort.

"I think I shall bring big Berger back with me from the other Maquis," Boulaya said. "And we will get Georges to look for a location for our new Command Post. Something a little distant from this Maquis. And we must try to build a rainproof hut if we can get no tents. Of course you will postpone your trip to Besançon today."

"Why? I might as well be there in the rain as sitting here dripping in the woods."

"I do wish you wouldn't go. There is no point in doing silly things just now. But if you plan an operation on the depot or the station I shall come along as second-in-command."

So I told him the plan. It was an idea that the Frisé had given me when we first discussed the lay-out of the station. In the very centre of Besançon itself the lines running to Belfort and Vesoul, to the east and north, as well as the lines to Dijon, to the west, and Dole, to the south, fanned out. I wanted to attack all the points on this fan. Control Post No. 3 and the "Bahnhofs" seemed to present the only difficulties. Opposite the fanning-out of the lines was the rest-room for the German railway workers, whom the Maquis always called the "Bahnhofs". These workers had been "injected" into the French railway system to make it more "honest and efficient" from the German point of view. Each of them was armed with a pistol, and we had to be prepared for trouble from them. And near the fanning-out, but on the other side of the lines from the "Bahnhofs", was Control Post No. 3, where there was always at least one pointman on duty.

This pointman would not presumably be antagonistic to us, since he would be an ordinary "cheminot". But he was dangerous in that he was in constant telephone communication with the depot, and if he was excited or frightened the people at the other end of the line would know from his voice that something was going wrong at the Control Post.

The German guards from the Besançon "Feldgendarmerie" had been stiffened around and in the depot since the attack on the "plaques-tournantes", and extra German patrols with Alsatian police dogs were seen occasionally in the station itself.

"We shall probably need you to go and reason with the man in Control Post No. 3," I told Boulaya. "To reason with him by means of a Sten 'mitraillette' of course, but at the same time it requires somebody who can keep absolutely calm himself, and talk smoothly and fast so that the pointman can continue to give the right answers on the telephone with the minimum of hold-up."

Everything was so wet that it was impossible to light a fire for breakfast. In some ways the lack of forethought of these people was simply staggering. Although rain had seemed possible when we went to bed, they had not bothered to protect bread or sugar or firewood against a possible soaking.

"Yes, indeed," Boulaya said, sadly facing a cold and breakfastless morning. "This Maquis needs a little discipline and organisation."

They dressed me up in workman's "blues" to go to Besançon, and we set off, the Frisé, Maurice, and I, as soon as our bicycle-tyres were pumped up. We took the track leading from the fields beside our wood to the village of Merey. The Maquis lay roughly between the two villages of Vieilley and Merey, although it was farther up the hill than either of them. Farther downhill, in the valley and beside a magnificent clump of tall pine-trees lay the small railway station of Merey-Vieilley. The four places formed roughly a square with sides about a mile long, with the two villages ending one diagonal and the Maquis and the station the other.

But whereas Vieilley as a village had a clean reputation from the Resistance point of view and was watched over by Georges Molle, the other village, though smaller, had two black marks, one doubtful family of Italian blood and another family which had relatives in Germany and which was reported to favour a German victory. Merey was supposed to be out of bounds for the Maquis.

Frisé led the way through Merey and then turned sharp left on to the Besançon road. He rode the small silver woman's bicycle that he had "found". He apparently judged it more comfortable to ride this machine standing on the pedals. Like this he advanced very swiftly in a series of rapid jerks, his tail wagging sharply from side to side, and the bicycle leaning over to the right. Despite the three speeds and satisfactory performance of my "Corsair", I found it most difficult to keep pace with him except on the down-hills. I already knew from experience that, while I could walk or run the average young Frenchman off his feet, he would completely master me the moment he mounted a bicycle. With Boulaya we had always sensibly dismounted when we encountered any hill which made cycling a strain. But to the Frisé and Maurice every hill seemed to be a challenge, something to be mastered at all costs. Because I was too vain to admit defeat by dismounting while they rode, I count that hour's ride to Besançon as one of the more unpleasant experiences of my life.

The attractive old town of Besançon, lying on a loop of the wide river Doubs, is entirely surrounded by hills. I did not see the town until we came over the hill above the small village of Valentin, and here the Frisé and I turned sharply to the left. Maurice continued straight on, for his papers being "en régle" he did not fear the German control post that was always situated at some point between Valentin and Besançon on the main road. Maurice had some messages to collect for Boulaya, and was also going to see some friends who knew the station well.

Twisting and turning through the narrow lanes of the suburbs, the Frisé led me down into the hollow of Besançon itself and finally turning sharply under a railway bridge halted beside the railway lines. I at once saw Control Post No. 3, an imposing two-storeyed edifice with the glass windows on my side covered with war-time blue paint. There, almost in front of me, was the great fan of railway lines, and on the opposite side the black hut used by the German railwaymen.

"Better not stop here too long," the Frisé said. "Just have a piss alongside the gate here, then we'll take the 'velos' across the railway to the other side. There are two plain-clothes men watching farther down, but don't worry too much about them. I know them by sight. They're French, from the Secret Police."

Carrying "Corsair" across the railway, I counted the "cœurs d'aiguilles" that would need charges. There were twelve of them. And that did not include the main through line to Belfort. I could see it forking away about two hundred yards farther in, nearer the actual station. That would take four more charges, making sixteen in all.

"Quite true," the Frisé agreed when I pointed this out. "I'd forgotten about them. But don't you worry. I'll do those boys while the rest of you are doing the others. I know the station so well that in the dark it'll be no trouble at all."

In a hairdresser's shop beside the station I bought a large pipe and a tobacco-pouch. These were presents for Boulaya. I planned to seduce him from his love for the star-spangled pipe. A militian and a German were having their hair cut. They were agreeing in French that the Americans would have to give up trying to take the Cherbourg Peninsula and that all the Allied bridge-head would soon be non-existent. To my horror the Frisé joined in this conversation.

"Heard the latest 'rumours' on the Allied radio?" he asked.

"What's that?" answered the militian, screwing round his head to look at the interrupter.

"The Anglo-Saxons are planning to land eight million men between Marseilles and Nice," lied the Frisé.

"Liars. All lies, lies, lies," said the German. "Just filthy propaganda. You French people are too easily swayed by words." We left the shop.

"Stupid fool," I told him. "You must be more discreet, at least when you are with me. And remember nobody is supposed to listen to the British radio."

"That's a joke, Émile," he answered surlily. "Everybody listens to the British radio, the Stolls do it just as much as we do."

I ordered him to show me the rest of the station and depot, and asked him curtly in doing so neither to get into conversation with the enemy nor to mention my identity to any of his friends. To pay me back he set off at a great speed and paraded me through almost every main street in the town. I was obliged to follow him, for I did not know my own way about. Occasionally he would stop, point in the conspiratorial manner at a large building and say: "La Geste" or "Feldkomandantur". To add to his other accomplishments he spoke a few words of German, and he enjoyed shouting "Guten Tag" at every German he saw on the pavement. There were many of them. Some wore naval uniforms, and I noticed a large number of smart young Marines. Finally, the Frisé ended our parade in the small café where they had waited for the attack on the "plaques-tournantes". From the upper window I was able to see that one "plaque" was indeed being worked by hand-gear, and they were fitting a new electric motor to it. The other appeared to be abandoned. The "plaques" were now well guarded. I saw five or six uniformed Germans in the depot. Two of them carried Schmeisser machine-pistols, things I never cared to see (and still less hear) in the hands of a sentry.

Maurice arrived with his information, which amounted to this: There were two German patrols which visited the station and patrolled across our objective, the "cœurs d'aiguilles" at irregular intervals during the night. One of these patrols were Cossack, the other was German. The Cossacks were reported to shoot at everything they saw. They were quartered in huts not far from our route in and out of the town. As far as the approach and the withdrawal were concerned, we should just have to take our chance. Normally a German patrol made rounds immediately after the curfew at 11 p.m. and before the curfew lifted at 5 a.m. Sometimes, too, they put standing patrols here and there in the town. If they saw a man walking the streets after curfew they opened fire.

None of this pleased me overmuch. I had not thought that the place was so closely surveyed by the enemy. That was stupidity, for with three thousand and more troops regularly in the town it was fairly obvious that soldiers as competent as the Germans would have a good system of guards and patrols, if only to keep their own people in order. I was careful not to show any disappointment to the two Maquisards, but rather pooh-poohed the whole thing, saying "Good" or "Fine" each time that Maurice mentioned another patrol.

Then, asking them for a list of restaurants where we might eat, I selected the one nearest the Gestapo with an airy:

"We might as well have some fun while we eat."

There was something like admiration in their eyes as we left the "bistro". I had no intention of going out on all operations with the Maquisards. But when I did there was everything to be gained by making a good impression.

It was a bad restaurant, but there were table-cloths and waitresses in starched dresses, and the Frisé, to my astonishment, did it the honour (after five minutes of seated consideration) of taking off his beret. There was no difficulty in getting plenty to eat if the customer had plenty of money. There were several "suppléments", and these we waded religiously through from steak and mushrooms to "crêpes suzettes". Neither of them bothered about the wine. They were abstemious youths. But Frisé eyed so wistfully a golden-necked bottle of "Mousseux" going over to some Germans in the corner that I bought one for him. The price was 240 francs, and I suspect that this influenced the Frisé to pronounce it "first-class".

These two were Bisontins born and bred. They had spent most of the war in Besançon, and during much of that time they had been at grips with the existing law. They were able to show me many of the Gestapo as they passed in the street. They looked solidly respectable, these Gestapo men. Like successful stockbrokers or bookmakers who had toned themselves to a look of easy opulence. It struck me forcibly that they looked happy, too. As though their life were good, and as though it were permanent. They passed our restaurant without a glance. One did not eat well enough there. They often had women on their arms or in their shining cars. Most of the women were German importations. One of them had two Gestapo men with her, one on either side, and each turning a dazzling smile on her. She was a German girl in the twenties with a mane of corn-coloured hair and a strongly pretty youth-movement face. A brown pale-lipped face without a trace of make-up. She looked like a girl on holiday. I hated her.

Our stodgy lunch had toned down the Frisé's energy so much that he cycled like a reasonable being going back to Vieilley. Just outside Besançon he took me off the road and we climbed a cherry-tree, filling our mouths and then our pockets. It was a gloriously hot afternoon. My cherries lasted nearly all the way back.

Now the charges had to be made. Sixteen standard 1½ lbs. charges took a good deal of making sitting on wet pine-needles with only novices to help. And the only type of explosive remaining in the Vieilley stock was a kind we called "808". This was excellent stuff, but it had two drawbacks. It had a powerful and sticky smell, and when you handled any quantity of it you got a bad headache. Some people actually got sick. I said nothing about the headache, but got them to heat a sufficient quantity of the stuff in boiling water until it was soft enough to handle. With many complaints about the smell they got down to making the charges. To save material I put only one primer in each charge and sixteen fuses for the sixteen charges.

When the charges were all made up and sewn into little linen bags, Maurice returned. He had some messages for Boulaya, but these were put aside while I gave out orders.

"Please watch as closely as possible the way that I explain the operation," I told them before I began on the actual orders. "Because if all goes well in this Maquis we shall be using you men to teach other Maquis. Now, firstly, when you are giving your instructions (I jibbed at the Army word 'orders', it implied too definite an idea of status and discipline) you must never allow anyone to interrupt until you ask at the end 'any questions?'" This gave me peace for ten minutes, and I explained the whole thing to them in detail.

Frisé had to raise a point.

"Unless I am mistaken, you propose that we walk there?" he said.

"You are not mistaken."

"Why can't we ride bicycles?"

"Because there are only four bicycles. The others would have to walk. But I don't approve of riding bicycles at night. Bad enough going there before the curfew. But coming back after the curfew and with all the Boches in creation looking for us because the station has blown up. No."

"Couldn't you and I and Boulaya and Maurice go on bicycles and let the others walk?"

"No."

"But," said the Frisé desperately, "I will have to go on a bicycle. I can't do that walk again with my bad leg."

After thinking this over I agreed. I knew that he was eager to work, and that he was quite honest about his leg. We fixed on a rendezvous by an electric pylon where our path from the forest ran into the suburbs of Besançon. He was to be there at 10 p.m. "Not a second later, Frisé," I warned him.

"Agreed, Émile." And the Frisé went off to get some sleep while we prepared to leave for our twelve-mile walk over the hill. Just as we were leaving, Boulaya came up to me with a long face and a message from the "patron". The message said that Boulaya was appointed second-in-command of the whole area, and that in the event of the arrest or death of the "patron" Boulaya must take over from him. The message ended: "I forbid you to risk your life in sabotage operations at the moment. This is an order."

"You cannot come then," I said. Regretfully he agreed. With Georges at his side, he stood and watched us crossing the fields.

Maurice led the way. We were a party of five. As we walked towards the forest I looked at the men with me and ran over once more in my head the tasks they would have to perform.

I planned to approach the station by the small back roads, walking in three pairs fairly widely spaced and arriving near Control Post No. 3 just before the 11 p.m. curfew. There we would hide in a convenient private garden. At midnight we would move out together and do the job, entering by the gate which the Frisé and I had used to cross the "cœurs d'aiguilles" that morning. The men carrying the charges were myself and Maurice, who had six each, and the Frisé with four. When we got to the "cœurs" I would begin to work across from the Control Post side, while Maurice would first cross all the lines and then begin working back towards me. The Frisé, who knew the station best, was to go on up the line towards the station and place his four charges on the Belfort line points. The other three carried Stens with three magazines per gun. They were to dispose themselves with Buhl watching and if necessary interfering with the Control Post, the Pointu watching the "Bahnhof's" hut and guarding Maurice and me from surprise from the open end of the tracks, and Philippe was to go in with the Frisé and protect him, and at the same time our rear. I calculated that the whole attack should take not more than ten minutes, that would give us roughly twenty minutes to get clear of the station before the first charges blew. And it would take us about forty minutes to clear the suburbs and reach the edge of the friendly woods. We would have to withdraw by the approach route. I did not like the withdrawal, and I could see plenty of holes in the whole plan. I sincerely wished that it was all over, and I simply could not imagine what had bitten me, what had made me so determined to initiate the thing.

We had three halts of ten minutes on the way, one climbing the hill, another on the descent to drink at a well in the middle of a lot of empty huts, and a third at the edge of the forest. The second halting-place, six or seven empty army huts in a clearing, was called "les grandes barraques". I was to see it again later in more dramatic circumstances. At the third halt we were only five minutes' walk from our rendezvous with the Frisé. And we had an hour to wait. I made them all lie down, and Maurice and I put detonators on to the charges so that all was ready for the actual placing. We had still an hour of approach march ahead of us, and in England at the schools the teachers would have frowned on preparing the charges so soon, would have called it "dangerous". But it is remarkable how real danger, in the shape of a possible enemy patrol, will familiarise you with the idea of carrying around something that might by accident blow you into powder.

"And after all things are weighed up, being blown up by a 1½-lb. charge is probably the best death on earth," Boulaya used to say. "For one's dependants it saves cremation fees and it also saves coal. One is scattered to the winds in a single operation."

We thought of applying to the Church after the war for sanctification of this method. We might then go into business in opposition to ordinary burials and cremations. We would set up our business on a high, wild hill. The funeral cortège would wind its way to the top. The mourners would take up their stand behind blast-proof shelters fitted with thick bullet-proof glass windows. They would gaze upward at the bier. A formidable explosion, and they would gaze at nothing. Bier, coffin, everything would vanish into nothing.

At ten o'clock we were at the rendezvous, but there was no sign of the Frisé. We climbed through the hedge, and sat under the exact pylon that had been fixed for the meeting. It was now dark, but not pitch-black. We waited for an hour and a half. Spirits which had been reasonably good up to ten o'clock, sank completely to the lowest possible limit. All of us now had bad headaches from handling the "808". It is at such times that you see what men are made of, when you are cold and there is an uneasy feeling in your stomach, and all the worst part of the job to be done lies right ahead. Maurice, Philippe, and the Pointu were surly and annoyed, but they held staunch. Buhl, the self-styled leader, the oldest man of the four, was the one who turned sour.

"Well," he said at 11.30. "All that long walk for nothing."

"What do you mean, nothing?" I answered angrily.

"Obviously, we can't go on now."

"And why not?"

"The Frisé isn't here."

"Maurice and I can still lay our twelve charges."

"Yes, but if the Frisé isn't here it means he's been picked up by the Boches on the road here. With all that stuff on him. They'll know he's only one of a gang. The whole town will be watched. Even if he doesn't shoot his mouth off."

"The Frisé wouldn't talk," said the Pointu. "We're not all like you." Ordinarily the Pointu was the Frisé's bitterest critic.

"There is nothing to suggest that the Frisé has been taken," I said, although secretly I thought it might be so. "He has slept in at the camp, or he has gone straight to the depot on his bicycle before the curfew. Well, there is nothing for it but to go on without him."

"But it's long past the curfew time, and we've nearly seven kilometres to walk through the streets," said Buhl.

"What about it. We must go as a patrol, that's all. Maurice and Philippe will go ahead as scouts. I will follow a hundred metres or slightly less behind them. You will follow on my heels, and Pointu behind you. No talking. The scouts will stop every few hundred metres to listen; we should hear the Boche easily. When the scouts stop we stop. If surprised by the Boche, fire and fall back. Let the scouts come back through us, and give them covering fire. Walk only on the edge of the road."

We set off, gingerly at first, and then, as the scouts gathered confidence, at a rattling pace. Buhl behind me kept up a constant flow of whispered remarks. I pointedly paid no attention.

"Madness," he said. "One needs to be too well trousered for affairs like this. Why shouldn't we do sensible sabotage in the country? Let the Bisontins look after Besançon. It's not sensible, that is all I complain about. Throwing ourselves away like this. Listen to the noise we're making. Oh, God. A regiment of Dragoons would make less noise. . . ."

With his last remark I secretly agreed. I had already made up my mind on two things; that I would never again venture on a job with Monsieur Buhl, and that for future night operations I would insist on everybody wearing "espadrilles" or rubber-soled shoes. I had wanted to wear ordinary footwear to the place where the Frisé should have met us and then change into something more silent, but I had been over-ruled by the others who clung to their heavy boots. Never again.

After thirty minutes' swift progress we were in the town proper. And two policemen in dark uniforms, wheeling bicycles, came round a corner and face to face with Maurice and Philippe. It happened that we were close behind the scouts at that point. I heard young Philippe say something to the pair in his low, hoarse voice. At the same time he made a sweeping motion with the fierce muzzle of the Sten he carried in both hands, and the two "agents" dashed up an alleyway and out of sight. I heard Philippe laugh, and the scouts moved swiftly on, so I did not interfere with them.

Next, as we were gingerly coming down the last slippery hill between high walls before the station (I could already see the blue lights of Control Post No. 3) the beam of a headlight swung around the corner and a small motor-cycle came panting up the hill. An enormous man sat stiffly upright in the saddle. All of us flung ourselves face downwards in the gutter. The motor-cycle panted on, and stopped about two hundred yards up the hill. The rider appeared to adjust his coat, then he continued on his way. This reassured me. If the man had seen us he would not have dared to have stopped. On the other hand, he was almost certainly a German. No Frenchman would use a motor-cycle at that place and hour. For a second or two I actually thought of turning, I am ashamed to say. But I soon urged the men on, and we found ourselves by the spot where Frisé and I had first looked at the night's objective.

All the landmarks were clearly discernible as I pointed them out to the four men. But the station seemed a million times more busy and noisier than in the morning. This was largely due to one engine, which was shunting carriages and trucks about directly in front of us. There were three or four railway-men engaged on the shunting work as well as the driver and fireman of the engine. We saw the door of the "Bahnhofs" hut opening and closing fairly continuously, and Buhl, who had his eyes riveted on the Control Post, reported that he had seen a man looking out from there over the great fan of the "cœurs d'aiguilles".

I had no intention of keeping either myself or the men waiting too long here. It was bad for the nerves. My watch said 12.30. When we had tied handkerchiefs around our arms in imitation of the brassards of the "gardes-voies" I said to Maurice:

"Right, Maurice. You see your 'cœurs'?"

"I think I see where they are."

"We'll go first. Go straight across the line and begin working opposite me. Don't forget to wedge your charges against the V-shaped casting, either inside the V or, if it's blocked with wood, on one of the wings. Let's go and get it over."

We slouched into the lights, walked down the railway line, and with a brief glance around, I got to work. I felt for the first charge or two as though I were working on the stage of the Palladium. Then I got used to the lights, the noise and bustle. And I had all six charges down and wedged and initiated in less than three minutes. I stood up. Maurice was crouched over the points and working slowly towards me, his haversack holding the unused charges hanging in front of him. Philippe was far down the lines towards the station, leaning casually against a hut. Buhl, his Sten gun held along his leg so that it did not show, was facing the big Control Post, and the Pointu was lurking in the shadows by the "Bahnhof's" hut. But they were not isolated figures in an empty scene. The place was fairly busy. There were people moving about everywhere. Far from frightening me, the bustle of the place gave me confidence.

Maurice had finished. Good and conscientious workman, he was nervous about his work.

"Hope I've done the right ones," he said. I gave the whistle that was the agreed signal for withdrawal. Pointu, being the nearest, was with me first. I told him to go and tell the "cheminots" working on the shunting to clear off, that the station would go up in the air in twenty minutes. The lanky youth did this with alacrity, showing his "petrolette" a little more obviously than was necessary as he did so.

As we made for the gate there came an announcement from the control-tower:

"All 'cheminots' leave this area at once and return to the depot. This is urgent." And then, very faintly, the metallic voice added: "Vive La France." The men doing the shunting had chosen this method of spreading the Pointu's warning. Frisé met us at the gate.

"Where have you been?" I asked him, and followed the question with some vile French.

"I was at the rendezvous," he lied. "But this is not the moment for conversation. A Cossack patrol has just passed the railway bridge at the corner. When are we going to do the job?"

"The job is done, or at least our part of it. The charges will begin to go in fifteen minutes."

"Name of God, and me with my detonators not even attached yet. I must be off." He placed his bicycle against the wall, and went slowly through the gate fiddling about as he went with a tangle of charges and adhesive tape.

"Where are you going?"

"To place my charges, of course. Like to come along, Philippe, in case I need protection?"

"We'll wait at the rendezvous," I told the Frisé. "Philippe knows how to find it." I knew it was useless trying to stop him, and two men would do better for the job than a greater number. So the four of us set off on the long way back through the town. We had done nearly a quarter of an hour's hard walking, and were not far from the Cossack's barracks when the first charge went off. The whole town was in a hollow, so the noise sounded particularly impressive. There was a vivid flash too. From then on, at irregular intervals spaced over nearly forty minutes, the explosions came. As I counted thirteen, fourteen, fifteen, sixteen, I knew that the Frisé also had succeeded. And not one charge had failed.

The sound of machine-gun firing came from the Cossacks' place. We learned later that they thought it was an air-raid, and they were proving to their Germans masters that they were awake by firing a few bursts into the air. I was glad that they did fire, the noise sobered my men a little. They were inclined to get too jubilant, and too noisy despite my injunctions before we had started that the withdrawal was the most dangerous part of the whole operation, and must be performed in silence. The good suburbanites of Besançon were crowding to their garden gates to stare down-hill into the dark bowl, watching for the flashes. Most of them thought it was Allied bombers. This annoyed the young men with me. So much so that passing one house the Pointu waved his Sten at the inhabitants and shouted:

"Enough of this goggling. Get inside. And don't say that you saw us."

The people stared at him with amusement. A little fat man and his wife and four children.

"Would you gentlemen not care for a glass of indifferent wine?" asked the little man. And his button-eyed stare said:

"So it was you who did it, eh?" Stupid Pointu. When I thought of the boastful Frisé following behind without my controlling presence I went hot and cold.

He and Philippe did not keep us long at the rendezvous. We divided a small ginger-bread cake that Buhl carried into six pieces and ate it, drinking water from a water-bottle. First I asked the Frisé where he had been.

"I was here at the right time," he said.

"You were either at Vieilley, asleep at that time, or you were with your friends in the café in Besançon. You risked the success of the whole expedition and the lives of your comrades. Why can you not work for the others as well as for yourself?"

"Émile, I am sorry. I was so ill tonight. I had a dreadful headache. I will never do it again." He was nearly in tears. But he did not say where he had been. And he suddenly burst out in a suffocating snarl. "And don't let anyone say that I did not do my part."

"There was no need to shout your name around the station," said Philippe. It appeared that no sooner had the Frisé placed his charges than he shouted into the station itself (from where he stood he could just see its dark mouth):

"Stay in your holes, 'couillons'. There are sixteen mines in position, and the first man to interfere with them gets filled with lead. I, the Frisé, guarantee it."

"Another thing, Philippe," I said, when I had stifled my laughter at the Frisé's stupidity. "What did you say to the two policemen we met on the way in?"

"I told them that they had seen nothing, and that they were lucky that we had not the time to take their 'velos' and their uniforms too."

"But the 'agents' are friendly to us. You must try to be more polite."

"Polite to the 'flics'!"

"Politeness would be going enormously too far," said the Frisé.

We set off on the interminable walk back. The path through the forest was wearisome, despite our light hearts. I was touched by the obvious intention of the Frisé to make me forget his delinquencies. Instead of taking the road back he rode along our paths, and often held branches back for me to pass. But the discomfort caused by his presence far outweighed any gratitude I might have felt for such services. For the paths were often precipitous and it was dark under the trees. No fewer than three times going down steep places the Frisé fell on top of me, bicycle and all.

We hobbled into camp in the pine-trees at five in the morning. Boulaya and Georges were already up waiting for us with coffee and a huge omelette. They were jubilant, for they had counted sixteen explosions. I was interested to note that Buhl was now the most boastful of all, even outdoing the Frisé in his accounts of the fearless way in which he had conducted himself and the boundless assurance of success which he, Buhl, had conserved throughout the entire operation.

I was glad to see my bed under the pine-trees and to get into my quilted sleeping-bag and lay my head upon my leather jacket. This was the beginning of our offensive on the "cœurs d'aiguilles". An offensive which was to prove so successful that the "patron" when asked to choose a motto for the sector chose:

"Haut les cœurs—d'aiguilles."

CHAPTER X

BOULAYA was a skilful propagandist. He could get the maximum of effect out of our small actions. For he was something of an artist with words, and while he lived in the Maquis himself, he was able to regard the Maquis and its work with outside eyes.

Following the sixteen-charge attack on Besançon station, he began at once to send out his waves of propaganda. The waves travelled insidiously, slowly, at first. Then; gathering momentum and power, they swept on until they were lapping at the rocky base of German over-lordship of Besançon. Boulaya created his waves by calling to the Maquis at Vieilley leading men from different sections of the population, or by sending out to selected recipients carefully written notes and exhortations in his beautifully balanced handwriting.

At first I was worried by his propaganda. I took a narrower view of the Resistance than Boulaya. I wanted to have something manageable and compact, something that we could reasonably expect to control. I wanted to shoot at the Germans first of all with sabotage, to stop loot leaving France through our territory, and war material passing into battle against our armies in the north of France; and later I hoped to be strong enough to attack the Germans in guerrilla actions and kill them. Those were my aims. But Boulaya took a broader view. When I listened to some of his plans I was tempted to sniff. It often seemed that he was trying to erect a building without foundations. When he talked over plans for governing Besançon after the victory, I preferred to turn my attention to derailing the 5.20. Boulaya, although he was much too diplomatic and polite to say so, must have thought that my ideas were narrow. For he, like the talented Albert farther south, tended always to think upon grandiose lines.

He never spoke of politics, and in all the "Équipes Boulaya" politics were a forbidden subject for discussion. But I felt that the grandest of Boulaya's plans must be linked with politics, and I held severely aloof from them. There was a complete understanding between us about this, although we never discussed the matter. The line his propaganda took was symbolised in the report he wrote to the "patron" following our attack on the "cœurs d'aiguilles" at Besançon.

"The Maquis of Vieilley, led by the British officer, Émile, have today saved the city of Besançon from Allied bombing," he wrote. "This is the first aim of our Maquis, to make Besançon useless to the enemy and to save the town for posterity and for France."

This line of talk was the kind best calculated to attract the respectable people of that area. Already there had been far too much banditry committed in the name of the F.F.I., particularly in the neighbouring department, the Haute-Saône, where the worst offender was a madman named Sauvin, who preferred to be known as "le Diable".

"Le Diable" rushed about the country in stolen cars and progressed with his bands of Maquisards from one act of brigandage to another. Such actions turned ordinary Frenchmen against the Resistance. And Boulaya understood that to gain power he must attempt to make his own Maquis respectable. There was little but his own silver tongue with which to give this impression, although in point of fact we were respectable. And to our weird headquarters in the pine-wood respectable citizens began to make pilgrimages. Their arrival in the Maquis was a constant worry to me. But Boulaya always insisted that they were eminently trustworthy citizens, and all in one way or another members of the Resistance movement. Sometimes they would take taxis, and alight at the cross-roads below Merey or at the restaurant in Bonney, the next village, and then trail up through the woods on feet unaccustomed to such rude walking. More often they came on carefully preserved and polished pre-war bicycles with large bags and other receptacles strapped on them so that they looked like ordinary black-marketeers out hunting for food.

Lawyers, doctors, architects, business men, priests, professors, butchers, they arrived sweating in their pompous cityfied clothes at our haunt in the pine-trees.

This is what the first arrivals found. A trodden circle among the pines with a "floor space" perhaps twelve feet square and with narrow "alcoves" leading off it to our sleeping places beneath the trees. In this space would be crouching or reclining perhaps, if we were all there, Boulaya, myself, Georges, and the five Maquisards. Or at meal-times they would find us in the hollow at the edge of the pine-wood, squatting around an open fire and eating some kind of meal out of dirty dixies. If these visitors were thirsty they got nothing better to drink than stinking water out of our own spring. If they were hungry they could eat what we ate. Few of them were hungry.

They must have thought us a wild-looking bunch. Boulaya and myself soon got that leathery look of people who are never indoors. It rained so frequently that the mud seldom dried out of our severely limited stock of clothing, and often we had neither the time nor the energy to wash. To keep up the proprieties, both of us shaved every second or third day.

I tended to resent the sleek-looking civilians who arrived from outside, and who talked smoothly with Boulaya about plans for the F.F.I. when the "situation developed" (in other words, when things got easier). Often I asked myself why more of them did not emulate Boulaya and actively do something. The answer, of course, was that this area, being far from British airfields, near Germany and strongly held by the Germans, was behind many other areas in organisation of the F.F.I. and especially in armament. Georges resented these "outsiders" too, and he never ceased to warn Boulaya that this coming and going was certain to be causing dangerous comment in the area, even if the strangers themselves did not talk too much in and around Besançon about what they had seen at Vieilley. Often, fortunately, they did not realise that I was not French. When there was a stranger there I kept my mouth shut, and Georges and the Maquisards seemed to form a protective screen around me.

After the attack on the "cœurs d'aiguilles" the enemy made lightning repairs by cannibalising existing castings and doing some expert welding. I watched his repairs with interest, for I thought that they would show which railway line he considered the most important. And to our amazement he opened first of all not the big main line to Belfort, but the smaller line Besançon-Vesoul. This was originally a French military railway, but the Germans, when the advance into Russia began in 1941, had considered it of such secondary importance that he had taken up one set of tracks, and carted off all the material thus gained to build up new railways on the Eastern front. If he was going to concentrate on the Vesoul line the single-track line would help us a lot. And for sabotage on that railway running up the valley of the Ognon, I was perfectly situated with the Maquis at Vieilley.

We decided to blow up all the "cœurs d'aiguilles" from Besançon to Vesoul. I studied my Michelin map (No. 66) and made the rounds of the stations, seeing what points there were to be destroyed, then planning the attack, and sometimes carrying it out myself with one or two helpers. At first I moved carefully about the countryside, often after dark, and I travelled normally on foot. I was careful never to make too many attacks close to Vieilley. This obliged me to take to cycling again.

It was high time to relinquish my "Corsair". The new bicycle the "patron" had promised me was a large and handsome machine of a pale-biscuit colour, but it lacked the charm of "Corsair", and its name "Griffon" did not appeal to me. Maurice rode "Corsair" away to Dôle, with my first messages for Albert since the fiasco at La Chevillotte.

Mounted on the new machine I began to make longer sabotage expeditions, nearly always accompanied by one of the Maquisards. The first of these took me north-east towards Rougemont, to the village of Cendrey. There I met the young ex-airman, Gros-Claude, to fulfil my promise to instruct his Maquis and to look at his arms dump.

The dump, the parachuted contents of one Halifax aeroplane, was exceedingly well-housed in a small deserted toll-house alongside a road. Gros-Claude had a mason among his men, and with his expert help and advice they had built-in a deep false floor in the toll-house. All the material, in absolutely perfect condition, was hidden in this space. It made my mouth water. There were even a couple of Bazookas, and there was a fair amount of explosive with all the necessary etceteras.

Seeing all this shining new material in Gros-Claude's dump made me change my plans. I had intended to return to Vieilley in time for a derailment we had planned at Miserey, near Besançon. Instead, I decided to stay out here in the open country and do a job myself. It would be good for Gros-Claude and his men, I persuaded myself. They were a soft lot. Apart from attacking the pump at Loulans with hammers they had done nothing since the start of the war. Their Loulans effort made me dislike them quite bitterly; for I had sent Berger there to get me information and he had done it thoroughly, so thoroughly that I had even made up two nice charges, and I was all prepared to go and destroy the thing neatly myself, when news came through that these oafs had done it crudely with hammers. I had been looking forward to that pump. I found myself obliged, following the orders of General Koenig, then chief of the F.F.I., to restrict myself to rail and telephone sabotage. The more varied industrial type of destruction appealed to me strongly.

Gros-Claude took me back to Cendrey, where I dined and stayed with his right-hand man, a small foxy-looking person named Manien. Blonde young Madame Manien was there, and Gros-Claude's friend, the Parisienne, who was schoolmistress at Cendrey. Why is it that in France the schoolmistress is often the most attractive woman in the village? In England this is seldom the case.

While we made up our charges on the dinner table after a splendid meal (Manien was district chief of food supplies), Gros-Claude was able to bask in the soft and admiring glances of his lady. I could not help smiling at this; it seemed typical of women and the general idiocy of the law of selection for the sexes. She admired the young man as a dare-devil. He had not bothered to excuse himself to me for having all that material in his dump, and not one reasonable attack on the Germans to his credit.

I let one or two sharpish remarks fall, and I could see that he was out to do his best to keep up the flashing reputation he had gained around his home villages. He was a slim youth with snake-hips, which he showed to advantage in a short-sleeved shirt, wide khaki trousers with zip-fasteners at the sides, and sandals. The sandals, or "naked-feet" as he called them, were locally made on the black market. I was able to order a pair.

While making up the charges there was much talk about a certain Jacques Paincheau, the Resistance chief at Rougemont. I had already heard Paincheau discussed, but by Buhl, the only one of my Maquisards whom I disliked. I am too ready to take quick prejudices against men, and I had taken one against Paincheau. I looked upon him more as a gangster than a leader. I had even gone so far as to consider building up Gros-Claude to be chief of that region, instead of Paincheau. Paincheau, chiefly to cover his numerous Resistance activities, was like Manien, a chief of food administration.

Most of the following sunny summer day I spent lying reading a French translation of *Bleak House,* under a vast cherry-tree, in Manien's delightful orchard. At intervals the obliging Gros-Claude climbed the tree and dropped me down branches laden with the cherries, which were very fine, being of the type known locally as "pigeon's hearts". Big, sweet cherries, with a skin of cream colour mottled with bright scarlet. The rest of the day I passed more conscientiously in instructing some of the local men. I noticed that most of them were middle-aged. Paincheau had drawn off the better young ones to his more spectacular type of Resistance. I determined to have a look at this Paincheau, and I was to get my wish sooner than I bargained for.

On the previous evening I had cycled with Gros-Claude to the station of Montbozon, and had selected there twelve "cœurs d'aiguilles" as objectives.

We left to make the attack after an agreeable dinner with the young women, who showed a marked difference of reaction to our manly activities. While the schoolmistress nearly swooned with admiration, Madame Manien treated the whole business with smiling scorn, and I could see that she would be quietly glad when I was gone. Her husband, unused to such goings on, was nervous and over-excited. The other two men we took with us were reasonable types. A little farmer named Charles, and a regular sergeant-major in the Colonial Army. We were going to Montbozon on foot, a long walk, but there were a great many Germans in the neighbourhood and I judged cycling to be imprudent. All of us wore "espadrilles". The others carried Stens; I had a big automatic in my belt and two grenades. I carried the twelve charges in a haversack.

We rode our bicycles as far as the sergeant-major's house, where his wife, a real camp-following woman, gave us champagne with the toast of "Great Britain". Thus fortified we padded off in cloudy moonlight. I was getting so accustomed by this time to those night expeditions, and things had gone so remarkably quietly for us, that such work was beginning to bore me. And I was over-confident.

After Gros-Claude had got us lost in a large wood, and we had torn our way out through an almost impenetrable forest of brambles, we finally came to the station. The sergeant-major was to come with me to learn how to initiate and lay charges. I had planned to begin at one end of the station and work right through it, covering all the "cœurs d'aiguilles" en route. Manien was to linger behind us as rearguard, and Gros-Claude and Charles were to go on ahead.

I was bending over the first set of points and the sergeant-major, a most fussy man about small detail, was asking if he might strike a light to see *exactly* how I did it, when I heard running on the permanent way. Gros-Claude was in the act of climbing out of the station. I heard his clothing rip on the barbed-wire fence. There were some figures coming along the lines towards me. The sergeant-major got going before I had time to take in these details. We were working in a deep cutting with steep sides, encumbered with prickly bushes. The sergeant-major and Manien, panicking, were noisily climbing up the side. Manien, running to get to it, had forgotten in the dark to avoid the signal wire, and, blundering into this, had made a tremendous noise. The alternative to going up the bank was to retreat along the lines away from the station, but in doing that I would eventually be silhouetted to the pursuers, and the cutting got steeper as one went in, so that if they had posted a sentry or sentries further along, which seemed not unlikely, I should be trapped.

Cursing myself and still more the bunglers with whom I was working that night, I set myself resolutely at the bank. Speed was the object. There was nothing now to be gained by silence, since the other two were making such a noise. At the expense of a torn finger, and many rents in the workman's overalls I wore, I got to the top fairly quickly.

Manien and the sergeant-major were running hell-for-leather across a small field to the cover of a wood some hundred yards away. I followed them. When I was nearly at the wood I looked round. Six men, half-crouched and in open order, with weapons that looked like sub-machine-guns, were slowly crossing the field after me. Gros-Claude, Manien and the sergeant-major, all greatly excited, were waiting for me at the edge of the wood. The six men in the field began to shout "Kamerad" and "Ami" in a strange guttural accent. Tempted as I was to think this a simple trick used by Germans, I went back to the corner of the wood to have a look at them, and they did not look like Germans. They were hatless—that showed up against the sky as they worked over the crest of the slope towards us. Getting the others to lie down beside me, I shouted in French:

"Halt, or we fire."

The line halted for an instant and there was a jumble of confused chattering. Then they came shambling on. Ordinary Germans would never have behaved like that. They must be German deserters, I thought.

"Halt," I shouted again. "Who are you?"

By this time the six were nearly on top of us. To make them halt before they got dangerously close, I ejected the top round from my automatic, and this noise stopped them. They stood, peering in front of them, unable to see us. One of them now put down his weapon and advanced slowly. I got up and went to meet him, saying loudly as I did so:

"Keep them covered, my friends."

"Parle Français," said the man in front of me, ungrammatically. But he evidently did not understand it.

"Who are you?" I repeated. "Are you a deserter? Why are you not in uniform? Are you German?" I tried the last question also in German. He answered in another language, and then I made out one word: "Russky."

"They are Russians," I told Gros-Claude.

"Ja, ja, Russky, Russky," they chorused.

"Oh well," said Gros-Claude. "That explains it. They are some of Paincheau's Russians. Escaped prisoners. It must be Paincheau who is working in the station here tonight. I heard the strange language and took it for granted they were Boches." The Russians now crowded around and we shook hands warmly. From them I learned with our combined few words of German, that they were indeed attacking the lines of Montbozon that night. They invited us to return with them, but I declined. I had no desire whatsoever to walk into a dark station, where I might be shot or blown up any moment by accident. They followed us for some way, endeavouring even with threats to make us return to see Paincheau at the station. At last they left us sadly, saying: "Auf Wiedersehen."

"How does Paincheau manage to keep all those Russians?" I asked.

"He has them planted out in the farms. They are good workers. They work through the day and at nights they go out with him. He has had them for a long time. They are supposed to have escaped from near Strasbourg. There were officers too, but they have gone."

Charles, who, like Gros-Claude, had run away from the station, had failed to put in an appearance.

In a thoroughly bad humour, like a dog that has been robbed of his bone, I led the others back to Loulans, where, fortunately, the "cœurs d'aiguilles" had not yet been destroyed. It was a long walk back, and Loulans was a less-important objective than Montbozon. The latter station has a vital fork near it, where a railway leaves the Vesoul track to run up towards Lure.

It was nearly 4 a.m., and we had been walking all night through long wet grass in canvas shoes when we finally reached Loulans station. Like most of those stations, it was some distance from its village, Loulans-les-Forges, and it appeared at that hour to be easy meat. I left Manien to guard us at the beginning of the station, and walked right through it and beyond to size up the objective. I saw that with twelve charges we had just enough for the job, and I worked carefully back, laying the charges and initiating them. The station was a long one, and when I placed the last charge I reckoned that we had only about seven minutes before the first one would explode.

And I was right. It took a little time to get started, and we were only about two hundred yards from the station when the first charge went off with a most tremendous noise and flash. So big a noise that I wondered whether the American explosive, which I was using that morning for the first time, was not more powerful than the others. But I soon ceased wondering. For the second explosion followed the first, and a jagged lump of steel the size of my head and shoulders fell in the pathway in front of us. My followers, who had wanted to stop and admire their handiwork, now changed their minds, and we set off rapidly for home. By this time I was as accustomed as a Basque to walking in "espadrilles" and my feet were not tired. But the others were footsore and bad-tempered. We had a good hour's walk to face from Loulans station to the house of the sergeant-major, where we were looking forward to drinking hot coffee, and then cycling home to bed. The dawn began to come up slowly over the hills between us and Germany. It was going to be a hot day, and at that hour, between 5 and 6 a.m., it was cold and clammy, with thick ground-mist hanging over the wheat- and corn-fields. Our path ran through stiff walls of the precious grain that we had sworn this year to keep from Germany.

We had come on to a small, hard-surfaced road and were

evidently approaching a village (I did not know the road since we were not homing on our outward route). Sure that the work was finished, the others stupidly had taken their Stens to pieces and packed them away in a haversack. Ordinarily, I would not have allowed them to do this, but I was half-asleep on my feet. It had been a long night.

Suddenly, there was the noise of many bicycle-tyres on the road behind us and a loud voice shouted:

"Stop!" That was the actual word used, and the accent was not French. A wheat-field was on the right side of the road. Gros-Claude and I were the slowest to react. He flung himself in the ditch, and I did about twenty yards through the wheat, then flung myself flat, drawing my big automatic from my belt. There was a confused noise of shouting from the road. Gros-Claude was getting out of the ditch. The men were all round him on the road. I thought that I saw a German helmet through the mist. There was only one thing for it. They had got Gros-Claude, they would soon get me. The sergeant-major and Manien had already streaked across the field towards the wood on the other side. They had got clear.

Giving myself no more time to reflect I leaped to my feet and charged across the field towards the wood, expecting to hear a salvo of shots. When you are very tired and very excited you do not see clearly; and in any case the light was bad. Going all out, I crashed head on into a rather high and solid fence. I managed to heave myself over somehow and raced on. Why were there no shots from behind? Perhaps they could not see me clearly enough through the mist.

Next thing I knew I was falling down an incline so steep that I could not stop myself. What had looked to me like a wood was simply a line of trees at the top of this incline. I met some small trees on the way down, but they were not sufficiently solid to stop my progress, and I did not manage to catch hold of anything. My descent continued for such a long time that I began to think it unending. It ended, however, with my leaving the ground altogether, and for what seemed a fairly long time I dropped through space. Then, with an appalling noise and an agonising pain in my behind, I dropped into a clump of thick bushes. I pulled myself out fast, because I was still thinking too much about possible pursuit to bother about small incidents, such as precipices. Then I had to pull out the sharp end of a broken branch which had embedded itself in my person to a depth of at least an inch. I remember that I moaned faintly as I did this, for the pain was considerable. But the other part of me, watching my flight as objectively as a football match, paid little attention to the moan. It was already looking at the terrain. For the day was coming swiftly up, and there was little time to lose.

The steep bank, ending in a rock-face down which I had fallen, continued for some distance, and appeared to form the base of a low triangle of flat ground. Some eight hundred yards from where I had fallen, this slope met a wood which filled in one of the angles of the triangle. I decided to make this wood my first bound, and set off. Another surprise. I could barely walk, let alone run. My left knee seemed to have given out altogether, and gave me strong shooting-pains every time I touched the ground with that foot. However, I had to force myself. So feeling now a shade heroic in my wounded condition, and with a large and bloody flap letting air in at the back of my trousers, I forced myself to hobble towards the wood.

When I got there I had a further surprise. The triangle of ground was bordered on the other two sides by a river, so wide that I realised that it must be the Ognon. I was therefore shut into a comparatively small space, which would be easy for the Germans to search if they felt like it. I hid myself in a clump of bushes right on the water's edge. I heard a large body entering the river a little down-stream from my bushes. Peering out in that direction I saw a man swim slowly across the river. He crawled out on the other side like a great dripping seal. It must be either Manien or the sergeant-major. Whichever it was, he gave himself a shake, and then moved off briskly from the river and was soon out of sight.

The situation was a shade complicated. I did not know where I was. I had followed a guide all through the night's wanderings, and now it was difficult for me to decide where Cendrey lay. After some careful thought, I decided without much confidence that it lay up-stream. What was I to do? If Manien and the other had crossed the river, it meant that they considered it to be unsafe where I lay. And with this leg I should certainly need all the start I could get. But the look of the cold brown water decided the question for me. And the absurdity of my situation once I was on the other side and soaking wet. If it had been in the Vieilley country I should have been all right. But this part of the world was still strange to me. I knew only the sergeant-major's house and the Maniens' house in Cendrey.

So I lay in the bushes until seven o'clock. Then, having hidden my pistol and hand-grenades, and the haversack, I brushed down my clothes, fixed the tear in the seat of my trousers with a safety-pin and rubbed dust over most of the blood, and cautiously limped down a lane which led up-stream. I came first to an abandoned mill. Seeing a rusty scythe in an out-house, I forced the door with my admirable parachutists' knife, and took the scythe on my shoulder. Thus disguised as a culti-vator, I hobbled down the lane, expecting to meet a Boche at every turning. I had done only fifty yards when I made a won-derful discovery. I knew where I was. The sergeant-major's house should be another hundred yards down this road. It was.

Gros-Claude and Charles were sitting in the kitchen. The sergeant-major's wiry wife gave me a chair by the fire and a bowl of grain coffee.

The two men appeared to be fighting with some hidden emotion. It was laughter. When I told the sergeant-major's wife that I had seen Manien or her husband cross the river "à la nage", the laughter filled the kitchen until it shook the bright copper-pans on their hooks. The good woman herself laughed more heartily than the men.

"Who were the men on bicycles who overtook us?" I asked Gros-Claude.

"Why, Paincheau and his Russians. We shouted to you when you ran across the field, but I suppose you were making so much noise that you did not hear."

"What did you shout?"

"Halt!"

"Yes, I heard that. But Germans would have shouted that too. Then I hit the fence. . . ."

"Ah yes, he hit the fence. . . ." The laughter broke out again.

We took our bicycles and rode back by a round-about route to Cendrey. I went to bed in the Maniens' best room, putting a cold compress on my knee before I went to sleep.

That afternoon, just before I left for Vieilley, Manien appeared, scarlet-faced and very smart in breeches and officers' puttees.

"I swam the river," he told me ruefully. "There was no sense in waiting. The sergeant-major swam it too, but higher up. This man, Paincheau, is a menace, circulating like that with thirty mad Russians on bicycles." To make Manien feel superior again, I asked him to supply wine for our Maquis. It was a good time to get something out of him. He agreed.

I made the long hot trip back to Vieilley alone and with great difficulty, for my leg had stiffened, and it was all that I could do to stay on the bicycle. It was Saturday, a good day to be on the roads, because that was the day when the Bisontins rode out into the villages to try to buy food supplies direct from the cultivators. I was grateful to see Vieilley. When I staggered into the kitchen the deaf Madame Marquis squealed like a trumpeting elephant:

"He is ill, this 'sacré' Émile." They found that I had a fever, so they put me to bed, and wrapped hot and cold compresses constantly around my knee. After two days of the compresses and starvation, I was able to walk back to the Maquis.

But I did not tell them how I had hurt my knee.

I was surprised to find how pleased I was to be back in the Vieilley Maquis. The best thing about it seemed to be the air of energy and goodwill that it wore. Maurice was now being used by Boulaya chiefly for carrying confidential messages. The three youngsters were constantly on the move and were turning into real soldiers. Any of them was now capable of leading other men on railway attacks.

There were two new arrivals, Berger, who had come across from the Champoux Maquis to be bodyguard and factotum for Boulaya and me, and a youngster who had been brought out of Besançon because he could cook. He was an ill-favoured youth, with an unpleasant way of telling dirty stories, and I noticed that he made himself unnecessarily smart when he went out to one or other of the villages to buy supplies. However, he seemed to be a good worker and a reasonable cook. His name was Jean, but he was always called "cuistot".

Boulaya had been promoted to the rank of major by the "patron", who was pleased with our work.

Since I was not fit for some time to go out on expeditions, I busied myself around the camp, helping and encouraging Georges and Boulaya to get things straightened out. The first thing was to choose our new headquarters. And for this Georges had selected a resting-place fit for heroes.

Half an hour's climb behind our Maquis, more than half-way up the hill to "La Dame Blanche", the massive, square, empty fortress on the skyline, a band of pine-trees separated the edge of the main forest of Chailluz from the topmost steeply-sloping hay-fields of Vieilley. Armed with saw and billhook the four of us climbed up there and in one day Berger and Georges—both countrymen and experts at such things—had made a very reasonable dwelling for two people. The cabin was rectangular, about twenty feet long by eight feet wide. One of the long sides was open, and faced, through a screen of pine-trees, a magnificent view of the Ognon valley and the hill-lands of the Haute-Saône beyond it. The roof—made of stout pine-branches, covered with small branches and then with straw—was about ten feet high at the open side and then sloped down to four feet at the back. Boulaya and I each had a bed made by cutting an indent in the clean soil and filling the indent with dry hay scythed in the field in front. At the other side from our beds was a table running all the length of the short wall and made with old boards salvaged by me from the fortress up above. Facing the table were two stout chairs made by driving forked branches into the ground, and adding a seat and back woven by Berger with the stems of supple creepers torn from the trees of the forest. On the seat we packed bright green moss, taken from the rocks above the place. You stepped from the open side of the shack to a three-foot wide terraced path, which led to two exits and to a look-out post, from which we could watch the roads and the railway far beneath us. Georges made the entry without cutting a single branch. You left a path through the wood, cutting through some bushes on a surface of broken branches which did not show tracks, then down a steep bank, and then, winding between small trees, and into the pines. The other exit was only for emergency use. We made a zig-zagging path through the pines nearly a hundred yards in length. Near the end of this path were the latrine and the refuse dump, and beyond them the concealed exit. If surprised in the shack the long pathway would give us extra mobility.

We moved up our rucksacks and there we were, installed in a new home. Berger slept the first few nights on a heap of hay beside the shack. Then he built a smaller reproduction of it for himself.

When the other Maquisards saw that we were shifting, they too left their old beds in the alcoves and moved off to other nests farther from the main camp. We did not tell them where we slept, and they did not disclose their new sleeping-places to us. In this way the Maquis became decentralised at nights. For we were nervous. Even the Frisé, who knew no fear when the sun shone, or when he was treading the night with his heavy "chassepot" in his hand, was afraid of being smelled out in the dark and quietly surrounded by Germans or Cossacks.

With me this became nearly a mania after a night spent in a house at Montbozon. I was passing through the small town late at night, with Berger cycling alongside me. And, since we were both tired and the curfew approached, we decided to stop the night. The house Berger chose to shelter us was opposite the hotel. We had to share a room. But what matter? I had my sleeping-bag and the floor was not too dirty. Berger had just turned out the light and moved across the room to the window to pull up the blind in deference to my mania for fresh air and early morning sunlight.

"Pssst," he hissed at me, and beckoned me across to the window. I got up in the sleeping-bag and crossed the floor in it like a child doing the sack-race. The night air struck chill on my neck and shoulders and I drew back, but not because of the chill.

There were Germans in the street below us. One truck already stood under our window, and while I watched another rolled silently in, with its motor cut. The driver must have squeezed gently on his brakes, for the heavy vehicle came so gradually to a stop that not a stone crunched beneath its tyres. From the hooded back leaped a string of steel-helmeted soldiers. They cast grotesque moon shadows. They were the first Germans I had seen that made no noise with their feet. They had taken off their boots. Berger and I stood there not daring to move. A deep breath would have sounded like a tocsin.

Like grey ghosts the Germans ran to their posts, surrounding the hotel opposite our window. Two medium machine-guns covered the street. Every corner round the hotel was covered by a grey figure tensely crouched on one knee, and holding a short automatic weapon.

A car came ghosting into the street and slid to a stop beside the trucks. Two officers in steel helmets got out, and stood stiffly to attention in the middle of the road. One of the kneeling grey figures detached itself from a shadow and came across to them. When they spoke the hearer put the side of his big helmet up against the speaker's mouth. There was something incredibly sinister about the silent conversation. Like a man who wants suddenly to hurl himself from the top of a tower, I felt like emptying the magazine of my pistol into the street. Then I remembered. I had no pistol.

The two officers tiptoed across the road. Unlike their men, they wore boots. They stood on the steps of the hotel for a moment. Now three men in stocking soles had joined them on the steps. One beat on the door with the butt of an automatic-rifle. The door opened quickly, too quickly perhaps. You would have thought that the hotel knew it was surrounded. The electric light from the open doorway shone out upon the Germans. I saw that they belonged to the "Feldgendarmerie". They wore great metal plaques hanging on chains from their necks. They stalked into the hotel, massive and magnificent figures, as proud of their power as two Great Dane dogs walking stiff-legged towards an amorous conquest. The proprietress, shining in tight black silk, held the door open for them, shut it behind them.

Then we heard them searching through the hotel. Heard bangs, and occasional, quickly muffled, loud complaining voices. The lights one by one went on in the hotel rooms opposite our window. One pair of shutters was not closed. When the light went on we got a flash picture of an elderly man in a fawn-coloured night-shirt sitting up in bed, his two arms reaching out to the pillow behind him, as though ready to propel him out of bed. Two Germans stood in the doorway looking at him. One of them, an officer, read a paper in his hand, probably the police list of the hotel clients. The other German crossed the room and pulled down the blind.

"Can we get out of here by the back?" I whispered to Berger.

"No. And who knows? The whole place may be surrounded. If one moves at all one is mincemeat when the Schleuhs hide themselves and wait like that."

The search continued in the hotel for two hours. Both the officers, as they left, said correctly to the black silk proprietress:

"Bonne nuit, madame. Merci."

The door shut behind them with the suspicion of a slam. The officers walked noisily back to their car, talking normally. They jumped in, the car started, the engine raced. The two trucks followed suit. All three vehicles pulled out into the roadway and roared away, the noise from their exhausts gradually dwindling to a suspicion and to silence.

Berger nudged me. His finger was on his lips, but there was no need to warn me to keep quiet. I knew already that the silent guards still kneeled around the hotel. Sleep was impossible near that strangely-terrifying man-trap. I lay down on the floor below the window, but Berger stayed there upright through the night, until my watch registered five o'clock. Then he gently kicked my feet, and I got up to see the Germans silently forming up in the roadway. One of them counted the others. There were eighteen of them. Each man got out a cigarette. Fallen-in, in threes, at the side of the road they silently smoked. I made Berger leave the window, and I watched them through the vertical slit between the shutter and the wall. Their eighteen glowing cigarettes-tips were pointing at us, and I feared that they might see into our window. When all the cigarettes were finished, they turned right to a muttered command and marched away. The leader was now at the head of the files, and they cast only one square, waggling shadow. As they grew distant, they looked like a grotesque rectangular animal sliding away into the bluish moonlight.

Next morning I was thankful to get clear of Montbozon. The "Feldgendarmerie" had not found the person they were looking for in the hotel. And we never knew who they were looking for. But their method never left my head. And the memory kept me in the woods at night, clear of houses and beds and villages.

Every night then, after the cabin had been built, when darkness was falling, and there was nothing more to talk about round the dying embers of the fire in the Maquis, Boulaya, Berger and I gathered our things together. There was no water up in the cabin, so Boulaya and I each filled a water-bottle at the spring we passed on the way up. Berger carried up milk and bread. The long, stiff nightly climb up the hill took the last ounce of fat off me, and made me equal even to Georges in covering country and going up hills. Boulaya made heavy going of the climb, and big Berger, bronchitic and a heavy smoker, only kept up with me with a great effort, and much panting and sobbing of breath. It was usually dark when we got near the cabin, and we had to find the way in with an electric torch. Once inside we got straight to bed and last thing before lying down each of us took a hearty swig of Marc from a tin cup. With this warming my inside I could stretch luxuriously on the sweet hay and look at the sky through the pine-trees.

It was not only fear and caution that drove me up to the cabin every night. For the height and peace and beauty of our life there, seemed to make a smoothness in me, to smooth away some of the silly torments that were still hurting me like sharp quartz rubbing on soft skin. Torments that had been forced into me in London. Sometimes I thought of them as parasites, and I made up my mind that they could not breathe in the purer air that surrounded the cabin.

Boulaya felt the same smoothing influence of the nights there.

He used to tell me of his ambitions, the loves of his life, and the steady basic affection that tied him to his family. I could tell him no ambitions, of course. I had none to set against his. If there were any ambitions in me they were so nebulous that I could not shape them in words.

Big Berger helped strongly to create the aura of peace that surrounded our cabin. He guarded us, worked with and for us, looked after us with a steady devotion that never faltered. He was a simple, a strong, and a good man.

Both of them were heavier sleepers than I. In the mornings I could see the blue sky through the screen of pine-trees. Sometimes I would waken when the dawn was just coming up and the valley was still a misty, wonderful sea below us. Sometimes the "8.10 voyageur", the little passenger train from Besançon to our valley would wake me with its noisy puffing.

From the look-out I could only see the farthest roofs of Vieilley, the nearer roofs ran too close into the swelling hill-side. If the "8.10" had wakened me the peasants would be already on their way out to the fields, and the fires would not yet be lit in the village. The peasants were an hour behind the clock. They refused to accept the advanced "German time". Even at that distance I would know a few of the peasants. I would know the Père Marquis, for example, by the rangy brown mule in the shafts of the rake he was driving down the road to Venise. Soon he would fork left for his hay-fields by the little bridge, where the old road to Moncey, long since no more than an almost unfindable track, passed below the railway. I would know that "platform" moving out to the potatoes nearer the station. It was a fine "platform", with modern rubber car tyres. Its driver, Gustave's nephew, was a friend of mine, and his "platform" was ear-marked for more stirring work when the nights got long enough again for the parachute droppings to begin.

What a splendid view it was. Over the shining and rich landscape I was able to see traces of our handiwork. That black stain just north of Vieilley, for example, was where we had crashed the two trains into each other. An almost bloodless little victory. They were empty trains that we set roaring at each other, face to face on the single line. One of them was a train that carried sweets, and riding in the van with his bicycle there was an officer in the "Feldgendarmerie", a lieutenant. We took the lieutenant's uniform and his bicycle, a heavy, solid, squarely ugly, typically Third Reich machine. The lieutenant also was a typical Nazi machine.

The remainder of the cargo was more appetising for the country people, with their war-time hankering for sweet-stuffs. It was a cargo of rather sticky boiled sweets in cheap paper wrappings. The two trains met head on, with a noise that could be heard in the valley for many miles. For an instant the two big locomotives seemed to pause buffers locked. Then they reared like two caterpillars meeting face to face, and both trains rolled clear of the line (unfortunately from the sabotage point of view).

When the villagers in the valley heard of the sweets spilling out of the railway wagons between the stations of Merey-Vieilley and Moncey, they sent scouts out to the spot. And following the scouts came long strings of lean children. Children who had scarcely tasted sweets in their lifetimes of war. Many of them had come, unthinking, with nothing to carry sweets away but their two hands. Others had receptacles like buckets, or even dolls' prams.

When we successfully attacked a train or a station we expected always to see one or two car-loads of Gestapo on the spot anything from half an hour to three hours after the train left the rails or the charges went. But this time, by a happy chance, the Germans were slow in getting to the trains. And early the following morning from my look-out high up on the hill I saw more strings of children winding their way by the paths from the villages to the railway. They came from Buthiers and Cromary, on the far side of the Ognon. From Devecey, Bonnay, Merey, Palise, Venise, and Moncey; from Chaudefontaine, Rigney, and La Barre, the children came to gather like ants around the fantastic train that lay still smoking in the Vieilley wheat-fields. And when the Germans came to the wreckage they found no sweets.

So later, when I saw that black spot in the valley, I still felt the thrill of a Pied Piper and remembered the children. When I looked out over the thin black line of the railway, then the winding, willow-fringed Ognon beyond it, and the villages that dotted the valley, I was looking at my country. Not at a foreign country. At my own country. There was not one of those villages in which I had no friends. There was not one of them that was not identified then and for ever with my life. For the war had given me, if only for a few months, this precious thing; it had made me a part of the villages and their fields. It showed me the life of the villages. When I went into any of them I knew which women were "enceintes", and whose men were in jail.

When I went into their grave-yards there were many names that were living names to me, for life is steady, and does not disintegrate with the generations in the Franche-Comté. I knew which house would offer me tart to eat, and which would have the strange, runny, local cheese in bowls. Although I do not personally believe in religion, I found peace in their village churches, with the tiled onion-shaped spires surmounted with fine wrought-iron crosses. And if the only services I attended were funeral services for my own comrades, then I thought no less of the dead man because I knew the names and often the small vices and virtues of the women in the choir, and because the saintly-looking acolytes were also very naughty little Francs-comtois whom I had seen in the village gutters and sometimes in the woods or on and in the Ognon river.

I loved the valley and the villages the more because I loved no one person there to the exclusion of other people, and no one place to the exclusion of other places. As I cycled through the villages there were always one or two people I hoped to see, and usually one or two people I hoped not to see; for as I learned to make friends in the villages, I learned too which people were dangerous.

Most of all this knowledge I picked up from Georges Molle. He showed me the valley as no other man could have shown it. I have said that Georges was the most celebrated amateur poacher in the valley. It was only natural that he should be. He had learned at the knee of Phillipon, the finest professional poacher in the valley.

Georges, who was always cautiously poking and prying in the village, as well as in the woods and fields around it, gathered all the news and warnings of the valley. He was the scout for the Maquis. When there were Germans near he usually knew.

And Phillipon, squatting in his self-built bothy between the forest and the village was our outpost. The only risk about this was that sometimes the outpost would tap a new supply of red wine or spirits. Drunk, Phillipon was more dangerous than the Germans.

After surveying the valley in the morning I wakened Berger, and we breakfasted on grain "coffee", heated on a fire behind the cabin, and bread and butter. Boulaya had much paper-work to do, and I usually left him there while I went on down to the Maquis to set about my part in the day's business.

Sometimes, instead of going down, I would go up and over the hill alone or with Boulaya to work with the Champoux

Maquis, or over the hills for twelve miles by woodland paths to the valley of the Doubs, up which runs the important railway and road from Besançon to Belfort.

One morning, while we drank our coffee, we heard shots from the valley immediately below us. So we took our arms and cautiously descended through the woods. Georges met us outside Phillipon's bothy.

"Be careful," he said. "Look out."

A sharp report came from inside the cottage: a bullet crashed through the rickety door and whistled out into the fields.

"Come on," shouted Georges. "We've got to get him now, it takes him time to reload."

Flinging himself at the door, he burst into the place, and then staggered out, locked in a wrestler's grip with Phillipon. The old poacher was strong (for at sixty-five he still climbed the "côte" almost every day, winter and summer), and wily, with the wiliness of a man who has fought scores of drunken battles. And the liquor ran in his veins with a potency ten times stronger than blood.

"Whoreson," he spat, tearing himself loose from Georges and kicking him on the side of the head as only a Frenchman can kick. "Midden, spawn of satan. I'll teach you to leave an old soldier in peace with his drop of 'goutte'."

But Georges gradually wore him down, and at last he sat on the old man's chest, panting from his exertions, soaking with sweat and bleeding where Phillipon's kick had torn his ear.

"The station-master wanted a hare for dinner today, and he offered Phillipon a litre of his best stuff, 'la goutte' at over sixty degrees," he told us. "Phillipon delivered the hare at dawn today, and drank most of the bottle before breakfast. When he does that he gets out his citations and his medals. Then he gets out his firearms, the twelve-bore and the pistol. Then he unburies his water-proof package of shells from the strawberry-bed. Then he begins shooting. It's always the same when he has a drop too much."

Phillipon had fallen asleep with Georges still sitting on his chest. He was a bony little old man, who had once been handsome. The features were still fine. The long sharp nose above the drooping moustache, and the firm lips, stained with tobacco and set in grey stubble.

Georges took us into the hut and showed me the results of Phillipon's excesses.

"This was last month," he said, showing a patch in the door.

"And this was Hitler's birthday—he shot him sixteen times." Hitler's birthday was represented by a hole in the roof four feet square, which had been roughly patched with timber and corrugated iron.

Phillipon, even in war-time, had all that he needed, except that drink and cartridges were scarce. Behind the bothy he kept a garden which produced every type of vegetable and fruit known in the region. There were a few plum-trees and a splendid cherry-tree behind the garden, and alongside it (for his home was above Vieilley) was his own vineyard, which normally produced enough wine to last him for nine months in the year. Then, behind him was the limitless forest full of game and wild boars that nobody could kill so neatly as old Phillipon. He was a great cook, an expert on herbs and a believer in simple classical cooking. Many a fine meal I ate with him. For if I fancied a hare I only had to promise him two litres of red wine (three-quarters of a litre to cook the hare, one quarter for the cook while cooking, and one litre for the two of us to drink while eating). The same system worked for partridges, woodcock, and other delicacies.

Hanging from the rafters of his bothy was his best suit (in beautiful thick corduroy, with brass buttons), several hundred leaves of tobacco (grown in his own garden), strings of onions and garlic, and little bags of everything from dried prunes to eleven different kinds of dried herbs. When Phillipon needed grease for cooking or for his boots, he used the grease of the wild boar, judged in those parts the finest fat on earth.

He was thought in the village to be one of the richest men. Not because he had much money—he did not want money—but because he had everything that he desired. He had no wife, he had the "Croix de Guerre" and the "Médaille Militaire", together with the best citations in all the villages; he only worked for himself and he shot like a god. That was the main envy. The way the old buzzard found his game and killed it. Every man in Vieilley, when he could get the stuff to make cartridges or snares, tried to emulate Phillipon. But the wily old man always worked alone or with his "adopted son" Georges. He had his secrets.

His kitchen range was an old broken one, and it stood on the triangle of grass in front of the bothy. It had just enough length of broken chimney to take the wood smoke clear of the pots that simmered on the range. When it rained he carried the range indoors and cooked with door and window open. His tame rabbits for eating were kept in a lean-to alongside the bothy. But there was one by name of Lebrun, a black-and-grey buck with one lop ear, that lived off the garden. Phillipon had tried to catch him when he escaped, then had tried to snare him for two months, and at last, in admiration of the animal's intelligence, tolerated it around the place. Its presence occasionally exacerbated him, and in those moments he would throw at it anything that happened to be in his hand, even his "Croix de Guerre".

Later, on the morning of the fight with Phillipon, Georges came to find me. I was eating cherries at the back of Vieilley. There was a large orchard there, and the trees were individually owned. I was sampling the fruit of the schoolmistress and finding it exceedingly good, although cherries to be at their best should be picked off the tree when the first sunshine of the morning has just touched their skins and the inside is still chilled from the coolness of the night.

Georges, usually so calm, was bursting with rage.

"Are you armed, Émile?" he asked.

"No."

"Then come with me."

He led me round behind the village until we could see the gardens of the four or five houses on the south side of the Vieilley-Bonney road.

Two Germans in uniform were eating cherries in the orchard of the Contini family. They were enjoying the cherry-trees as much as I had been doing five minutes previously. Shouting and laughing at each other, and at stout Madame Contini, who was at her kitchen window.

"What does this mean?" I asked Georges.

"They belong to a party that goes through once a week to collect special foodstuffs for the 'Feldkomandantur' in Besançon. These two were dropped off as the truck went through. They are friends of the Contini daughter. They carried a letter of introduction from the girl."

I knew about that Contini girl. She had worked in Germany and she spoke German. She was reported to have had German lovers. Now she worked as an interpreter for the enemy in Pontarlier.

There were two Contini families in Vieilley. This was the rich one, and the bad one. The other Contini were cousins. They were called the "top Contini" because they lived in the top of the village, and they had a beautiful daughter named Maria, beautiful in a thin, mouse-coloured, un-Italian way. She was to marry young ginger-haired Georges Pernod, who worked to supply our Maquis and was going to fight with us when we got more material. The top Contini parents spoke with Italian accents, but they were more French than the French. They hated the bottom Contini family. I had kept well clear of both families. The name and the accent gave me the jim-jams. But they had done us no harm and I wished them no evil.

"That will be all right, then," I said innocently to Georges. "Nobody must 'descend' the Boches, of course. We must draw no stupid trouble on the village."

"Émile, you are my friend, but now I see that a foreigner is a foreigner. You say it's all right. Yes. From your point of view. I don't suppose the Contini will dare to tell the Boches what they know about us and even about you. Probably there is no risk there. But do you not understand how we in the village feel about this? The insult. Boches invited to eat cherries in our own village. . . ."

"Nonsense. The Contini woman probably did not dare to refuse them when they asked if they could stop there till their truck returned."

"Did not dare. How can you say that? Look at her smirking at them while she peels her spuds. This must be wiped out in blood—not the Germans, as you say. Contini blood."

"In blood!" Surely Georges of all men would not stain Vieilley with blood. He was proudest of all of the clean record of our Maquis. Contini himself was quite a character in the village. He was a dynamic old fellow, something of a ranter and a bully and one of the men who laid down the law in the café and the bowling-alley.

I was obliged to ride away to Moncey to pick up messages from the Dardels. Janine, the quiet, ultra-respectable daughter, had begun secretly to work for me, riding on her bicycle or on the trains to Besançon, and even farther afield. She was brave, for in thus working she had to lie for the first time to her parents, and she held deep ideals of filial duty. I stayed for lunch in the cool, dark room with French windows opening to the garden's lusty sunlight. I stayed and enjoyed the change of atmosphere that a visit to that house gave me, but at the same time I was worrying. Something serious had gone wrong in Vieilley. Feud was in the air.

I hurried back to the Maquis, and found that a terrible thing had happened. The "patron" had arrived.

In other circumstances I should have been delighted to see him. Now this blustering, fierce, old war-horse was the last person I wanted in the Maquis. He was already engaged in fanning the flames. Boulaya had taken the same view as myself. He had ordered the Maquis to leave the Contini alone. The Boches had gone away peacefully. It would be silly now to rake up trouble. We had no blood on our hands. We were not there to attack old people.

But for once the Maquis were paying no attention to his words. They were sitting around like angry wolves. Even my friend Georges. Maurice had an incendiary in his hands. It was a fine incendiary, one of my most treasured possessions. It was the only one I had, and I was keeping it for something special like the petrol and ether refinery at Roches, on the banks of the Doubs, or a train of carburant.

"What are you doing with my incendiary?" I asked him sharply.

"We were hoping to use it on the Contini house, Émile, but Boulaya says no."

"I refuse to allow it to be wasted on a miserable farm. Put it back in the chest." He slouched away.

"Émile is right," the patron said approvingly. "Much better to go for this Contini and teach him a physical lesson he will never forget."

"I did not advocate that either," I told them. "This is none of my business. I have never interfered before in something that concerned only French people. Now I would beg of you not to bring violence to Vieilley. The Germans follow always in the train of violence. If you begin that sort of thing you will pay for it in blood."

"Agreed," said Boulaya.

But the "patron" took his old pipe from his mouth and spat into the embers until they sizzled. The Maquisards waited for him to speak, for they knew that he would say what they wanted.

"Go to his house tonight, Maurice. Take him outside and give him a beating up that he will never forget."

"But that is hooliganism," I protested. "Surely that is not justice. There is something messy about it. Much better to leave him entirely alone or execute him cleanly. . . ."

It began to rain heavily, and I hoped that this would damp their enthusiasm. Not so. That night, when Boulaya, the "patron", Georges and myself were walking through torrential

217

rain to Georges' barn to sleep in the hay, I saw a party from the Maquis cutting across the fields towards Contini's house. They were all there. Even the "cuistot" and Berger. Fortunately the blood-thirsty Frisé was away on a job. Lying in the big barn, itching in hay that was full of fleas and ants and mice, another sound bit into the noise of the rain on the old roof, it was the sound of a fusillade of shots. The fusillade ended with one whole Sten magazine fired in one burst. Justice had been done.

Next day we learned what had happened.

Maurice had knocked on the Contini door. Old Contini leaned out of a first-floor window. "What you want, young man?" Maurice asked for shelter for the night—said he had come from Besançon with an introduction from a mutual friend. Contini did not believe this, apparently. "Come back tomorrow morning," he said. Maurice lost patience. "Come out of your house, collaborator, or we will burn the whole place and roast you inside," he cried. "So that is your game," replied the Italian, and before Maurice could step back from the doorway the old man had fired once at him with a small pistol, and missed. All the Maquisards grouped around the house now fired one or two rounds at the lighted window. Finally, young Philippe let a whole magazine spray into the room where Madame Contini lay screaming below the table and Contini himself lay beneath the window-sill. Contini was bleeding from a terrible stomach wound when the firing ceased. But it was self-inflicted. For he had intended to throw a home-made grenade into the road. He had made this grenade for such an emergency with "terrorists" by filling a stout piece of lead pipe with black powder and sealing a length of fuse into one end. But his seal was imperfect. When he lit the fuse with his cigarette-lighter some black powder trickled down the fuse and the grenade exploded against his own stomach.

Everybody was pleased with this result except Boulaya and myself. The villagers went about saying that it had been well done. The old man had been taken away to hospital in Besançon. He was in agony. He would die. The Contini house was empty now, and its prim, two-storey, pink stucco front was splashed with bullet-holes.

The Maquis thought that Contini's miniature pistol and home-made grenade had put them in the right. Old fire-brands like Phillipon were not slow with their congratulations.

"Have you forgiven us, Émile?" they asked me.

"No, and I never will. You have changed everything. Now you have linked us with 'le Diable' and the rest of them. Contini showed that he was a man. He comes out as the hero of this night's work. You are a gang of thugs who found it necessary to go with six automatic weapons to take one old man, and then you did not even shoot straight. . . ."

"Terrible," agreed Boulaya. "For the first time I am ashamed of this Maquis. And there are a few rather influential people coming for lunch today. They should be here any minute. Attention now, not a word about this disgraceful affair."

"Please, Boulaya," I said, for this was the last straw. "Can't we just behave ourselves without all this respectability campaign?"

"We ought to be careful today," Georges put in. "The Boches may be sending troops to the village to find out why their friend got hurt. This is no day to have a lot of outsiders around the place."

"And there is no tobacco," said Frisé. "What about letting me and Philippe go and stick up the 'bureau de tabac' at La Bretenière. I heard they were expecting some supplies there."

"By all means, go and *buy* some," Boulaya said. "No nonsense now. You must not even carry weapons."

"Count on us," said Frisé, and the couple departed.

We were in the middle of a stilted lunch with three strangers and not enough eating utensils to go round when Frisé and Philippe, highly elated, returned. They had just derailed three locomotives in Rigney station in front of the crowds waiting on the platform for the two o'clock "voyageur" to Besançon.

"Afraid we had not the time to stick up the 'bureau de tabac', in fact we never got that far," said the Frisé, putting both feet right in it.

"Only his way of talking," Boulaya explained to the three Bisontins. "Frisé is one of our best and most conscientious soldiers."

"Passing under the bridge by Rigney station we saw the three 'locos' standing there hitched together and with steam up," Frisé went on. "I says to Philippe: 'Did you forget to leave your revolver in the Maquis as Boulaya said?' 'I did,' he answers. 'That's strange. So did I,' I reply. So we got into the station and I got hold of a 'cheminot' standing there, and make him show us how to fix the points and wedge them so that a train approaching at speed will derail itself. Then we walk back to the three engines outside the station. I jump into the cab of the first one and show them my persuader, Philippe gets into the rear one. 'Get going backwards,' we tell our respective drivers. When we had backed to about one kilometre from the station we all get out. I give them all a cigarette while the three firemen stoke the fires up good. The driver of the middle one is a bad lot. He refuses my cigarettes. 'Gitanes' they were, too. 'O.K.,' I says to the drivers. 'Hop in and give them full tubes.' They do as they are bid, jumping out as the engines get going. Only I noticed that the second one had not opened her full throttle. I give him a wipe across the nose and we move back to the station for our bicycles. The crowd at the station is jubilant. Three 'gonzesses' kiss Philippe. Only one has the temerity to kiss me, but she does it better than his three put together. The Gestapo passed us on their way out to see the wreckage. They were going so fast they paid no attention to us.

"I think the station is blocked," he added, looking at me. "The first and second 'locos' are dug in very deeply indeed."

"Blocked. The station blocked," I said. "That would mean the crane."

"The crane," they all repeated, with awed voices.

The three strangers looked at us as though we were crazy. They did not know that the breakdown crane was our Number One objective.

CHAPTER XI

THERE was only one railway crane in our part of France. It was stationed normally, we believed, at Dijon. And after the blockage at Rigney, which denied all traffic on the Vesoul line, we awaited its arrival.

It arrived late one night, while I was out working on something else. I came back, homing on Vieilley, the following morning and I was passing through Moncey when the mayor, an enormously fat man and one of the most formidable drinkers in the East of France, hissed at me from the door of his house:

"Pssst."

"What is it? Anything the matter?" I asked.

In answer he made an expressive and then popular gesture, relaxing the fingers of the right hand and shaking them downwards with a rotary movement of the wrist, as though shaking drops of water from them. But at this moment Madame Dardel came out of the grocer's, the "Docks", and whirled me away into her garden.

"Are you mad?" she said angrily. She imagined always that I ran the most fearsome risks on the roads. "Have you gone completely out of your wits? Don't you know that this place is simply stiff with Germans and Militia?"

"How did they get here?"

"They came with the crane."

So it had arrived. This was something different, something worth while. The Germans had run so short of railway cranes that they were making desperate efforts to preserve the few vital ones that remained for all the railways of France.

I left on my bicycle by the back paths along the river out of Moncey. And, still following small paths through the fields, came to the station of Merey-Vieilley. The station-master was a close friend of mine. He was a scraggy old Communist who talked in a perpetual shriek and with a great deal of spittle flying about. He edged up to you while he talked, and if you retreated from his advance he was apt to stretch out a hand and grab you. Despite this last failing, he was a good man and a real patriot. He was invaluable to me, for, having no ordinary station-master's work to do (owing to our labours), he spent the greater part of every day listening to the talk that passed on the railway telephone. When he had to go out he would put his wife or one of his two daughters on the telephone. There was little that he did not know about the railway.

"Ola, Émile. I told the girls you'd be along today," he shrieked, holding his hand over the telephone mouthpiece and his left ear to the earpiece. "Hey, Mother. Take this infernal telephone, that's just Vesoul talking to Miserey about coal. Let me know if they mention the crane.

"Now, Émile, don't go getting yourself shopped over an old forty-five-ton crane, my lad. Because they're waiting for you. It's a trap, that crane. Fifty Boches guarding it and sleeping in the first-class coach. And with them forty-odd militians. Nights they put patrols even far out in the woods. And the thing is stiff with guards. Machine-guns on fixed lines all round it. Before lark she'll leave work at Rigney and come back to Moncey for the night. Special guards on all the line between Rigney and Moncey. I tell you it's only a trap.

"Much better take one of the girls down to the river to bathe, eh, Émile? Which one do you like best, the white one or the black one?"

His daughters, blonde and brunette, nearly wriggled themselves off their chairs at the appalling directness of such talk

Greatly admired by the young men of the district, they were fine girls.

"Come, man. Which one will you take? White or black?"

"Perhaps the black," I answered.

"She's yours. I suppose you are rich. All of you people are rich, and they say you never make your women work."

"Such talk, 'chef', from a good Communist. Does it matter whether or not I am rich?"

"I know it shouldn't matter in theory. But it does. Especially with a foreigner."

Up in the Maquis, Georges was holding a council of war. His scouts had just come back with first reports on the crane. The Pointu had been stopped and asked for his papers as he passed Rigney normally on the road. Frisé and Philippe had lain watching it all night in the trees and had nearly been trodden on by a German patrol.

"What are we going to do about it?" he asked.

"Nothing for the moment," I answered. And later, when we were alone, I told him of my plan. The first part of the programme was to make the train, Germans, militians, crane and all plunge into a small chasm created by blowing a bridge immediately in front of the leading engine. Then, in case this did not suffice, we would send a locomotive down the line with open throttle to smash into the back of the train. The bridge I had already selected was only two kilometres from Vieilley, the little one beside Marquis's hay-field. Georges did not like this. The bridge was too near Vieilley. If the thing came off we should have Boches in the village for days, and worse still, the forty militians off the train. They would be dangerous inhabitants, fifty times more dangerous than the Germans. If they stayed more than twenty-four hours in the village they would smell out the Maquis.

"Then the Maquis will just have to move," I said. "The crane is more important than the Maquis."

"Who are going to do the job?" he asked.

"You and I. Nobody else must know about it. You must hang around the station to find out from the 'chef' what day, and if possible what time, the crane is coming back our way."

"Is there no other suitable bridge?"

"No."

"All right, Émile. How much warning will you need about the crane moving?"

"Two hours."

Three mornings later he arrived at the cabin as I was preparing to descend to the Maquis.

"They plan to take the crane away today, probably in the afternoon, but perhaps earlier," he told me. "She left Moncey earlier than usual this morning to finish work at Rigney. Once she's done that the rail will be open. Three railway engineers who've been stuck for two days on the other side of the cut at Rigney with a petrol-engined rail-car reported this morning to the depot at Besançon that they'll be home for lunch. Then the crane is going to pick up the derailed locomotive between Rigney and Moncey. When that's finished she'll leave."

Georges and I cycled by separate routes to the railway bridge. We were both dressed as peasants, and were unarmed. He carried a scythe on his shoulder and I carried a big hay-rake. We met under the bridge at ten o'clock. All seemed to be quiet around the railway. The hay-making was on, but by good luck there were at that moment no peasants near enough to the bridge to see what we were doing.

"Have you made up your charges?" he asked.

"No. I judged it too complicated. I am going to make the whole thing actually on the spot."

He cast around on his bicycle for a bit longer to see that nobody was watching. Then he climbed a high cherry-tree about fifty yards from the bridge. From the top he had a good post of vantage.

"Go ahead," he said.

I scrambled up the side of the embankment and walked on to the bridge. There were four cuts to be made in the two big girders supporting the rails and two cuts on the rails themselves, making six charges in all. I felt naked there with the railway lines running dead straight to past Merey-Vieilley station on one side, and on the other curving up for four hundred yards to the high iron bridge where the Venise-Cromary road crossed the railway.

It was quite a tricky job getting the charges on the girders in place and wedged. If my hands and wrists had been big I should not have managed to manipulate them through the narrow space between the surface planks of the bridge and the tops of the girders. The only explosive available was the American type. I fixed the charges in place with the help of stiff grease-proof paper stolen from Madame Marquis's kitchen and a quantity of whippy wooden wedges which I had previously cut to measure. When all this was done and the four big charges were linked to a "main" of detonating fuse running for twelve feet to the Moncey side of the bridge, I fixed on the two camouflaged charges I had already prepared for the rails and lastly the two "fog signals" and detonators which were going to set the whole thing off. Then I went over my work, camouflaging it wherever possible with the nearly white stone chips that lay beneath and between the sleepers and elsewhere with precious khaki adhesive tape. When I had finished Georges was getting restive.

"Forty-seven minutes you've been up there," he complained. "It's tempting providence, but I don't see anybody around."

I was quite pleased with everything. It was a solid piece of work with a good many semi-professional touches about it. The plan was that I should take up a position hidden in a bush on the embankment beside the bridge. Georges was to hide near the iron bridge crossing the railway. From there he could see down a five-hundred-yard straight to Moncey station. When he saw the smoke of a train he would walk out on to the iron bridge, where I could see him well. If it were not the train we wanted to kill he would hold out his left arm horizontally. In that case I should stay in my bush and the train would pass. But a signal of both arms outstretched would mean that the crane was approaching. I should then have time, we reckoned, to spring out of my bush, fix the "fog-signals" on the line and slide down the embankment, then to double under the bridge, pick up my bicycle and my rake which were hidden in some nettles on the far side, and take a path which ran alongside the railway for a thousand yards in the same direction that the train was taking. The train in theory would explode our "fog-signals", thereby initiating the charges and blowing the bridge immediately in front of the leading locomotive. A gang of our Maquisards back near Rigney were going to launch a runaway locomotive as soon as possible after the train was signalled as leaving Moncey station.

We were in our positions by midday. It was one of the hottest days of the summer. The noise of the grasshoppers in the dry grass was almost deafening. I had sweated a lot on the bridge without realising it. At one o'clock thirst drove me out of my hiding-place to the cherry-trees. Georges was there too. There was nobody else about. All the cultivators were back in the villages eating or resting—and drinking. My thirst was nearly unbearable. I ate hundreds of the small, half-bitter wild cherries. At first they seemed to help the thirst, then they made it worse.

"There will be a great many people in the fields this afternoon," said the knowledgeable Georges. "They will see that there is going to be a storm tonight and they'll want to get the last of the hay in." He was right.

All through the long afternoon and evening we lay hidden there. I imagined I could feel the extra heat emanating from the stones and the metal lines not far from my head. The villagers came out by whole families. There was old Marquis with the rangy mule in the rake. Madame Marquis and the two daughters were there (even the delicate one, Camille, who was not allowed by the doctor to work in the fields). They wore loose cotton dresses that swung open over their breasts as they stooped to work. They helped the tall, sunburned labourer and the little orphan boy to load hay on to the big "platform". Trip after trip it made to one or other of Marquis's barns in the village. Each time I saw it swaying away, drawn by the only two horses the Germans had left him, one light and one heavy, I thought: "They will be able to have a drink of water as they pass the village fountain." The women rested on the toppling load luxuriously stretching their thick Renoir limbs, and pulling their wide straw hats down over their sweating faces. But only for the first trip or two. After that the horses were tired in the heat, and the women walked or stayed behind. Marquis worked with the mule and swore at it and everything and everyone else. Gradually most of the remnants of the hay crop were tidied and carried away from the fields around me. There was something inspiring about the evening. About this community with almost all the families out doing the same thing on the land that they owned. And about the constant trickle of "platforms" that carried hay back for the winter to the old stone barns of the village that nestled so sweetly beneath the "côte".

But the train situation worried me. It was three o'clock in the afternoon when the first signal came from Georges—one arm. This turned out to be the engineers in their small rail-car. An hour later a single engine came puffing slowly round the bend. Georges waved to me to keep well down, and I did so, wishing my bush were both bigger and farther from the railway line. It was a German "scout" engine with two Luftwaffe Regiment men on it as well as the French driver and fireman. The Germans stood in the cab looking out over opposite sides of the line, their captured Sten guns ready to fire. After this I picked up hope, for I thought that this locomotive was probably an advance-guard for the crane. Only two goods trains passed, however, one of them carrying German wounded. At ten o'clock Georges went back to the station-master to find out what had gone wrong. The news was bad. The crane had had difficulty with the locomotive near Moncey. They had finished work at eight o'clock, but had decided to wait the night in Moncey and leave early the following morning. In case they had given this out as a blind, and intended to travel by night, I set the "fog-signals" on the rail, so that if a train arrived from either direction it would be destroyed.

Boulaya met us with a long face in the Maquis. The "patron" was arriving that evening and intended possibly to stay with us for good. He had enjoyed his previous visit so much. Both of us admired the "patron", but we found his company wearing.

Buhl had gone down to meet the "patron", who was dining in the village with Marquis. Since Marquis had a large cellar and was a generous host, and all three, Marquis, the "patron" and Buhl, were fond of "la goutte", we knew that we should have to wait a considerable time for them. At midnight a sudden burst of firing came from the direction of the railway. Probably a German patrol, we thought. Shortly afterwards we heard loud voices approaching. It was the "patron" and Buhl, both extremely loquacious.

"Don't worry about the shots," the "patron" shouted at us. "They are five hundred metres away." All the way up the hill to the cabin he talked at the top of his powerful voice. We had developed a discipline of silence, so that if we spoke, especially after dark, we spoke almost as low as a whisper. This habit appeared to madden the "patron".

"What are you all whispering for, damn you?" he bellowed. "I tell you there is no need to be afraid."

Nothing annoys Frenchmen more than such a remark, and the atmosphere was far from that "aura of peace" I have described when we settled down to sleep in the cabin. Georges slept with Berger. I gave my bed to the "patron" and slept myself, per-fectly comfortably, on the table. The aura of peace was still further lessened when, at 1 a.m., the long-overdue storm broke. After twenty minutes of really torrential rain our straw roof gave up the struggle and the water began to pour through. Boulaya and I were accustomed to suffer such misfortunes in stoic silence. Not so the "patron". He began fiercely:

226

"Nom de dieu de bordel." He then lay silent for a moment, sizing up the full enormity of the situation.

"This roof leaks," he said. Nobody questioned the profound truth of this remark. Annoyed by the silence, he next shouted: "Nom de dieu, answer me, somebody. Why does this roof leak?" I left the reply to Boulaya. And the following angry conversation ensued:

"Why did you not use corrugated iron?"

"There is none in all the valley except what is being used on houses. We cannot steal it from the cultivators."

"Why did you not fix up a tarpaulin?"

"We've given all the tarpaulins to the men. Most of them leak, anyway."

"Why did you not get someone to make a proper job with straw?"

"We did not want to give away our Command Post to outsiders."

"Is this the first time you've been wet here?"

"No."

"Then why the devil did you bring me here? And why are you not all dead?"

The last remark, comparatively innocuous in itself, was spoken with all the bitterness of which a regular colonel in the Colonial infantry was capable. After that Boulaya pretended loudly to be asleep. I actually slept, for I was tired and the sleeping-bag kept me warm, though not dry. I heard only excerpts from the "patron's" running commentary, which continued through the night, and woke with the dawn to hear him exclaim:

"Merde! Les deux fesses dans l'eau et gelées."

He was quite right. The indents which we had made for our beds were now pools of water. Boulaya still pretended to sleep, but I was able to leave the place with Georges, for I would have to make the bridge safe again before the "8.10 voyageur" appeared.

First, too, there were the shots in the night to investigate. We dropped down through the woods and cautiously picked our way through the wet vineyards to Phillipon's bothy. The old man heated me some grain coffee while Georges cycled across the fields to the station for news. The station-master told him that a German patrol had passed in the night, and had fired several rifle-shots, probably at some of the youngsters from Bonnay, who were out sabotaging the telephone-wires. The youngsters had done their job too thoroughly. The station-master had no telephone to listen to. A runner had come through though from Moncey to say that the crane would pass Merey-Vieilley about midday.

There was nothing else for it. We must make the bridge safe for the "8.10 voyageur". (We never attacked French passenger trains.) Accordingly, Georges took his scythe, I took my rake, and we cycled out to the bridge by our separate routes. I crossed the railway by the level-crossing on the road to Cromary, then rode alongside the tracks, along the path which was my route for withdrawal after the attack. I must admit that I looked carefully at every bush that I approached. But there was no sign of a living creature in all the rural landscape that had been so busy the day before. Georges met me at the bridge.

"I feel something's wrong," I said.

"That's strange. So do I."

"Well, at any rate, keep a look-out while I make it safe for the 8.10 to pass."

I mounted the embankment and took the "fog-signals" from the line, hiding them beneath a sleeper. Georges was pretending to scythe some wet hay while he kept a look-out. I examined the charges. Nothing had been tampered with. There were no footmarks around the spot. Despite this, I was uneasy. Georges voiced my uneasiness.

"I think we should be foolish to wait here all morning," he said. "Let's go back to the village. We can return here about eleven."

A sudden urgency to be off took possession of us and saved our lives.

We rode directly back on the track across the flat fields to Vieilley. The much-needed rain hissed into the earth, turning the surface dust to slime. Georges led the way pushing hard on a bicycle he had stolen from the Germans. The wheels slipped on the mud, and it was hard work since the fields sloped slightly in a steady incline from the village down to the railway. Suddenly an electric horn sounded in the village. Georges stiffened, whipped a look around him and drove his bicycle into a big patch of maize. I followed.

Two black cars turned off the road on to our track. In the first car were two German officers and three men in plain clothes, Gestapo. The second car was filled with Gestapo. Before they reached the bridge another Citroën thrust its black, front-wheel drive nose under the archway facing toward us.

"See that?" said Georges. "The swine approached the bridge

from both sides. Lucky we left when we did. Time to get out of here."

We left our bicycles lying in the maize, crawled through two orchards and a pig-pen, and then, carrying our scythe and rake, strolled slowly through the village and up into the woods behind. The sun was out now. The storm had suddenly ended. It seemed absurd that we had been so nearly caught.

Georges nosed around the village and the station and got the story. It seemed that two railwaymen who lived in little houses at the level-crossing had found the charges as they walked in to work at Moncey. After anxious discussion, they decided that they must report the matter, because they feared that the "8.10 voyageur" would otherwise be wrecked. At 6.45 the Germans knew of the charges. At 7.30 Georges and I were at the bridge. At 7.40 the Germans were there.

They stayed there all day. Four Gestapo men in hot, dark clothes sat with weapons in their hands staring out over the fields. The cultivators were busy around them. Sometimes the Germans would crunch across the stubble in their stiff town shoes to ask the workers what they knew of the terrorist attempt. Georges worked near them for a bit with his scythe, but I kept far away.

At midday the crane passed slowly down the valley. I sat alone on the little hill above the quarry from which stone for all the houses in the village had been cut. It was bitter to see it pass with its opulent first-class carriage of Germans and the hated militians leaning from the windows of the second-class carriage immediately in front of the crane. I had lost all our remaining explosives, and for nothing. They said that the German engineers who took the charges away had been surprised at the way I had tackled the problem. It would have been interesting to have discussed it with them. Bitterly I watched it pass, for I felt that I had failed in the eyes of the Maquis and even of the valley. And half an hour after it had passed a runaway engine careered after it across the landscape.

The crane, although I did not know it, was going to its death. Instead of returning to Dijon it turned left up the valley of the Doubs. And well up that valley a wily saboteur called Tito lay beside the railway, a string in his hand. The string was attached to a "switch" which was attached to a small initiating charge buried under the railway line among some 150-mm. shells. As the crane passed over the shells Tito pulled his string.

CHAPTER XII

GEORGES MOLLE introduced me to his village and his valley. He showed me the finest cherry-trees, the best strawberry-beds, the coolest cellars, the sweetest hay-lofts to sleep in on the hot August afternoons.

He showed me where the peaches and the plums and the best eating apples and pears were to be found among the vineyards. He took me to eat green walnuts, and explained where to find mushrooms, the white field mushrooms, and the woodland varieties of which we preferred the mysterious and beautiful "chantrelles".

From him I learned which were the curs and which the famous hunting-dogs that every man in the village ought to know by name. From him I learned which fountain had the softest water for washing and which the coolest for drinking. From him I learned the jack hare's habit of never going to a place and returning by the same route.

Best of all, he showed me the Ognon. A quiet, ordinary, brown river. On tranquil afternoons I often walked from the Maquis across the wide stretch of the Vieilley fields, past the dark clump of pine-trees by the station, and on down to the river. It was a long, hot walk, and if Georges accompanied me he liked to take the other route, cycling down the small road that ran from the bowling-alley in Vieilley to the level-crossing with its cottage where the woman always looked at me fearfully, thinking that I might kill her man, for he it was who had revealed my charges destined for the crane. After the level-crossing the road became a grassy path which meandered eventually to a part of the Ognon bank known as "the beach". The beach was a strip of shingle eight feet wide and there were usually two home-made fishing-punts tethered there. One of them belonged to Georges.

On the banks of the Ognon I spent many peaceful hours. Most of them were passed in solitude, but often Georges was there with me, and occasionally the station-master's "black" daughter, who disliked work, and tried to pass all her afternoons there lying alone on her back with her old liver-and-white pointer bitch sleeping beside her, scaring away the grass snakes.

It was a disappointing river for the keen swimmer, since the current was just swift enough to discourage you from swimming against it, and in few places near Vieilley was the Ognon so deep that I could not touch the bottom with my feet. Fish abounded, however, and these we caught in all conceivable manners, even (I regret to say and without the approval of Georges) fishing with explosives when the Maquis was hungry and much fish had to be killed in a short time. I bathed twice in the Ognon with the lily-skinned Boulaya, and twice with old Phillipon, who went there once a fortnight with a block of home-made soap with plenty of boar-grease in it. I always took soap to the water myself. The south bank of the Ognon was our bath-room. In the waters of the Ognon, too, near the end of our war, I made the mistake of telling the American, Captain Bazata, a large and ardent republican, that I *admired* Roosevelt.

I avoided parts of the Ognon where there were people, and when I went to the river I tried to remember to carry a pistol. We knew that the Gestapo knew that we frequented the Ognon. Before I arrived at Vieilley, five thugs from the Militia had come looking for Georges when they thought he was fishing with his punt secured athwart the stream above the island. They were right. He was fishing, but he saw them before they saw him, and when he noticed the sub-machine-guns in their hands he left for the Haute-Saône by slipping otter-like from the punt into the water.

"It would take one hundred men to find me in the Ognon if I did not want to be found," he used to say. He was right, I think. He was the greatest fisherman with his hands that I have seen, and he knew every bush from Buthiers to Cenans. I have seen him fish in his bathing-trunks and up to the neck in chilly water, mounting over three miles of the river, and taking out eighty fish, some of them five-pounders and over, all with his hands.

Then, later, the Gestapo were believed to send two women to snare me on the banks of the Ognon. It became too much known that I often swam in the evenings. And it is true that two strange women did sometimes appear when I was there. One was blonde and the other brunette. The only precaution I took against them was to wear bathing-trunks. Then, one evening, I grew angry with their presence, and had them obviously trailed by two particularly fierce-looking Maquisards. After that they did not reappear.

It was on the Ognon that I met Nono for the first time.

I recall that it was a cool Sunday afternoon, and Georges and I were hungry for the fried fish they call "la friture". So we took the round "épervier" poacher's net and went out in the punt. There were too many fishermen on the river. We were searching for an unobserved spot when we came on some youngsters by the side of the stream. One of them, a well-built youth with a long nose and a wide mouth, came and climbed into our punt. He wore a soft hat and a pair of old shorts. He talked to Georges and looked curiously at me, but I was intent on my fishing. I did not want him to hear my accent.

I knew about Nono. He was twenty years old, and the son of the lawyer at Bonnay. Nono led a Resistance gang of youngsters in the neighbourhood. He was intelligent and energetic, and had done much useful work. Such things as regularly sabotaging the telephone lines, and taking down the German road signs and putting them up again in the wrong places. His ambition was to get into our Vieilley Maquis.

He was a fine boy. I saw that at once in the punt. And a patriot. Next time his name cropped up in the Maquis I advised Georges to take him on. So he did. After refusing so many times that he was sick of the sight of the boy.

Poor Nono. It would have been better if I had never met you.

It was a pity you went down to the river that Sunday.

"It's a trap, Émile," said the "patron".

"Why all the guards, the obvious guards, if it's a trap?"

"Are the tankers full? And why should they leave all that petrol at Roches when they are dying for petrol for their aeroplanes and tanks and the army transport?"

"Yes, they are full. I had a railwayman, Jean Buthot, with me today, and he could tell by the springs. They are waiting at Roches for trucks to carry the petrol by road to Bordeaux. It is destined for the 'Luftwaffe' there. The labels on the tankers confirm that, and the guards are 'Luftwaffe' soldiers."

"How many guards are there?"

"Thirty-five, and a pretty sleepy lot."

"Think you can cope with them?"

"Yes."

"Well, it's your affair. Go ahead. But I still say it's a trap."

I was inclined to agree with him, but, as I told myself, when a thing doesn't look too easy you are always ready to think it a trap.

That day I had called in at the Champoux Maquis and cycled over to the small town of Roches-les-Beauprè, sitting on the banks of the Doubs. What interested me in Roches was the ether and petrol refinery. There were three big reservoirs of carburant there, and my better saboteur self was always having a constant battle with my better nature about them. I wanted to blow the reservoirs up. But in doing so I would endanger a fair part of the town, particularly the workers' houses around the factory. I realised that I should have to get special permission from F.F.I. Headquarters to do the job in that manner. But I had an idea that we might open some valves somewhere and let all the petrol run out of the tanks. We might even let a good deal of it run into some tanker trucks that Boulaya thought he could rake up in Besançon. The time was approaching when we were going to need all the petrol we could get.

There were twelve little drawbacks to my day-dreams about the factory at Roches—eleven German infantrymen and one "feldwebel". It was not that the Germans would be difficult for us to kill or make prisoner. But if we killed them in any ordinary way terrible reprisals would be taken on Roches. It was a nice little problem. Boulaya and I had often discussed it; we had even made trips to the valley in the hills above Roches, whence we could look down on the place in plan.

This time I took Jean Buthot, and "Chocolat" Missana with me. Missana because he had a great friend, another Italian, who worked in the Roches factory. When we had crossed the last hill and dropped down into the valley I changed objectives. Shunting about on the main line running through Roches station I saw a train of thirty tanker wagons.

So I gave Jean and Missana the task of finding out why the train was there, how long it was staying, and what it held.

After my talk with the "patron" I determined to have another look at the train the next day and then, if possible, attack it with the Champoux Maquis at night. One reason which encouraged me to try an attack was that the Champoux Maquis had now received a Bazooka, the American infantry anti-tank rocket thrower. And since I had asked London to send me large numbers of these weapons, I felt that I ought to use one. We were parachuted twenty rockets per Bazooka, so rockets were much too valuable to be wasted in useless practice. And if I had to fire the thing, it seemed to me that a nice stationary tanker wagon would be an encouragingly easy thing to hit. Being an American weapon, I did not know the Bazooka. In fact, I had only once seen the thing, at one of the schools in England. The British sergeant-major who had shown us the weapon had told us simply: "If you ever have to use this thing be careful not to drop the rocket—it's sensitive. Be prepared for heat when you fire it—you may get your face burned." I hoped that the parachuting factory had included instructions with this particular Bazooka.

For my reconnaissance I dressed myself up as the boy cyclist, wearing only blue linen shorts, bought for me on the black market in Besançon by the red-haired Countess of Thise, and the sandals that had been made for me at Cendrey. My personal weapons, clothes, and sleeping-bag I put in a rucksack. On the other side of the terrible hill to Marchaux, the cyclists' nightmare, I hid my rucksack in the woods, so that I could pick it up if I decided to return to the Champoux Maquis and call them to action.

Then I departed on the ride to Roches, feeling particularly innocent. And it was as well. Two hundred yards before Roches, on the main Belfort road, I ran into a German control. There were five or six soldiers and an officer and two N.C.O.'s in the "Feldgendarmerie". They searched my trousers pockets and the bags on the carrier of the bicycle. All they found was a handkerchief, a little money, my papers, and a bag of plums. Who could suspect a half-naked youth on a bicycle? The "Feldgendarme" officer fairly beamed on me:

"You are very bronzed, Monsieur," he said to me as he waved me on towards Roches. I had never seen a control there before, and I wondered whether their presence had anything to do with the petrol train at Roches.

They had split the twenty big tanker wagons into five groups of four, with about sixty yards gap between groups. The wagons lay between two small level-crossings, and on the north side of the railway they were screened by a small pine-wood. On the south side the country was open fields, with a certain amount of low cover in the shape of banks and bushes. There were cows in most of the fields though. That was bad. Cows at night can make a lot of trouble. And we would obviously have to attack from the open side. On the other side there was no field of fire for the Bazooka, because of the pine-wood. Not only that, but there were German sentries in the wood. I saw that as I cycled slowly round the objective.

At the first level-crossing I got a good view of the enemy quarters. Fifty yards from the crossing they had the last group of tankers, and attached to this were a third-class passenger carriage and a wagon. It seemed that the Germans slept in the carriage, and their cooking was done in the wagon. There were two "Spandau" machine-guns on tripods beside the carriage, swivelling out along the line. I noted that one of them had quite a nice field of fire over the fields on the southern side.

The Germans were enjoying the sun. All of them had their tunics and shirts off, even the young sentry on the level-crossing. He looked approvingly on my nakedness and my blondness. He was a well-built youth in a shambling way, but his skin looked dirty. There was a streak of sweat running down the centre of his chest, and just to the left of it there was a strange tattooing of an eagle carrying a bear in its claws. Below the picture the tattooer had printed "Russia, 1942". A fairly professional enemy to stand against Jean's Maquisards. The other Germans looked about the same type, I thought. I cycled slowly round the place, stopping for a little on the north side at the château, to see if our friend, the countess, knew anything. She gave me a fine brandy, but all she could tell me was that there were some Poles among the German guards, and they had told her Polish farm servant that they were "most nervous about terrorists". I rode on to Thise to call on another friend, this time Barbier, a working man whom Boulaya and I called "naked torso", because he never, even when dining ceremoniously in his own house, covered the upper half of his muscular body with so much as the skimpiest singlet or shirt. "Naked torso" gave me some quite remarkable plum brandy of his own distilling, but he knew less than the countess about the train. I cycled slowly south and over the other level-crossing. Here there was again a German sentry, and I saw the other end of the train about four hundred yards down the track. Just on the other side of the level-crossing a youth stopped me.

"Afternoon, chief," he said.

"What d'you mean, chief?"

"Come off it, chief. I saw you over here the day the troop train was upset and the Boches fired into the fields. Thought we'd see you around here today. I did really."

"Who the hell are you with that careless tongue?"

"I am Marcel Blanc, a 'garde-voies'. I have told your Pointu that I want to join the Maquis. Last time he was here I helped him. Look. I have been watching the Boches around this train."

"Is there a sentry on this level-crossing at night?"

"On this one, no. On the other, yes. They draw the sentries close in to the train at night."

This level-crossing would be a danger spot. We should have to arrive from the north, walking through the forest. We would cross the railway here. Then it would be necessary to make the attack from the fields. It would be fairly unpleasant if any big German convoy came down the road while the fireworks were on, since we should then be sandwiched between the railway and the road, and our only line of withdrawal was back across the railway. There were about four hundred yards of flat fields between the railway and the big road. German convoys had begun to pass through Roches at 4 a.m. that morning. The situation was not favourable to an attack with untried troops. I wished now that I had arranged to do it with my Vieilley men. With the Frisé, the Pointu, Maurice and Phillipe to stiffen the Champoux lot I should have felt all right about it.

The day was now so hot that I decided to go and have a look at the Doubs. I ate my plums as luncheon beside the broad river. Watching the many bathers gave me an irresistible desire to bathe myself. I cursed my forgetfulness in not bringing any suitable garment. My shorts were war-time things, and I dared not trust them in the water.

A party of eight German soldiers from the petrol train solved my difficulty. They came down to the river and taking off all their clothes without any evidence of modesty, were soon enjoying themselves in the water. All the French people in the vicinity sheered away in disgust, leaving a wide empty space on the river-bank. This was irresistible. I moved my bicycle close to the German party and in a few seconds, dressed exactly as they were, I was lying on my back in the water looking up at the magnificently cloudless sky. After half an hour of floating down-stream and slowly swimming back, I dried myself in the sun, and cycled to the Belfort road to look again at the objective. This time I picked out two places for the attack; one for the Bazooka party, the other for a party who were to approach behind the small houses on the south side of the level-crossing and attack the German guards in their carriage. There was good cover for a night approach at this end. And the second party would have an easier withdrawal, they could cross the railway where they liked.

The Champoux Maquis were for it. Tonight they would have their opportunity to get even with the Vieilley boys, of whom they were insanely jealous. Crossing the hills again—I had chosen for this operation the worst country for hills in the whole sector—I dropped down into the village of Marchaux. Here thirst drew me to the "Hotel de la Poste", where there was always a glass of wine or beer and a warm welcome for me. The buxom hostess led me as usual into the small, fly-infested kitchen. When she gave me a glass and a bottle that had been standing near the cold tap, she got out a loaf of bread and a china bowl of runny "concoillotte" cheese. Then she said:

"Lots and lots of Boches around today, Émile."

"Where?"

"Oh, I don't know. There have been a lot on the roads. Some people say they plan to attack the Maquis."

"Who says so?"

"Oh nobody special, you know. Just everybody really."

"No news at the Gendarmerie?"

"No, only rumours. I saw Madame Chapuy an hour ago. Her man is still in the jail. They haven't tortured the poor soul. Not yet, anyway. . . ."

I paid little attention to this talk. Marchaux was a breeding-ground for rumours. There were too many policemen there. Up in the Maquis there appeared to have been some kind of celebration. One half of the men were spread-eagled on their beds, although it was only 5 p.m., and the others were talking a great deal. Perhaps the most talkative were Jean, the chief, and Missana. I had grown so used to such things in my stay in France, that it took me some time to realise that this Maquis had been collectively drinking. A well-wisher had sent them a cask of wine, and they had been soaking it up during the afternoon. I could hardly blame them. Their existence was drab enough.

I expected my announcement of the night's programme to produce the ecstasy such announcements created at Vieilley. I had even thought out a little speech which mentioned the honour of using the "secret weapon" (the Bazooka) on the enemy and the honour which fell to their Maquis of carrying out a real attack on the Germans. I ran over the lay-out of the train and its guards and told them that I expected to take the train itself, with much booty in the shape of arms, German clothing and equipment. All this was greeted with apathy.

As I read the instruction booklet on the Bazooka I wished fervently that I had a few of our Vieilley tigers to put some life into these men. "Chocolat" Missana did his best to make up for the others' lethargic attitude with a burst of prophecies of how we, and he, were going to "carve up the Boches". After an hour's work on the pamphlet, I selected a tall youngster with a hard face to be loader to me with the Bazooka. We practised the drill with the tube and the bombs again and again, and at the same time I showed all the others how the weapon (I thought) should be used. Then we ate.

A lusty dinner seemed to improve the men's feeling about the night's operation, and Jean improved it still further by announcing that he intended to carry four full water-bottles of wine when we set out. French water-bottles are very large, but I did not dare to question such a popular decision. I felt that we needed all the enthusiasm we could get.

The orders were given out in the light of an acetylene-flare, just before we departed on our long walk through the forest. To reinforce and protect the tall youth and myself with the Bazooka, I chose two good rifle-shots and a third man with a Sten. The two with rifles were railwaymen, whom I knew to be good soldiers. The man I chose to carry the Sten surprised the rest of the Maquis.

I chose Minari, the foxy-faced "false militian". Young Minari, who looked like a Hollywood villain, had joined Darnan's Militia, he claimed, to find out their secrets and pass them to the Resistance. He had indeed done this to the best of our knowledge. And he had "descended" a militian himself in his home village of Venise. He was a difficult man to work with, unpopular with some of the Maquis, and considered untrustworthy by many. I had an idea, however, that he was sound. And in any case, if he were unsound, it would do no harm to have him within range of my Colt .45. He appeared to be gratified that I had chosen him. His bony grey face creased in smiles.

Jean was to lead the other party. He had ten men to smash up all German resistance around the railway carriage. I ordered them to wait, hidden as near the carriage as they could get, until they heard the first round fired with the Bazooka at the train. That was to be the signal for the riflemen with me to open frontal fire, and for Jean and his party to massacre the Germans in their carriage. All his men carried Stens and grenades. With surprise and darkness on their side, I reckoned that they should at least kill a lot of Germans, giving us time to have a good go at the train. Since some of the rockets for this Bazooka had not turned up, I only took six for the operation.

After three hours' walk through inky-black woodland paths, we skirted the village of Thise, and were near the level-crossing.

Here, with a silent prayer, I split forces and allowed Jean to lead his party on ahead. They passed the level-crossing without being challenged, and five minutes later we followed them. It was a tricky night for this operation, extremely still and silent, and with an electric storm to the south that occasionally lit up everything with brilliant and sustained flashes. Natural Very lights. Following the route I had observed after my bathe, I led my four men to positions along a small bank that ran parallel to the railway lines. It was difficult to judge, for the light was bad between flashes, but we seemed to be about one hundred yards from the train. We could hear the German sentries moving about, and once one of them secretly (as he thought) smoked a cigarette among the bushes.

When I had got my men posted and had moved them about several times, getting myself thoroughly wet crawling with them through the dew, my first worry was the cows. These maddening animals had rushed away in terror as we entered the big field; now that we were crawling gently about or lying still they were beginning to evince a certain powerful, though scared, curiosity. They walked cautiously towards us. These cows were half-brown and half a brilliant white. The white parts showed up well in the night. As though they had not drawn enough attention to us, they next stood in rings around each of our little positions and mooed. But the German sentries were probably townsmen. They paid no attention.

My next worry was Jean's party. Were they going to be able to make their approach without disturbing a dog or falling over something? At any rate, if anything like that happened, my party were now all ready to open fire and cause a diversion. I tried several times to align the sights of the Bazooka on the tanker wagons, which I could just pick out with the naked eye. But it was too dark to see the sights against the dark background of the accursed pine-wood. Well, I had warned Jean and his party that I would perhaps wait until the dawn before I opened fire. That would mean a two-hour wait. Fortunately, it was not cold. If I had been as sure of the other men as I was of the two riflemen and my loader, all would have seemed rosy. Minari, whom I had put behind me to guard our rear and watch the road, had behaved well up to now, and the final approach had been fairly tricky.

No, it was Jean's party that worried me. If they rushed the enemy by copiously spraying the carriage with lead the moment I opened up, all would be well. Surely they would. Jean hated, and had reason to hate, the Germans. But he had a wife and several children in Besançon. He was not the fire-brand type, despite his virile appearance. For dash and vigour in the attack I would rather have the young Frenchman than any other man. A 1944 patriot, no matter how good he was, was better, in my experience, if he was unmarried and had no relatives that mattered desperately to him. Then the Italian boxer, "Chocolat", was a weak link. He, the loudest mouth before we started on the night's trip, had been obliged as we neared the railway, to make frequent halts to lower his trousers. And his brave boasts had altered to injunctions to the men to "keep lying down" after they opened fire. One weak man can weaken a whole group. Especially when there is a long and nervy delay before action. After thinking this over I again tried the Bazooka sights. It was no use. I should have to await the dawn.

There was a certain amount of German traffic on the road. But the only thing that would really be dangerous for us would be a big convoy. Anything small would tend rather to accelerate if it heard firing so near the road. I waited, watching the wheatfield between me and the train becoming more and more detailed. I could see the men in my own party looking round at me to see why we had not opened fire. At 5.30 it was really daylight, but each time I put the Bazooka to my shoulder the train still seemed to be shadowed by that damned wood. However, in view of the difficulties of withdrawal, I felt that I must have a go. So I checked up with the little red light on my Bazooka and told the hard-faced youth to load it.

"Fire;" he said, and I pressed the trigger. There was a warm feeling all over me, but especially on my unprotected face, eyes and hands. The projectile was low. It struck underneath a wagon and pieces of rail and other metal that appeared to be red-hot went spraying all over the place. At once my people opened up a steady fire, and I heard the rattle of sub-machine-guns from the right.

"Fire," he said again. This time I was a shade to the left. More metal splashed over the target though. There was no reply from the German sentries in front of us. One of them had been killed by the first rocket. But now they were firing in our direction from the wood behind the train and from the carriage. I could hear no firing from Jean.

"Fire," he said again. A direct hit, smack in the middle of a tanker. I heard liquid gushing out, but it did not ignite as I had hoped. Standing up as I was to clear the tops of the high grain in front of me, I knew that each time we fired the Bazooka the flames shooting out of the back of the tube were showing us up to the Germans. A nourished and fairly well-directed fire was now coming from their flank by the railway carriage. And all of it was directed on us. What was Jean doing? My own men on either side of me were firing like veterans. After one rifle shot we heard a high scream from beside the train. The Spandau now got going and fired across our front. The rounds were cutting into the wheat just ahead of us.

"We'll fire one more round," I told the youngster.

"Very good. Fire." Another direct hit, and no explosion, no flames. I was able now to see the sights, and we still had two rockets. But things were getting too hot. And the rockets seemed to be wasted. Accordingly, I gave the whistle which was the signal for withdrawal, and we waited for the men on the right flank to come through us. The loader coolly picked up his cardboard cases and the remaining bombs. Minari, who had also behaved well, now lay on the ground and seemed reluctant to get up. But he followed us, conquering his fear of the whistling air. There was a good deal of fire now. The five of us, running behind banks that sheltered us slightly and helped by the occasional fire of the two riflemen, managed to get back to the level-crossing, and from there into the forest, where nobody was likely to catch us.

We had been lucky to get out of that with nobody wounded. But once we were safe in the forest and foot-slogging it for home, a good twelve miles away, I began to get annoyed at the whole business. We seemed to have wasted four good Bazooka rockets. My reputation was not ruined, because fortunately I had told the Maquis before we started that I did not know the properties of the rockets, and did not know whether the tankers would explode and burn when hit. Then Jean and his men had definitely failed to play the part allotted to them.

We went home by the same paths as on the outward route, through a part of the forest that I hardly knew. But going home it was light, and I was able to study the paths. It was as well that I did so.

Up in the Maquis Jean's party had already settled down when we arrived. That is to say, they had made coffee and eaten bread and butter, and now they were lying down. But fierce arguments were raging. Jean was accusing Missana of cowardice. Missana, for his part, was affirming that Jean's leadership had lacked dash. and was offering to fight with bare fists anybody who dared call him a coward (I have noticed that pugilists are apt to make this kind of gesture). Piecing their heated talk together, it was evident that they had not even stopped to pour a really good burst of fire into the German's sleeping carriage. And when they were hurriedly withdrawing, leaving us unsupported in our exposed position, they had seen a fine thing. The "feldwebel" from the Roches factory was leading six of his ten men through the streets at the double to go to the help of the train. Jean and his men had not even fired on them, and in a sneaking way I was glad. I admired the "feldwebel" who led out his puny force to help comrades who were over a mile away, in what could be considered hostile country.

Honours for that early morning's work went to the Germans. Without waiting to talk the operation over, I picked up my rucksack and left their Maquis.

Often when one is tired the best thing to do is wash and shave. Having once more negotiated the hill between Marchaux and Vieilley, and that immediately following my efforts of the last twenty-four hours, I thought that I would shave in the Marquis's kitchen.

I went into their house as usual by the back way, through the byre, then up five narrow steps to the kitchen door, which had a small window through which I always checked up on the kitchen's occupants. A good-looking young woman whom I had not seen before was doing her hair in front of the mirror. Camille Marquis was there, talking in a friendly open way with the stranger and occasionally shooting unfriendly piercing looks at her back. I waited until Camille came near enough to the door for me to signal to her. She came out to the steps.

"Who is it?" I whispered.

"Oh, it's quite all right. It's a friend of Boulaya."

So I went in and shaved. While I did so the strange young woman came out of the dining-room and watched me for a moment.

"You wouldn't be Émile by any chance?" she asked.

"No."

"Can you tell me where I can find Boulaya?"

"Who sent you?"

"Charles Maurice."

"I will try to get a message to Boulaya."

She said indignantly that she was in a great hurry and that she had urgent messages for Boulaya. But they always said that. And one could not be too careful with women. The Resistance used them a lot. So did the Gestapo. And on principle we mistrusted the young and pretty ones. They might have bad lovers. Or they might want money for clothes, or parents, or lovers.

Boulaya was the first man I saw. I met him as he was coming down from the Maquis.

"There is a blonde waiting for you at the Marquis' house," I told him.

"Who is she?"

"Calls herself Jeanette."

"And her password?"

"Says she comes from Charles Maurice."

"Never heard of him. It is a trap, I swear," he said, and he accompanied me back to the Maquis. "Maurice and Pointu," he said. "I want you to bring me the young woman who is at Marquis's place, a blonde calling herself Jeanette. Go armed, and bring her whether she wants to come or not. You understand. . . ."

Boulaya already had details of the attack on the train. A considerable number of tankers had been pierced by our fire and there were several German dead and wounded. But the contents of the tankers were now said to be part petrol, part diesel oil, and part water. Tankers with water in them were interspersed with the others.

"I said it was a trap," said the "patron". "And I stick to my original opinion."

"If it were a trap we would not have got out of it, or at any rate we would have been chased," I answered.

"The attack was useful, Émile, because they think they were attacked by a light field-gun. That's good for the morale. Now leave it at that. No use bothering about it any further."

"They say the petrol is all at one end of the train?"

"Yes," he answered.

"Then it should be at the end farthest from the carriage where the Germans sleep. In that case it could still be attacked."

I felt that the train at Roches was a challenge. And I began to think that I had been wrong to attack it in force. It looked like a job for two men. The approach was possible. They could crawl along the embankment from the level-crossing which we had crossed. They would have to keep between the railway and the wood, and stalk one, possibly two, German sentries, to find a gap in the guard. Then one of them could climb on to a group

of tankers and fix on say three charges (magnetic charges—
"clams" would be best) linked to an incendiary. The other man
would have a Sten. He would lie under the tankers and give
protection until the job was done.

"I want one volunteer to go on a job with me tonight," I said,
and I had the impression that someone else had spoken the
words.

All of them were there around the fireplace in the new living
space, further into the forest than the old one, and with a tented
cover over a huge table built of birch branches. They were
eager to come. I looked around their faces and weighed them
up as companions for the night's job. It must be someone
young, agile, able to crawl and to run if need be. Otherwise,
there were no important qualifications. I would place the
charges myself. As I ran my eye around the circle of eager faces,
I could not help noticing that Nono, who had been for about
one week in the Maquis, looked ready to burst into tears.
Philippe, and one or two of the others asked me to take them.
But Nono was too shy to ask. I saw that it mattered terribly
to him.

"I'll take you, Nono," I said. "I'm going up above to sleep
now. I'll be down at four in the afternoon. We shall go on
bicycles and you'll want a rucksack with soft shoes, a Sten, and
something to blacken our faces and hands. Wear dark clothes.
And look me out three "clams" and an incendiary with a small
roll of detonating fuse, some ordinary fuse, one of the small
boxes with two detonators, and a roll of adhesive tape."

"Very good, Émile." He wrote it all down. "When do we
start, Émile?"

"Leave here at five o'clock. You might ask the 'cuistot' to
have something ready for me to eat at four."

"O.K., Émile, and," he cleared his throat and looked
sheepish. "And thanks very much, Émile, for taking me and
all that sort of thing."

I did not get much sleep. No sooner had I got into my
sleeping-bag in the cabin, it seemed, than the gentle Berger
wakened me. Jeanette had turned out to be a messenger from
Albert. She carried urgent messages for me, and she would have
to depart soon after two with my replies. She was returning
to Dole, and there was only one train from Besançon.

So all the sleep I got was a couple of hours lying in one of
Berger's home-made benches alongside the table in the Maquis.
When I awoke Nono was sitting beside me like a dog, waiting

for me to take notice of him. He had laid out everything neatly on the table and had checked all the articles off on his list. This was his great day. He looked happy. And the glances he threw casually at the other Maquisards were full of friendly superiority.

They gathered around to watch me eating two fried eggs and making up the charges for the night's job. They asked me where we were going, and when they were denied a reply they said they knew. And, indeed, a half-wit could have told that those charges were designed for something made of metal that held an inflammable liquid. They told me that there was much talk in the district about the attack on the train at Roches. The Germans had threatened reprisals on the town of Roches itself.

I had brought down a small haversack for myself. I only had my "espadrilles", my washing-things and my swimming-trunks (I had not forgotten the river Doubs) to put in it. Nono insisted on putting everything in his rucksack.

"You are tired, Émile," he said accurately, but too solicitously.

I checked over my clothes as usual before setting out. I wore the grey leather jacket and corduroy trousers in which I had left London. On my feet I had the light, rubber-soled sandals made at Cendrey, and I put a beret on my head to try to look more French. I stuffed my pistol into my right-hand trouser pocket, and put two spare magazines in the other pocket.

My idea was to cycle in a leisurely fashion over to Thise, dine there with the hospitable Barbier, sleep for a bit on his sofas, and then go out and do the job about one or two in the morning. Then we would return, pick up our bicycles and ride into the forest, where we could sleep some more. Sleep was playing a big part in my thoughts, you notice. That is always a danger sign.

Nono was in high spirits, spirits that even the long walk uphill towards Marchaux failed to damp.

"Do you think that I shall ever learn to work with explosives, like the Pointu and Philippe do, Émile?" he asked.

"Certainly. I remember well when they knew nothing."

"Explain the theory of explosives to me again, would you mind?"

Stifling the annoyance of fatigue I forced myself to explain once more. Then he took another line. He was going to come to England after the war. Where should he go? What should he see? How did you say this and that in English? I was relieved, indeed, when we got to the top of the hill and mounted our bicycles for the long descent into Marchaux. Nono rushed down the hill without touching a brake. He was whistling and singing all the way. I could not help being a little elevated by his pure high spirits. It was a lovely evening too, but heavy. There would be a storm that night. All the better for our job. A good rainstorm would be perfect.

"If Jean and the others had done their job better I would be in bed now," I told myself. And I cursed the wine they had drunk in the Champoux Maquis and again en route to the railway. Jean was of the old school, who believed that the soldier should have wine, that the "poilu" only reached great heights when he had plenty of "pinard". That was not my view, although I am no wine-hater. For I had noticed that when our Maquis had no wine, and we went out to work on nothing stronger than brackish water, the jobs were better—even more courageously—done than in the later, richer days, when we normally had wine to stimulate us.

Madame Chapuy was sitting in her window looking out on the road running through Marchaux. I had to stop and talk for a few minutes. She was unhappy about her husband in jail, grateful to the Resistance for the help they were giving her and her children, and mainly just anxious to talk. Nono sat his bicycle in the middle of the road, fretting with impatience.

"Really, Émile," he said, when we were once more moving. "Your pistol is a bit obvious. It was hanging right out of your pocket when you were talking to the woman at the Gendarmerie."

This was the sort of thing I was always getting angry with the Maquisards for. I detested any kind of display of arms around the villages. Obediently, therefore, I put the pistol deeper into my pocket.

We were approaching a road fork, and I had a crucial decision to make, although I did not know it. We could take the small road to the left, and go over another hill nearly as bad as the Vieilley-Marchaux one, dropping down into the valley of the Doubs by Amagney. Or we could continue on the Marchaux-Besançon road for some three miles, and turn off into the woods at Braillans, whence a path led to the back of the village of Thise.

I chose the second, and easier, route. My spirits began to rise. I was hungry again, and looking forward to my dinner with Barbier. You ate well there. We passed the spot where

I had seen the "patron" for the second time, and whence I had
so admired him when I watched him cycling off alone in the
rain towards Besançon. It entered my head then that one's
understandings constantly change, and one's admirations with
them. I still admired the "patron", but not because he had
the little courage it took to ride alone along that road. My
admiration now was founded on his worthy qualities as a leader.
Nono interrupted my thoughts.

"Your pistol's hanging out again," he said.

This time I turned it around and pushed it right up into my
pocket until the butt stuck. I could not draw it quickly now,
but I was tired of being told that it showed. Nono began to sing
again. A charming song, which went:

> "Sur la route qui va, qui va, qui va,
>   Et qui ne finit pas. . . ."

"How old are you, Nono?" I asked when he had finished.

"I'll be twenty in one month."

"You'll just fall in for your military service when the victory
comes."

"Yes. I look forward to that."

"What are you going to be?"

"A lawyer, like my father."

"I would give a lot to be twenty again."

"Why do you say that? It doesn't feel so good to be twenty."

"I know, but so much lies ahead."

We had begun to mount a longish hill with a curve at the top,
and a wood on the left of the road. The slope was just negoti-
able on a bicycle. My "Griffon" groaned as it took the strain.

"What age are you?" asked the curious Nono.

"Thirty-three."

"God, so old. One would never think you were so old."

"I have never done one thing long enough, or loved one
woman long enough to grow very old," I said.

"What did you do in peace-time. I suppose you were a
soldier, an officer."

"No. I was a newspaperman."

"For a newspaper in the provinces?"

"No, in Fleet Street. That is in London."

"Which paper, Émile?"

"The *Daily* . . ."

The words died on my lips as though my larynx had sucked
them back to silence. There was a German soldier in the wood

on the left. He was only a yard inside the bushes. He did not seem to be paying any attention to us. We cycled on for two or three yards, breasting the slope, then both of us saw what lay ahead—several German lorries pulled into the side of the road and Germans in uniform examining the civilian who had been riding a bicycle about three hundred yards ahead of us—and both of us said simultaneously:

"We must turn back."

Nono had been riding on my right. Now we swung round as quickly as we could on the roadway and he was on my left. As we turned one of the Germans bellowed down the road, obviously to men concealed behind us:

"Terrorists . . ."

And before we had got any speed up on the down-hill the man we had seen in the bushes had come out to the side of the road, slightly in front of us. He was a short, square German soldier, and I shall remember his face as long as I live. It was a strong, shiny, very-much-washed-looking face. It was pink and white, and the paint-work on his heavy helmet was deeply scored with criss-crossing scratches. There was no fear on it. Only satisfaction. I struggled to get my pistol out, but, thanks to Nono's admonishments, it would not move from my pocket. There was only one thing to do—ride for it. The German had already raised his rifle to the aim position. I would pass him at two yards' range. I was between him and Nono, and I assumed that I was as good as dead.

We were side by side picking up speed, when the bang came, close to my right ear-drum. I could not believe that I was still careering down the hill, swerving my bicycle from side to side. They were firing at me from behind and from both flanks, especially from the left flank, where they had men hidden in the grain. I could see them like scarecrows in the grain. They had come up to the kneeling position to fire at me.

"Poor Nono," I said as I flew down the hill. "Poor Nono." And something told me that I was going to get away, because they had killed Nono instead of me. I had to get off this road though. There was an up-hill beginning where the down-hill ended. They had got some kind of machine-gun going now. The steel was zipping off the road metal. If I slowed on the up-hill they would certainly knock me over easily.

There was only one piece of available cover. The wood on my right. There were Germans in that wood, but probably they were all higher up. At the bottom of the hill, without slow-ing down my "Griffon", I swung it to the right into the deep ditch. As the machine dropped I tried to shoot myself up, and my momentum carried me sailing head first through the thick scrub bordering the wood.

For a fraction of a second I lay there, winded, grateful for the cover from fire. The firing was still wildly going on, but now the steel was cutting through the upper branches above my head. I heard shouting too, and the sound of a car's starter, and heavy boots running on the road.

At no ordinary time would I have bothered to walk through such a wood, even hunting for "chantrelles". Now there was nothing else for it. I hoped that I was in a tongue of the southern part of the forest of Chailluz, that part of the forest that we had traversed twelve hours earlier, returning from the attack on the train. On my left was an open glade running up to a small farm. I dare not run up the glade because it was observed by the Germans, and if they were at all intelligent, they would send a party up it and completely cut me off. On my right I could hear Germans smashing through the small trees and bushes. My only hope seemed to be to break through and get to the top of the "tongue" and into the forest before they cut me off.

Although I was pouring with sweat, I kept my leather jacket on, since it protected my body from scratches. My face, hands and bare toes and ankles were soon running with blood, for much of the dense undergrowth was bramble. In places I had to slash a way through with my sharp parachutist's knife. It was a race all right. I could hear the Germans each time I stopped, and they were edging ever closer to me. To make the going harder, the wood ran up a steep hill. I had never in my life felt a more numbing physical exhaustion. Every branch seemed scientifically designed to claw at my arms, legs, and head, or to drive little dagger-like shoots into my eyes.

Georges' teachings helped me, for I came to a tiny clearing where wild boar had rooted in the ground. I followed their tracks, and so came on a path. It was extremely narrow and low, as paths go, but it helped me considerably. Now I seemed to be gaining on the Germans on my right and I was nearly opposite the head of the glade on my left.

When I reached the edge of the forest proper, I paused for a moment. The Germans were struggling through a thicket perhaps fifty yards behind me. After a second's reflection I drew my Colt and sent two .45 shells thudding into this thicket. There was an instant answering salvo with a sub-machine-gun and rifles, but when I had fired I had dropped down a bank and now, fairly silently on my rubber-soled sandals, I was running through much opener woodland.

With all their other faults, the bushes and trees through which I had torn my way had been hanging with moisture. My corduroy trousers were soaked through, and so heavy that it was difficult to run. I stopped to roll them up over my knees. While I stopped, I heard another party of Germans arrive at the farm in what sounded like two trucks. My line of escape was to circle to the left and try to cross the Marchaux road lower down. I must therefore try to make a circle round this second party. The first party had not stopped long after my shots. They were already on the move again. But I was confident of outstripping them. I got out the excellent compass they had given me in London, and checked up on my direction. Until I found a path I knew I would have to go through the forest by map memory. Then I set off at a steady run. I am fond of running long distances, and I was then extremely fit. But my breath was coming in the deep gasps of an animal that is hunted. The battle through the wood had taken a lot of the energy out of me.

After half an hour I struck a path that I recognised from our withdrawal that morning. If I had not known it I should have hesitated to take it, thinking that paths were dangerous since one might find Germans on them. But I knew that the entry to this one was fairly well hidden in the woods, and it was just what I needed to take me round the large German party that was now cutting deep into the wood from the farm. I continued, running down the path for perhaps two miles. All sounds of pursuit had now died, and I was nervous, for an unheard enemy is sinister. I had a feeling that we had bumped into an ambush set by the advance-guard of a large body of German troops. If they were very eager to get me it was possible that they had set guards along the Marchaux road which I was now approaching.

At the edge of the clear space that bordered the road at the point I intended to cross, I pulled out the small flask they had given me at the airfield in England. After drinking nearly half of the "calvados" it fortunately contained, I felt equal to the crossing and the climb which now confronted me. Using all available cover, I worked nearer and nearer to the road. There were three young children there, but I was not going to bother about them. I tried to clean the blood off my face with a handkerchief damped with spittle, took off my tell-tale leather jacket, rolling it into a shape that was easily carried. I changed the magazine in my big Colt and thrust it loosely into my trouser pocket. As I did so I remembered with a twinge that if I had been able to draw this weapon Nono would possibly still be with me.

I strolled across the road, as though I were a cultivator returning from his work. No Germans were in sight. But the road was busy with peasants. As I mounted the hill, for I was now on the western end of the plateau between Marchaux and Champoux, I heard the church bell of Marchaux begin slowly to toll. I was sure that it was tolling for Nono. And perhaps for me too. I cut straight up the hill. At the edge of the forest I stopped to look west. I was astounded at what I saw. Two large bodies of Germans were working their way up towards the edge of the forest. That could only mean one thing. They were going to search the forest, and on our side of the Marchaux road, the northern bit of the forest. There were not more than two hundred Germans in these parties, however. Unless they had other parties operating on the other side of the "côte" from Vieilley, Bonney, or Devecey, the search could not be serious for me, though it might menace the Maquis.

Pushing myself to my fastest pace, I climbed the long hill to the path that I knew so well running along the summit. There was no sign of Germans on the top, and I made good time back to the cabin, and, since there was nobody there, down to the Maquis.

Boulaya, the "patron", and Georges were there with most of the Maquisards. They were amazed and relieved to see me, for already the rumour was going that I was dead. A heated argument developed around the dinner-table in gathering darkness. We had as yet no confirmation that Nono was dead. We hoped, naturally, that he was. If he was not dead he faced torture and then death. When the Gestapo saw the nature of the things he carried in his rucksack, they would certainly want to know whence he came and who were his friends. Under the kind of torture the Gestapo gave, anybody might talk. The "patron" thought that the Maquis should move across the Ognon into the Haute-Saône that night. Georges and Boulaya held this to be unnecessary, and indeed impossible, for we had at that hour no means of rapid transport. I was too tired to take part in the argument.

It was a cold night. Sinister black clouds with greasy golden edges hung over the hill as we climbed to the cabin. We all knew that it would rain in the night, but it was too risky to sleep in a barn or in the village. I was shivering and weak with exhaustion when I got into my sleeping-bag. Boulaya had insisted on my having my own "bed", and the "patron" slept beside me. Boulaya and Georges shared the other cabin. Berger was away carrying messages from me to Albert and Paul. He was expected to return early in the morning.

The first rain came about midnight. I was only half aware of it, and tried to sleep on. But the "patron" would not tolerate that.

"Émile," he said, leaning over and shaking me. "It's raining."

This was followed by his usual stream of colonial reflections prefaced with "Nom de Dieu". Luckily that day, in response to my appeal for some kind of waterproof fabric for enveloping charges, one of Boulaya's respectable go-betweens in Besançon had produced a roll of pale blue rubberised fabric. I cut two long strips off this, gave one to the "patron" and took the other myself. I thus contrived to sleep, warmly damp. When the others went off, still in the rain, at breakfast-time, I continued to sleep. At ten the faithful Berger arrived, followed by Boulaya. They had decided that, as the rain seemed to have set in for some days, they were going to vacate the cabin and move into Georges' barn on the outskirts of Vieilley.

"Isn't that a little risky?" I asked Boulaya.

"No. Of course I had forgotten. We've been saved by a miracle."

"After yesterday I am prepared to believe in it. What is your miracle?"

"The Junkers have tried to murder Hitler. The army is fighting the S.S. in several places. There have been shots in the barracks in Besançon. This has certainly saved us. The Gestapo have their hands full for the moment. Otherwise . . .

"In any case, I am sending the Maquis to their homes, those of them that have homes. The others will shelter in the usual barn until the rain and the immediate danger cease. The Champoux Maquis have moved. Just as well too. They moved whenever they got our message last night. An hour or two later the Boches were at Champoux. They did a drive with six hundred men all along that side of the 'côte'. They were searching for you."

"And Nono?" I asked.

"Nono is dead. He was killed there, beside the road. They took his body, riddled with rifle and 9-mm. rounds, to Marchaux. The officer in charge even handed over his papers to the gendarmes in Marchaux."

"His real papers? But I told him not to carry papers."

"He must have forgotten. Yes, his real papers with his parents' names, and the address at Bonnay. A month or two ago his father and mother and all of us would be in deadly danger. Now I think the Gestapo are too busy. Poor Nono. He must have a hero's funeral. I am sending Pointu and young Georges Pernod to Besançon with eight thousand francs (£40) to buy the finest wreath they can find. Then we still have some of the wreaths we had made for July 14th."

While he talked I had made up my mind to go and rest for a few days with the Dardels. Nobody except Boulaya and Berger suspected that I knew them. I did not share Boulaya's optimism about the Gestapo. It seemed likely to me that they would follow up the Nono clue. Bonnay was the next village but one to Vieilley.

As Boulaya packed up his belongings Berger prepared for me a bowl of hot milk with some alcohol and sugar in it. Then when I climbed out of one dirty wet pair of trousers preparatory to putting on a clean wet pair, he took a soft cloth and wiped the blood and dirt off my legs. There was nothing that Berger could not do. He himself was soaked to the skin, and his bronchitis was worse. The rain poured steadily down. I felt surprisingly weak going down the hill. For some reason the Nono affair had knocked me up. Probably the reason was Nono.

The train had gone from Roches now. I had thrown a life away by my eagerness to avenge my first failure, an eagerness that had prevented me from resting properly before I tried again. In an ordinary frame of mind, if I had to carry weapons and explosives, I should have walked over the "côte" to Thise, instead of risking the bicycle trip by Marchaux. The Maquis were disturbed about it too. While we lay warming and drying ourselves on Georges' hay, Maurice, who had now been made chief in place of Buhl, came in. His face did not show the usual ruddy, gap-toothed smile. In fact he scowled at us as he said:

"Why are we running away?"

"Explain yourself," replied Boulaya.

"Well," said Maurice, taking off his streaming oilskin and

seating himself truculently on the hay beside us. "The boys say that the officers are running away, and they want to know what it's all about. They say that you've told everyone to go home and hide, whereas we feel that this is the moment to go out and avenge Nono."

A lot more followed. Instead of answering somewhat curtly, Boulaya took each point in great detail, showing that the officers had not run away, that he had sent warning to the Champoux Maquis, that he had arranged for a grand funeral for Nono. An argument then swung from one side to the other with Maurice, rather enjoying the part of playing the stubborn honest sergeant, gradually being won round by Boulaya's eloquence. Finally, Boulaya had wound himself and everybody else up into such a frenzy that he, the "patron", and Georges all went out on a longish walk through the downpour to pass on all that had been discussed to the men. There had been much talk about that strange thing "morale" in this discussion. And when they all came back a few hours later they told me that the morale was now good. It reminded me of a French war communiqué in May, 1940, and demonstrated finally to me that only French officers could lead Frenchmen. I had not the kind of patience needed to talk to my subordinates about morale, nor to hear them question my own motives and moves as Maurice had done. Boulaya was a pattern of an officer for the Maquis. He led the same life as his men, he looked after them, took no nonsense from them. He never curried favour with them, yet he was popular and respected. If he thought it necessary to do all that talking about morale, then I knew that it was necessary.

Personally I was going to "run away" whether they liked it or not. I told Maurice this in plain words. But he only smiled at me.

"It's not the same for you," he said. "You're a foreigner, Emile, and we've no complaint about your behaviour. You're a friend, but you're outside all this sort of thing, if you understand what I mean."

I thought I understood.

It was dark and still raining when I arrived at the Dardel's house. I had chosen the darkness because I did not intend to let myself be seen there. They were expecting me, sitting up in the kitchen and rather flurried. I had sent Berger that afternoon to warn them that I would arrive to stay for a few days and the good soul had told them that I had been through a "terrible experience". They had not seen me for some time, and in the interim I had lost a good deal of weight. Also my clothes, after the rains hitting them frequently in the waterlogged cabin were now so creased and generally in a ghastly condition.

They put me to bed in the salon on a comfortable divan with clean linen sheets. When they had all said good-night and gone off to their beds, I turned on the bedside light and inspected the books laid out for me to read. One of them was the unabridged version of *Lady Chatterley's Lover*, translated into French. I read this extraordinary book all night, and the following day, apart from having a lasciviously pleasant hot bath and eating three meals, I slept.

For four days I allowed myself to relax in the comfortably family atmosphere of the house. On the first day of this holiday Monsieur and Madame Dardels went to Bonnay to attend Nono's funeral. It was the biggest funeral ever seen in these parts. There were more than three thousand mourners and every village sent its contingent. There was a guard of honour of our Maquisards dressed in their khaki uniforms and carrying Sten guns. They guarded the tomb, which was covered with wreaths and the beloved German-banned tricolour. Pinned to a cushion paraded at the funeral was the "Croix de Guerre", awarded posthumously to Nono. Standing over the grave in the sunshine Colonel Fournier of Venise, who had been a great man in the Daladier war government of 1939, made an impassioned eulogy of the dead boy beginning:

"Soldat de France, mort pour la Patrie. . . ."

Nono was a youngster who had a talent for leadership. Even after death this talent seemed to persist. His dead body was an inspiration to the valley

When I listened to all this, and later when I visited his two parents, leaving guards outside the house to see that there were no Germans about, I felt angrily that, had I been sufficiently energetic to walk to Thise, Nono would have been something better than a little hero of the Resistance. He would have been alive.

I told his parents that he had been killed instantly there, beside me on the road. But a cultivator of Marchaux who was working in some pear-trees on the hill-side and claimed to have witnessed the whole thing, said that Nono was only wounded on the roadway. He dropped his rucksack and ran across the field to a little wood, and from there managed to make his way to the forest at the bottom of the "côte". He was tying up his leg wound when the Germans caught up with him. He fired with

255

his revolver. They filled him with lead and dragged him back by his heels to the road. When they saw the contents of his rucksack they kicked his dead body. Then they threw it into a truck and took it to Marchaux. They also took my bicycle, the "Griffon".

But apart from the funeral sortie the Dardels, as always, held aloof from the Resistance. The problems of the day were domestic ones. Monsieur Dardel had little work to do, since his factory was hardly ever open. So he occupied himself in other ways. One day he fitted up a grotesque machine in the garden, started an engine in the machine, and sawed wood. Another day he made soap. This was made by boiling equal quantites of fat and a solution of caustic soda. Where the "savon Dardel" was something special was that it had some resin in it. My identity had to be kept secret from the two boys in the house, Claude, the son, a muscular and obstreperous boy of fifteen, and Roger, the fat boy, a refugee from Paris. Claude's aim in life was to be in the Resistance. When he was not fishing in the Ognon or smoking cigarettes in the woods, he was playing at being a Maquisard. He was scornful of his parents and his sister, finding them far too law-abiding for his taste. As for me, although he was inclined to think of me at first as a mysterious stranger, he was finally duped by the words of his cunning father into thinking that I was just an insurance agent. He was not allowed to speak to me. I gathered that the excuse given for this by the Dardel parents was that I suffered from some dreadful nervous ailment. But when I asked the exact nature of the ailment they had described Madame Dardel always went a bright pink, and once she actually had to leave the room. I heard her then having hysterics of laughter next door. She and her daughter fussed around me while Dardel himself looked on with his affable, though faintly cynical smile.

The daughter, Janine, went through agonies of conscience about the work she was doing for us. Although dangerous, it was harmless work, since it consisted only in carrying messages to "cover" addresses, usually innocent and respectable houses, like the château at Thise. But although she was twenty, Janine still believed that to tell a lie, even for one's country, was a deadly sin. She was a shy person. In fact she was as tortured by shyness as I was at her age, and still am sometimes.

It was known all over the district that when strangers called at the house in Moncey, Janine Dardel was in the habit of

whisking through the kitchen, the bathroom, and then up the
back stairs to her own bedroom. This was a charming room,
very white and virginal with a lot of good books, including the
poetry of Baudelaire and Rimbaud (which she said she disliked), and the poetry of Verlaine (which she said she liked).
On the wall was pinned the cover of a 1939 number of the
magazine *Match*, which showed a camera portrait of a man in
a glengarry who seemed to be a private in the Highland Light
Infantry. Janine asked me if I did not think him photogenic.
I answered that I did not. The poor thing was disillusioned by
my appearance. She had been dreaming that all Britons were
like the private in the H.L.I. Young women are always apt to
be silly, no matter how many exams. they have passed.

Before I returned to the Maquis and my work, Janine did
something disastrous. She gave me a brown leather bag that
she used to carry her music. The kind of satchel in which young
schoolchildren in Britain carry sandwiches, a box of coloured
crayons, an apple, and some school books.

This innocent gift was destined to cause her great anxiety
and to wipe that naughty boy smile from the face of her father.

CHAPTER XIII

I FOUND changes in our Vieilley Maquis. They were un-
welcome changes to me.

In the first place Georges was about to move the Maquis
itself, to move it higher up the hill, more behind Vieilley and
Phillipon's bothy. Still, he had chosen a good place for it as
usual. The approach, up a path running into the hilly fields
from the bothy, was not easily marked and was easy to guard.
And the Maquis would be farther from the villages.

Now we had several new Maquisards, and some of them, led
by the "cuistot", who, as I had always suspected, was a good
worker with bad habits, were dragging down to the village of
Merey at nights. It was easy for them to womanise, for many
women, fired by the exploits of the Vieilley Maquis, were only
too proud to render any services. Georges planned to ban the
villages completely to the men. But it was a rainy time then,
at the beginning of August, and he had to build them a weather-
tight habitation. This was finally achieved with the capture of
more tarpaulins from the railway.

More serious than the moving of the Maquis was the change in the habits of the officers. I had expected to find Boulaya and the "patron" reinstalled in our high cabin. But owing to the rain, and the severity of our last drenching there, they had decided to leave it altogether.

They were not living in the woods any longer. They were living in the village, and going to the woods for their meals. They slept in two places. One, called the "Ritz", was Georges' big barn. The other, called the "Carlton", was in the old château. The château had not been occupied by one family in living memory. It was occupied now by several farming families, and it was the most squalid place in Vielley.

Both château and barn had two exits, one into the village and one out to the orchards surrounding the village. But this gave little security. If the Germans came to Vieilley we knew that they would probably surround the whole village. And the back exits from both places gave on to the flat and comparatively open low country on the north side of Vieilley.

The "patron", who had many times been nearly caught by the Gestapo, was the most emphatic of us all that this system of life was absurdly dangerous. But it was he with his work who kept us tied there. For now that the war was moving obviously in favour of the Allies, and the southern and western areas of his territory were beginning to receive parachuted material, the "patron" had an enormous amount of organising and paper work to do. Boulaya was obliged to help him with this. The "patron" seemed to feel that some disaster was hanging over his head because almost every day he reminded Boulaya:

"You are second-in-command. You must know everything in case anything happens to me."

And the energetic Boulaya, who disbelieved in paper work, was obliged to tie his volatile nose to a desk. The "patron" got through a vast amount of paper work in a day. A vast amount too much, I thought. And occasionally his passion for paper cost us dear.

Once, for example, he suggested a scheme that greatly attracted me, a grand attack on Vesoul railway station and depot. Vesoul was outside the territory I had interested myself in. But the "patron" wanted me to lead a picked team up from Vieilley and do the job with one hard blow. I calculated that with four men in under an hour I could put the station out of action for many weeks. Our journey to Vesoul had been minutely planned, also the hide-out in the town to which we would retire when we had done our work.

"Splendid, go ahead, Émile," said the "patron" when I reported all this.

"Yes, but hold on a moment. We have precious little explosive."

"How much have you got?"

"We can scrape up eleven kilos."

"How much do you need for Vesoul? Don't stint yourself now."

"Sixty kilos."

"Don't worry, Émile. I'll write today for your sixty kilos. You can prepare to do the job in about a week's time. I'll ask Paul at Montbeliard."

He wrote a letter addressed to Paul, naming me, asking for sixty kilos of explosive with primers, detonators, and detonating fuse, and stating that the stores were required to perform a large-scale attack on Vesoul station. He sent this letter to one Rita who operated from Rioz, in the Haute-Saône. Rita had instructions to pass on the letter.

But in the meantime Rita and his men had made prisoner two women who worked for the Gestapo. And Meisner, the Gestapo chief in Besançon, had ordered Rioz to be burned in reprisal.

So on the morning after the "patron" had sent his letter to Rita, the inhabitants of Rioz awoke to find that Cossack troops had surrounded their village and the Gestapo were rounding up all the men and forcing them into two or three houses under armed surveillance. The Cossacks were then allowed to burn eight houses and commit at least one rape.

Rita, the "patron's" letter still in his pocket, was seized by the Gestapo. He managed to knock over the two men who held him, and he escaped. But he left all his papers, including the letter, in the hands of the Gestapo.

That ended all plans for Vesoul.

Village life passed for me in a kind of haze, a haze of mistrust and fear and pleasure mixed in with a great deal of work outside the old Maquis area. It was a time of expansion. Every day twenty or thirty people would arrive to see us in Vieilley. Some came in cars, some on bicycles, some on foot. Some were Boulaya's respectables; some were messengers working for the "patron", for Boulaya, or for me; some were just thugs looking for a job, and some were French specialists who were working for the F.F.I., people who had been trained by the de

Gaullistes in England and parachuted into France. For one particularly of these men I had the highest esteem. We called him Ligne, and he was a thin, suave and charming regular officer in the French Army. He acted as a kind of secret Regional Commissioner for the Resistance, and he could not have been more capable or more helpful. Perhaps there was something odd about a Regional Commissioner who rode round under an assumed personality on a bicycle, and who risked his life every time he left his office, and every minute he spent in his office. It never seemed odd at the time.

Gone was the enchantment of my mornings on the hill, with the view and the exaltation of being in the woods and so far from the working valley. Strive as I might to change their way of life, I could not do it. For the new existence was convenient and almost comfortable. When I complained the argument always ended with the expression "fear nothing" or the old favourite: "Ça ne risque rien."

Instead of the lonely exaltation of the cabin I now awoke in a room just large enough to hold four men stretched on the floor. Georges and Boulaya slept on one mattress under the window, the "patron" slept beside me on a "single" mattress, and I slept in or on my sleeping-bag. This room had reached a pitch of dirtiness that was simply fantastic. Before Georges "converted" it for our use, it had been a receptacle for rubbish. A pile of old sardine-tins, chamber-pots, and medicine bottles lay on the one small rectangle of floor space that we did not use. There was a cooking range standing at the foot of my "bed", a range that had seen much service and then apparently had cracked in many places from over-heating and old age. It was a "Venus". Imagine that. Two tommy-guns and a bottle of potable and digestive alcohol sitting on "Venus" were what my waking eyes now alighted on. Then one of the other three would be snoring. And if the night had been cold the small window with its cobweb curtains would be closed.

I was always the first to waken, and dress myself in shorts and sandals, and perhaps my leather jacket. The "patron", sound old soldier, was a profound believer in the saying "a good soldier always sleeps in his boots", and he was outspokenly horrified at my habit of sleeping naked. The "patron" was the most practical man about these things that I met in all the Resistance. Once when he and I were setting off on a long journey to visit Albert and Colonel La Guarde of the F.F.I. on the plateau of Meche, I saw how a real soldier does his toilet.

We were sleeping in the barn beside our bicycles, for we had decided to depart at six o'clock. I awoke at five a.m., washed myself at the pump outside, and at twenty minutes to six I wakened the "patron". He rubbed some sleep out of his yellowish eyes, rolled off the hay, swept his hair back from either side of his forehead with three or four jerky movements of his hands, put on his beret, seized his bicycle, rode out of the door, and looked at his watch.

"Nom de Dieu, why did you wake me so early?" he asked. It was sixteen minutes to six.

In the mornings we left the château by one of the back doors. Usually I was alone. Sometimes Georges was with me. And we washed and breakfasted in the most dangerous house in Vieilley, Georges' house. The important thing of the day for most people was the early morning news programme of the Swiss radio. That was at 8.15. Although most of them listened a great deal to the B.B.C., it was the Swiss radio which interested them and swayed them. It was the more truthful. Georges had an absurd little radio in his kitchen. When it ceased to work you gave it a hard blow with your fist and it worked. It was a German radio.

For breakfast now we usually had bread and butter and honey. The honey was given to me by Madame Dardel, who had got it into her kind head that I suffered from a sugar famine because sugar made energy. Every time I went there she gave me honey from her own bees, and a bag of sugar bought on the black market. Then Madame Poirier, wife of the "garde-pêche", often gave us some very indigestible plum- or apple-tart.

The stream of visitors began soon after breakfast, and often they would take five or six of them up to the Maquis at mid-day to eat. The Maquis commissariat was now well organised, and the "cuistot" had regular fatigues to help him. It was summer and food was plentiful in the neighbourhood. The more so for us because Philippe and Maurice had captured a German lorry containing fifteen large pigs designed for eating.

One day after lunch Philippe asked if he might take some of the others out and do a job on the Vesoul railway. We had just heard a train pass below us in the valley, and this was such an unusual sound that it roused us to action. Boulaya refused permission, but I persuaded him to let Philippe take out the Pointu and two new lads, Communists whom Maurice and Philippe together had rescued from imprisonment in the German hospital in Besançon, where they had been convalescing from German-inflicted wounds. The four of them departed happily on foot, carrying an arsenal of miscellaneous weapons and the heavy tools we used for unscrewing the railway lines. They promised to work as far afield as Miserey. Things appeared to go badly. That afternoon we heard the sound of firing, and the story came back to us that while they were derailing a train near Miserey a German truck full of soldiers passed on the road and opened fire. The Maquisards replied and then withdrew.

One by one that evening the young men dribbled back into the camp, bringing with them all their weapons and the tools. The story of the Germans was true, but Philippe had turned their arrival to our profit, for while the little battle was going on he had walked into Miserey station, found another train there and obliged the railwaymen to start it at full speed. This, crashing into the derailed train in the cutting, broke up the battle and allowed the other three Maquisards to withdraw in good order. On the way home Philippe and the Pointu seized a third train near Devecey, made all the occupants descend, and hurled this train on to the wreckage near Miserey. This was a wonderful day's work. I cycled out to see it, and I knew that if the enemy still had a crane he would need it for this, and it would be a long job. The cutting was deep, and the wreckage was well wedged in.

But our Philippe was irresistible. Boulaya gave him a holiday in Besançon to celebrate this important victory. He spruced himself up and left on a new bicycle. (We had just taken eight new ones from the police in Besançon, and Boulaya and I each bought one on the black market, so we were now astoundingly well off for bicycles.) Bronzed and bleached by the sun now, Philippe looked more cherubic than ever.

Unable to avoid the scene of his crime, he cycled past the still smoking remains where the Gestapo were examining tracks and questioning civilians and railwaymen. He saw another locomotive in Miserey station. Unarmed as he was, he cursed and swore at the railwaymen until they sent their engine rushing down the track. It hit the wreckage while the Gestapo were still there, and jumping, said onlookers, thirty feet into the air it landed upside down on the other side of the heap of twisted metal. Its wheels continued to revolve for some time. Already crowds were gathering for this fantastic sight. Cycling excursions were setting out from all the villages. Many of them were to have their money's worth. Philippe, tranquilly continuing on his way to

Besançon, found another train and again, with only his gruff and determined voice to help him, succeeded in getting it launched at full speed on the right rails. In front of a large audience this train added itself to the heap in the cutting.

Sightseers were still visiting the place six weeks later. And it was known locally as "the mountain of Miserey". This closed the Vesoul line until (and, alas, after) the Allied Armies arrived.

As the crowds of strangers increased in the Maquis, and meals there became more and more social affairs, I withdrew myself, jealously regretting the old freedom and the old hardships, and jealously resenting the intrusion of newcomers who had slept softly in beds and had thought of our Maquisards as terrorists or wood-lice only a month or two previously. I withdrew myself and I began another phase of my life so different that it amounted to a new life.

It was well for me that this new life presented itself, for with the shortage of weapons and explosives, and the railway battle virtually won by our side, there was now little enough for me to do if I continued in the old way.

I became a gangster with genuine regret.

Had I been born ten years later, this might not have been so. During the formative years of my childhood, the leading inhabitants of my imaginative world were, in the following order: sailors (Drake especially), Romans, Napoleon, cowboys and trappers, Christ, Robin Hood and all outlaws, King Harold (because he lost the Battle of Hastings, I think), and Tallulah Bankhead. The only two of this list who have not slipped away are Napoleon and Christ.

I do not think I ever seriously considered the merits of gangsters because I do not think that I heard of them before it was too late. I have always felt a strong, and I believe thoroughly healthy, antipathy for anything in the shape of a policeman. This antipathy is possibly what prevents me from reading any book about crime or detection.

The necessity to become a gangster was more or less forced upon me by the shortness of the summer nights, which precluded the possibility of supplies arriving by parachute.

And the Maquis was growing fast. Our work was growing. The young men from Vieilley were going out now to do the training which I had done in the beginning. They spoke with the authority of blooded warriors. They led attacks with other new Maquisards, many of whom I had never even seen.

With our new formations which were beginning now to

263

encircle Besançon, Boulaya had ordered a great offensive drive against the depot's water supply. After swaying one way and another the battle had been won again by the Resistance. The outlying pumps had been attacked, then the three sources of water for the depot itself. The Germans were reduced to sending empty locomotives under tow to collect water from far distances, even to calling on the fire brigade for water.

When we thought that each goods train might carry four hundred tons of French food or merchandise into Germany, or four hundred tons of German war material to the Western Front, it was good to see the railways dead. But there is a sadness, too, when one phase of the battle is over, and it has been won. The athlete who ends the first lap in the lead would rather the race ended there. I wanted to finish the race alive, and the pace was increasing.

The battle was going our way. The fame of Boulaya was growing in the land. We were expanding cautiously, as surely as possible. But there were annoying, maddening difficulties of supply.

Food for the Maquis was normally obtainable because the country people were generous, and the F.F.I. now usually had adequate finances sent out from the French headquarters in England. But there were other things that the Maquis needed desperately. Things like boots, bicycles, tyres, petrol, blankets, socks, grease, biscuits and tinned food or chocolate for emergency rations. We could not get those things from England, and when the parachutages began every cubic centimetre of container space would be wanted for weapons. But the German garrisons in our part of France possessed those things. Boulaya and I had to see how thefts, large-scale thefts, from the Germans could be organised.

Our existing Maquis were unsuitable for such work. They were serious, almost military units. If we allowed them to become gangsters for one week they would never return to their regular work. It looked as though we must have another organisation of gangsters, separate from our ordinary, our "respectable" terrorists.

Our old friend the Frisé became the first of the gangsters. In reality, the Frisé had to be banished because his indiscretions grew so grotesque that his presence endangered the whole organisation centred on Vieilley. He was sent with a friend named Marcel, another ex-sailor, to form a new Maquis near Franois, west of Besançon.

Frisé departed with an air of "you just wait and see", and within a few days he had produced fireworks, killing some Gestapo men and making their "traction avant" his own car. Wearing captured German uniform, he and Marcel began to tour the area. At first they only had one uniform. So Frisé wore the tunic and Marcel wore the hat. We expected them to get caught almost immediately, but they were a wily pair, the Frisé knew every road and track in the area, and many times they passed through impossible situations by sheer dash.

At first the Frisé confined his sorties to sabotage expeditions on the railways and telephones. But soon the necessities of his cars (after the first week he was not content with one, but always had two or three Citroëns in his woodland "garage"), obliged him to make almost constant expeditions in search of what were now necessities to him, petrol, oil, and tyres. Despite this, we began to find the Frisé useful because he was mobile, and he was afraid of nothing.

When Rioz was burned and the "patron's" letter taken, the Frisé played the lead in what, for him, was not an extraordinary incident.

Hearing that two friends of his were among the men rounded up by the Germans inside Rioz, the Frisé took off with Marcel and two others in their fastest car. They were able to direct themselves on Rioz by the smoke that was already floating in a horrid, oily column above the village. There were groups of Cossacks guarding the roads with their shaggy ponies and little anti-tank guns. When they saw the Frisé's German uniform they jovially waved the car past. So they drove into the centre of the village, and by luck they found the house where their friends were. When they had released the prisoners and tied up the guards, they naturally took all the German arms that they could find. And the Frisé saw something that made his mouth water. It was a 9-mm. Italian sub-machine-gun, and it seemed to the Frisé to combine the beauties of the little American Winchester, the Sten, and the Schmeisser. He took it and checked that the magazine was full. Then he saw something else that interested him.

Sixteen Germans were sitting in a café across the street having a glass of marc (or schnapps, as they called it, the barbarians). With the Frisé the two coincidences were strongly linked. Finding a dream weapon and seeing the dream target. The others had gone back to the car, for they were anxious to leave Rioz. The Frisé wiped his sweaty hands on the seat of his pants, took the new gun in his hand, walked across the road and kicked open the door of the café.

The Germans sat at marble-topped tables around the room.

"One good swinging burst, and I have the lot," thought Frisé. His prospective targets sat frozen momentarily in terror, gazing at the figure in the doorway with its fierce frizz of hair.

Frisé squeezed on the trigger. Nothing happened. He had forgotten before he crossed the road to see how this weapon worked. Now it was obviously on "safe". He searched desperately for the safety-catch with his spare fingers. He was still searching when he noticed that the Germans were getting busy. Four or five of them were drawing guns. He leaped backwards and sideways out of the doorway, a stream of bullets following him. Doubling round the corner he found the car, started up and all ready to go. The same Cossacks who had waved them in waved them out. Sixty yards beyond their post the Frisé told Marcel to stop.

"What is it now?" asked Marcel and the others.

But the Frisé was leaning half his body out of the window. One shot rang out from his new sub-machine-gun, a pause, then a short burst.

"Drive on," he said. But Marcel did not need to be told because the Cossacks had flung themselves on the roadway and were busily answering the Frisé's fire.

"I just wanted to see that it worked," the Frisé explained. "You see, it's got two triggers. The front one fires single rounds, and the other bursts. That will take a little getting used to."

Apparently it did. The following day when he was explaining the new weapon to me he accidentally put a short burst within two inches of my right big toe.

Yes, the Frisé was wonderful. But Paincheau was the real discovery. Paincheau was supreme. And the strange thing was that before I met him I disliked him. I never wanted to meet him. Especially after my accident due to my own nervous disposition, to him, and to his Russians. Perhaps I never should have met him if it had not been for a strange and dreaded figure that had constantly flitted across our horizon—La Marche, the tall French ex-officer who worked for the Gestapo.

One evening Berger, who had been visiting his baby son in Montbozon, came up the hill to the Maquis and told us:

"I saw Paincheau take La Marche."

He described the scene he had witnessed on a road near Rougemont. Paincheau was cycling along. He stopped. A tall,

266

dark man following him casually on a bicycle also stopped, pretended to be adjusting his saddle.

"Anything the matter?" Paincheau asked softly, dropping his own bicycle and walking back towards the other.

"No, thank you very much indeed. It's only that this saddle keeps slipping." La Marche looked down at the little man confronting him, and his glistening smile was full of bonhomie.

"You are La Marche, are you not?"

"Why, no. You are mistaken. My name is Beaufort."

"My name is Paincheau. You are under arrest." Paincheau held a big automatic pointing at the other's stomach.

"Under what authority do you arrest me?"

"I am an officer in the F.F.I."

"My dear fellow, so am I," answered La Marche easily. "I shall willingly accompany you to prove it."

"Well, just drop that bicycle and clasp the hands behind the neck. I think we should take this path into the wood. The road is a shade public for us members of the F.F.I."

Next morning Paincheau himself arrived to report. His appearance at first repelled, then interested me. He was a short man, extremely lightly built with the slender wrists and ankles and the long bony fingers of a mandarin. His features were small and featureless, except that his eyes were the soft tea-pot brown eyes of a woman, and I was to learn later that when he was disturbed emotionally as he easily was, the eyes could fill with tears. His voice was low and soft. It had a tender, purring quality that never seemed to vary.

Could this be the firebrand and killer I had imagined?

He was going a little bald on the top of his head, and he wore his hair, which grew in baby curls, extremely long and fluffy at the sides of his head, and elongated into a pair of enormous side-whiskers. These stretched down below the bottoms of his ears and stuck out, stirring gently in the air, on either side of his small, sensitive face. The effect was to give an unnaturally domed and shining look to his forehead.

Among us of the Maquis his odd appearance was further exaggerated by the fact that he affected slightly foppish, city clothes, except that he wore no tie, but had a spotlessly white shirt-collar which hung open Byronically to show the base of a hairy neck. His suit was blue, with wide trousers and a long square-shouldered coat fitting his hips and pinched at the waist by a little belt at the back, and pleats. Out of the twenty-odd men there in the clearing, he and I were the only two who wore shoes, not boots. Paincheau's shoes were black, well-cleaned, and thin-soled.

We were eating a good mushroom omelette with sauté potatoes, and he took some on his plate. But I noticed that he only pecked at the food. I saw him glance quickly once at the surface of the plate, and I guessed that it was not clean enough for him. He smoked incessantly, and his fingers and nails, otherwise immaculate, were slightly coloured by tobacco.

Accompanying Paincheau was his lieutenant, bodyguard, and gunman, young Jean Viennot. I already knew Jean well by name, for he and his brother were farmers at the hamlet of La Barre, which was one of my favourite haunts. But for months the farm had lacked its two stalwart owners, and had been managed by a married sister who had come from a city job to keep the place going. Jean had spent six months in Gestapo hands earlier in the year. Then for some reason they had released him. They returned later to the farm to rearrest him. But it was a misty morning, and Jean ran out of the back door, leaped a stone wall while they fired their pistols at him, and vanished into the mist.

He was a splendid young man. In appearance a virile and bigger edition of Byron at his best. Like his chief, he wore huge side-whiskers, and these gave to his chiselled features a look of ancient and poetic nobility. Jean did not copy Paincheau's clothing. He was dressed extremely Maquisard, in breeches, high boots and the fur-collared short coat they call a "canadienne".

While I was taking in the two strange and florid figures, Paincheau told his story. He told it simply and without stressing any points or gloating over what the others regarded as a great achievement. You saw from his quiet way of talking that he was used to authority, and he was not over-awed by the presence of his superior officers or myself. Indeed on me he turned only one blandly curious glance and then never looked again. He was an introvert. He was wondering what impression he himself got from what he said.

He had walked La Marche into a wood. Two of his men were waiting there with a car. They drove La Marche to another wood, a small, isolated wood. There were still five hours of daylight. La Marche showed signs of nervousness when they arrived. He was not allowed to sit down, and they made him stand beside an open grave. So while Paincheau softly questioned him, asked him the same questions again and again, he occasionally stole a took at the damp woodland earth in the grave, earth with worms in it and the roots of trees. The freshness of the summer evening must have come seeping down into the wood. La Marche confessed.

"Why did he confess?" asked the "patron".

"He saw that we knew all about him."

"You did not torture him?"

"No. He just got tired of answering questions."

They gave La Marche a piece of board, some pages from his own notebook, and a pencil. He was allowed to sit beside his grave while he wrote his miserable confession:

"Money had always been necessary to me. . . . I did this work for money. . . . I was paid a fixed sum per month and a reward for prisoners and for information given to the Gestapo during the month. Most months I earned ten thousand francs (£50) or more. The following are my accounts for the past six months. . . . I would be willing now to work for the Resistance. I denounced the following French men and women to the Germans. . . ."

The name "MOLLE, Georges, Vieilley terrorist", figured in his list.

When he had finished, read, and signed his confession, they made him stand again by the damp grave. He was shot and his body fell into the grave.

"Why was he killed so quickly?" demanded the "patron". "It was a case for expert questioning. We might have got much more out of him than that."

"He was a dangerous man, and it was my responsibility to guard him," Paincheau answered.

"Who killed him?" The Maquisards crowded silently closer. There is something terrible, something enthralling about the taking away of that incredibly fragile thing, life.

"I did." Now his eyes were hard china. "I got one of the men to attract his attention, and when he turned his head I shot him twice through the temple."

"How was he at the end?" they asked.

"He was nervous. Shaking. But courageous. Frequently he took out that picture of his wife and kissed it. One of the men said to him: 'She's pretty, your wife.' He replied: 'Yes. But you ought to see my mistress.' He had courage, the swine."

Next time I met Paincheau was on the high road, near the village of La Tour de Scay. I was on a bicycle and he rode a small, noisy Peugeot "petrolette". His side-whiskers were wind-blown. And his hair. Otherwise he was immaculate in his own strange way.

"I have been thinking that you and I could work together," I said to him.

"So have I, Monsieur Émile," he answered. "How do you want to work with me?"

"I will tell you that definitely when I see your work. But I think I would like to arrange with London that you should be allotted a ground or grounds for parachutages."

"That is important. Can you come to Rougemont tomorrow? Good. I will have a man waiting on a big motor-cycle with a pillion seat one hundred metres this side of Vieilley at, say, 11.45, if that suits you. You will know that it is the right man if he is turned with his back to Vieilley on the left side of the road, and if he rests a hand on each thigh, thus."

And there he was. Not a minute late; five minutes early. I saw the big motor-cycle sweep over the hill from Venise, its following fan of dust a soft grey like good pearls with a warm glint of the sun in them. So Paincheau cared about time. I had been seeking for three months a man who was there at the given time, and not at least half an hour behind time. Punctuality was the rarest of virtues.

He had not sent just "a man", he had sent big Jean, and I knew that he had sent him as a compliment to me. Since we were going to ride a machine that had been stolen from the Gestapo, we would have to endeavour to shoot our way through any control we might be unlucky enough to meet. So I carried my large "chassepot", and Jean had a couple of grenades handy for me in the side pockets of his "canadienne", and a revolver stuck in his wide, military-looking belt.

It was a fine day and the motor-cycle was powerful, being a five-horse-power Swiss competition model. Riding a motor-cycle seems to me to combine something of the horse and the aeroplane, I get a passionate and childish satisfaction from it. Now, sitting on the pillion behind the muscular and ardent rider, I tasted the thrill of speed again—and the days of my contented walking and bicycling were over. I opened my mouth to sing and the wind caught it and filled it like an old wind-sack. My nose and eyes and hair filled with dust, and through the grey-white dust of France I smelled the hot oil and petrol fumes of the motor. It was wonderful. Odd that the smell of petrol, which you had always thought you disliked, could be intoxicating and heavenly after a long abstinence.

We rolled into Rougemont, a handsome little town some twenty miles up the Ognon valley from Vieilley. This was my first visit to Paincheau's town. Not that he was a Rougemont man. He was the son of an architect in Besançon. But he had taken the town and organised it for the Resistance. It belonged to him and it loved him.

The town was out to see us roaring through the twisting, hilly streets. There were waves and smiles. And curious looks at me. Jean flung the heavy machine into a sharp turn and we shot under an archway into a court-yard behind the small "Hôtel de la Réunion". There were several other motor-cycles in the garage.

"This hotel is our headquarters in the town," said Jean. "We have another Command Post in the Maquis. My sister and her husband own and run the pub."

"Isn't it dangerous? It all seems very open. After all, there are Boches at Montbozon, Villersexel, Vesoul, Valdahon, Besançon. Some of them must know that there is a strong Resistance at Rougemont. They will descend on you one day."

"Yes, but Paincheau has things so well organised that we shall get plenty of warning."

"Has he?"

Since this was new territory for me, I had to submit to being kissed by Jean's sister, who resembled him, being tall, dark and handsome, and all the hotel women. Then the little husband sat us in a dark parlour and brought us a good drink for that stifling weather, a Montrachet, deep gold in colour and drunk with water and ice. Ice was a rarity in this part of war-time France. If I examined my conscience I might find that my frequent meetings and great friendship for Jacques Paincheau during the remainder of that hot summer were in some measure given a deeper, a more lasting quality because there was a refrigerator at the "Hôtel de la Réunion".

Upstairs in a room that had a balcony with a wrought-iron railing luncheon was set for about ten people. There were flowers on the table and white linen and knives, forks and spoons shining with cleanliness. Paincheau wore the usual gleaming shirt, he was shaven and as soft and clean and fluffy as always. The other people there were the chief men of his group.

By the end of the meal I knew that in Paincheau I had found something really valuable. The man was an organiser. A very rare thing. He gave orders to all the men and sent them off, except for three who were coming with us to inspect possible dropping-grounds. We left to inspect them on motor-cycles, and Paincheau had an advance-guard cyclist out in front and a rearguard half a mile behind.

At the end of the day we went to his garage. This was a deserted farm in the middle of some quiet woods. There he kept his cars and trucks which were being serviced by two excellent mechanics, and when French mechanics are good there are none better. Early grapes were beginning to ripen on the walls of the garage as Paincheau and I talked about the future. We made plans for the expansion and motorisation of our forces. In Besançon and the district there were still many private cars hidden away in garages. We were going to need some of those cars to give us more mobility and also petrol-driven trucks to transport arms and sometimes men. Anyway, every car that we left in a garage was a potential gain for the enemy. Already he was hunting round for them, for he was desperate for transport. We planned to get every good car we could lay our hands on. They were not to be stolen (except from the Germans), but were to be taken for official use and paid for with Requisition Bonds printed by the headquarters of the F.F.I.

What particularly pleased me in Paincheau was that he was fussy about detail. All his vehicles were properly looked after, his men were properly dressed and did not behave like hooligans. That was always the danger with the youngsters whom I preferred to work with. They were brave and admirable while they worked and then, naturally enough, when the work was over they liked to pretend to be very tough indeed. Paincheau *was* very tough indeed, and he pretended to be soft.

When he climbed into the driver's seat of a shining Citroën "traction avant", in which we were to drive back to Vieilley, he found that the motor did not run as smoothly as he would have wished. Immediately the mechanic was called to the side of the car. He was a fearsome-looking individual, the type that will push you around in some wayside garage when your car breaks down in France after the war. But he quailed under Paincheau's soft eye, for the chief found his explanations unsatisfactory.

Thinking over the day's work that night as I lay in the heaving darkness of our confined room in the château, I was sure that it was good. Then I remembered something a little unusual: I had heard Paincheau deliver reprimands to a fair number of men that day, but I had never once heard him swear, and I had never heard a man answer back.

Yes, it had been a good day's work.

On the following I had a fine car for myself. Berger took delivery of it. It was a black Citroën with red wheels, almost new, and with a large roomy body, suitable for carrying a good many men or vital light material from the parachutages. It was the type known (oddly enough) as the "familiale". Then there was a nice petrol-driven truck and a big five-ton lorry complete with a driver who understood its ways. I had fought down the temptation to get a motor-cycle, and I had made up my mind only to use the car for absolutely necessary operations. Rolling about on the roads was too dangerous for us in such close proximity to Besançon. In three weeks the Frisé and Marcel had been obliged to change their Maquis location seven times. Berger, Georges and I made a hidden garage in the forest, driving the vehicles up a narrow track and into a thicket which nobody would ever penetrate.

To increase our mobility and speed communications, Berger got his own motor-cycle from Montbozon. He succeeded in getting all the necessary papers for it so that he personally could travel about on it in safety (except for strangers in the Resistance, who were naturally suspicious of motor-cyclists who possessed German permits). I did not enquire how Berger got the permits. He said vaguely that a woman in Vesoul had helped him. Probably this tall, dark-chinned Berger was not always as gentle as he seemed.

Now with the Frisé and Paincheau to do any jobs of a rougher nature (such as hunting down Gestapo agents and killing them), with Berger to carry important long-distance messages, with Janine Dardel and one or two other girls ready to carry ordinary messages, and with the red-haired countess at Thise to buy anything we might want on the black market, I felt that things outside the regular military work of the Maquis were organised and might develop.

There was nothing, apparently, that the countess could not get for us. One day I said to her that we might like to have a few bottles of gin, to give a party in celebration of the Allied victory which seemed still far distant. I also knew that Albert liked this drink, and I wanted to send some to him and to Paul. Next time I saw her, she said:

"I have got one hundred and ten bottles of gin."

The difficulty about the countess was that she was hard to see. Her husband, Jacques, had been in the Resistance at the start. It was he indeed who had enrolled men like the Frisé and Jean

Buthot. But he had been obliged, about the time of my arrival in the Franche-Comté, to fly to Switzerland. The countess was Swiss herself, and she was under constant Gestapo supervision. She was a striking woman, tall and Grecian looking (Boulaya always compared her with the head on Marshal Pétain's hundred-franc notes). Much too conspicuous a person for clandestine meetings in woods or cafés. So we tried to go over occasionally to Thise. When we arranged to meet the countess at Barbier's little house all went well. But when we wanted to taste the fleshpots at the château something always went wrong. Once, when Boulaya and I were on our way through the forest of Chailluz to the château, a distance of ten miles across country, with much climbing, the bad luck that attended this journey might have cost us our lives.

We were walking gaily along down a path which traversed the clearing occupied by the military huts known as "les grandes barraques", the huts I had stopped at on my first sabotage trip across the hill to Besançon, and had since passed many times. We walked into the clearing, still discussing something cheerfully, and then Boulaya stopped stone dead and said:

"Merde."

I came out of my trance and looked around me. We were surrounded by militians, the men we feared above all. A group of nearly twenty lay on a grassy bank beside our path, only ten yards ahead. There were others in a group behind us, and indeed they were dotted all over the clearing. Some were playing cards, others cleaning weapons, but most of them seemed to be staring at us. They were well-dressed as usual in blue ski-ing type uniforms and berets.

Fortunately the gallant Boulaya pulled himself together and asked the nearest one the road to Thise.

"How should I know?" the man answered roughly. "Better ask the 'cuistot', he comes from this detestable part of the world."

"Where would I find the 'cuistot', please?" Boulaya asked politely.

"Where d'you think? In the cook-house of course."

"That hut behind you," said another, a shade more graciously.

We strolled over to the hut he had pointed out. I was waiting for the question which should come any moment: "Who are you?" But it did not come. The cook showed us the path we already knew, and we walked out of the camp. It was as easy as that. Boulaya was magnificent. He cast jocular remarks to one side or the other as we passed through these brutes. As though we had not already been lucky enough, we happened to be sitting down behind a bush when an officer of the Militia walked down our track, going towards the camp. He was a tall, sour-looking person. We both agreed that we would never have passed through the middle of the camp without questioning if an officer had been there. We were well-dressed for the part of holiday-makers or Bisontin black-marketeers, since I wore my shorts and was naked above the waist except for a rucksack which held some rations and a bottle of wine. Boulaya, too, was not looking as Maquisard as usual, since he was spruced up for the countess. Each of us had a pistol hidden in his trouser pocket, but those would not have been of much use. The militians were good fighters in a brutish way. When the big charge exploded which had been placed on the Militia headquarters in Besançon by our people to celebrate the night of July 14, 1944, the militians came out into the streets like a swarm of angry wasps, and they came out running, with weapons in their hands, and with a drive one would expect from only the best of troops.

Next time Boulaya, Georges and I were invited to Thise, with such delectable additions to the attractions of the countess as "pâté de foie gras" and chocolate soufflé for lunch, we crossed eleven of the twelve miles through a rainstorm, gathering "chantrelles" on the way. Boulaya had even prepared an elegant little entrance speech to accompany the gift of the basket of golden mushrooms. Having completed the eleventh mile, we found ourselves on the southern edge of the forest of Chailluz, looking down into the valley of the Doubs, with the château, and beyond it the railway where I had attacked the tanker train, then the Belfort road and then the river Doubs. To the right of the château, between the railway and the road, lay the small Besançon airfield. The Germans had not used this field since their first advance in '40. They had used French labour to cut ditches and put up fences on it to prevent it from being used by the Allies, just as we in England put up posts along the London-Brighton road in '40. But now an extraordinary sight met our eyes. There were thousands of horses grazing on the disused airfield. And a lot of men about the hangars.

"Cossacks," said Georges.

We heard firing, too, from the wood beside the château, and worming its way around the château boundary fence was a fighting patrol in German uniform.

Boulaya, standing out on the hill-side, made one of his dramatic gestures.

"Farewell, beautiful Countess, duty will not permit that we descend," he cried. And added, with feeling: "And farewell, chocolate soufflé."

"Come off that hill-side if you want to make histrionics," Georges told him sharply, for, faced with the prospect of another two and a half hours' walk in the rain without food, tempers were suddenly short.

"Give me that basket," said Boulaya, and clutched at it. "The lady shall not be robbed of her mushrooms. I, Boulaya, will carry them to her; nothing shall stop me."

We prevailed upon him, however, to do no such thing, and forced ourselves to return gloomily to Vieilley, where we cooked the mushrooms ourselves, first gently boiling them and then frying them in oil perfumed with garlic. That ended our last attempt to walk to the château of Thise.

Although she was vastly useful, the countess could only get comparatively small things, personal things, or presents for my friends and helpers. For the bulk needs of our headquarters or the Maquis we fell back on Paincheau.

The first thing I desired to end was the tobacco situation. And Paincheau ended it for us. He sent some men and trucks to Besançon and, working with a gang he ran in the town, they went to the place where French tobacco for the use of the German military garrison was stored. Breaking into the warehouse, these men coolly loaded their trucks with hundreds of cases of cigarettes. Germans passing in the street never imagined that anything illegal was going on. One night's work in the grand manner had provided enough cigarettes for all our Maquis for months. Paincheau had killed the "bureau de tabac" menace.

Next we asked him for boots, and these he supplied in the same grand manner. The Frisé also captured a truck-load of boots. All the Maquisards, including the officers, now appeared in brand-new lemon or banana-coloured boots. This became such a menace to security that we had to issue an order that all boots were to be dirtied or stained dark before worn. It was said that when a customer entered a shoe-shop in Besançon to ask for a pair of boots, the salesman said:

"But why not join the 'Équipes Boulaya', monsieur? There you gets boots without disbursement and without coupons."

The next thing was petrol. Paincheau already had fairly large stocks of this which he had requisitioned. But he decided that these must be increased. With his Besançon gang he devised the following plan. The main German petrol supply in Besançon was kept in tanks which were in a guarded building. One night Paincheau's men drew up in a large tanker truck beside one wall of the building which was not guarded. One of the men was a mason. Scientifically and silently he cut a hole in the brick wall. His comrades ran a pipe through the hole and into a tank in the interior. All night they pumped petrol out of the German store into their truck. As the first light of dawn came over the hills surrounding the city they stopped pumping and the mason rebuilt the wall. The tanker returned to Rougemont to empty its precious load. The following night the operation was repeated successfully. But now the level of the petrol in the tanks had sunk so drastically that the Germans discovered the loss. Since there were always guards on the door of the building, the Gestapo arrested all German soldiers who had been on this guard in the past seven days. Paincheau decided that we would get no more petrol. So that night four of his men volunteered to go back into the store building, to put two hundred pounds of sugar into the remaining stocks. They entered the building by the same route. The same mason closed the hole after them. The operation was an entire success.

Once Boulaya was short of money. All our Maquisards were paid like soldiers regularly by the week on a fixed scale according to the number of their dependants. Their pay was small, but it was important that it should not be interrupted. Paincheau could get anything from a bottle of absinthe to a funeral cortège with a black-and-silver hearse, lilies, and black Belgian horses. He met us in a wood between Devecey and Bonnay and unstrapped from the back of his "petrolette" an enormous sack.

"What have you there?" Boulaya asked.

"Eight million francs," he replied calmly.

It was Gestapo money deposited in banks in Besançon. Paincheau explained that four men had succeeded in getting this money by several visits to banks with an accomplice, a woman who worked for the Gestapo. But the story was so complicated that I could not follow it. Perhaps it was because he spoke so softly. At any rate, the men who did the coup had only, we understood, kept two million of the German money for themselves, and the rest they presented to the Resistance. They were real patriots. Boulaya and I were greatly touched by the patriotism of the experts. We laughed a lot.

Jacques Paincheau was a magician. With his help we were able to organise the food situation. Where lesser beings thought in kilos, he thought in terms of truck-loads, barge-loads, warehouses. He could produce sugar, rice, gruyère, yes, even tyres for vehicles and chocolate by the ton. And all taken from the enemy. Although, like a skilful prestidigitator, he produced all those valuable things without apparent effort, his coups were all the result of faultless planning and execution. He worked everything out to the minutest detail, and he was prepared to lead his men into anything that he planned. He and I became close friends. We were not able to meet very frequently because we were both too busy. But each time that I met him I found that his mind was packed with ideas for work, and each time they were new ideas. Like the Frisé, Paincheau wasted no time on women, or playing around.

When Laval fled to Belfort with his retinue of Darnan's Militia and German S.S., Paincheau sent up three of his best men in a car to see if they could get near to Laval. One of the men, the leader, was the young brother of Gros-Claude, a powerful, squarely-built young man, and a crack shot.

I happened to be with Paincheau in his Rougemont headquarters when young Gros-Claude returned.

"Hullo, he has a new car, anyway," said Paincheau.

It was a small but smart black car with whitened tyres. A car that reeked of Paris (or Vichy)—and women, and furs, and perfume.

"Guess who this automobile belongs to?" shouted Gros-Claude. "To Darnan himself. And we took two people in it, a man and a woman."

They had found at Belfort that Laval was too well guarded. They could not get near him. But they picked up the black car and its occupants, who appeared to be stragglers from the entourage. Gros-Claude wanted the car, so he pushed his pistol in at the window and told the man sitting at the wheel to get into the back beside the woman. The driver appeared greatly perturbed, but he obeyed this command without recourse either to the handsome sub-machine-gun that lay all ready with a round in the breach on the seat beside him, or to the American Colt, also loaded, that filled the well-polished leather holster nestling under his coat. The woman had a gun in her handbag. But only a tiny, mother-of-pearl affair. There was nothing unusual in that. She was beautiful too, said young Gros-Claude.

He had left one of his companions in the other car with orders to follow the black machine. He now took his place behind the wheel of this new one, and drove out of Belfort. His companion on the front seat turned half round so that he could watch the man and woman they had taken, and he held a pistol just in case they were troublesome, but they chatted and smoked all the way and assured their captors that they were charmed to be charmed away from the Laval entourage. They had wanted for a long, long time to join the Resistance. The Maquis was the life. . . . They had met continuous German convoys on the journey back from Belfort. One German officer had tried to stop them, but they had run past. There were two bullet-holes in the back car. . . .

"Where are the prisoners?" interrupted Paincheau.

"Up in the wood."

"And their papers?"

"Also up in the wood. We took them from them at Belfort. I hadn't time to look at them."

"Come on. We may as well see who they are. The car is pleasant. Well done."

The wood covered only an acre or two. It was isolated, and had to be approached by rough farm tracks. People were brought here for questioning. It would have been dangerous to take even innocent strangers to an ordinary Maquis. And here La Marche and other traitors had been killed.

Two fat wallets and a woman's handbag lay on a tree-stump. As Paincheau looked at the first wallet, an expensive affair in real leather and silver, his breath came in a sudden hiss. He whipped round, looking at the two prisoners who sat smoking on a bank. And he spat at them one word:

"Miliciens!"

He went through document by document, photograph by photograph, the contents of the two wallets. They were the records of vile lives centred on Vichy for two years. Both the man and the woman had possessed two identities, it appeared. Both had passed to the "Hôtel du Parc" at Vichy for their "special police duties". In both wallets were addresses of "suspected criminals", and following each address were short notes such as: "Denounced as listening to British radio. Believed to have 50,000 francs secreted in the house in British and Swiss money." What a picture of crime and bestiality the two wallets showed. The man's wallet contained photographs of his companions in uniforms and in over-smart civilian clothes, and snapshots of women, many of them wearing few or no clothes and posing lasciviously for the photographer. And the woman's wallet held, among the pictures of cafés and bathing-parties and young men, a signed portrait of Darnan himself.

"Stand up," said Paincheau. His face and the face of every man in the circle was full of loathing as he looked at the traitors who had lived in the rich and gruesome slime of the Militia.

How did they look, the traitors? The man was weak. You could see that by his effeminate pointed face and the little mouth that had a homosexual look to it (despite his wallet). He was a tall, and at first sight a strapping man. But his neck was too long, and his legs were knock-kneed. His hair was greased back and shone like a solid surface. At the back of his head the long hair swept back from his ears, met in a kind of interlocking parting. He was dressed a little like Paincheau, except that he wore a pale tie to accentuate his olive tan. A brown leather glove, the top folded carefully down so that it did not touch his shirt-cuff, encased one of his hands, the other played incessantly with the buttons on the front of his coat. It was a coarse hand, like a peasant's with a slab of dead, immobile flesh on the back of it, and many black hairs growing out of the flesh and lying along it like healthy creepers. His nails were carefully kept, and they shone. His eyes wandered round and round the clearing and its occupants, except for Paincheau. He avoided looking at Paincheau. You felt that his face would have been more comfortable with a little worldly smile fixed on it below the thin line of moustache, but that he was forcing a more serious expression because he did not want to annoy the men who stood around him. He answered Paincheau's questions in a voice that was rough, with a lot of slang and bad grammar. You knew what he was feeling there in the middle of the circle. He was feeling: "So this is what it is like to die." And then: "It cannot be me. This only happens to other people."

The woman was not so frightened. She thought too: "This cannot happen to me." But then she had more reason for believing such a thing, even though she admitted to all the facts that her wallet declaimed. Oh yes, she had been in the Militia. Yes, Darnan had given her the picture.

She hoped that her physical attractions would still pull her out. Gradually as they were questioned she increased the space that separated her from her companion, as though she was dis-sociating herself from him, disowning him. He was going to be killed. But not her.

Her eyes did not avoid Paincheau, they scarcely looked at anyone else. You could see her weighing up his clothes, his side-whiskers, his softly persistent, controlled voice. Again and again her eyes sought his. And he occasionally looked into her eyes, but his look said neither yes nor no. This was a woman of the type that the French would call a "poule", but that the English would hesitate to call a "tart". Tall and rather beautiful and voluptuous, she was quietly dressed with no jewellery except for two rings. Her dark hair looked soft and expensive. Her face was heavily made up with a very dark, purplish mouth. She was proud of her strong teeth, for she chose every opportunity to open her lips in a wide smile. Her nails were very long and pointed and of some clever colour between pink and red. They failed to elongate her hands. Ugly hands, the hands of a woman who might cook and make love well, but who would dislike doing the flowers.

Paincheau finished questioning the man first. When he had admitted to the story that the papers told, Paincheau left him coldly and began on the woman. The man had been uncomfortable under the questions of course, but now that Paincheau was finished with him, he seemed to find it unbearable there, doing nothing.

So he was given a spade and a pick and told to dig a grave. Paincheau did not ask the woman many questions. Soon the two were digging under the trees while the others watched. They might as well have dug one grave for the two of them. But without being told, they worked on two separate graves. They had been lovers in life too. At least the man had said so. The woman had said nothing when this question was put to her. It was surprising the trouble they took with their graves. Was it only that they wanted more minutes of living? Or was it that they desired to lie well-covered under the trees in their traitors' graves?

The man asked for permission to go into the trees and ease himself. Paincheau nodded. Two men went with him. He was a long time there. The woman worked alone in the clearing. Occasionally she gave a dry sob as she laboured. The earth was hard packed, and there were many slender tree roots below the surface. She was making so little impression on the roots that Paincheau told a man to help her. She threw out the loose earth while the man worked with the pick, loosening the earth and wood for her. The smell of her perfume hung vaguely in the clearing. Her handsome, Chinese-looking shoes were shapeless now with the wet earth that clung to them.

When the man came back from the edge of the clearing, he stood for a little time looking down into the hole he had made for his body. Then a long shudder caught him. As though he were touched by an electric shock that began a shaking between his shoulder-blades and stretched out in both directions up to the greased hair, and down the legs in their wide trousers. When the shudder stopped he ran for it.

He ran perhaps fifteen paces and then Jojo shot him with a pattern burst of the Sten gun, five rounds thudding into the small of the back. When he fell he skidded for a bit along the surface of the ground. His body was limp and disjointed. He had an easy death.

Paincheau did not like a mess. He made two men put the body in the grave. The woman now climbed out of her grave. You got the impression that she had been waiting for this. Indeed, she said:

"Now that he is—gone. Now I can say that I tried for a long time to leave the Militia. I hated them all and their brutality. I always tried to help any of you boys. I always wanted to be on your side. Take me in the Maquis. Please take me in the Maquis, Monsieur Jacques. I will cook or fight or spy or anything. Please, please, Monsieur Jacques." As she spoke she took little swinging steps closer to Paincheau. Now she was kneeling hands locked together and forming a rest for her up-thrust chin.

"Think of the ways I could help you," she said hoarsely. "I could lead you to militians who are hidden away. I could show you where to find money, cars, jewellery. I will do anything. I will tell you what I could do. I could get Darnan for you. Give me the car and send someone with me to Belfort. I will deliver Darnan to you. Please, Monsieur Paincheau."

"Perhaps there is something in what she says," one of the men said.

"Get up from your knees," Paincheau told her. There was no expression on his face or in his voice.

She rose slowly from her knees and her outstretched hands caught on Paincheau's clothes and pulled herself up towards him. He put his hands behind him, the two arms rigidly stretched backwards so that he would not touch her. But perhaps she did not notice.

"Please, Monsieur Jacques. Please." Her voice was softer, more caressing. Paincheau jerked his head at a man standing behind her, and bringing one of his hands round her body, made a slight sign. The man approached quietly, and raising his pistol while the woman still clutched at the motionless Paincheau, he blew away the back of her head.

CHAPTER XIV

ON the morning of August 15, I awoke with the free feeling of holiday in the air. I awoke in the château. There was the old range with the two Sten guns and the bottle of alcohol sitting upon it, there was the pile of refuse, increased now by one or two empty bottles, and there were my three companions, all of them sound asleep. It was 7.30 by my watch.

I had that feeling because August 15, being the Feast of the Assumption of Our Lady, was a holiday in the village, and I intended to take a holiday myself. I was to spend the morning bathing and fishing in the river with Georges. Then a mammoth luncheon with the hospitable Marquis family. And dinner in the evening with Phillipon, who had shot "something special" for the occasion.

When steps approached our door I did not worry. The old man who lived alone above the "Carlton" always passed down the narrow stairs at this hour. But today the steps did not pass. I heard somebody fumbling with the pile of faggots which we always arranged to block the entrance and make the landing look disused. Taking my pistol from below the leather jacket that served me for a pillow, I awaited events. The others still slept.

Without knocking, the old man put his head inside the door. "Stay there. Stay where you are," he quavered. "They are everywhere."

"Who are everywhere?"

"The Boches. They are all round the village, and in the orchards and streets. Stay where you are. Stay there calmly."

Calmly! We were all wide awake. This was what everybody had been saying would happen. And we had continued to sleep in the rat-trap for fifteen days. Fools. All of us were madly dressing, except for the "patron", who, according to his custom, had slept, despite the summer heat, without even taking off his tie or his boots.

"Nom de Dieu de bordel," he muttered, jumping off his mattress. While we were putting on our clothes he slipped out of the door and was gone.

It took me less time to put on my shorts and sandals than it did Georges and Boulaya to lace up their boots. Georges' brow was furrowed in concentration. I was ready, but I waited for him, for I trusted him. It was his village. If anybody could lead us out of this mess, he would. But it seemed a slim chance. We knew how the Germans went through a village when they bothered to encircle it. When we first slept in the "Carlton" we had discussed with Georges two methods of hiding from the Germans. One was to jump out of the window (we had all practised this, even the "patron") and crossing the orchards and three back gardens, including the garden of Georges himself, to hide ourselves in the mouth of the Vieilley sewer. Plan two was to mount into the roof of the château. Georges said that strangers might move around in the attics there for days and never find the hiding-places he had used as a child. I wondered which he would choose. When he had laced his boots he called the old man.

"We are going out, and the moment we are gone you must hide everything here," he told him. "The guns, the Englishman's sleeping-bag, the bottle. Take the mattresses to real bedrooms and put them on the beds."

"Stay tranquilly here," said the old man. "I beseech you to remain here."

Georges was at the small window, cautiously peering out. Then he turned into the room.

"We must try to reach the aqueduct," he said, and he used the complimentary word "aqueduct" perhaps to conquer any reluctance we might feel for going there. "There are several truck-loads of Boches in the road already. I'm afraid it's a thorough search, and they've caught the village with its pants down because today's a holiday and all the cultivators lay late in bed." He looked at us. "Where in God's name is the 'patron'?" he asked sharply. The old man, who still stood in the room, answered:

"You mean the old gizzard? He went straight down the stairs and out of the door. Guess he went out the back way."

"He'll get us all taken," said Georges angrily. "Why couldn't he wait? Does he know the aqueduct?"

"No," Boulaya said.

Georges decided not to go out by the window. I tiptoed behind him down the stairs and out of a kitchen door into a run full of ducks, hens and rabbits. We could see a German sentry. He was about one hundred yards away, in the cherry orchard (not far from my favourite tree, the big tree belonging to the schoolmistress).

"Don't run," Georges told us. "Until I tell you to. They can see us for the next fifty metres." We climbed out of the hen-run and walked slowly across an apple orchard.

"Now run like hell," he said. And we flung ourselves over two fences and a wall. We were in his garden. We lay there in the high tobacco plants for ten minutes while Georges crawled around. He came back to us, as low to the ground as a good crawler can get.

"The bastards are in my house already," he said. "When we cross the path and the wall, there, we'll be in view if anyone's looking from the back of the house. We must do it, though, and there's not much time. They'll be chasing through these gardens as soon as the sentry who saw us leave the château gets in his report."

He crawled across the path and swung himself over the wall. I gave him two minutes to make the tunnel entrance, then I crawled with a prayer from the tobacco plants to the edge of the path. I could see the back of the house now. A sheet was hanging from the first-floor window. That was the tenant's signal for us. There would be one hanging in front of the house too. The signal meant "Keep away". I could see no Germans, so I snaked across the path and pulled myself on to the high stone wall. I could lie on the flat coping for a second, for there I was screened by a couple of bushes. Boulaya was already pushing his head out of the beautiful tobacco leaves. His face looked funny, gummed up with sleep and with his hair in wisps around his small blue beret. From the top of the wall I had the width of one long narrow field to cross. There did not appear to be any German posted on the outer ring of sentries who could see into this field. The other danger came from the centre of the village, for the main roadway, in which the German lorries were grouped ran past the head of this field, which was screened by a high wall with a large ornamental iron gate in it.

Running out below this wall in the far corner from where I lay on the wall was what appeared to be a small and dirty ditch. This, I knew, was actually the mouth of the "aqueduct", as Georges called it, a vaulted tunnel which ran underground for a distance of two thousand yards, from the topmost extremity of the village to this point. Boulaya was already crawling to the path. I lowered myself gently, crossed the field upright and slowly (for I am a great believer in the maxim that slow move-

285

ment does not catch the eye where rapid movement does) and dived into the ditch.

In the ditch was a trickle of water and a thick mud bottom. I was careful to crawl in the centre of the mud, and to wipe out all traces of my passage as I went in, pushing aside the over-hanging bushes. The mouth of the sewer was a low archway into which you could crawl comfortably.

At first it seemed impenetrably black, and a flow of nauseous air caught me by the throat. I sat myself on small cobbles just inside the mouth, cobbles down which liquid seeped into the ditch outside, and fought with my nausea. After a moment it departed, and I ceased to pay much attention to the smell. Also my eyes, which rapidly accustom themselves to changes in light, were able to distinguish Georges, who was seated, back to the wall, beside me. I even began to see my legs, sandals, and shorts, which were now covered in slimy mud. Boulaya came in, choking and gasping in the foul air.

"Did you leave any tracks in the ditch?" Georges asked us sharply. We both said no, but he crawled out himself to make sure. When he came back we heard a fusillade of shots, then a rushing of heavy German boots on the road immediately over our heads. Then more shots. A light machine-gun was firing out over the fields to the north, between the village and the railway.

"That's the 'patron'," we told each other. Georges cursed the old man. "Why could he not follow me like you others?" he said. "If I had been caught in his village I would have followed him."

He stopped his whispering complaints when we heard German shouts in the gardens we had crossed. Then the ornamental gateway into the field was creakingly opened, and somebody said in German:

"Search all those gardens then. They can't have gone far. Take twenty men." Heels clicked and we heard the nailed boots thudding over our heads.

"We must get back at least two hundred metres from here," Georges told us in the lowest of whispers. "Not a sound going back, now, because there are certainly sentries on the road, and this tunnel is a sounding-box since there are small drains running into it from the gutters. If the Boches find the mouth they will probably fire up it with rifles. Then we must lie down. One hundred metres up, if I remember, there is a slight bend, so they won't hit us directly, but they might touch us with ricochets.

286

It's up to anybody who gets wounded to make all efforts not to cry out. Agreed?"

"Agreed."

Georges led the way. I followed him. After a few yards we were off the cobbles and crawling through soft mud. The bottom of the sewer (for now none of us could use the more distinguished name, aqueduct) was constructed with a series of little dams, so that for the numerous strange animals that skated about on the thick surface of the liquid slime it must have appeared to descend in a series of large steps. And for us the liquid was sometimes so deep that it came up to our elbows and we wondered if there was room for our heads between the surface and the small stone vault. Then gradually the level would descend, and progress would be less nauseating. The slime in which we crawled was alive with leeches and with worms, large and small. You could feel them on your hands and legs. And it was filled in places with broken glass and old tins with jagged edges. Before we had gone far I had cuts on the hands and knees. Now when you looked back the mouth of the tunnel, which not so long ago had seemed pitch dark, was a patch of bright light. You were crawling by feel alone, in absolute darkness. When we rounded the bend which Georges had mentioned, we saw another much smaller patch of light perhaps one hundred yards ahead.

In this light Georges stopped. It came from an opening into the gutter of the road above us. Under the hole was a large heap of old rubbish. By pushing your head right up into the hole, you could get a whiff of fresh air and you could just see the surface of the road to one side and get a worm's eye view of passers-by up to the height of their knees, and possibly a little higher. Georges and Boulaya seated themselves on the upper side of the heap of rubbish and I sat below it on a big stone I had found among the slime. Here the bottom was cobbled again, and it seemed clean after what we had been through.

Georges explained where we now were. The village of Vieilley has roughly two main roads in it. One, the road running through it and up the valley, the road on which the houses of Georges and the Marquis were situated with the war memorial and the more modern and imposing buildings of the village, and the other which ran out of this at right angles, forming a T-junction by the big fountain, and wound up towards higher Vieilley, the spur of houses and barns that ran right into the hill-side. The hole above our heads lay exactly between the bowling-alley and the "bistro", that is in the smaller road running up the hill, but near the T-junction.

The Germans all seemed to be gathered in the bigger road, outside the house of Georges. Now, for the first time that morning, we began to feel that we could relax a little and take stock of things. There was little doubt in our minds that the "patron" had either been killed or taken. What else could the shots have meant? Further danger for us lay in two places, in Georges' barn and in his house.

In the barn the "patron" had worked most days, and it was there that he hid all his papers. He hid them in two biscuit-tins among the hay. Also hidden in the barn was three hundred gallons of captured German petrol. As if that were not enough, five newcomers from Besançon and Berger with his motor-cycle had spent the night there. Berger's papers were all right, and he was probably shrewd enough to look after himself, so long as neither the incriminating papers nor the petrol were discovered. But the five others were Bisontins of the middle-class type, young men who belonged to mountaineering clubs. They were about to open a new Maquis overlooking the Belfort road, and they had come to Boulaya for instructions and material. We could not depend on them not to make fools of themselves. In Georges' house there was more danger. The "patron" had also worked there, and perhaps he had left papers lying around. In the kitchen were two British wireless sets, one the ordinary midget set and the other my more tiny short-wave receiver which I had sent the Frisé to collect from Albert. Boulaya, it was true, had wrapped the two little sets in brown paper the night before and hidden them on the top of the high kitchen dresser. But that could hardly be expected to pass a German search, and we could hear them all the time banging things about in the house and carrying loads out to their cars. In the inner room was all the clothing of the "patron", Boulaya, and myself. Furthermore, the night before Berger had returned from a quick trip to the Maquis of Jacques, which was still in the same place, north of Dijon. And he had brought with him the big suit-case I had left at the farm when I first went away with Albert. This suit-case contained many shirts, handkerchiefs and pairs of socks and valuable odds and ends like towels, soap, tea, and the colonel's gold cuff-links. Still, we could not worry about such property. Life is the main issue.

"I can stay here for two days if necessary," Georges said. "And if we hear them investigating the sewer, we'll just crawl

up it in front of them. I don't think any soldier would bother
to go much farther than this, unless they know that we are
definitely here."

"Why not go right up it now, and out at the top?" I asked.

"Because the top entrance is not quite clear of the village,
and they should be around the whole place. Also they have
probably attacked the Maquis at the same time. It won't be
healthy in the woods around here for some days. If we cannot
stick it down here for longer than today, we must try to crawl
out and through their cordon at night. At night we could work
across the fields and over the river into the Haute-Saône."

Boulaya, who was older and stiffer than either of us, was finding the sewer desperately uncomfortable. He repeatedly shifted
on his stone and groaned and muttered.

"What about a cigarette, Georges?" he said in the wheedling
voice of the tobacco addict.

"All right. Light one carefully and we'll see where the smoke
goes." But the smoke was sucked straight up through the hole
above our heads. "Put it out at once," Georges ordered sharply.
Boulaya sadly complied. I was beginning to feel desperately
cold in my shorts. Outside it was a hot day, but no heat pene-
trated to the sewer. Every time footsteps passed Georges poked
his head up towards the hole to hear what was said.

But the only villagers who passed were women, hurrying cattle
and horses back to byre and stable. There were Cossacks in
the village too. Georges did not see any of them, but we heard
their horses clattering along the big road. They made a noise
like thunder in the sewer. We could tell the Gestapo "traction
avant" cars, too, by the throaty tone of their exhausts. There
was a lot of coming and going. Georges was worried about
the Cossacks.

"If only they don't burn the village," he said, and occasionally he reviled poor Boulaya for the carelessness of the 'patron'
in leaving papers about. "You could have stopped him,"
Georges said bitterly. "But, of course, this isn't your village.
If they burn so much as one cottage here or rape one girl, I am
finished. They will never forgive me. They will not forget for
five generations that it was Georges Molle who drew this on
Vielley."

The church bells went at eleven o'clock for the High Mass,
to celebrate the Assumption of Our Lady. Normally, the whole
village, with the exception of a few old cynics like Phillipon
and Marquis, and the most ardent of the fishermen, would have

gone to the Mass. But few feet passed our drain, and Georges reported again that there was not a man or a young woman among them. The banging had now ceased in Georges's house.

We had been four hours in the sewer when the German trucks all seemed to depart, and half an hour later we began to hear Frenchmen's voices in the street. Georges recognised the voices, and, after listening for some time, decided that it would be safe for us to go to the mouth of the sewer. Crawling out, now that fresh air was an immediate prospect, and fear had lost its impellent force, the vileness of our surroundings struck me more forcibly and I was sick several times.

At the entrance we waited for some time in the warm sunlight, beside the ditch, so that we could go in again quickly in case of danger. From the houses on either side we had news. Madame Poirier, the tenant's wife, leaning out of the back window of Georges's house, told us that the Boches had taken all our things and had carried off the "patron" and several other men. They were believed to be attacking the Maquis at that moment, but no shots had been heard. Two young girls who lived in the house on the other side came to the fence to gaze upon our wretchedness. We were covered from head to foot in mud and worse. Hearing that we had not eaten, they ran in to get us hot milk and bread and honey. As one of the girls bent across the ditch to hand us a bowl, I noticed with amusement how Boulaya appreciated the milky skin of her bosom, which showed where her best Sunday dress opened at the neck.

Georges led us in single file through the village. Passing the mayor's house I saw the anxious face of Madame Dardel peering through the window. I knew that she sometimes bought butter in that house, and thought it likely that she had made the trip to Vieilley to find out what had happened to me. When she saw me she flung her hand to her throat and vanished. Twisting round by the paths that led behind the church, Georges led us by the lover's lane, to the place above the quarry, where the village boys took their girls on the warm evenings. Hidden in the bushes up there we could see all round us, even behind to the vineyards sweeping up to the forest. There was a great deal of German traffic on the road below, and we saw German trucks in the village of Merey, which I had always mistrusted.

Our party had now been increased by Georges Pernod, the ginger-headed youth who had organised the feeding of the Maquis, and by one of our Maquisards, a midget called Démaï, who was ill with bronchitis, and who had been lying in bed in the upper village when the Germans arrived. Georges Pernod was also in the upper village. He and Démaï had managed to escape through a hole in the German cordon, which had failed to close completely round the north point of the village.

Beautiful Maria Contini, with the older Marquis girl, climbed up the quarry at two o'clock with food for us. They could give us only a garbled account of what had happened. But it was clear that the Gestapo had descended on the villages because of the attack on the lower Contini and the death of Nono.

Old Contini (even the terrible stomach wound had failed to finish him) had been in one of the German vehicles with his wife, and it was evidently they who had vindictively denounced the men for whom the Germans searched. One name on the list was, of course, Georges Molle, another was Georges Pernod, two others were old Contini's cousin and nephew, father and brother of the fair Maria. Both of them had been caught, tied up and thrown into a lorry beside the "patron", who sat there, said Maria, with a bloody face that appeared to have been battered in on one side, but he was still able with one eye to cast looks of fierce hatred at the Germans. Vieilley was the centre of the German descent, but they had also visited and searched the neighbouring villages of Devecey, Bonnay, Venise, Cromary, and Moncey. From each they had taken some prisoners or hostages, apparently working on old denunciations. Since the French peasant will do anything to his neighbour when sufficiently pushed by personal hatred or jealousy, most of these denunciations took effect on people who were innocent of the crime the Germans took them for—"terrorism". The Contini father and son, for example, sympathised with the Resistance, but had never actively done anything for it. They were all taken to "La Butte", in Besançon.

When darkness fell Georges and I descended with pistols and torches to the village. We climbed in at the back window of Georges' house. All of his ground floor rooms had been looted by the Germans, but not thoroughly searched. All of our belongings had gone, except for those that the Germans had rejected as being not worth taking. But they had not found the two British wireless receivers on the top of the dresser shelves.

"That has saved the house and perhaps the village from burning," said Georges. "I see what happened here. The Boches came in and saw all those fine clothes and suit-cases lying around, so they decided to loot instead of searching. Don't fear for your British-made clothes. You will never see them again, but they will never be passed on to any higher authority. The Boches are collecting civilian clothes already for their own flight. Look, they have not left a single suit-case or bag of any kind. They've even taken that leather satchel you brought back after Nono's death."

"My God, so they have."

"What does that matter? It hadn't your name on it."

"No, but it might have somebody else's." It would have been just like the Dardel girl to write her name inside the thing. Schoolgirls always did that with everything. But I was inclined to agree with Georges. It looked as though the Gestapo had been looting on their own account, instead of searching for evidence. After collecting my sleeping-bag and the other things which had been successfully hidden in the château, we went to the barn. Berger had ridden away on his motor-cycle, but we were told that he had buried everything suspicious, including the "patron's" papers and our petrol in one of the middens up the street. The five young men had got out by the back way and through the vineyards. The Germans had fired at them. One was believed to be wounded.

Apart from the taking of the "patron" we seemed to have come remarkably lightly out of things. We now repaired to a wood directly behind Vieilley, part of the main forest of Chailluz. And there at night most of our Maquisards rejoined us. Fortunately, the Maquis had not been numerous that morning, because Maurice and Philippe had led a party into Besançon to investigate a false report that a certain factory there was making parts for the robot bombs that the Germans had begun to send to London, and the Pointu, with another party, was carrying out a little outside sabotage for me at the town of Roches. The remainder, mostly new hands, were under the command of an old sergeant in the French Colonial Infantry. This sergeant looked like a lizard pickled in alcohol, and spoke with a voice hoarsened by the parade ground, spirits and tobacco, to such a pitch of huskiness that I found him entirely incomprehensible. But he was such a divine shot with the light machine-gun, and so cool in action, that we were simply forced to give him some kind of command. He was not at all the type that was wanted, but he did his work so well that you could not overlook him. Except when the sergeant was drunk and unmanageable, Boulaya and the others pointed him frequently out to me as proof that my contention was false that the young Frenchmen were the best.

The sergeant found himself that morning in the Maquis, with Germans believed to be surrounding the wood and all his officers believed dead. The rumour had instantly shot through the valley that Boulaya, myself, and Georges had been killed and only the "patron" made prisoner. The sergeant therefore gathered all his men, weapons, and ammunition together, and took them to the hill that made the centre of the wood in which the Vieilley Maquis had always lived. He had about ten men with him, and they were armed to the teeth. The sergeant grouped them on the very top of the hill, told them that the first man that coughed would get his teeth knocked down his throat, and that if the Boches found them they would fight to the last round. They lay there on the little hill-top all day. Most of the day there were German sentries within one hundred yards of them. A strong German force, led by young Contini (son of the lower Contini), had passed through Merey and gone directly to our old Maquis sites. They had found the first two, but the third, well-hidden, and some distance away on the other side of the wood, they did not find.

At nightfall the sergeant found out from Phillipon where we were, and brought his men over.

On the previous night Phillipon had drunk the alcohol I had given him as a bribe to shoot "something special" for my dinner on the feast day, with the result that he spent the night cooling off in the vineyard behind his bothy, and awoke in the morning to find German soldiers searching the vineyards. They had not found him, but he had forced himself to lie out all day on the scorching lumpy earth between the rows of vines, because, in his dazed condition, he was certain that the Boches had come to look for him and for him alone.

That night he was over to ask us whether we could possibly "advance a litre or two of wine", as he felt particularly thirsty. Nobody had told him where we were, but he knew everything about the woods. We spent an uncomfortable night, with sentries out, and standing patrols above and below us.

Next day I went down to the village, because I could exist no longer without washing from my body the remains of the Vieilley sewer. I now felt that I had a more intimate connection than ever with this village. But the part of it that Boulaya, Georges and I now visited was new to me. It was the top part, the arm that ran into the hill. There was really just one steep, narrow little lane, with a house here and there along it. The lane was cluttered with reapers, carts, and live-stock of all sorts.

Our host was Gustave, a tall man with a sour smile and such a slow way of thinking, that you were surprised that he ever got anything done. He did though. He ran the illicit oil trade of the village. People brought him the grain and he produced cooking oil in his workshop. In peace-time he was a mechanic, reputed to be the best in the village. The Germans had caught him making oil in '43. They had endeavoured there, among the presses, to give Gustave a beating that he would never forget. They did this to dissuade Gustave from making oil. Gustave did not stop making oil, though now he only made it for people that he knew, not for stool-pigeons. But he will never forget the beating. He will take it out on every German he meets for the rest of his life. And Gustave is a "Franc-comtois", who is as large and as powerful as he is single-minded. Fools believe that "a good flogging will make him mend his ways". They are people who have never been flogged themselves. There was nothing like a good German flogging for building a good French patriot. And that is the type of patriotism (or hate) that does not end with a peace.

So Gustave, who would, I think, have been a mild sort of man, was very fierce. I washed myself in a basin perched on the shallow stone sink in the kitchen. He lived with his sister, an elderly person with an undiscriminating hatred for the people who had broken Gustave's face. When we had washed they gave us some coffee and bread. The Maquis was already set up in the new wood above, and the "cuistot" was preparing a midday meal for thirty.

We had slept right at the edge of the wood, for Georges thought the best kind of security was to be warned in advance of the enemy's approach, and he preferred always to be able to see a long way from the Maquis, but to have the forest behind him for an unobserved escape. It was an uncomfortable wood to sleep in. The trees were too close together.

In front of the wood, sloping down to the woods bordering the narrow cut that held the topmost houses of Vieilley, was a splendid field. There were seventeen trees dotted about this field, like trees in an English park; twelve apple-trees, two cherry-trees, and three superb walnut-trees. We spent hours sitting in this field, while Boulaya "received".

Now Boulaya's status had changed, and he found himself compelled to be the big chief. He would rather, in many ways, have remained the dashing junior leader. But the "patron's" arrest thrust heavy responsibility on him, and he rose to it.

The "patron" had raised him to the rank of colonel some time previously, but Boulaya had remained so quiet about it that I think nobody knew of it, outside the "patron", George, and myself.

Those were difficult days, for German supervision was fairly tight on the area and especially around Vieilley, yet Boulaya was forced to show to all the chiefs of the Resistance in his vast sector that he was still there. In the first day no outsiders came to see us, for they believed that the whole Maquis, complete with headquarters had been taken, and the village itself razed to the ground. Then, after a day or two, they all came. They arrived in the village in droves, and mounted to our field with the seventeen trees, to see the new chief and swear eternal obedience. Boulaya was more adroit than the "patron" at getting through with such interviews, but he was compelled, nevertheless, to see all who came, just to show them that the F.F.I. headquarters still stood firm.

Georges, who feared greatly for his village, made continual protests at the ever-growing stream of "foreigners". We developed a system whereby strangers were given rendezvous at a disused barn, which was the last Vieilley building on the road to Marchaux. There we kept two Maquisards perpetually on guard, and when somebody arrived who gave the correct password, one of them brought the visitor up to us in the field. At first I felt that it was my duty to be present at Boulaya's conferences and interviews. But two or three days of them left me nauseated with talk and adjectives, and longing again for the undiluted company of simple men who knew you well enough to say what they wanted without dressing up the want in sugary words.

One story these talkers told which interested us. The story of the "patron".

When he left us dressing in the château, the "patron" slipped quickly downstairs and peered out into the château courtyard. Seeing Germans there he went out by the same kitchen door that we later used, determined to make a break for it by the fields. A suicidal idea. He was, had he but reasoned the matter out, the fortunate possessor of a Vieilley identity-card, a false card issued to him by our friend, the mayor. If the "patron" had calmly put on an old pair of clogs, taken off his coat and collar and tie, and strolled out into the courtyard in his braces and his clogs, chewing away at his dirty old pipe, he would not have been taken. As it was he began to make his way, now crawling, now running, towards the open fields and the railway, through the orchards from which the German sentry later saw the three of us. Of course, the "patron" was seen. There was no cover. Called to a halt, he broke into a run. Three sentries fired upon him, one with the light machine-gun we heard. They missed. The "patron" was now running across the fields towards the railway. Here he made another tragic mistake. Forgetting that the Germans had cars in the village, he ran straight on, across flat country, and between two small tracks. Two cars of the "Feldgendarmerie" raced out, one down each track. When he realised his mistake and tried to bear left, into more hilly country where cars could not follow, it was too late. He was forced to give himself up. The soldiers of the "Feldgendarmerie", as was their custom when they caught somebody who had tried to escape, gave him a severe beating, turning the right side of his face to a ploughed mass of thick blood. Then they took him back to Vieilley, where he was interviewed by a Gestapo man. They could not see anything suspicious in him. He looked like an old peasant. He was asked however: "Why did you run away?"

"Because I was afraid," answered the "patron". "I thought you Germans had come to burn the village and kill the men."

"And why are you all dressed up like that? No other old man in the village is dressed up at such an early hour."

"I always dress up no matter what the hour."

Because he had attempted to escape he had his hands brutally tied behind him, and was heavily guarded in the truck that took him to Besançon. And there they found that he had a large amount of money in his wallet for such an ordinary-looking old peasant, and his wallet also contained (incredible though this seemed to us) no fewer than three identity-cards, each card carrying his picture, with a different name. All three cards certified that the "patron" was domiciled simultaneously in three widely separated villages. Up to now the Gestapo had been slow. Rewards had been offered frequently for information leading to the arrest of Colonel Morin. His picture had been issued to the Gestapo and the "Feldgendarmerie", and had been in the "rogues' gallery" book that they often carried when they made snap road blocks. But the 'Feldgendarmerie" had made such a mess of his face when they took him that he was unrecognisable.

Now they did what all of us feared would happen if we were

taken. They confronted him with Tom. And Tom gave away his former chief.

After that, although Boulaya made strenuous efforts, some of them at the greatest personal risk, to get him out, either by force or by secret negotiation with the wily Meisner, Gestapo chief in Besançon, he was unsaveable. The slightest attempt to rescue him would have killed him. He was the prisoner of the "Feldgendarmerie", and we were told that after his capture he was neither beaten-up nor tortured. When his face had partially recovered, they took him away to Germany.

The Gestapo had come to the valley mainly to avenge themselves for the great funeral that had been given to Nono. They were busy with their own Germans at the time of the funeral, but they had several informers there. When they were told that the Colonel Fournier had made the oration over Nono's body, the Gestapo decided that Colonel Fournier was chief of all the Resistance in the valley, and probably largely responsible for all those horrible accidents to the trains. So poor Colonel Fournier, who up to then had not been connected with the active side of the Resistance, had to hide like any hunted dog of a Maquisard. Not that Colonel Fournier could ever look like a dog of a Maquisard. He had snow-white hair, fine features, a rounded and flowing voice, great personal charm and a great war record in at least two wars.

But the omnipresent Boulaya saved Colonel Fournier as he had saved me. A lesser man than Boulaya would have let the colonel do a little of the running away that he himself had been forced to do, in the times when the Resistance was less respectable and more difficult. Not Boulaya. He took Fournier under his wing and then produced him as his equal. Of course, there was a method in all this. Boulaya was good at paper-work, much quicker and neater than the "patron" had been, and he was security-minded, which was more important. Boulaya did only the necessary paper-work, and he sent his messages in code. But he always found this work a profound bore. So when he dramatically produced the Colonel Fournier on his staff with a position equal to his own, he also blandly announced that from that day all paper-work would be in the capable hands of Colonel Fournier. Everybody was pleased, except perhaps a few people who disliked newcomers.

Besides hunting for Colonel Fournier, the Germans made trouble at Bonnay, Nono's village. The mayor was away when they arrived in Bonnay, on August 15, so they took his deputy instead, and dragged him into the graveyard to the tomb of Nono, still decorated with palms, wreaths, and the Tricolour, and covered with flowers. While German soldiers tore the flag from the tomb and burned it, the officer made an oration.

"This man was not a soldier, he was a gangster, a criminal, a terrorist, and a murderer. He did not die the glorious death of a soldier, he was shot because he was a criminal working against the government of his country and the government of Europe.

"Yet this village has idolised the man in death as though he was a hero. He was not a hero, he was a pig. If all the signs and words painted on his tomb, if every flower and every wreath is not removed within eight days, we will return, and the village will suffer heavily for its false idolatries." He ended with the peroration: "You French are dishonest people. Fundamentally dishonest. You are such swindlers. You return generous treatment with secret curses and secret threats. You are cheats and murderers."

I might be tempted to continue this last episode in my little story of Nono in an heroic vein. But you cannot make heroes out of people who decline to be heroic. The mayor of Bonnay decided, with sound common sense, that, for the good of the community as a whole, the grave should, for the moment, be cleared of its wreaths and patriotic slogans. When the Maquis heard of this there was a strong urge among some of the young hot-heads to prevent the execution of the mayor's orders, or to re-decorate the grave. But I spoke strongly against this. On the whole, I am against throwing away for sentiment alone, human lives and houses that do not let in the rain. I think that my advice was taken, because the Germans carried out no punitive raid on Bonnay.

"Was your name on that satchel you gave me just after Nono's death?" I asked Janine Dardel.

"Why, no."

"Because the Gestapo took it with them the other day."

"Wait a minute. . . . Yes, I think, I am sure that my name was inside the flap. Yes, I remember. At school. I printed it in gothic lettering. Oh, my God. My poor parents. There, you see. I knew something appalling would happen. This is the reward for my deceit." Large glistening tears rolled off her rounded cheeks. This was a fairly terrible thing. The Dardel house really was in some considerable danger. I certainly could not use it again as a hiding-place. Or the girl as a messenger. She might easily be followed.

"Better not tell your parents," I told her. I always take the easy way out whenever possible, and I could see no point in worrying her people. Also, if the Gestapo did arrive at the house with the incriminating satchel, the Dardels would give a better impression of innocence if they knew nothing about the affair. Dardel himself had such an unblemished reputation so far as the Germans were concerned, that they were unlikely to do very much to him.

"No, I won't," agreed Janine, but she rode away in such a state that I had my doubts. These were confirmed a couple of days later, when I called at the Dardel house to collect a letter.

"Reckless dare-devil," Madame Dardel greeted me. "Don't you know that the shadow of the axe hangs over this house?" Janine came out into the garden with downcast eyes. "This idiot girl has told us everything," her mother continued. "I cannot blame her for working with you, I should have done the same at her age. But the stupidity of leaving her name on that thing. To think that I could produce a daughter capable of such a thing. What is she going to do when she gets married? Her husband will know everything, every little thing." The girl took all this with downcast eyes, as though, conscious of her sins, she offered her bare and bleeding back to the lash.

"Where is Monsieur Dardel?" I asked, more to change the subject than anything else. To my amazement Madame Dardel sat down on a wheelbarrow and laughed until her feet beat little taps upon the dry ground and her fine hands knotted themselves into red fists. Janine gazed on her mother with a sad and sorry limpid air, that made me want to stick a long pin in her.

"I really should not tell you," gasped Madame Dardel.

"No, mama, don't, oh don't tell him," said Janine hastily.

"But I must. Oh yes, I simply must. It is so *damned* funny, this extraordinary creature that I married twenty-one years ago. I tell you, Georges (she always called me that because she rather admired the King of England), I tell you, incredible as it may seem, he is building a 'cachette'."

"Who for?"

"Why, for himself. In case the Gestapo come. He has had a mason in to cut a hole in the wash-house wall. From there he can get under the stairs to the cellar. He's doing the rest himself. Making a secret door, etcetera. Oh, it's divine. I tell you he has not been so busy since 1938. Hasn't time even for his 'belotte' at the pub. Even though I am so frightened, I just laugh and laugh and laugh all day."

"I think you are most unkind to poor daddy," Janine said. "And it's all my fault."

Hastily taking my leave, I roared off to Rigney. For I had, momentarily succumbed to the urge for speed. At this time the Germans had attacked all the local Gendarmeries. The gendarmes had escaped, since they were waiting for some such move. And knowing that it was coming, they had managed to hide away the majority of their transport and petrol. The motorcycle I now rode was one of their giant five horse-power Terrots. A clumsy machine, but smooth and powerful on the open road. I went to Rigney to have my photograph taken by old Letallec. He posed me beside the lemon-trees in tubs, and his daughter held a large scarlet and orange-striped parasol to shade one side of my face from the burning sun, while he took the cover off the lens. I was having this picture taken because I had changed my appearance and my papers, following confirmed reports that the Gestapo were searching for me personally in Besançon, and up the valleys of the Doubs and the Ognon.

My appearance had been changed with the aid of two bottles of extremely superior hair-dye belonging to a woman acquaintance. She was a well-preserved woman, who did not like to show grey hair, and she changed the colour of mine in one evening of hard work. She did my hair and eyebrows and I did the rest later, making a thorough job of the whole thing. I was now a fantastic-looking creature, with a lot of strange-looking auburn hair, which always looked to me like a wig, but which gave me great confidence as I began to move around the country again. My new papers were for nothing grand like an insurance agent. Now I was just a plain peasant, domiciled in Vieilley. Since I had lost all my belongings people had showered clothes upon me, but they were all old, and the ones I liked best were the comfortable blue denims, faded by much work and washing in the sun.

The red-haired countess ordered me a fine suit from a black-market tailer in Besançon, as I thought that I was going to have to make a trip to see someone at Lyons. But the trip fell through, and I never did more than look with awe upon the suit, a striking-looking "zazou" garment in brilliant black-and-white tweed, with drain-pipe trousers and ultra-long coat.

After having my picture taken I rode back to the top of

Vieilley, where I was expecting an important messenger from Albert. And at 10 p.m., in pitch blackness and feeling dreadfully alone, I climbed the hill behind the village.

Georges that day had moved our Maquis from Vieilley to the other side of the river. He was not scared for the Maquis, but for the village. The Germans had now, we knew, formal orders to burn down any village where they found signs of the Resistance. And he and I had prospected on the other side of the Ognon, in the Haute-Saône. There we had found a delightfully clear and cool little stream, in which there were many fine trout. The trout settled it. Georges moved the Maquis there, to one of the shady banks. Boulaya was off on a long expedition to Montbéliard. Berger I had sent away to the other side of Dijon to see a French wireless operator. So I was alone in the dark.

I am afraid of the dark. If there is one person with me, or even a dog it is all right. Or once I can get moving through the darkness I forget my fear. But if I have to sit alone and listen to the noises of the night I have to fight against fear every minute. I have tried to conquer this absurd fear, just as I tried, with more success, to conquer my fear of the dentist.

The fear of the dark I must attribute to an evening's "fun" in 1916, when we were playing hide-and-seek after a tea-party in a tall house near Troon. And two sisters ran out upon me as I sat fearful and alone in the dark attic. They were dressed in white sheets and made strange and horrible noises.

So this night in 1944 I lay down alone in my sleeping-bag, listening to noises of the field-mice and the owls and wishing that I had even a German or two to keep me company.

CHAPTER XV

"LA langoureuse Asie et la brulante Afrique." This charming phrase filled me with joy.

I had first heard the phrase on the lips of Geneviève d'Estournelles, when she was reading Baudelaire to her grandmother one afternoon beside the river on the terrace of the Château de Créans. I was eighteen then, and the phrase caught my imagination, and was the beginning of my interest in Baudelaire. When I sent code messages to London for my parachuting grounds I had remembered excerpts from his verses.

This meant that during the night there would be two aeroplanes coming out from England to parachute on my Vieilley ground.

I went out and along the street to warn the "garde-pêche" Poirier, Georges' tenant, that the message had been passed, and that he must get his men to the ground that night. Georges was there too. He jumped on his motor-cycle (another giant from the Gendarmerie) and rode off to tell the Maquis. I insisted that my code messages on the wireless remained a secret shared only by the chief and his assistant for each parachuting ground. Unless you were particularly careful about this the whole valley knew the message. Since I was often away from Vieilley on business, I had further check there in Camille Marquis, who listened for me for three months. She was a thin, tight-lipped girl, slightly shrewish and unpopular in the village. And she was jealous of the close association between us, since she did two confidential jobs for me, the radio watch, and my laundry. She was inclined to look on me possessively as her own private little Britisher. But she was a most useful colleague.

Poirier had twenty-two trusted peasants to warn for duty that night, and four of them would have to be away early to the parachuting grounds with their two-horsed rubber-tyred "platforms". These long hay-carts were admirable for carrying containers. Two of them were capable of dealing with the contents of one Liberator, with a few odds and ends left over.

In the Maquis we had another twenty men available for the night's operation. I would go down later and have dinner with them beside their trout stream. In the meantime, I must go to the ground and see that all was well there.

Another thing had to be seen to. That afternoon, not far from Buthiers, only two villages away, but on the other side of the Ognon river, the ferocious Rita, Haute-Saône Resistance leader, often known as "le fou", had slaughtered four Germans, and had been obliged to leave their bodies lying in the roadway, because more Germans arrived shooting just after the killing.

There were four German patrols out now, around that spot, only eight kilometres from our parachuting ground. I sent beautiful Maria Contini over there on her bicycle to find out exactly where the patrols were, and whether they were stopping there the night. If they did that I would be forced to call Jean's Maquis from the other side of the "côte" to liquidate the Germans. This parachuting *must* be a success. Not only was it the first in the Vieilley area, but I was expecting parachutists, as well as desperately-needed weapons.

London had told me that they were sending three people to help me, two captains and a radio operator. As I cycled to the ground Berger came riding after me on his motor-cycle.

"Jean's Maquis was attacked this afternoon by two hundred Schloks," he reported. "Jean has moved four kilometres up the Rougemont road in the woods. No casualties. This afternoon Jean attacked a convoy on the Belfort road. Three trucks burned, eight German bodies."

"No sign of Germans high up in the forest?" I asked.

"No, mon Capitaine."

"Get out my car. Take a small cask of wine and a bottle of Marc to the château at La Barre. Tell Madame, with my compliments, that I hope by tomorrow morning early to give her the three guests I promised. Have the car on 'Onion' by 2300 hours."

"Onion" was the code name for the Vieilley ground. To get to it I rode down past the Merey-Vieilley station. The gates of all the railway crossings stood wide open all the time now. Since Philippe had made the "Mountain of Miserey", one month previously the cultivators had been able to graze their beasts on the grass patches alongside the railway track. I rode on past the station for five hundred yards, then left my bicycle in some bushes and cut across the fields. My ground was a big rectangle of over one thousand square yards. It was bordered on the north side by the Ognon, which made a good landmark for the airmen, to the south by a large wood, to the east by a line of poplars and to the west by a wire fence. Despite the poplars and the fence to the east and west, the ground really continued beyond them in a succession of wide, flat, rolling fields. Since our prevailing winds there, "the Bise" (dry weather) and "the Wind" (wet weather), blew from the west and the east, the ground was a good one. I had chosen it for this operation because it was fairly well screened from most of the surrounding roads.

London had demanded bonfires for this dropping, because it was to be carried out in the dark, inter-moon period. Bonfires show up for a long way at night, and I heartily cursed "le fou" as I walked over the field. It was a hot evening, and I would have liked to have bathed in the big pool I knew beyond the end of the poplars. But there was not time. I found our three litre bottle of paraffin and six jealously-guarded books of matches in a tin box. These stores were for lighting the bonfires. And farther on, among the high bulrushes, I found the

303

nicely-tied bundles of dry pine branches that Georges and I had made nearly a month before, when we first picked out this ground. In my mind I ran over the other stores we should need. A big jar of wine for the workers. Four round loaves of bread and half a dozen tins of "singe", the French equivalent of bully-beef. Four aluminium cups for drinking the wine. A bottle of spirits in case one of the parachutists hurt himself and to give them all a nip in the morning if the aeroplanes did not come. At least four electric torches. These were difficult. At that time only four torches were available in the whole area of Vieilley. One of them belonged to me, another to Boulaya, the third to the Curé, and the fourth to a man outside Vieilley who was considered too much of a talker to be let into the secret. His wife (believed to be more discreet) stole the lamp from him each time she was informed by us that it would be needed. That ended the list of extras. The small comforts were necessary. If the parachutage arrived the work was long and back-breaking. It took four strong men to lift each container. If the aeroplanes did not arrive the wait was a long one for men who had been working hard through the day. If they did not arrive that night it would be the third time that Vieilley men had kept watch in vain. And it was the season for hot days and cold ground mists that came creeping across from the river at nights.

Back in the village, Gustave was waiting with one of our trucks to take me over to the Maquis. He was glad to have a petrol-driven truck in his hands again. He had not driven one since the battle on the Marne in 1940.

"Say, Émile," he shouted above the noisy engine as we rattled down the dusty white road to Cromary. "If the weapons arrive tonight, will you arm us boys in the village?"

"Not this time, Gustave my friend. But next parachutage perhaps, if it is a big one." My dearest wish was to get enough arms to make an armed nucleus in each of the villages. Already we had picked the men, and a skeleton training had been given to them. They were all men who were good shots and keen sportsmen. Fine material. And Georges was to have command of them. They would come from six villages and form a guerrilla "company" about three hundred strong. By this time I had seen villages burning when I had gone sniping on the Belfort road. It was a terrible sight, the filthy smoke, the dead cattle and horses, the screams of the women, the murdered, mutilated men. The time was approaching when the villages must protect themselves or be swamped in a horde of Germans.

But my first responsibilities were to the first men to join up in the Resistance, and these mainly came from the workers in factories or towns. We had to arm the existing Maquis, and all the groups that had been waiting, some of them for over a year, and who were ready to take to the woods the moment we gave them arms. The workers had been the best men for the sabotage. You could not forget them now that the character of the Resistance war was changing. Now there was no more sabotage (except road destruction) to be done. There was only fighting.

And for the fighting the peasants, the men of the land and the woods, were probably the better men. You liked the men of the land. You had to like them as you liked the trees and the haystacks on the land. But you had to admit that the men of the land had not suffered as the other workers had suffered. The peasant had continued to cultivate his land while the enemy ruled his country. He had kept as much food from the enemy as possible. He had cheated him thoroughly because a Frenchman is as clever as a German is heavy-witted. But the peasant had lived the good hard life on the land, and he had often made money from the war by selling his produce to the townspeople at black prices. Now the war was sweeping up to the peasant's soil, not to attack the false God patriotism, but to the fields his sweat had fertilised, to the village and his own people. The peasant wanted to fight. He would fight. But you had to give the first arms to the worker, who had been in the battle longer because he had no fields to draw him out of the war, no crops to drug his hatred of the oppressor with their work-earned peace.

The Maquisards had already begun their meal when we arrived. They were sitting at a long table beside the clear stream. Georges had developed an admirable technique now for the Maquis. There were none of those smells that had offended me when I first parachuted in. (Or was it that familiarity had changed my sense of smell?) Meals now functioned with the smoothness of a well-run house or restaurant. A battery of aluminium cooking utensils that would have graced any restaurant had been supplied (almost free of charge) by Dardel. We all ate together, of course, and we all helped each other. Now I found an elegant visitor, the Colonel Fournier whom I had last seen in full bloom at a conference in the Paris War Ministry in '40. His next door neighbour was the Frisé, and they were carrying on an animated and friendly conversation.

I was delighted to see the Frisé, who had been badly wounded in a road skirmish not long before, and who had come to rejoin our Maquis at his own request.

"How's the leg?" I asked him.

"As good as it ever was. My legs were always failures, eh, Émile?" He put a quarter of a pound of underdone steak, a mushroom, and two sauté potatoes in his mouth, submerged the food in red wine, and continued to speak through the process of eating. "But no more cars for me. It was cars that got us into our little mess. No. Give me motor-cycles now. And say, Émile," he continued angrily. "The other day I took the trouble to kill a Stol and take a brand-new one-and-a-half-horse-power Peugeot from him—can't manage anything more powerful yet. And today the new major tells me he wants my 'petrolette'. Now is that playing the game?"

"I venture to suggest that I needed the thing for more pressing business than wasting petrol running around the country for the sake of a thrill," said the "new major", Maître Corneille, an advocate from Besançon.

"For my part, I don't mind giving him the 'petrolette'," Frisé said. "Only it means finding another, and if he likes that better will he not take that? Where will this all end? Can the status of officers as compared with the Maquisards not be elucidated?"

"Say, Émile," shouted the Pointu from the other end of the table. "If there are any American carbines in this parachutage, can I have one?"

"Can I? And me? Can I?" chorused a dozen voices.

"Can I have a new Bren?" hiccuped the Colonial Army sergeant, who had taken advantage of an extra glass of wine issued in honour of the night's operation. He exchanged cigarettes with the youngsters against their extra wine, and then exchanged his plate of meat against four cigarettes. During the remainder of the evening he cadged cigarettes off myself or anybody else soft enough to humour him. Sometimes if you gave him a cigarette he told you a mercifully-incomprehensible, vulgar story (Colonial Army brand). I had got to like the old beast. And the more he drank the better he handled the Bren.

"Where are Maurice and Philippe?" I asked.

"Why, they've gone off to do the job with the Poles."

"But we were still checking up on the contacts."

"Maurice decided to go all the same."

This worried me. I had arranged with the Besançon railway-man that fifteen Polish mercenaries who were doing essential guard duties in the depot were to escape one night and be met by some of our men, who would give them blue overalls in exchange for their complete German uniform, kit, personal weapons, and one heavy German machine-gun with ten thousand rounds. Maurice and Philippe had volunteered to do this job, the rendezvous had been fixed in a court-yard at St. Claude, suburb of Besançon. But somehow I had an uneasy feeling about the whole thing, and although the heavy machine-gun was desperately tempting, I had put the date off and off. Now, it seemed, Maurice had himself set the thing in motion. He and Philippe had driven off that evening in one of our Citroëns.

"We can't afford to lose Maurice and Philippe now," I said.

"Why lose? There's nothing to it," said the Frisé.

"Then why did you refuse to go?" asked the Pointu.

"Because I thought Émile would be more likely to give me an American carbine if I worked on the parachutage, and I wanted to ask his advice about my 'petrolette' being stolen by the major."

"I am not interested in your 'petrolette'," I lied. The Frisé was a menace running round the country on his motor-cycle. But he was such an old friend that I would have given him anything.

We managed to pile all twenty-two plus Gustave, myself and the jar of wine into the truck. As we hurtled through Vieilley we saw the Marquis family standing in their lighted doorway to see us go. It was 10.30. I was already beginning to yawn. The past two weeks had been exhausting because the parachutages were beginning in my area and also the first signs of the backward German rush were apparent. We had changed to more open tactics. We were attacking the roads with parties of sharpshooters. I had been sleeping most nights on the bank in the topmost garden of Vieilley, twenty yards up from Gustave's house. It was a pleasant, wild garden, and I enjoyed sleeping there. Usually Berger and Boulaya slept there too. Often we did not get to the garden before five in the morning. Then we would be wakened at nine or ten in the morning by messengers or one of Boulaya's new secretaries. When it rained we slept in Gustave's barn, which had a secret exit into the woods behind. If we slept there we had nine boys between the ages of seventeen and twenty for company. These were "refractaires" boys of the upper village who should, had they obeyed German orders, have been working in Germany. Like us they were hiding at night. During the day they worked with their fathers and brothers and sisters in the fields.

Once arrived at the ground, there was too much to be done to remember tiredness. I allowed the Maquisards to lie down in a circle and sleep while Georges and I got the villagers to place their bonfires. The other peasants were divided into working-parties, and, once the parachutes were all down, it was the lusty countrymen who would load the heavy containers on to the "platforms" which now were waiting discreetly in a wooded corner of the field. I had learned that you had to keep them fairly far away from the aeroplane approach. Otherwise the horses were likely to panic. The Maquisards had already been detailed off into three parties who were to guard the field, escort parachutists to me, and act as "long-stops" for containers or packages that might drop before or beyond the fires.

All was ready by 11.45 when Berger arrived in the car with Maria Contini, whom he had found searching for me with her report. German patrols and sentry posts near Buthiers had departed for Besançon at nightfall. They were as nervous as I was in the dark, and with better reason. I told Berger to take Maria back to her home in the car. It was no time for respectable and good-looking girls to be alone on the roads after nightfall.

We settled down to rest and sleep. Most of us had brought some sort of covering. I had my sleeping-bag of course, but the sky was seldom without an aeroplane of one German kind or another. When I first arrived at Vieilley there had been much German air activity in the area. During the day flights of fighters passed, small courier aeroplanes buzzed down the valley at regular hours, and twice a day we had the reconnaissance plane they called the "mouchard". But at the end of June all air activity ceased. Towards the end of August it came back with a rush. And now, through the day, the German aeroplanes hedge-hopped up our valley. This was an encouraging sight, for although we never saw an Allied fighter, we knew that the enemy was afraid of them even in our valley. At night the most frequent passers across the sky were the throaty and pretty Junkers 88 night-fighters. We feared and hated them. They were hunting for our four-engined friends.

At 1.12 there was a deeper roar from the north-west, coming from over the lovely hills of the Haute-Saône to the right of Buthiers village. Georges and I both sat up at the same time.

"Quadrimoteur, Georges," I said.

"Yes, it's them."

It was too dark to see the solitary aeroplane, but it was a four-engined one, there was no doubt about that. Georges yelled at the teams around the fires to light up. Meanwhile I ran to my place and began to flash the signal letter, pointing my torch at the noise of the four engines as an American called Bob once taught me to do in one of the odd schools in Britain.

All three fires flared almost simultaneously. The men only had to pour on a little paraffin and strike a match. Within a few seconds the whole field was picked out in yellow, flickering light. The men around the fire looked wonderful, like giants. I concentrated on my letter L. The aircraft was miles away now, it seemed to be paying no attention to us.

"Merde," shouted Poirier behind me.

"What's the matter?"

"The 'cochon', he's paying no attention to us."

"Wait a minute. These big ones take nearly eight kilometres to turn in a circle."

"Here he comes," screamed Georges. "Look out, it's a Junkers."

An aircraft seemed to be diving at great speed towards us. Georges claimed, like all professional aviators, that he could tell any aeroplane by the noise it made. When he said this, therefore, I thought it prudent to run a little, away from the fires. So did everybody else. Lately reception committees had been machine-gunned and cannoned by German night-fighters. But the aircraft that swooped down over our fires was a Liberator. I saw the first cluster of parachutes, twelve of them, the containers, leave the hull.

"Oh, God," I said. "Let there be Brens." Everybody else was shouting. We had been taught at the school that "the whole operation must be carried out in absolute silence".

The Liberator, passing low over the fires, with the swishing of her body through the air plainly audible, was one of the beautiful sights of my life. I saw other Liberators before and after this. And Halifaxes and even the mighty Stirlings which carried most of all. But this was the first aeroplane to come to Vieilley. And I owed Vieilley so much.

"She is like a trout," I cried. "Georges, she is like a trout."

She was. Her graceful belly, its tones warmed and merged by our fires looked just like a fish seen in a beautiful pool, like the big brown pool of the Dulnain that we used to fish.

On her second run the Liberator dropped three men, followed by some packages. She was late with this drop. The first man fell well behind our fires, and the others must be far out. Frisé had collected the first parachutist; he came up leading the uncouth figure by the arm and carrying his parachute as I had instructed them to do. I had forgotten how silly men looked in the rubber helmets and parachuting overalls. This man was a Frenchman.

"Chapelle," he said, holding out a steady hand.

"Émile; congratulations on your arrival. Are you all right?"

"Perfectly." He was a cool customer, and I noticed he spoke with the local accent. That was good.

"Anything you want? Not hungry or thirsty?"

"No, thank you. That is, unless you have some wine. I have not tasted good 'pinard' for years." They gave him some wine in a tin cup. Not vintage wine, but the honest rough twelve-degree stuff that on some occasions tastes better than the best bottles in the Rothschild cellars.

There were no aircraft to be heard now.

"Put out the fires," I shouted.

"Jump to it now. Out with the fires," Georges echoed. "And get ready your paraffin and small stuff for the next 'zingue'."

Berger came up with the second parachutist, a tall, square American. He was as excited as the Frenchman had been calm. He had a loud laugh and handed out delicacies like chewing-gum and chocolate. A long tail of my workers followed him. I got angry with them and ordered them sharply away to their posts. The American said that he was proud to meet me. He had heard a lot about me in London.

"This American likes France," Berger told me in an awed voice.

"Yes, I expect so."

"No, but not just calmly like you, mon Capitaine. Passionately. You see, he landed head first, and his face hit the ground. Then he got to his knees and he took two handfuls of earth and raised them to his lips, and said: 'I love the bloody soil of France.'"

"I expect he meant 'sacred soil'," I told him. "The words are easy to confound for a foreigner." I asked the American: "Berger here says you landed upside down. Are you all right?"

"Sure I'm all right. I'm just so glad to be here. We've been waiting to come for three whole weeks."

The third parachutist arrived at our group. It was dark now and I shone my hooded torch on him. He was another American, tall, thin and very young and silent. There was no time to say anything to him. We heard engines again.

"Light the fires." I ran back and began to shine my L into the sky again. Two of the fires were blazing, the third had not lit and Georges was screaming curses at them. The second Liberator came over just as the first had done, quickly and silently. She dropped her twelve containers well beyond the fires, circled and dropped some packages close to. This time there was something more like silence. The men had begun to work, gathering the heavy containers into piles. The "platforms" were already creaking out from the corner by the river. I got the three parachutists together and told them that I was taking them away in a car immediately. They moved in a dazed manner. It was difficult to get them going in the same direction. I knew how they were feeling, and I chivvied them along, bossing them. We were half-way up the open slope towards the car, parked on the edge of the wood, when the Frisé came up to me shouting.

"Emile, Emile, here's another parachutist."

"Buckle your lips, I can hear, and so can everybody else within ten kilometres." The man who followed him introduced himself in a smooth voice, first in French, then in English, with an excellent accent.

"Captain Mesure."

"Enchanted. Emile."

"Is the Colonel here?" he asked.

"What colonel?"

"Why, the Colonel who was in the aircraft with me."

"Did he jump?"

"Yes, he jumped before me. I was miles away. Perhaps over a mile behind the field." I secretly blessed the chance that had made me select a ground with a clear run of cultivated land on either side.

The colonel came up while we were at the car. He had taken a long time to find the field. All of them said they were all right. They were beginning to worry, as travellers will, about their luggage. They all began to ask questions at the same time about packages and things.

"Don't worry," I told them airily. My worry was to get them well away from the ground in case of a German search that night or the following day. I pushed them all into the car. Fortunately it was the "family model". Berger took the wheel, the young American sat next to him and I was on the outside with a Sten gun poking out of the window. The other four, enormous in their parachuting clothes, had squashed themselves into the back.

What respectable parachutists they were compared to me, I reflected as the car felt its way silently in the darkness along the tracks leading from the woods. I had been trained to discard all signs of being a parachutist on landing. Some of these men still wore rubber rings round their foreheads, and they wore knee-pads and everything. They were in uniform too. I thought I would shake them up a little bit.

"Shall I use the lights mon Capitaine?" Berger asked when we hit the road between Bonnay and Vieilley.

"Yes, put them on 'code', not full on. We must get away from here as quickly as we can."

"By the direct route?"

"Yes, through Venise, Moncey, and Rigney. Cut the lights when we take the hairpin two kilometres before La Barre, and go slowly to avoid leaving tracks. We'll turn down the lane at the end of the property and walk across the orchard to the château."

The others were listening to all this.

"I suppose you are all armed?" I asked them. "Good. This road is a secondary one and is not generally used by the Germans. Do any of you know this part of the world?" As I expected, one of them did, the first arrival, the calm Frenchman who spoke like a Franc-comtois. But he had not been there since his childhood.

"Do you know where you are on the map?" I asked. Yes, they did, but they were slightly out. They thought they were on the other side of the Ognon. I had given co-ordinates of the ground in the North side, between Buthiers and Cromary to London, and had changed the ground at the last moment because of the Germans stirred up by Rita on that side, and because of a doubtful family in the village of Cromary. I told them where they were and how to ask for help if we should be ambushed and separated. That quietened them down a lot. The boy beside me had been silent all the time.

"When will the war be over?" I asked him stupidly, really just to hear myself speaking English again. The two Americans hardly spoke French and understood less. And only Mesure of the three Frenchmen spoke English.

"Can't say," was all he answered. He was very sleepy.

"Nice automobile. Runs kind of smooth," he added, feeling perhaps that he had dealt with my question too abruptly.

"Yes, it's front-wheel drive and has no chassis."

"That so. Where d'you get the gas?"

"We steal it."

It took us some way to find our way out of the orchard and through the garden. Then Berger gave the rattling signal on the kitchen shutters and the girl pushed her head out of her bedroom window on the third floor of the high château.

"Coming, Monsieur Émile," she said softly, and soon we were all inside. The girl and her mother were alone in the château; for the moment they had no servants. But Jean Viennot's sister, from the farm across the road, came over to help them, and brought them hams and rich yellow butter from the farm. The girl and her mother were both thin and wonderfully polite. They sat up very straight, not touching the backs of their chairs, and their distinguished faces showed exactly the right mixture of welcome, compassion, and politeness. They talked easily and without embarrassment. It was a soldier's family. The salon held a portrait of Madame's late husband in full uniform and there were swords and wild Moroccan arms on the walls. They were not dismayed at having two extra guests sprung on them at half-past two in the morning. And they were not nervous. The old lady feared nothing. Her word battles with the Boches were legend in the district. She was mayor of the hamlet, and the enemy was obliged to come to her with requisitioning demands. The château had sheltered many Russian evaders too. That appealed to me. Once, when I had congratulated the hawk-faced die-hard on her broad-mindedness in taking in our allies, and risking herself, her daughter, her château and her village for them, she replied:

"Of the five men we sheltered here only one had not had his home destroyed by the Boches. They could have had anything they wanted from any of us, and they wanted so little. Besides," she added, "I am a soldier's daughter and a soldier's wife. Stalingrad and Leningrad cured my old-fashioned ideas about Communists." She noticed me looking at a portrait of Marshal Pétain that hung on her wall. "He *was* a soldier too," she said.

I did not bother to look much at the new arrivals. Berger and I still had a lot of work to do, and we took our leave in a few moments. The room overflowed with their belongings as they stripped off their parachutist's overalls. They were all dressed up in uniform hung with equipment and weapons. Except for the French colonel and Mesure, they were rigged up like British paratroopers with assortments of fancy knives and gadgets sown into them and their uniforms littered with all the funny wings and things one expects from those people. The Americans asked for coffee.

When Berger and I arrived back on the ground, Georges and his lusty gang had nearly finished clearing the containers away. There were only a few odd ones to be cleared up by the truck. When those had gone we formed a line and swept the ground for over one mile behind the field. We got a good haul of packages like this. One of them was a leg-bag. It contained twenty-four million francs in notes. At the end of our beat, to my horror we found a nice silk Nylon parachute lying stretched out across the haricot poles, just as it had fallen. I had been taught that it was the parachutist's greatest crime to leave the 'chute. It belonged to one of the two in the second aircraft. I was angry, for it showed thoughtlessness on the parachutist's part. There would be many German aeroplanes flying up the valley during the day. And already the early dawn was beginning to light the sky. I was worried too, because I failed to identify all the luggage that the five told me they had brought with them. One package with its parachute could give away the whole operation. If the enemy found it he would comb all the villages and woods around.

However, it was getting late, so Berger and I loaded the car with the packages, and I ripped open the unaddressed ones to try to find the American's wireless transmitter. They wanted to make contact with London early that morning. Berger and I took all the stuff we had found to La Barre again. We just dumped everything and left. They were all asleep in the château. We were getting chary about using the roads now, for if the parachutage was suspected we were liable to be nastily surprised at any of the corners.

Camille Marquis was waiting for us at the entrance to Vieilley. Two farm boys of Bonnay had found parachutes in the fields between that village and the river. There was nothing else for it, we must push on down there at once. We stopped the car in the back of the village and made discreet enquiries. It was the butcher's son who had seen the parachutes. He had hidden them, sensible boy, in a field of potatoes. Already the German air stream had begun hedge-hopping up the valley in the direction of Belfort. We told each other that the big Junkers 53s contained senior officers leaving their troops down south. Probably most of them held wounded. We saw Georges as we went racing over the level-crossing to look for the parachutes. He had heard the rumour too. We found three more packages and one man's parachute. This was where Mesure had fallen then. He had been perfectly correct when he said that he had walked a mile and a half to the ground. Both he and the colonel had left their parachutes lying on the ground to betray us. I was enraged at them, and told them so later. Berger and I drove to La Barre for the third time. All their luggage had now been found. Berger and I hid the car and then went to sleep for a couple of hours in the château garden. I left him sleeping there and went into the house, eating plums and small sweet pears as I went. Inside the hall there was a long mirror and I suddenly saw what an extremely odd figure I made with dirty shoes and worker's trousers, a leather jacket, a shock of queer dark reddish hair, a massive pistol stuck into my belt, and dark bags under my eyes.

There was chaos now in the living-rooms of the château. These people had brought mountains of equipment with them. The two who had abandoned their parachutes were sharing a room upstairs and were less encumbered than the others. They had arrived to report to Ligne, and were going to help Boulaya. Both of them had already put on civilian clothes, and were in full question-asking form. Receiving newcomers under such circumstances is like being at the same time a mother, an enquiry bureau, a lawyer, and a very young officer who is obliged to give orders to a very old officer.

The other three formed a "team" which was to work with me. They were still in uniform, for they had been sent as soldiers. I soon had them out of their fancy uniforms though, telling them that, even in civilian clothes it would be unsafe for the moment for them to put their noses out of doors. These three had brought with them a simply fantastic amount of stuff. I nearly wrote "junk", but the equipment they carried with them was the pick of both American and British officers' equipment. They had apparently been encouraged to bring everything that appealed to them. They all carried a variety of arms, contained in the most complicated and wonderful series of cases and holsters hung on belts and shoulder-straps. Each of them had an enormous rucksack festooned with all kinds of rolls and appendages. Not one of them could have carried his rucksack two miles, and all of them had much more luggage than this. I noticed to my amazement extras like cooking stoves. And Chapelle, the Frenchman, who might have known better, had even brought a small axe with him. It was a fine axe, made somewhere in America and with a nice leather hood for the gleaming blade. They were dripping with compasses and all sorts of cunning devices, of course. As for knives, each of them had at least three. And maps. I worked with one old Michelin map stuck in an inside pocket. They had huge British map-cases filled with all kinds of alarmingly coloured masterpieces in different scales. And boots. Each of them appeared to have three or four pairs, including at least one pair of the high brown American parachuting-boots. Where and how was I going to hide these gentlemen? I would need a pantechnicon. Then the Americans did not speak French.

I should have to give up the life I liked, the solitary life with friendly interludes in the Maquis and in the villages. I should plainly have to be with these three, at any rate, until they had got over their first feelings of strangeness, and were acclimatised.

But when they talked, or rather Bazata, the big American who was the dominant character, my reluctance faded into the background. Bazata was a blustering man with a heavy, Russian-looking face. He was a quick, eager talker, and he picked out and hammered on the salient immediate supply necessities of the area as a good newspaper editor might have done. He was a get-things-done man.

Floyd, the second American, was only a child. He was some kind of sergeant, and looked well under twenty years of age. Dark, handsome and quiet, he held Bazata in great awe. The Frenchman, Chapelle, was also silent. He came, I found out now, from the other side of Besançon. He had been a regular soldier before the war, and he had risen to the rank of captain in the de Gaulliste army, and to this special job. Where Bazata was brilliant, and liked to sketch things in with broad sweeps of his imagination and his ever-active tongue, the Frenchman was solid and persevering, and thought, as a thoroughly trained soldier will, in great detail. Once they had found out what I wanted and where, they got their wireless going, and sent and received messages almost all day and all night.

Bazata was forced, by a serious leg injury, to keep fairly quiet for a day or two. His leg had been hurt when he jumped. Through a mistake in balance he had made a head-first exit. The static line he used was of some metal composition and this caught between his legs, tearing the flesh. He was lucky to be alive. Their preoccupation with the radio and Bazata's injury gave me time to go round my sector for another two or three days.

I arranged with Paincheau to move with my three new comrades and Berger to the Convent at Huanne. Among the nuns and sisters I thought that we might conveniently hide our accents and national discrepancies. Also the convent was well situated, being farther up the valley, well to the north-east of Vieilley, in Paincheau territory. Tactically, it was a difficult place to surprise, for it was perched on top of a cliff down which there was a secret path. But to be perfectly frank, the main thing that swayed me was my desire to live in the convent. Like many irreligious people, I am profoundly attracted to religious buildings and institutions. When I saw the scrubbed bareness of the long empty rooms with their faint odour of soap and soda something drew me irresistibly to the place.

Nobody could have been keener to have terrorists in her house than the Mother Superior, a delightful person. She arranged our quarters. We were to have six rooms. I could not help noticing that she took some pains to see that we should have no doors or corridors which would permit us to mix socially with the nuns and sisters in her charge. But then, I was accompanied by the swarthy Berger, whose sulphuric masculinity was advertised by his blue jowl and shiningly greased hair. Also he wore tight tweed knee-breeches and long stockings which demonstrated the strength and suppleness of his powerful lower half. Possibly also my dyed hair gave me a slightly sinister turn of countenance. At any rate, I comforted myself that had I been my normal sheep-like, blonde self the Mother Superior would have feared nothing. The male gardeners were decrepit old men. One of them accompanied Paincheau, Berger and myself on our rounds of the convent. Paincheau warned him fiercely at the end to keep his mouth shut about our pending arrival.

I considered the monastery well situated because I wanted, with the three newcomers, to expand to the north of the small area I had been working in, and to take in much of the Haute-Saône.

Things had been cleaner in the Resistance there since the worst brigand of them all, Sauvin, had been liquidated. Sauvin, "le diable", raped three women whom he had taken to his Maquis as suspects. They were raped before they had been tried, and this time he had to suffer the consequences of his terrible deed. The "patron" (just before he was captured by

the Germans) called a court-martial of three Resistance officers.
Sauvin was condemned to death. An executioner was appointed.
Sauvin was kidnapped (no easy matter), taken to a wood, shot,
and buried.

With the amount of material Bazata and his friends hoped to
get for us, all of our Maquis around Besançon would soon, I
hoped, be equipped. Then we must expand the service and try
to help the Haute-Saône, so far badly neglected. Accordingly I
wanted to be somewhere near Loulans-les-Forges, on the north
side of the Ognon. Since I did not know that part except by
sight from two or three small sabotaging expeditions, the best
compromise while the new boys were still new, seemed to be to
live in Paincheau's area, where we would be under his wing,
and at least warned if danger directly threatened.

When we had made our arrangements at the convent we drove
back to Vieilley for the distribution of the material received the
night before. The village of Vieilley for four generations had
dumped its hard rubbish beside the lane that ran past a copper-
coloured spring that only dried up on the hottest summer days,
and so along just below the trees that thickly covered the hill as
far as Venise. The wily Georges had chosen the rubbish-dump
as a depository for his containers. The "platforms" had been
directly unloaded on the dump, then age-old rubbish was forked
over them. As we opened the containers on the dump an inven-
tory was made and the arms were handed directly to representa-
tives of several Maquis who had been notified to attend.

It was a good parachutage. There were a lot of rifles and
Brens, which were what we needed for ambushes and sniping.
At the end of the afternoon the whole dump was closed down
and everything incriminating disposed of. The last convoy
waited to go off. It was our own truck which was to run a
selection of arms for one hundred men down to the country
near Bouclans. There one of Boulaya's Besançon companies
that had been waiting so long had finally taken to the Maquis,
and they were without arms. The Pointu, the sergeant of
Colonial Infantry, and little Démaï were in the back of the
truck, sitting on top of the deadly cargo. Pointu had three
phosphorous grenades rolling inside a captured German helmet
handy to his right hand. A supply of these grenades had arrived
in this parachutage and they were invaluable for this type of
work, particularly if you were pursued.

Paul, the American radio operator, for example, had been
chased a week or two previously in his car by a car-load of

318

Gestapo men. Paul knocked out the back window with his pistol-butt, threw one phosphorous grenade out backwards, and the enemy, car, Gestapo and all, disintegrated in a cloud of white smoke with a stabbing flame. Paul was now a veteran gunman. He had established his headquarters in the cellars of the old château at Ronchaux, and he had killed two other Gestapo men with my small .38 Colt.

The Frisé was most keen to use the phosphorous grenade. He was really a child. When there was some new weapon he simply burst with curiosity until he had tried it out on the enemy. He was going to act as advance-guard for the truck—or the "arms convoy", as they called it—by riding ahead alone on his little "petrolette". In that way if there was any trouble the Frisé would buy it alone. He liked working like that. Before he left I searched the insecure carrying-bags of his machine. As I had suspected, they contained two ordinary hand-grenades and four phosphorous grenades. I took them out while he eyed me sadly.

"Fool," I said. "You want to burn yourself. Why do you take such stupid risks?" He laughed at that, for he was always quite pleased when you got angry with him. Then he rode away. I watched them skylined for a minute on the road to Venise. The Frisé jerking along on his little motor-cycle and the truck following five hundred yards behind. And my heart filled with joy and pride that these men undertook gladly such dangerous missions. We had told them that the Germans now guarded several and perhaps all of the Doubs bridges. But it was vital to get the arms through. It was no use sending inexperienced men on such a trip. They were fired on that evening at the bridge of Laissey, below the tunnel of Champlive. They got through two days later, on their third attempt.

Vieilley was a madhouse now, compared to the early days when Boulaya and I had begun to work there with the five men in the Maquis. Now every day there were rumours of the German retreat that was certainly coming up from the south to swamp us. Boulaya was smothered with men who wanted to see him. Some of them wanted to fight, and asked for arms. More of them were interested perhaps in the composition of local government in Besançon when that town should be liberated. From all these strangers I kept severely aloof. I wanted to give arms to all men in Besançon who had worked for us and who were members of the companies that had been formed there when times were difficult in the Resistance, and the ultimate issue still hung in the balance. Personally I did not want to accept as recruits any newcomers from the town.

Women, as well as men, began to pester the dashing Boulaya. He never paid more attention to them than French courtesy demanded. But they came, and in ever-increasing numbers, to the muddy village where this extraordinary and fascinating soldier had his headquarters. They were women from Besançon. Wives and friends of those respectable bourgeois who had spoiled our Maquis even in the early days. The women, once they knew about Boulaya, could always rake up an excuse to attempt to see him. They were carrying messages, or bringing gifts, or, more blatantly, they had an invitation for the Colonel Boulaya. In self-defence Boulaya was obliged to withdraw from his headquarters at Vieilley. He put the new parachuted colonel there and Colonel Fournier, and several others whom I scarcely knew. These men were working fairly openly in Georges' house. They supposed that the Gestapo in Besançon were too busy packing up and getting their hands on all available loot to bother with the new dangerous sport of hunting out the Resistance. For the Resistance was changing rapidly. Georges had moved the Maquis again. Bad weather had driven them from the pleasant wood because torrential rain swelled the clear trout stream until it overflowed its banks and the Maquisards found themselves swimming for it, or at least crawling through water. So Georges had taken over Palise, the small hamlet that he and I had previously earmarked for the winter. If forced to spend winter 1944-45 in the Maquis, we intended to put the Maquisards in the disused church there and in the six or seven houses which composed the place. Palise was well off the beaten track. It lay on the south bank of the Ognon and it was a dead end. Small roads, so soft and bumpy that they were just possible for cars, linked Palise to the back of Moncey and to the bridge across the Ognon below Cromary. Now Georges had accelerated our plans. The Maquis was about thirty strong, and there were already two prisoners, drivers of captured German cars. The prisoners did the fatigues, and were quite reasonably treated. Certainly better treated than I was as a prisoner after the Germans had handed me to the Italians.

Before I left Vieilley I went out for an afternoon to fish this new part of the Ognon. I knew the river pools only up as far as Cromary. In the afternoon we punted up through the new pools. New to me, anyway. Georges occasionally dived off the punt to search under some bush and come up with a fish or two, mostly perch or barbel in his hands. Well up-stream, near a one-room bungalow that belonged to some week-end fisherman from Besançon, we tied the punt to the rushes and went in for a swim. Here the river was very deep and slow. And the water was warm enough to sleep in. Several times I floated down until I found myself bumping on the shallows below, and I swear that I was half asleep.

I believe that when lovers weep at their parting they weep not for each other, but for the thing they had together, the experience, the event, which is ended for ever. For if they love each other again it will be a new experience, and the old thing they had together will never be revived. So I knew that this was the last afternoon of my Maquis existence. Next day I was going to the new people with their radio. And I would be dissociated from the Maquis just as the difficult time began. I was sad that I must leave the Maquis and Georges and the Ognon. Sad that I would only have time now to travel in cars and on motor-cycles. I remembered the days in the early summer when I had longed for the process of development. Before the new phase had begun I was regretting the simplicity of the old phase. You could not talk about such things to Georges of course. He would have asked if you were ill. We discussed the normal things. Talked about the Junkers 53s that passed up the valley and the fish we had taken from the river.

Back in the Maquis there was terrible news. Maurice and Philippe had been taken by the Germans. An ambush had been set for them inside Besançon. The enemy had caught them with explosives and weapons in their possession. The car they had taken to Besançon on the night of the parachutage still stood outside Maurice's house. Nobody dared to touch it in case there was another German ambush there. I would never see them again. They were two of the best men.

We slept in one of the Palise barns. There were guards outside in the road, Maquisards carrying Sten guns. We spread out silk parachutes on the hay, lay on them and used other parachutes as blankets.

"I would rather be in the cabin on the hill than here," I said.

"Certainly. So would I," said Georges. "But this is more convenient. We have not the time to hide away now."

"No. This is convenient."

CHAPTER XVI

"THIS cannot be the right house," I told Berger. "It must be a school."

"Oh yes, this is Monsieur Landel's house, mon Capitaine. You see, he has ten children. And some of his children have children. And there are probably some friends of the children . . ."

"Stop. Imbecile. How can this Landel help us when he is cluttered up with children?"

"But Monsieur Landel is not like other men. He will help."

We were sitting in our muddy car on the gravel carriage-sweep of a medium-sized, square house. It was a pleasant, box-like house. A Pandora's box. No ordinary house could be expected to contain so many children. They poured from every balcony and doorway to goggle at us; and others clustered around the swing or played with the donkey on the lawn. The air smelled sweet and fresh, for the rain had just stopped and the sun was out on the lawn and on the wet ultra-green leaves of the big plane-trees. The children were round and fat and healthy-looking with pink cheeks, well-scrubbed bodies, and glistening eyes. The little girls had their hair carefully arranged either like Alice in pig-tails or in careful creations that piled a mass of hair on top of their heads and then released it in a contained surge to the backs of their necks, like the plumes of the Life Guards. The little boys were thin, energetic, dark. Each wore his thick black hair cut short and carefully shaped back from the "brosse" in front. They were correct children, more energetic and more disciplined than the normal run of French children.

Bernard came out of the house. He was the oldest son of Monsieur Landel, aged about twenty, tall and quite good-looking enough, even with his hair "en brosse", to walk straight on to the films and play juvenile leads: but charming all the same, serious and unspoiled. I had met Bernard before. He was a Maquisard.

"My father is coming, mon Capitaine," he said. This was Landel, mayor of Loulans-les-Forges, owner and manager of the cheese factory, the richest man in all the rich valley (one could reckon his riches in hundreds of pigs), a patriot who ran a small Maquis himself and went out on night patrols with it, and the father of ten children. I had half expected to meet a huge man, rather a gross man reeking of pork fat and butter fat. But Monsieur Landel was very small and very thin, and his movements were the quick, agile movements of a bird. He had what I consider the finest type of French face, a fierce, narrow, intensely thoughtful face. He wore his white hair "en brosse" and he had a small dark moustache. He smoked all the time, lighting one cigarette from the stub of another until his cigarettes were finished, then suffering silently until somebody produced more cigarettes for him.

"I am a British officer," I told him. "My name is Émile, and I have not so far had the honour of your acquaintance. I have been working round Besançon, and until now have avoided the Haute-Saône. I have three comrades, two Americans and a French officer who have arrived to work with me. We have a radio with which we transmit messages to England, and I will not disguise that that is dangerous for any house that shelters us. But the work is important. I must find shelter. And the house must be discreet, because the Americans speak little French.

"Berger advised me to ask your advice since you are known as a patriot and you know all the big houses in the neighbourhood."

"I would not ask any of my friends to take a risk that I would not take myself," Landel began uncompromisingly. "I will take you here myself. You want a house for tonight? Very good. Bernard, ring up Sophie. No, wait, fetch your mother."

Madame Landel was a stout woman with a good, brown, religious face. The face of a woman who has patched up children with every kind of wound and ailment, and has arrived at a state of complete self-confidence and charity.

"I want two rooms and four beds for Captain Émile and his friends tonight," her husband told her. "Monsieur Berger will sleep opposite in the little coachman's room, and their car can go in our garage. Now all you have to do is get rid of enough children to clear the two rooms, and send away the younger ones who might be indiscreet."

"But can any children be discreet?" I asked. "I really feel that you are too generous. I must remind you that you are risking your home, your children, everything if you take us in. I am overwhelmed by your generosity. But is it prudent?"

"Our children will not talk if they are told not to," said Madame Landel, as though she were quite offended at the idea. "Only the very young ones might let it slip. Besides, Captain Émile, we are quite aware of the risks, and we are French.

People like us, who have been fortunate through the war, cannot hesitate when there is a chance like this to make any small contribution to the victory."

"Yes indeed, yes indeed," agreed Landel.

"I'll telephone Sophie and ask her to take the eight young ones this evening. Sophie is my sister, Captain Émile. She lives in the next village and she was married to my brother-in-law who died last year. The eight children she will take are not all mine. Some of them belong to friends. Here with the 'laiterie' we can always get milk, butter and cheese." She was able to make you feel one of her clean family. She told you the details of her entourage without embarrassment, and the details were strangely important and strangely dear to you.

Berger was happy as we drove away. It was he who had recommended Landel, and he saw that I liked the place. I told myself that such a house was a crazy hiding-place for the five of us with our radio. Everyone said you should never go into a house with children. If anything went wrong and the house was destroyed, the parents and children murdered on our account, we should never clear our consciences. There was one advantage, however. There was so much coming and going about the Landel place, because of his duties as mayor and because of the factory, that we would be less noticeable than in a quiet place. Then there was the question of food. Landel would find it no burden to feed five extra. I would give him a quantity of sugar and coffee and tinned sardines (all stolen from German stores by my gangster friends).

I dropped Berger at Montbozon, where he was going to pick up his motor-cycle and do some odd jobs for me, then drove down south of Rougemont to the dark mill. I had parked the other three there on the previous night. There had nearly been an accident over the convent.

Having severed my permanent connection with Vieilley, heavy at heart, I had dined at La Barre with the three of them. The old lady and her daughter cheered me up, for to my surprise I ate the very best meal I tasted in about eight months' experience of occupied France. They understood that good cooking is a matter of selecting the finest of everything, preparing it with all the laborious care of a chemist carrying out an experiment which may alter the destinies of empires, then cooking the prepared substances with sure vigour, dash, courage, and judgment.

There was wine too, for I was able to supply that. As we were

324

leaving for the convent, a despatch-rider from Paincheau arrived to tell us to wait, and hot on his heels came Paincheau himself. He was in his mood of cold and deadly rage. I took him alone into the château kitchen and he stood and shook with anger for some time before he could bring out a word.

"It's the old gardener," he said finally. "You remember the old pig who came round the rooms with us. He kept his unwholesome tongue still until today when, at midday, he went down to the café and announced that tonight Supreme Allied Headquarters were to take up residence at the convent and begin radio emissions straight away. What shall I do to him, Émile? Don't let me go there now, or I shall kill him. Don't let me . . ."

"Leave the fool alone, Jacques. Now where are we to go? I don't like to leave these people here any longer."

"Take them to the mill."

"The mill it is."

I found the mill a depressing place. But it was safe for one night, anyway. And there was plenty to eat. A mill was always a big centre for black market. You could get beautiful bread in this one. Absolutely white bread.

Back from Landel's, I found that both millers had got together and were entertaining my friends with luxuries like champagne and roast duckling. I had listened to the radio on the way. There were more parachutages on our grounds for that night. One of them for Paincheau. But it was a terrible night, blustering wind and torrential rain.

In the middle of our celebration dinner as guests of the millers we had to leave the table. A little strong, bald man called Menigoz, who operated in the north-east of the Haute-Saône, came in with big news for us. He and another F.F.I. officer, by assiduous flattery and other wearing work, had succeeded in debauching the Ukrainian major commanding a group of six hundred German mercenaries, all Ukrainians, who had been stationed for some time near Vesoul. The Ukrainians were ordered west to a barracks in Dijon. But the Frenchmen had seen that the major was wavering. In the cafés and restaurants of Dijon they continued to pour their subversive talk into the Ukrainian's hair-filled ears. Their words bore startling fruit.

The Ukrainians were given a move order. They were put into a special train which moved slowly eastwards from Dijon through the Haute-Saône. Not far from Menigoz' country, the

Ukrainians butchered all the Germans with them, officers, N.C.O.s and interpreters. They thought there were about fifty (but had not bothered to count). Menigoz led them then to the forest of Cherlieu. The local French cultivators agreed to feed them and to hide up and feed their horses, for they were complete with all their weapons and horse transport. And now they were barring one of the important roads for the retreat into Germany. They had already stemmed small German attacks on their position. But they needed arms and munitions. Would we ask Britain to supply them? Menigoz, a bundle of energy, frothed at the mouth like Mussolini as he spat out his final demands.

"What are the Ukrainians like?"

"Splendid fellows," Menigoz replied. "Bursting to have a go at the Boches."

"Yes, and if the invasion had never come, or if the Boches were still winning the war, they would be bursting to have a go at us 'terrorists'. They are traitors, my friend. And their major, does he not mouth German propaganda?"

"He is anti-Communist. He wants to fight against the Boches, but he is not for the Russians. The men all say they were forced to fight for the Boches."

"They all say that. Every Pole, Cossack, Ukrainian, Austrian, and Pomeranian we have captured says he was forced to fight for the Boches. In my view, these men are all traitors. Another thing, I notice that ninety per cent of the Germans we capture say that they are Austrians, Poles, Czechs, or even Ukrainians or Cossacks forced into the Wehrmacht. The remaining ten per cent is German, but *very* anti-Hitler. I am sick of these traitors, but if they are fighting the Boches we must use them. The Russians will be capable of dealing with them after the war. After all, we are plus six hundred well-armed men, and the enemy is minus six hundred; therefore we are plus twelve hundred."

Bazata, when I had translated, took the same view. We would ask London if possible to parachute captured German ammunition for the Russians. And also an assortment of anti-tank weapons. They were afraid of tanks, Menigoz said. When this interesting business was concluded, down to the mutual hand-shaking all round (which still amused Bazata and Floyd), we got back to our duck. It was cold duck now, and warm champagne. I liked being with the Americans. They amused me as they accustomed themselves to all the little domestic habits of that country. For example, when the host offered you a drink in the ordinary houses there he filled all the glasses, then everybody sat for a decent interval (it might be ten minutes) talking, and never looking at the glasses. Then the host would take his glass in his right hand. As though a secret signal had run round, everybody would suddenly and mysteriously be holding his glass. The host then picked his glass up and clinked it against that of his neighbour or the most honoured guest. Immediately everybody clinked glasses and drank, but not too much. You could empty with safety up to half the contents of your glass. Then you could have another swallow or two a little later. But you must not actually empty the glass before you were rising to go. If you wanted the host to refill your glass, or at any rate had a mind to accept if he offered you some more, you were still supposed to leave a few centimetres in the bottom of the glass. The first few times that the Americans' glasses were filled they were immediately emptied, down to the last drop. Emptied sometimes before the host had finished pouring out the other people's drinks. Then all kinds of amusing situations arose. The host might start the preliminary conversational ball rolling. Then he would notice that two glasses were empty. He would usually falter. Perhaps he would refill the two glasses. Perhaps he would clink, empty glasses or no empty glasses. The whole rhythm of the drinking process was altered, and the most absurd things were liable to happen. But Bazata was too sharp. He soon adopted the local habits with various enjoyable flourishes and exaggerations, for he was a born clown. Floyd would probably not have noticed, but he disliked drink and was generally working so hard on his radio that he had little time for it.

Driving north that night to Loulans through terrible weather, we came on Menigoz' car parked by the roadside. The little man was out sniffing the wind and the rain. I pulled in behind his car. It was quite difficult to stand up in the wind. I still had no raincoat of any kind, and I was annoyed at being wet at such an hour.

"What is the matter?" I shouted.

"Four-engined aircraft," he shouted back. "One came skimming over the hill, so I stopped the car. There must be a parachutage near here tonight." There was, I knew. On one of Paincheau's grounds. We could hear engines, but only fitfully in the wind. I was sorry for the airmen up there. I did not know whether they were British or American, but I respected them for being so low in the air and so far from home on such a night. Boulaya used to call these airmen "flying diplomats", and it was true that each flight they made successfully was worth more diplomatically than months of work by me—especially when they flew through such dangers as this night. I felt a warm glow in me as we drove on through the rain, especially warm, since these comrades in the air were servicing Paincheau on the ground, and Paincheau was a staunch and useful friend to me. He had laryngitis, but I knew that he was there in the rain. There might be odd differences—like language and side-whiskers—between Paincheau and the airmen. But they had a lot in common.

Landel opened the door to us. He wore a long woolly dressing-gown of the sort that comfortable English boys take to their preparatory schools. I was glad to be there, for I disliked driving through the night. It was too hit and miss, since there were no friends about after curfew to warn you of Boche posts or ambushes. I was trying to institute a system whereby the mayor of each village in the sector would send out a boy on the road to a distance of one kilometre on either side of the village, if there happened to be Germans inside it, the boys would stop all Resistance cars and warn them. Even that would not work at night. The peasants were heavy sleepers.

Next day, after a family breakfast—big bowls of milk with a dash of ersatz coffee in them, toast made in the oven, butter, honey, and lots of children with strawberries-and-cream faces—Bazata, Chapelle and I went over to tackle Haute-Saône headquarters, leaving Floyd to send and receive messages. His transmitter was powered by a neat, hand-turned generator. A most practical thing, since it made him completely independent of electrical supply. Bernard, or one of the girls, was turning the handle as we left. The generator made a faint, high-pitched whine through the house.

The Haute-Saône chiefs lived in a gamekeeper's house in the middle of a dense wood, situated about a mile from our new home, and on the other side of the Loulans-Rioz road. There was too much offering of wine and too little talk about business at the headquarters. The senior officers there, unlike Boulaya, had no direct knowledge of what was happening in the sector. They had to make a lot of appointments with underlings, who would meet us the following day and give us the details we wanted. All this lack of knowledge was dressed up in long speeches. Bazata, less experienced than myself with the profuse

328

oratory of Resistance chiefs, was maddened by the smallness of what we had been able to achieve in a whole morning of talk. Chapelle, however, was admirable, pushing the pompous officers into corners and obliging them to make promises, some of which they would probably keep. The area was in a bad way, we thought. But we could arrange for them to be armed, and I believed that the three of us working together and separately, would be able to help them to quick progress. If we had the time. Reports from the battle-front to the south were getting wilder and wilder. Most days we had a rumour that the American 7th Army was approaching Besançon. And it seemed that unless the Germans could hold them on the line of the Doubs, they would move fairly steadily to the Vosges and the Belfort gap. The last few days were going to be the most tricky. I would have faced them confidently had I been alone. But I was worried for the two Americans.

When we got back to Landel's house I was horrified to find that Floyd's room was still littered with all his equipment, including the wireless set. We had made a kind of hiding-place in a cupboard opening from a bedroom in the top of the house. It would not pass a proper search, of course, but at least we could hide there all the weapons and incriminating gear. I had told Floyd to hide all his belongings there, but he had not bothered. He had no idea that he was living on the edge of a precipice.

Nor, apparently, had the Landels. They were the least "windy" people that I ever stayed with in occupied France, and they had more reason to be windy than any of the others.

Our work went on for three days. Organising the Haute-Saône and sending long messages to London. I toured the area by car and motor-cycle, arranging for the distribution of parachuted material. Bazata was usually with me.

On the fourth day we drove to Vieilley. We were going to cross the "côte" after lunch, with Corneille, the new major who had taken over the Vieilley fighting command from Boulaya, since the "patron's" capture. When we sat down to lunch with the Marquis, we knew that there were Germans in Devecey, but nobody quite seemed to know what they were doing there. When we had finished the soup somebody came in with a warning that a large party of German infantry and gunners had arrived at Bonnay, next village down the big road. And half-way through the entrée, Madame Marquis came in shouting:

329

"Be off with you. Out of this house. The Boches are coming here from Bonnay."

At this moment Chapuy, the Brigadier from the Marchaux Gendarmerie arrived. He had just been liberated from the Butte at Besançon.

"All the Boche civilians are going today," he said. "Only the army remains. The Americans are on the south side of the Doubs. They are shelling Valentin." Indeed, now that there was no conversation around the table, you could hear dull explosions from the other side of the "côte". Another woman came in to tell us that a large party of Boches were approaching the village. So we got into our cars, both of which were in Georges' barn, and drove quickly away in the opposite direction, taking the small roads to Palise.

We received the message: "La langoureuse Asie et la brulante Afrique," while all this bother was on. We separated, after a conference in the woods near Palise, Georges and his carload to go to the Maquis, while we returned by field tracks to Moncey, and so to Loulans, where we had some interviews for that evening.

There were to be no interviews, though. Loulans was full of German soldiers when we arrived. Landel's house was on the edge of the village, and we were able to slip the car in by the back entrance, and run it into the garage without being observed. I was thankful to learn that Floyd had been taken away that morning by Chapelle, to work at the Haute-Saône headquarters. They had a plan of withdrawal from there in case of attack, and I was glad that they were there rather than with the Landels.

Bazata, Berger and I would leave that evening for the Vieilley parachutage. We were determined to have it if possible, although it would clearly be madness to light bonfires with Germans in most of the villages. We would guide the aircraft in with four electric torches. With this dropping we intended to arm the villagers.

The Germans were in retreat, there was no doubt about that. Loulans was full of them, because a continuous stream was passing down the Rioz-Montbozon road. The majority passed straight through the village, but some of them stopped to get water by the pump, or to try to buy milk or wine or fruit. Bazata and I strolled down to the cross-roads, where there were perhaps sixty Germans, common soldiers and a few N.C.O.s. They all looked dirty and exhausted, but not beaten. The villagers were surly with them, and refused them favours, but they seemed to take this as a matter of course. There was no looting or hooliganism. Their transport was appalling. Much of it was made up of French civilian cars, and all of it was falling to bits. Their retreat was a heartening sight for someone like myself, who had seen their robot advance into France in 1940. But you had to respect them in their retreat. They were still orderly, and even if their clothes and transport looked as though they only held together by the dirt that cemented them, they still looked like men, and like soldiers. I was afraid that Bazata might give himself away if spoken to, so I persuaded him to walk with me up to the Haute-Saône headquarters.

When we came back, perhaps an hour and a half later, there were still more Germans in the village. To cross the road in the centre of Loulans we had to push our way through them as though they formed a football crowd. There was a rank smell about the crowd.

Berger met us at the top of the side road, just outside Landel's gateway. He was dancing his breeched legs about in a frenzy. He did not dare to speak to me, but gestured towards the garage door. There were two Germans in there. They wore panzer uniform, and they were examining our gleaming black car.

"Go and get the officer," one of them said.

"Go yourself. My feet hurt."

"All right then. We'll both go."

It was quite evident that they were going to take the car. Fortunately, the ignition key was in Berger's pocket, otherwise it would already be gone.

"Any word of Boches on this back road?" I asked Berger.

"None have passed this afternoon, mon Capitaine."

"Good. Are we all ready? We must leave this instant for Palise." We flung in our sleeping-bags and carbines and were off within one minute. The smiling Landel family watched us go. It was a watery kind of evening, and all of us were nervous about the road. There were so many Germans on the Rioz road, that it was possible that we would find traffic even on this small side road. Tanks had been passing through Loulans when we left.

The annoying thing was that there were no peasants about. I wanted to question someone to find out where the enemy was. However, five hundred yards before the village of Cirey we came on a cultivator standing in front of his little farm. He said that he had not seen a German all day, but that he had heard "a great noise of horses on the roads".

We could not turn back for "a great noise of horses", and anyway, there was nowhere to turn back to. We were now about eight miles from Loulans. I told Berger to drive on. He obeyed, sweeping round the last corner before the village of Cirey.

It so happens that that village is built in a hollow, beside a marshy belt of fields, at a place where the Ognon overflows in winter. And before the dip of Cirey itself, on the small road to Loulans, stands a modern bungalow so wonderfully wrong that it would be difficult to find its superior among all the architectural monstrosities in the Chinatowns of London's suburbia. The blatant bungalow always drew my eye as we passed. It hypnotised me.

"Stop," I shouted to Berger. A woman was standing behind the bungalow wildly signalling us to stop. That could only mean that there were Germans in the village. I jumped from the car and opened the fancy and rickety double iron gate that led into Ye Olde Rock Garden, in front of the bungalow. As I opened it I saw two German sentries come up the road. They had heard the noise of our car. Berger was doing his best to turn, but it was difficult in that narrow roadway, and the bungalow's gateway was awkwardly set, and just big enough to take the wide car. My carbine was in the car, so I could do nothing to stop the two Germans, who began shooting at us from sixty yards. One of them had a sub-machine-gun, the other had a rifle. I leaped into the car. Just as the first burst came from the sub-machine-gun, Berger finally got turned round and stamped on the accelerator. There was no time to fire, and what is the use in firing from a bumping car. I hunched forward in the front seat, ready to seize the wheel if Berger got hit. The firing behind us became hotter. With every rev. of the engine I expected the car to be riddled, or to catch fire. But we turned the corner, having covered perhaps one hundred yards under fire.

There was not one single bullet-hole in the car. Bazata had been lying on the floor at the back. When he came up we laughed heartily together. And thanked God that the Germans could not shoot.

We drove on as fast as we could down the road to Loulans. The only thing to do was to attempt to hide the car. We found a track running up a thickly-wooded slope on the left of the road. Berger swung in. Bazata and I took time to efface the tyre marks. The car just managed the ascent. At the top of the track Bazata and I got out and made Berger drive into the bushes, perhaps fifty yards from the track. It would have to be hidden there for some days. When I went down towards the road on foot to see that we had not left too many tracks, I did not like the look of that wood. There had been Germans through there that day or the night before. There was a still-smouldering fire. A pair of German military boots and a grey Wehrmacht shirt lay below an oak-tree, and it looked as though two or three men had slept on the moss beside the abandoned clothing. Vehicles passed now on the road on which we had fled. And once over the tops of the trees I saw three American Thunderbolts racing across the sky. The sound of bombing came from the Doubs valley, and over towards Besançon a brown cloud of smoke hung in the air. Before I had got back to the others, horse traffic had begun to pass along the road below us. We carried our sleeping-bags up higher into the wood. I made Berger take out the key of the car and the distributor rocker arm. I did not think we would see the car again. It looked as though every square yard of wood would soon be filled with a German. The evening was drawing to its close and we could plainly hear bombs and artillery. The three of us lay down in a little group to sleep.

We were hidden by high bracken, and this was just as well. Some of the cavalry and horse transport we heard continuously on the road below, decided to rest in the wood for the night. The place seemed to be alive with them. Voices carry loudly in the darkness, and towards eleven o'clock we heard German spoken all around us. Things looked unpromising for the morning. Bazata and I decided that if the Germans were still there at four-thirty we would have to try to clear from the wood then, in the hope of finding a less densely populated place when daylight arrived. It began to rain steadily.

Soon after midnight I heard our four-engined aeroplanes. They came nosing up the Ognon, and I was certain that they followed the river, looking for our "Onion" ground. But I knew that the column of retreating Germans probably extended down the river as far as and beyond Vieilley. The parachutage was clearly impossible. Again and again the big aircraft circled round. I could hear the German cavalry panicking on the road below. They were crazily frightened by the sound of aircraft, for they had been harried by aircraft up the Rhône valley, on the long retreat to Germany. It was agony, lying listening to our aircraft. They were very low, searching round. Some people fired on them from the ground, but they paid no attention. At last they went slowly away, as though disappointed. Berger often snored. I had to wake him each time and he was terribly apologetic. But he was so tired that each time he went immediately to sleep again. He muttered stormily in his sleep, when he did not snore. The near-accident had shaken him badly, not because of himself, or even me, but because of the danger to the car, which he adored.

At four a.m. the Germans packed up and left the wood. At six a.m. we hid our sleeping-bags and other belongings in a hole and cautiously followed them to the edge of the wood. Berger knew some people in a group of six houses near-by. After questioning an old man picking mushrooms, Berger led us into the back door of a surprisingly filthy cottage, where a kind woman, whose husband was a prisoner in Germany, gave us fried eggs, bread and butter, wine, coffee, and calvados. All this was most welcome, for we were soaked through from our night in the rain. Bazata decided to go back on foot to Loulans, keeping to the fringes of the woods. I wanted to go to Vieilley, to find out what had happened about the parachutage; we should have to give news of that immediately to London. I had a bicycle at the Dardel house, and I planned to take the roads to Moncey, a long walk. I could pass as a peasant, and my best chance was to go unarmed. I gave my Winchester and pistol to Berger, to carry back to Loulans.

War was coming to the valley all right. By the look of things, the Germans were still holding the Americans on the Doubs. Albert must have been "liberated" I knew, Boulaya too, if he was still alive. He had departed in a taxi from Besançon a day or two previously, to have a conference with Albert and Colonel La Guarde on the Meche plâteau. The villagers were plainly scared. There were few people in the fields, and the villages were full of rumours. I passed through Cirey, and stopped at the bungalow. The woman who had warned us was at the back door. She recognised me.

"Come in, monsieur; I was afraid they would catch you," she cried.

"I won't come in, thank you, madame," I hastily said, recoiling slightly, for I was afraid that the interior of the bungalow might be disappointingly ordinary and functional. And I thanked her as well as I was able. The Germans, she said, had pursued us with three cars. They had accused her of sheltering

334

us, for they were under the impression that we had driven out of her house. They had punished her only by taking all the food in the house. There had been about six hundred of them in Cirey when we approached it in the car.

Six of them were still there as I walked through. They were lying in the swampy grass near the mill. Ground-strafing Thunderbolts had shot them earlier that morning, and their comrades had left them there. I thought that—although one of them wore no boots—they looked rather fine, lying in the sun. When I died, I thought, I would instruct my executors to have me embalmed and lay me out in the sun on a private beach, where rain and vultures never came.

I had passed odd parties of Germans when I arrived at Moncey. Janine Dardel was pining for something to do for "La Patrie", and I thought I should look definitely unlike a terrorist with her, so I borrowed a clean shirt and shaved myself with Dardel's razor, and then rode out, the picture of bourgeois youth on holiday, with the well-dressed Janine riding at my side.

Georges had saved the parachutage. At first I could not believe my ears. He, too, had given up all hope of taking it. And he had been worried by my non-arrival. Jacques, husband of our red-haired countess, who had returned from hiding in Switzerland to be in at the kill with the Maquis, had arrived in the course of the evening. The old "Onion" ground was clearly impossible. There were Germans all round it. They were kept away from Palise, on one side by the river, and on the other by low-lying damp woods. Georges wondered if it would be possible to receive the dropping on the one small field that lay between the woods and the river. The others said no, it was too encased. Georges and Jacques were still arguing this out late at night, so they decided to sleep out under the trees at the edge of the field in question. When the rain began, Jacques went back to the church, but Georges could sleep through any weather, and he declined to go.

When he heard the four-engined aircraft he sat up, as I was doing a few miles away. He listened until he could bear it no longer. He ran out on to the middle of the field flashing our code letter with his electric torch.

To his amazement and joy the two big aircraft—they were Stirlings, the biggest of all—dived on him, one after the other, and released half their containers. Then they circled and dropped the other half. Although it was raining, and they only had Georges' torch to sight and judge on, they landed forty-five out of forty-eight containers on one small field. A wonderful achievement. The remaining three containers had fallen into the river, but when I arrived they had already been fished out, and their well-greased contents were none the worse for the immersion.

There was no time now for inventories. The new teams came from the villages and each man took the weapon and ammunition assigned to him by Georges. He had a piece of rag in his pocket, and with this he cleaned his new weapon. Then he loaded it and went back to his home in a fighting patrol. Now the villages had stings.

Bazata and Chapelle came over that night on borrowed bicycles. The German traffic stream had eased off on the side roads, they reported. They thought that things would be quieter now, until the main body of the German army came back from Besançon, where they had succeeded in blowing the bridges across the Doubs. This was a defeat for us, for counter-sabotage on these bridges had long been part of our plans, and we had teams of men all ready to attack the German engineers when they did this job. But this was not the type of army sabotage, when the rearguard is preparing to leave, and a couple of engineers, practically unprotected, blow the bridge. This time the excellent German engineers were working in the middle of their own army, and the demolitions were carefully guarded, for by now the enemy was very experienced regarding "terrorists". Our people killed a few engineers, some of them probably important. Our own losses were heavy in these operations.

The three of us ate in Palise with the Maquis, who now had a dozen prisoners. They had been carrying out road blocks during the day, and they had a great deal of booty taken from German officers they had killed. Jean, the "cuistot" whom I disliked, had killed a German major, and proudly showed us the papers of the dead officer. The German had a wife and four children in Dresden. They looked charming, and he, from his photograph and his record on the battle-fronts, must have been an admirable person in some ways. He had been twice wounded, once severely, in Greece, by British shrapnel. And now he had fallen to the "cuistot's" Sten gun. He had died painfully, too. Gasping and cursing beside the Buthiers-Cromary road, heaving and twisting in agony, until blood bubbled from his mouth. It seemed strange that the cook should claim such a valuable victim.

That day, before the arms had been issued to the villages, a deadly insult had been put upon Vieilley. A party of thirty German soldiers had descended on the place in a truck. They had carried off three horses. Two of them were the worst horses in the place, but the third was the magnificent Sara, powerful bay mare, and pride of the village. News was rushed down to the Maquis at Palise, but all the Maquisards were out in two parties doing road blocks. The Germans got away unharmed with Sara.

Now, the villages decided, things were going too far. On the following day they were going to barricade with felled trees all the small roads leading to the villages, and the barricades would be defended. I would have liked to have worked with them, but Bazata had other ideas.

Certain information which had come to us that day had to be taken through the German lines and handed to the Americans. After some argument (for Bazata's adventurous spirit was a menace), I agreed to have a go at this with him, provided Chapelle went back and attempted to send the information by radio to London to be passed on by other channels.

Frisé came in on his "petrolette" as we were retiring to our barn to sleep. He had a German prisoner sitting on the carrier behind him, arms clasped around his waist. The prisoner had a livid bruise near the point of his jaw. Frisé explained that he had taken this man near Cirey. Held up at the point of the Frisé's pistol, the German surrendered. But ordered to get on the back of the small motor-cycle he quailed. He was frightened, with perfect reason, of two things: firstly, of sitting behind the Frisé, and, secondly, of being ambushed or even seen by other Germans. So the Frisé had hit him once on the jaw.

"Then what happened?"

"He fell down, and when he got up he agreed to sit behind me," answered the Frisé.

"That is untrue," interjected the German, who spoke reasonably fluent French. "When you hit me you wept tears and you apologised. Then I saw that you were a decent fellow, so I agreed to sit behind you."

"Liar," shouted the Frisé. " 'Cuistot,' give this pig of a Schlok something to eat." Then he handed me a message he had collected from Gros-Claude, the elder, who was leading a band that attacked the Belfort road. They had killed seventy-five Germans that morning. Gros-Claude was improving.

We slept on the parachutes in the barn. There was artillery

fire all night. At five o'clock, before dawn, the firing increased in tempo and volume. Georges and I awoke. He put on his boots and got up, telling me that he wanted to set a road block on the other side of the river. I followed him out of the barn. The gunfire was lighting the western sky. I stood watching the flashes for a time. They were plainly over towards Besançon. I had the feeling of restlessness that obliges a man to do something. I thought I would cross the river, walk through Cromary, and climb to the upland by taking the road towards Buthiers. Up there it would perhaps be possible to get an accurate idea of what was passing near Besançon. Just as I made up my mind to do this Bazata came up. The noise had wakened him too. He agreed to come with me. We searched each other for arms or incriminating documents. It was better to go with nothing, in case we ran into the German main body.

I led him down to the Cromary bridge. We went that far on bicycles. There we hid the bicycles in the wood, and continued on foot. Just across the bridge there was a dead German, lying spread-eagled on the road. We nearly fell over him. It was still very dark. Just beyond the body there was a bicycle, which he had evidently been riding. The bicycle had no tyres. Some of the deserters, we knew, were trying to make a get-away by riding like that, on the rims. After a few miles the wheels fell to pieces. This German had his head beaten in. He was a bad thing to leave on the road so near the Maquis. We hid him and his bicycle in the ditch, and walked on through the sleeping village of Cromary.

We drank and washed our sleepy faces a little at the fountain, and then turned left towards Buthiers. As the dawn came we walked steadily west on the Buthiers road. There was no sign of traffic. The gunfire round or in Besançon had faded away. Now we could hear firing and see flashes over our left shoulders, more in the direction of Clairval, in the Doubs valley. Probably the Americans were trying to force the river there, to by-pass Besançon.

Bazata was a delightful companion. While the adventure merely made me feel dead inside, cold and almost bored, it stimulated him to talk about himself, his home in Washington, his departure from America, his business before the war. After a little, as we walked briskly down the road with the light gradually seeping into the sky behind us, I began to take a real interest in what he said, to seek out his personality from his

338

stories. He seemed to be made of tugging contrasts; an unhappy man and a gay one. A strange mixture of rapacity and generosity, of laziness and industry, at the same time sensitive and crude. He could not walk very well, because of his leg, damaged on the drop. And he could see that it was a very long way to Besançon. But he was quite determined to get there. I was afraid that his determination would lead us into German torture cells. Walking with the tempestuous Bazata towards the German lines was like riding a horse with a mouth of iron towards a precipice that the horse knew nothing about.

At the edge of Buthiers it began tempestuously to rain. Both of us were in thin suits, without hats. We dived into the first barn we saw. It was part of a farm building. When we had sat there for a little, an old man came out and chatted. Bazata answered his questions willingly, despite the man's look of staggered amazement at the peculiar French. A young man next came into the barn. He also seemed quite dumbfounded by Bazata's French. He gave us both a piercing look and then came over to me.

"You are from Vieilley," he said.

"That is right."

"Come in, with your friend, and have some breakfast."

His wife was sitting in the kitchen, feeding her baby. She was a rather fine-looking young woman, with the carroty hair not uncommon in the Franche-Comté. Her breast was of an unbelievable whiteness in the dark, dirty kitchen.

"You would think there was a light inside it," Bazata pointed out to me in English.

"There is a light inside it."

"Émile. You should have been a preacher."

The young woman asked us if we liked dancing. We said that we did. So did she. So did her husband. But we did not dance the Java in America, did we? We asked if there were any Germans in Buthiers. Yes, there was a very big headquarters in the château. It was said that the Marquis de Buthiers had been so rude to the uninvited square-heads that they had shut him up in his own room.

They gave us hot milk to drink. I had some of Dardel's sugar in my pocket, so we were able to sweeten it. Bazata, who was something of a gourmet, tasted it with mistrust, but finally drank because he was damp and hungry. Then we began to nod with sleep. The rain was still solid outside. There was no point in going out in that. Dressed as we were we should arouse too much suspicion. We climbed up into the attic of the barn, and went to sleep in the hay. It was good to be inside and hear the rain lashing at the pantiles. Each of us made a hole in the hay, and we slept thus for three hours.

German traffic on the road outside woke us. It was a fairly long and heavily-armed convoy. There were light uncovered vehicles with machine-guns mounted on them. The occupants all wore steel helmets, but many of them looked like officers.

"It's the headquarters moving from the château," I said.

"That means they're pulling out, all of them," said Bazata. "Come on, let's go. We've got to get through those lines."

"Hold on. Don't forget these people are going to run into our road block four miles down this road."

"That won't stop them."

But soon we heard a loud explosion from the direction of Cromary and a considerable volume of small-arms fire. The convoy came racing back. We saw it turn right in Buthiers, taking the road to Vesoul.

"You mean to say Germans run from a single road block like that?" Bazata said.

"They don't know how tough the block is, and they cannot spare half an hour to an hour of scouting and fighting to find out. They see on their maps an alternative route by Vesoul, so they turn and take that."

"I guess we could go now."

"All right. We'll walk quietly through the village. I know the mayor's wife. We'll go and ask her for news."

But as we strolled down the road in the drizzle, we saw that there were a great many Germans in the village. Down in the little square stood four big buses camouflaged in the jaundiced colours of the German Africa Corps. Infantrymen, in full battle-kit, were hanging around. There were gunners, too, and several guns, 88s.

"What are you stopping for?" Bazata asked me as I turned off the road into a big court-yard, with an open barn making the far side of it.

"You don't think I am going to walk through those Boches, do you?"

"Why not. We look like civilians, don't we?"

"Yes, civilians. But first we are not dressed like villagers, second we are too muddy about the trousers, third we have neither brushed our hair nor shaved this morning, fourth we are both too tall for Frenchmen, fifth many of the Germans speak excellent French, and you have not got into the way of speaking it yet."

"Quit riding my French."

"I refuse to take you past those Boches."

There was a young man in the barn, sheltering. He was a Maquisard, I saw at a glance, and he knew me. He was a fat youth, and he chattered with terror or cold.

"Where are you from?" I asked him.

"Gros-Claude's group, Captain Émile. I carry a message for Marcel. But seeing the Boches here I stopped. They would certainly take my bicycle from me."

"Yes, certainly. In Besançon yesterday they were taking not only bicycles from women in the street, they were taking their rings as well."

"The pigs. What shall I do, Captain Émile?"

"Hide your bicycle in Buthiers somewhere, and go on foot."

"Here is my cousin, Captain." The cousin came walking briskly down the road, and as he came he shouted at us without obviously turning his head.

"Get out of that barn. They are sending gunners to shelter there. They've arrested the mayor and ten others already."

The young fat boy was beginning to panic. He darted into the hay and uncovered his bicycle. I climbed out of the side of the barn, followed by Bazata.

"Whatever you do, don't appear to be in a hurry," I told him. "There are probably Germans all over the place."

"There are," he answered cheerfully. "See there, other side of that orchard?"

We switched left, along the back gardens of the houses and into a little lane. There was a group of Germans ahead of us, looking directly at us. There was only one thing to do. I walked in at the door of the first house, as though it belonged to me. Bazata followed. As I turned in I saw the fat boy running across the field towards us, pushing his bicycle. I hoped he had not seen us go in. He would get us all shot. There was a pale, nervous spinster type of woman in the kitchen, and two children with Parisian accents, evacuees.

"Good morning, madame," I said to her in my best French. "Would you kindly permit us to shelter here for a few minutes?"

"Certainly," she answered coldly. "Please seat yourselves." She thought we were Germans. I dared not tell her the truth. I feared that she might scream with fright. To my disgust, the fat boy chose this moment to enter. I began to swear at him

tor running in the field. He was humble. He had hidden his
bicycle on a rubbish-dump. After this conversation the woman's
attitude became much more friendly. She saw that we were
Resistance.

"Monsieur is Alsatian?" she asked me. "I am so sorry that
I was rude. I thought you were German." I still did not dare
to tell her who we were. Bazata felt the same, for now he only
spoke in whispers. I asked the woman to go out and find out
what the Germans were doing in the village.

She came back with bad news. German infantry and one
battery of artillery were taking up positions in and around
the village. It was thought that they were going to round up
all the men in the village. Nobody was allowed to leave. The
German interpreters in uniform seemed to be Frenchmen,
militians, it was feared.

"Couldn't be worse," Bazata agreed with me laconically.
"We got to get out of here."

"Too true." Looking out of the door, I saw something that
gave me an idea. Two old people were moving about in the
fields with baskets.

"Do you know a mushroom when you see it?" I asked
Bazata.

"I might do. Kind of white, isn't it?"

I borrowed two old blankets from the woman, and we strolled
out, bowing our backs to look as old as possible. The heavy
rains and intermittent sunshine periods had lashed the mush-
room-spawn into a frenzy of productivity. I have never seen
so many field mushrooms. Bazata and I picked busily in the
fields, and as we picked we edged further and further away
from Buthiers in the direction of Cromary. After half an hour
of this each of us had several pounds of mushrooms, and we
judged that we were far enough way to step it out across the
fields.

When I looked at Bazata's basket it was half-full of puff-balls.
He convulsed with laughter when I told him they were inedible.

"I'm hungry," he said. "Can we get these mushroom
saviours of ours cooked up into a good hot stew?"

"Yes, at Palise." And we did. All the men-folk of Buthiers
had been shut up and questioned. A profuse growth of mushrooms had probably saved our lives.

I would have been quite content to leave our attempt to cross
the German lines until at least the following day. Not so the
indefatigable Bazata. He insisted that it must be done that

afternoon. I doubted if his leg was strong enough for the walk, and there was definitely no question of the trip being possible any other way. However, he was an expert at getting his own way, and I was half afraid that he might realise that I was not certain in my mind whether reason or cowardice made me resist the project. At length I agreed, and got the Frisé to act as guide. He knew the woods of the Haute-Saône and the western approaches of Besançon. And if there were still Germans in the town, the Frisé would know how to avoid them.

Before leaving I borrowed changes of clothing for us both. We now wore peasant caps (more useful in that country than berets), and Bazata had an amazing corduroy shooting-jacket, with vast pockets, capable of holding two hares each. I had an old peasant's working jacket. We looked a real pair of thugs. The idea was to ride our bicycles as far as Bonnay, and walk on from there.

But just before Vieilley Georges caught up with us in a car. He had been out looking at a road block and had heard of our plan, which he disliked as much as I did. He insisted that the only possible way into Besançon was across the "côte", and he was the only person capable of guiding us over that way. Colonel Ligne, who was with him, had spent that night lying on the floor of a house at Valentin, just north of Besançon, being shelled by American guns. He had walked out in the morning, and had been questioned by Germans three or four times on the way. With good papers and a cover story he had just got away with it. But he would not do it again, he said. We should have no chance of getting through that way. After hearing this, even Bazata agreed that Georges' plan was the only way. Accordingly, Ligne took the wheel of the car, which had a German prisoner in the back, and the abandoned Frisé sadly relinquished his bicycle to Georges.

Cutting out of Bonnay opposite the house of Nono's parents, Georges led us diagonally up the slope, keeping the fort of "La Dame Blanche" well on our left. Soon the paths he followed led us into the woods. I began to wish now that we had brought arms with us. More than ever when, rounding a bend in the path, we came face to face with a German soldier, who was walking in the opposite direction.

Georges, who was leading us, hesitated, and so did the German. Then they advanced gingerly towards each other. We followed Georges. The German was clearly not a deserter. He carried all his weapons; his rifle, barrel pointing downwards,

343

was under his right arm. He was quite obviously afraid of us. And we were afraid to overpower him in case he was under observation by his comrades.

"Americans there?" he asked, pointing in the direction we had come from. We shrugged our shoulders.

"Germans there?" Georges asked him, pointing in the other direction.

"Germans, yes."

"Far?"

"Two minutes."

He shambled away down the path. Georges turned up the hill on our left, and we climbed steadily for ten minutes, then had a rest while Georges climbed a high tree to see what he could see.

"We must avoid all paths," he said when he came down. "I believe there are large parties of Boches in the forest, mostly ahead of us, probably on the slopes looking down on the plain north of Besançon. You want to go on?"

"No," I said.

"Yes," Bazata said.

"All right," I said.

It was tiring work, fighting through the bushes with the left foot always much higher than the right. We traversed a big distance like this. Once we heard Germans on our right. With Georges I was confident. He walked so steadily that it was difficult for me to keep up, and it was probably agony for Bazata. But Georges took no risks. His eyes were always searching for a footprint or a broken twig.

"Boches," he said pointing down to the surface of a path that mounted the hill directly. "At least fifty of them." He picked up an Austrian cigarette that lay in the grass beside the path.

"It is unwise to continue," said Georges.

"If you don't go on, I will, alone," said Bazata. Plainly, he had made up his mind now that both of us needed stiffening. "What do we risk, anyway?"

"All right," I said. It was no use beginning to explain these things now. Five men of Poirier's Maquis had been found dead in the woods above Bonnay that morning. A little further on Georges found a corpse. We did not bother to examine it, for it was already beginning to smell. The woods opened into a glade. Georges walked out first, and across the glade to farm buildings, mainly hidden in a thicket. After a time he reappeared, and signalled us to join him.

344

"There are no French people about, and I don't like that," he told us. "And there are Boches' tracks everywhere."

He led us now down into more open country. Fields with scrub and small woods between them. We could see some of the German lay-out for battle. It looked as though they were withdrawing from Besançon, and were defending the edge of the plain to the north, that Georges had mentioned. On the edge of the Haute-Saône woods we saw anti-tank guns taking up positions and infantry digging. Artillery was firing from Devecey, immediately below us, from Buthiers, and from two other points in the woods. They were firing almost over our heads, either on Besançon, or just to the west of the town. Bazata marked in the batteries on his map. We came to a valley and then climbed up a road to a village. There was an orchard on our right, of very special-looking trees and a "Keep out, private property" sign, the first I had seen in all this part of France. The sign gave me an uncomfortable feeling, like Throgmorton Street. Above the orchard there towered another big fort, the fort that had kept the Germans out of Besançon in the 1870 war, when the Bisontins had formed human chains to pass the munitions which its guns showered down on the enemy, attempting to cross the plain. We suspected that there would be a German O.P. in the fort now, working for the guns that were throwing the shells whistling high over our heads.

On the other side of the lane was a field with a score of fine milk cows in it. The cows were in agony, dying to be milked. Up in the village at the top of the lane we heard children and women weeping. Then we heard the cause, the measured tramp of German jack-boots over the cobbles, followed by a harsh command. Georges turned and led us back. Working out to the right, towards the plain we came to the edge of a belt of German anti-tank defence. We counted some twenty guns dotted over the hill-side. Even Bazata agreed that it was impracticable to go through that way. As a final resort we climbed straight up the hill behind the village and the fort. We could now plainly see German 20 mm. anti-aircraft guns on the latter. Georges' objective was now a village called Tallenay, on the other side of the crest of the hill, and at the head of a small valley and clearing that ran into the forest. We were now at the Besançon end of the "côte", the long ridge that ran right up the side of the Ognon valley, as far as Rougemont. Darkness was falling, for by this time we had walked a long way over slow and tiring country.

345

Georges halted us in a small scrubby wood overlooking the village of Tallenay.

"What's wrong now?" asked Bazata angrily. He was sick of our careful progress.

"Don't like the look of Tallenay," Georges muttered.

"Why doesn't he like it?"

"No villagers about," said Georges. "Nobody about at all. We must wait here until we see some movement. The moment we show ourselves in these fields we are finished if there are Boches in position here."

An Allied reconnaissance plane did us a great service. It came flying low over the fort. The guns there opened an intense burst of fire, which was taken up madly from the fort past us, and all over the scene that one second before had appeared to be peaceful. The Germans were firing tracer, and we saw now, clearly, that we were right in the middle of them. The village was full of machine-guns. There were positions down both sides of the clearing and positions behind us.

Without opposition from us, Georges led the way into the heart of the thicket.

"We must stay the night here," he said. "In the morning we shall see if the Boches go. If they stay we must go back. We cannot get through them here. They are too thick on the ground."

"Why not make a try for it tonight?" said Bazata.

"Hopeless, moving at night in the forest. At night all noises are magnified, and you can see neither where to go nor what enemy waits for you."

So we spent a terrible night in the thicket. It was cold, and the sweat in our clothes soon became clammy. The earth was soggy, and when you lay down you formed a kind of puddle. Georges made no bones about the situation. He lay down, and was almost instantly asleep. I managed to doze off for a short while, when the heat of the walk was still in me. I awoke, cold, to find that Bazata was still standing beside us. He now suggested that the three of us should lie close together for warmth. We all lay on our right sides, with Georges in the middle. Every ten minutes Bazata said in a firm voice: "Turn over." And we disengaged ourselves, turned to the other side and fitted together again. I did not mind this, but Georges, who managed comfortably to sleep, was considerably put out. At midnight the turning process ceased, however, as heavy rain began to fall. All of us stood up and faced the wet night, doing the cabman's exercise to keep warm.

"If only it would *rain*," said Bazata with a high laugh.

"*Please* ask this American to be quiet," Georges said. Bazata and I stood and talked until dawn in low whispers to pass the time. Georges sat with his back against a tree and slept. At six o'clock the rain stopped and the sun touched the edge of our wood. We crawled over there, to get into the warmth of the sun and to examine the valley. The Germans certainly were not moving. There was firing to the south, but our sector was calm, except that a lot of traffic was moving on the precipitous road leading to the fort. Near the head of the Tallenay clearing a German stood sweeping all round him with field-glasses. Then he walked out into the fields of the clearing, crossing them with a healthy young swagger. He was a Panzer lieutenant, we thought, doing the rounds of his defensive posts. He wore a black uniform, with a white peaked cap, a bad uniform for work in the woods.

I agreed entirely with Georges that we could not go further. After half-an-hour's argument, Bazata was persuaded too. We started on the long walk home, which, fortunately, was uneventful. In the Marquis kitchen in Vieilley we ate one of their local breakfasts, with wine and coffee, bread and cheese, meat and fruit. To end up with there were eggs cooked in their local way, fried in butter, with a large amount of fresh cream added a minute or two before the frying is finished. Bazata approved.

CHAPTER XVII

THE retreating German Army came pouring into the valley, until in many places saturation point was reached, and there was no small space that did not hold a German. In places the valley smelled of death, and the woods were stained with a stain that would not wash out in years of wind and wetness, the stain of human rot and blood and pus.

There were two American armies pushing at the Germans, sweeping them clear of France, the 7th sweeping from the south, beginning from the shores of the Mediterranean, and the 3rd, sweeping down from the north-west.

Vieilley village formed a boulder against the grey tide that, obeying the eastwards surge towards the Fatherland, pushed up the Ognon valley. The main German traffic flooded the big roads that ran by Vesoul and Belfort. It was a backwash that

347

flowed up our valley. Sometimes it flowed as far as Bonnay.

But the villagers of Vieilley, helped by our Maquis, went out in the night and felled the big trees across the roads. When all the men and boys were needed for the work or for fighting the young girls kept watch for the German convoys.

Normally when the convoys approached the blocks of felled trees they turned tail. If they tried to pass the rather pathetic barriers they were fired on by Gustave and Gustave's nephew and the thin boy with the squint, and all the others who were lucky enough to have weapons. Sometimes the villagers would be helped by the Pointu or the fierce Frisé with a band of Maquisards. They would lie in the ditches and blast the enemy with Mills grenades or burn him with phosphorous.

So, by a miracle, Vieilley kept itself entirely clean of the German waves. Not one house was burned, not one girl was outraged. The only battle scars on the place were the aging bullet-holes in the prim stucco front of the lower Contini house. And since Vieilley formed a brave little buttress to the tide the other villages that I knew immediately behind it, going as far as Rigney, were also saved. They helped to save themselves too.

Even Dardel, whom I had never regarded as a man of war, abandoned his now perfected "cachette" beneath the cellar stairs, took his rifle to fight with the Moncey armed bands, and carried himself like a stout and muscularly stiff edition of the man he always pretended to be. In Rigney there were long faces in the "Hôtel de la Gare", for old Letallec had at last got his call to arms and had tramped off with a sub-machine-gun to the woods.

But other villages were not so lucky. Marchaux was swamped and partly burned. Rougemont was sunk deep in the German tide, while the young men fought with Paincheau on the outskirts and on the roads. And up the left bank of the Ognon, from Buthiers to Loulans and beyond, the Germans were thick. I continued to admire the German enemy, for he kept his soldier's pride and he was always ready to answer shot with shot. Not so his miserable allies and levies, the Austrians, the Poles, the Czechs, who were only too anxious to give themselves up if they felt they could do so safely.

Based on Palise, and continuously reinforced from other Maquis that were carved up or overrun by the enemy, the Vieilley Maquis survived, although often there was fighting with Germans even at the entrances to the hamlet itself. They fought on the roads and patrolled the woods, and they stiffened the Resistance of the villagers. Over on the other side of the "côte" in the valley of the Doubs all the Maquis had to fight to exist. The German was so numerous that it was a question of holding some piece of ground, some corner of woodland, and in clear spaces going out to hit him on the roads. Jean Buthot and his Maquis fought well and managed to survive. So did Gros-Claude.

During this time I was obliged to be almost constantly at Loulans, for instructions were coming in so fast from London that we had great difficulty in coping. Chapelle, cementing his association with the Haute-Saône, was often away. Menigoz and his Ukrainians seemed to be doing well in the north. The parachutage to give them munitions arrived one night when none of us could get through to them, since they were surrounded by bodies of well-disciplined enemy troops. But they managed to take the dropping. To our horror the following day, we learned from London that an American colonel with a "mission" of some kind had also been dropped there. The ground was unsuitable for receiving "bodies" (as we called parachutists). And Russians, Colonel, and "mission" were now surrounded and fighting. From then on our lives were made difficult by stories of more and more "missions" to our part of the world. The "missions" were to deal with all sorts of things from intelligence to communications. They seemed to be mixtures of all nationalities. They might have been useful, but to us they were a headache. Because neither Bazata, Chapelle, nor myself would take the responsibility of accepting a parachuted "mission" in those days. You could not find enough ground unencumbered by Germans on which to have a parachutage. I became sick of our life, hidden at Loulans and coding and decoding most of the day and night. Floyd was nearly dead on his feet.

"I'm going to Vieilley this evening," I told them. "I'll go on the big Terrot. Bernard has offered to go down the road in the afternoon to see if it's clear."

"And I'm coming with you, maybe there'll be a chance of going through the lines," said Bazata. "If only it would *rain*." (This was his stock expression since our two nights in the open.)

Berger came in on his motor-cycle as we were finishing our coffee with the Landel family in the salon after luncheon. I was thankful to see him, for I had sent him off two days previously with an important message for the south, and had regretted sending him ever since he departed. He was slightly wounded in one ear, and three times had been forced to ride for it while stray Germans beside the road shot at him. For now the soldiers did not care whether Berger had German papers or not. All they wanted was his motor-cycle to provide quick transport to the east.

There were long messages to send that afternoon, and for some reason I was particularly nervous. Bernard was winding the generator handle while Floyd worked away on the Morse key. He had a strange method of sending, for he insisted on stretching his long body full length on the floor. Paul, on the other hand, had always demanded a table. He fixed his key on the table with two screws and only began to work when everything was properly arranged and he was comfortably seated in a chair. Paul was Navy and Floyd was an airman, perhaps that explained the differences in their methods. It was odd how vulnerable you felt, sitting in the room there with the key tapping out signals that were audible in America. I was afraid that some message would come through so important that we would be forced to cancel the trip to Vieilley.

Young Bernard came in with news at 4.30 p.m.

"There is a rumour that the Americans are at Rigney," he said. "But I doubt if you can get through to them if they are there, because it looks as though the Boches are preparing to blow all the bridges across the Ognon. They say that the Ollans and Cirey bridges have gone already, and your Maquis are fighting a big battle now to preserve the bridge at Cromary. Also, as I passed the Cenans bridge, I saw some Boches on it with funny bucket things held on sticks."

"How many on the Cenans bridge?"

"About ten, not more, with two trucks."

"Get all the men you can from your Maquis and wipe them out. How strong is the rumour that the Americans are at Rigney?"

"Gros-Claude told Erneste that he had just had a drink with them in the 'Hôtel de la Gare'."

Bazata came out from his bedroom where he had been decoding.

"Get a load of this, beautiful," he said. "They want us to give them a ground and reception for sixteen hundred parachutists. How about it?"

"We must ask the Americans. They are supposed to be at Rigney. The only ground still possible for us is the one near

Rioz, but that is probably too near the American spearhead to be worth while."

"You're right. Let's go."

"Just one thing, they are blowing all the Ognon bridges. But it seems the engineers are just beginning on the one at Cenans. What about that?"

"We can rush them, can't we?"

"If you can hold on behind me, I dare say the bike will go fast enough to take us through."

I got the big Terrot from under the weeping willow-tree beside the river where it had lain hidden for days. Three of the boys helped me to push the monster clear of the holes into which it had sunk. It started easily, and seemed to be running well. I let it run to get warmed up. It was not far to Cenans, the next village. We both carried our pistols.

"Don't let go to shoot at them," I warned Bazata. "You will need both hands to hold on. The roads are bad at Cenans."

He had only once, it seemed, sat on the pillion of a motorcycle before, and that was when I had brought him from Vieilley to Loulans. All the Landel family waved us good-bye. Berger was running round and round me like an anxious old hen. I slammed the machine into second and allowed all its five horses to bite into the stiff hill that mounted from the Landels'. I wanted Bazata to get used to the speed. We covered the distance to Cenans at something near seventy miles per hour. The road was full of pot-holes and sometimes Bazata nearly bounced over my head. The tears were pouring from my eyes. I shut the engine to coast more silently down into Cenans village. We had a sharp turn left there, then perhaps one hundred yards of down-hill straight to the bridge. The Terrot had four forward speeds. Third gave plenty of getaway and plenty of speed. I slipped her into third and took the bend as fast as I dared. Then I gave her full throttle and prayed.

The bridge seemed fairly to leap towards us, in a blur of speed. I saw a few figures there and two trucks drawn up at the side of the road. There was a bump at the entry to the bridge that I had forgotten. The big machine seemed to buck clear of the ground and I was afraid she would twist in the air, but somehow we kept going straight and Bazata was still there. In the noise of the engine I heard no shots, although Bazata said he did. Soon we were round a bend and heading more steadily for Rigney.

We came up the hill, approaching Rigney from the station

end, and there, at the top of the hill, was an American sentry, a corporal from Texas. I don't know that I have ever been more glad to see anyone. He was tall and dark and extremely polite. There was a lieutenant working in the station waiting-room. He sent us back to his coloncl, who was working in a house behind the premises of my wine merchant. When he heard what it was about and saw Bazata's papers (I had none), the colonel pushed us into a jeep and sent us back to brigade headquarters. Brigade sent us to Division (sitting in the middle of Besançon), and Division sent us back to Corps, where we gave our news and information to General Truscott.

The general sat in an austerely comfortable little caravan and one of his staff officers gave us dry martinis made with real gin, French vermouth, and ice.

We dined alone in the general's mess-tent, eating the nourishing American canned food, which I found nauseatingly sweet after some months of simple French cooking. Then we followed a white tape which led us through the darkness to our waiting jeep. Bazata and the driver talked all the way back, along the road to Marchaux and Rigney that held memories for me. Here was where Boulaya and I had crossed the road after seeing the militians. Here Georges had chased a hawk through the trees, finally making it drop the dead partridge it was carrying. That wood where American tanks were parked had been a good wood for "chantrelles", but they would be finished now. Here was the top of the hill where Nono had been killed. The gendarmes were back in the long, pale yellow gendarmerie at Marchaux now, and Madame Chapuy had her husband, the *brigadier,* back with her. The whole village still smelled of singeing from the burned houses.

They were the 3rd Division, the American troops. They turned all my landscape topsy-turvy. It seemed like the end of the world, not the end of the war. The driver said the 3rd were the finest troops in the U.S. Army, and I could believe him, for I saw at once that they were good troops, not well but brilliantly equipped. We had heard rumours that the men were tired after their long advance from the south coast, but they showed no signs of wear. I had only seen Americans in England before, and mainly around Piccadilly. I had not expected to like them so much in the field and to be so impressed by them as soldiers. I noticed that their senior officers, even the general, were dressed exactly the same as the ordinary soldier except for their rank badges. Nor could they have been better dressed.

The excellence of their transport and equipment after the patched and rickety passage of the Wehrmacht, gave you an overwhelming and false sense of security. But the tension had to be screwed up again.

Rigney was still a front-line village. The Americans had consolidated a little, but had advanced no farther. It was midnight when we arrived there, and most urgent that we get to Loulans right away to send a message to London.

"You're crazy," said the American lieutenant. "That's no-man's-land out there. You can't go there on that thing." The "thing" was the Terrot. We thought of taking the jeep as far as Loulans, but decided that we would not be justified in asking the driver to go and then come back alone through the lines.

I knew perfectly well that Bazata was crazy. Nothing would stop him from going back to Loulans that night, and I was not going to waste time arguing.

It took a slight wrench to unliberate yourself seven hours after being liberated. The Terrot had no battery, and therefore no lights. The moon was just strong enough for me to see the road. The Germans, the American lieutenant told us, had blown the bridge we had crossed that evening, but the bridge at Cirey was unblown.

We felt our way cautiously. Soon after Rigney we saw figures ahead and I stopped dead. It was a large American patrol. They challenged, and were very prudent. They were flabbergasted when Bazata spoke to them in their own language and stood solemnly eyeing us while we started up again. Some providence gave us an open road back to Loulans. I cut the motor and coasted down the hill to the Landel house. While Bazata went in to wake Floyd and get the message into code, I hid the motorcycle under the weeping willow.

Evidently there were Germans in the village. There was a lot of singing coming from the cheese factory, and I could hear the stamping of horse lines. Strange that we had not been stopped on the way in. Perhaps the sentries had been asleep. When Floyd opened up on the wireless, Berger and I crept around the outside of the house to make sure that the carefully closed windows were containing the whine of the hand generator. You could only hear it if you stood directly below the first floor window of the bedroom where he was working.

For some time I stood stupidly in front of the mirror looking at strange bruises on my waist. Then I realised that these were the places where Bazata had hooked in his big hands as we crossed the bridge at Cenans.

It was a lovely morning, but it did not look so good to us. Two German officers were standing on the gravel in front of the house when I awoke. The fat cook was holding them at bay. At length she slopped into the house in her felt slippers to fetch Landel himself. He talked to them for a moment, then the three of them moved off across the narrow foot-bridge to the "laiterie". I overheard the German spokesman tell Landel that he was a colonel, and that he needed space for one thousand men, and a large house for a headquarters.

"But surely you are not stopping here?" said Landel.

"Why on earth not?"

"Because of the Americans."

"Stuff and nonsense, the Americans are still on the other side of Besançon," the colonel lied airily. "May I ask if you put your own house at our disposition, sir?"

"Certainly not. There are empty houses in the village. I have ten children and several employees sleeping in my own house."

When I was dressed I walked down to the factory to look at the Germans. They were reasonable-looking troops, but a poor lot compared with the Americans I had seen the day before. The only thing they had more of was discipline. They were eating a stew made up of captured tins of American meat mixed with German tins of potato and vegetable.

They had put out blocks on all the roads leading from Loulans with thirty to fifty men and mines in each block. When I walked back to the house the children were talking with two German cavalrymen who had ridden into the garden. They were blond, friendly young Germans who were trying to get somebody to offer them something to eat or drink. Nobody did, of course. The children were horrified by the saddle galls on the hairy ponies. A young foal had followed them in. The Germans explained that they did not understand horses. They were U-boat sailors from Bordeaux, mounted and armed and uniformed in grey to fight their way back to Germany.

Floyd had a lot of sending to do while the Germans were there. I improved the hiding-place for our weapons and equipment by getting one of the married daughters to put her baby to bed in the room, and we pushed the baby's cot against the door of the cupboard. Berger and some of the sons or cousins patrolled all the time around the house to see that none of the Germans wandering about could hear Floyd working. It was a

354

glorious day. The Landel family seemed to treat the whole thing as a joke. We all sat down as usual to eat at one o'clock. I counted seventeen at the table. Two of them married daughters who were *enceinte*. A general air of fecundity seemed to hang over that house.

Madame Landel was just as particular about the small things (where people sat, et cetera) as usual. She sat with an American on either side of her and a Britisher at the end of the table and discussed differences between the French, English, and American systems of education. Twice during the meal, once during the pork-chops and once during the plum-tart, her husband was called by the maid from the room to speak with German officers. The front door where he spoke to the Germans was immediately beside the dining-room door. We could plainly hear the loud German requests and Landel's acid replies. Yet plump, practical Madame Landel never as much as interrupted a sentence.

If she had been poor I should have found her nerve less remarkable. But she was rich in the things that money cannot buy, in old furniture and silver and linen that she and her husband had inherited, in the funny old square house with its associations of ten successful accouchements and thirty years of happy and prosperous married life.

That afternoon, since it was not possible to use the roads, Bazata, Berger and I went out with Bernard and another man to try to get some sniping at the enemy on the Rioz-Loulans road. I was put off the sniping by the smell of the wood. This road had been one of the main lines of retreat for the German columns, and there had been frequent killings in the paths of the woods that hemmed the road in for several miles. It was a hot afternoon and, surprisingly enough, there was no traffic on the road. We knew that the Americans were pushing up through Rioz, and we expected a German retreat along this line.

While we lay there four or five shells came over and exploded behind us, in Loulans, it seemed. Bazata came along through the wood to see me.

"Are those German or American shells?" he asked.

"Don't ask me. If they are German, it means the Boches have cleared out of Loulans since we left towards Montbozon or Rougemont."

"What about you and me going back and having a look?"

When we got back as far as the Landel piggery we could see that the shells were falling near the road just beyond the Landel's house. We saw an American armoured car come

355

snaking over the road. It sat watching the shells for a few minutes, then darted past the danger spot and into Loulans. Two seconds later we heard a tremendous explosion from the centre of the village. The American vehicle had found the German engineers' truck loaded with their too sensitive explosives and had exploded it with the first burst of fire. Following the armoured car came three Sherman tanks loaded with infantry.

Loulans was liberated. I called Berger. I wanted to go to Vieilley to tell them we had cancelled their parachutage for that night, now that the Americans had passed them, and also to find out how the Maquis had made out in their battle for the bridge. Berger was to come with me to get his ear dressed by a doctor.

It was a glorious late summer evening, with yellow sunshine and brown shadows. We rode away from Landel's on two motor-cycles, Berger leading. It was good to be moving again and to be able to overtake whenever I pleased since my machine was the more powerful. We crossed the river at Cirey and headed up for Rigney. Coming to the top of a hill, we had a clear view of Rigney station. The road between us and the station circled slightly in and out of a dip. I heard an explosion, but paid no attention, thinking that it came from Berger's exhaust. Another, however, followed immediately, and I heard the whine of a bullet. This was preposterous. The Americans were behind us at Loulans and immediately in front of us at Rigney. There is something infuriating in being fired at when you supposed yourself to be safe. But there was no future in being infuriated. Berger and I lay forward over our petrol-tanks and made good time all the way down the road. In places there were high banks to give us cover. The firing was coming evidently from a wood on the right of the road. Neither of us was hit. We roared on into Rigney, past the same corporal from Texas, only now he was lying down behind the wall. Two Americans, entirely unprotected, were standing out on the small iron balcony on the first floor of the end house, calmly exchanging shots with the Germans in the wood. And the last hundred yards before the station was dotted with dead German infantry, evidently knocked out as they charged the place with fixed bayonets. The one who had got closest to the objective lay spread-eagled on the roadway within twenty yards of the "Hôtel de la Gare". He was an elderly man, a common soldier with fluffy hair and a bald pate. The villagers had already taken his rifle and his boots.

Riding into Moncey we met an extremely flash German car, painted a pale khaki and carrying an enormous Union Jack on one side and an enormous Tricolour on the other. Citizens lining the streets were raising a thin shout of "Vive le colonel" as this vehicle passed. I paid no attention to it, but it turned round and pursued me, overtaking me between Venise and Vieilley. Waving me to stop, Boulaya got out and we shook hands. Strangely enough, we had stopped beside the lime-tree under which he had met me when I first approached Vieilley.

"A coincidence," he agreed when I pointed this out. "Gone are those bad old days, Émile. Now a new era is opening here and everywhere else."

I was not so sure. We sat down under the trees. The brakes of his car standing near-by smelled strongly of burning. He was depressed because Corneille, who had taken over the Vieilley command, had been killed in the defence of the bridge at Cromary the day before.

"The funeral is tomorrow morning in Vieilley," he said. "And I have promised that you will attend it."

He walked over to his car, opened the back, and produced the little yellow suit-case that I had left, long ago it seemed, in the house at l'Eglise. My old battle-dress was still inside it.

"I collected this for you from Albert," he said. "Because I promised that you would attend in uniform." He told me the long story of his escapades since he went down south to see Albert and ran into the liberators, in his case Spahis of the French 1st Army. He had established himself in Besançon now.

"In the University City, the only offices in the place with bathrooms," he said. "Although, of course, there is no water yet. And I have a flat for you. The finest apartment in all Besançon awaiting your pleasure. All the war correspondents have asked for it, but I said no, that is for Émile."

"War correspondents, my God. You are keeping high company."

"I know how you are feeling, Émile," he smiled at me. "You are regretting the old days. But now you must change a little. Relax and enjoy yourself. Come now. We'll go and have a drink with old Marquis. He has some Pernod."

The Maquisards were preparing for the night in the church when I arrived with Georges. They were going to bed early because they had done clearing patrols in the forest starting at dawn. Over in one corner a man lay his head swathed in bandages.

"Who's that?" I asked.

"The Frisé."

"How did it happen, Frisé, my friend?" I asked, sitting on the floor beside his bed. "Was it at the bridge?"

"Bridge nothing," he replied gruffly. "I am in this trouble because of you and your damned phosphorous grenades, Émile. Now the least you can do is to get me out of it."

"Yes, of course. What happened?"

"I was riding my 'petrolette' through Venise. There must have been a phosphorous grenade lying in the roadway. Before I knew where I was I found myself enveloped in white vapour. I went to the fountain to wash it off. An agonising pain began. There is only a little on my face, but it hurts."

"Who had left a phosphorous grenade lying in the middle of the roadway at Venise?"

"Well," he admitted. "I had three or four in the bag behind on my carrier. Maybe one of them fell out. The road is hellish bumpy in Venise."

"What are you going to do now, Frisé?"

"Boulaya has offered me a job as a kind of ceremonial body-guard in his office. But I was never made to be a lap-dog, Émile. I think I'll go into the army."

"Why not the navy?"

"The army has the work to do now. Besides, with my knowledge of demolitions and the German language, I should be useful when we cross the Rhine."

The remainder of the Maquisards, led by the old sergeant, told me the story of their fight on the bridge. It was like any other story of any other fight. They had two dead, and they had not saved the bridge. They looked incredibly encrusted with dirt. I had never previously remarked how dirty their teeth were. They seemed quite pleased with their immediate future of doing patrols behind the Americans (instead of out in front), and of doing police work on the roads. I knew they would soon tire of it, although they did not yet see that the anti-climax period had begun. I saw that I had grown away from them too. Pointu and the Frisé were the only originals who were left. The Pointu was already talking about going home "on leave" and then joining the army. He was a fervent young patriot, the Pointu.

Back in the village they insisted on my going to see the body of Corneille. He lay in Georges' inner room, opening off the kitchen. It was the room where I had sat through interminable discussions with the "patron". The room where the Gestapo had found all our clothing.

His body was laid out in candle-light on a red, white and blue bier. He looked strangely normal, lying on his back. In life he had always worn a rather fixed expression, an expression which became a prominent lawyer. I remembered that he had been fond of fishing and also of aeroplanes. One night Boulaya and I had stayed with him in his hide-out, a fishing cottage in a village on the other side of Besançon. He was destined to become the military governor of Besançon. Now he would fill a hole in the Vieilley churchyard. He had been killed, almost by accident, while stepping out of his car on the edge of the skirmish. If he had lain down like the cunning old sergeant who was stabbing at the enemy with five-round bursts from his Bren, all might have been well. But a German machine-gunner on the other side of the river got his sights on him and tore out his back. He died one hour before all fighting ceased and the Germans were cleared from that part of France.

Next day in the church they called him a hero. Women who had called him a foreigner only a few days ago because he came from the town, now wept for his memory. I was in the front pew beside Boulaya. The choir, girls and young women in stiff Sunday clothes, cast furtive looks at my strange uniform. The Vieilley Maquis formed a guard of honour for the coffin and six of them had carried it, with a mighty effort, up the hill. They were dressed up in khaki jerseys and new khaki trousers. They seemed to be sunk in the rich pathos too.

But one Maquisard was not there. The Frisé had refused to come, giving his wounds as an excuse. While the service went on I heard the impudent sound of his "petrolette" passing through the village on the way to Besançon, where he was to get treatment from the Americans for his burns.

Another man, a prominent figure in the village life, was not there. This was Phillipon, and I knew where he was. I had seen him slinking off across the fields towards a certain private property reputed to be richly stocked with game. Moreover, I suspected from his walk that he carried his old twelve-bore. This was not obvious. For he had his own method of carrying it, which was much less tiring than the normal method. The barrel was attached to the stock by a piece of string just long enough to go round the back of Phillipon's neck. Both barrel and stock thus hung beneath his long jacket, "out of the rain", as he used to put it.

Georges was standing on the other side of Boulaya. He was all dressed up in French airman's uniform. He had three medals, I saw, one of them the "Croix de Guerre". He had plastered his hair down with water. His face looked fresher and rounder. More satisfied with itself. The girls looked at him more admiringly. Frenchwomen have a strangely accentuated weakness for airmen. I saw that there were two sides to my friend Georges. But after all, there is a good bit of the peacock in most men. And the other side that I liked would overcome the other more and more as he grew older, and fiercer, and wilder. That was good because Phillipon had a weak chest dating from the Salonika campaign of World War I, and could not be expected to live much longer. Then, unless Georges took his place as the greatest poacher in the valley, there would be nobody to plunder the richest coverts during public holidays and feasts and funerals and marriages, while lesser men were mixed up with the women and the joys of the table.

I was glad to get away from Vieilley after the funeral. And I did not see it for some time, for my work took me to the Haute-Saône. When I returned to the village I was leaving the valley. I was in a car with Berger and Bazata, who sat heavily in the back nursing a hand wounded a day or two before in some German shelling of the village of Dampierre.

Vieilley looked dark and muddy, almost as impersonal as it had done on the day of my arrival. I did not feel like saying good-bye to anybody. Perhaps I would have liked to have walked up to the woods to look at the empty Maquis sites, where I should probably have seen a few old papers and tins and a worn-out bicycle tyre beneath the trees. But all I did was to ask for Georges.

"He is spending the day on the river, Émile," said Madame Poirier. "He said it was so long since he had the peace to enjoy a good go at the fish."

We drove on to Besançon, and I envied Georges in his punt on the smoothly slipping water.

In the streets of Besançon I met my old and good friend Eric Sevareid, dressed up in American uniform, and looking otherwise just as I remembered him on the Boulevard St. Germain.

"What are you doing here?" he asked, looking at my peculiar civilian clothes.

"I don't really know, Eric. But I'm going home now."

"And do you want to go home?"

There were tall windows stretching the length of one wall in the bedroom of the flat Boulaya had found for me. Outside the windows there were metal shutters. Inside there were long white, transparent curtains. Between the windows and the curtains there were lamps concealed in the floor to throw light into the embrasures. It was that kind of flat.

I closed the shutters and the curtains and went to bed, hoping to sleep for thirty-six hours. I was limp, as though I had been drugging myself for a long time, and now the drug no longer worked. And I wanted to forget the Besançon outside in the street where men of the F.F.I. strutted along in strangely variegated uniforms with weapons slung on their shoulders. They were men of the F.F.I. whom I had never seen, most of them, although one month previously I had known every Maquis in the area. I had met some French friends, too, in the streets, among them the Frisé and Marcel. They were quietly dressed, I was pleased to see, and neither of them carried a weapon.

"Where are your guns?" I asked.

"Back in the barracks. If we always had a rule not to frighten the civilians, why begin now?"

"In the barracks?"

"Yes, we're in the barracks now with the old Franois Maquis. But it's time to end all this. All we want to know is, if we go into the army now, can we go into the navy after the war?"

They were quite right, I reflected, lying on the square and enormous bed in the middle of this room with the over-emphasised windows. The episode of the Resistance was ended for me too. And I had no wish to try to hang on to it. I pulled the sheets over my head to shut out the grinding rattle and clatter of the street below.

CHAPTER XVIII

BOULAYA stood beside me at Amberieu airfield, sniffing the petrol and dust on the air the taxi-ing aircraft hurled at us. There were flocks of Thunderbolt fighters with scarlet splashes on their stubby silver bodies, and clumsier twin-engined D.C.3's bringing in hospital supplies. We were waiting for the Hudson that was to take me back to England.

Bazata and Berger had also made the long trip from Besançon to Amberieu to see me off. Berger stood looking at me with sad brown spaniel's eyes.

"If it would only *rain*," said Bazata. He thought he would follow me to England in a few days, and he wanted to go with me. But, although I was reluctant to leave Berger and Bazata, it was of Boulaya that I thought most as we stood on the tarmac. Perhaps we had not achieved much together, but it seemed that we had always been working together and always sharing things. He had come a long way since the day he picked me up at the farm near Salins. Now he was important. He had won his own little battle. There would be many other battles before France was well again. Honest and brave Frenchmen like him would be needed. I remembered something.

"The march through Besançon, Boulaya. When is it?"

"The march. Oh, that takes place tomorrow, Émile. I had always imagined that you would be there."

"Yes, I know. I am sorry. . . . There is a Hudson," I said. "They say it will only wait ten minutes here."

"I must make a confession to you, Émile. I have never flown before."

"Before? But how wonderful. You are coming to London?"

"I cannot see all those gleaming aircraft without deciding to come to London."

"But the march through Besançon?"

"Damn the march through Besançon. Fournier will do that better than I could."

For some reason the sight of the cliffs of the Channel coast of England affected me more deeply than usual. I could not take my eyes from the funny higglety-pigglety country that lay below. I had never been more glad to come home. We landed at a British airfield, and one of the first faces I saw was that of a major who had lectured to me at one of the schools. He did not recognise me. Why should he? Now I was one of a crowd, not a creature under a microscope any longer. Not Émile, who might be whispered about, but an ordinary sheep-faced British officer, like tens of thousands of others. I liked that feeling. It was comfortable. And I felt like saying to the major:

"Thank you so much for not recognising me, and would you mind telling me about the flying bombs."

A lot of other queerish people had arrived from France. While they gave us all tea and glamorously white bread and wedges of bully-beef at the airfield and while they rushed us to London in a bus, I thought about the flying bombs. I remembered that the last time I had longed so desperately to be back in London.

And when I arrived, nearly everything that I had looked forward to had been killed.

The bus stopped outside some American place in Brook Street. Boulaya had to be shut up that night in a special house because of the Immigration people. So I got out in Brook Street. I could easily carry my luggage. The rucksack on my back was only one third full, and the yellow suit-case was still emptier. I crossed Mayfair on foot. It was dark and quiet as I remembered it before the invasion of France. My hotel was the same. They asked me if I had come from Scotland.

B. answered the telephone herself, sleepy after the day's work. She had not been touched by the flying bombs, and after five minutes of shy conversation, I thought that she had not changed about me. Only then did I look around me and see that I really was in London and say to myself: "It cannot be true."

The doorman at the aquarium did not remember my name, but he remembered just enough about me to let me in with a polite: "Morning, Captain Ur." The brown-eyed blonde on the telephone did not remember either.

"I know you so well by sight, but I cannot quite remember your name. So many pass through . . ."

Mrs. Pollock swept in with an orchid spray and said sharply:

"Hullo, Millar. Where have you been mercifully hidden all this time?".

"Good heavens. You remember my name."

"Of course I do. You were one of the most difficult. Horribly self-satisfied. But I remember you gave me the most gorgeous roses once."

"That was to get compassionate leave to Scotland."

"I know, I know, but there is no need to shout." She looked around her apprehensively. We were pressed in the middle of a swaying mass of people. This was a party at the aquarium. Soon there would be no more need for the aquarium. And that afternoon General Koenig, still head of the F.F.I., was to speak to us. Albert, tall and short-haired in his uniform, stood near me looking down his nose at everyone. He was not glad to be back, for he had enjoyed the fighting.

"Where's Paul?" I asked him.

"Out with some sailors."

Most of the aquarium officers were there, looking more at their ease than I felt, since they had not got out of the habit of such parties. Boulaya came in with one of the French Army

363

friends he had found in London. He was to leave for Besançon that night, flying to the airfield beside Thise, where he and Georges and I had once seen Cossacks. Boulaya wore French uniform now, a pale, rather nasty uniform, with wide dark stripes down the sides of the trousers. His face was browner and leaner than most of the faces there, but in uniform he lost his swagger, became over-respectable. General Koenig made his speech. One of the officers translated sentence by sentence. It was a speech of thanks. When it was over we went upstairs to a room where a bar had been set up. Boulaya was presented to Koenig, then he presented me. The two of us from Vieilley retreated to an empty corner. Neither of us had drinks in our hands. We shook hands and said good-bye. There were tears in his eyes.

I walked downstairs as quickly as I could. B. was waiting for me in a big car outside the aquarium.

THE END